Latinos/as and Mathematics Education

Research on Learning and Teaching in Classrooms and Communities

A volume in
Research in Educational Diversity and Excellence
Yolanda N. Padron and Hersch C. Waxman, *Series Editors*

Research in Educational Diversity and Excellence

Yolanda N. Padron and Hersch C. Waxman
Series Editors

Educational Resiliency: Student, Teacher, and School Perspectives
Edited by Hersch C. Waxman, Yolanda N. Padron, and Jon P. Gray

Research on Technology Use in Culturally Diverse Settings
Edited by Hersch C. Waxman, Robert L. Blomeyer, and Tirupalavanam Ganesh

Latinos/as and Mathematics Education

Research on Learning and Teaching in Classrooms and Communities

Edited by

Kip Téllez
University of California at Santa Cruz

Judit N. Moschkovich
University of California at Santa Cruz

Marta Civil
University of Arizona

INFORMATION AGE PUBLISHING, INC.
Charlotte, NC • www.infoagepub.com

Library of Congress Cataloging-in-Publication Data

Latinos/as and mathematics education : research on learning and teaching in classrooms and communities / edited by Kip Téllez, Judit N. Moschkovich, Marta Civil.
   p. cm.
   Includes bibliographical references.
   ISBN 978-1-61735-421-2 (hardcover) – ISBN 978-1-61735-420-5 (pbk.) – ISBN 978-1-61735-422-9 (e-book) 1. Mathematics–Study and teaching–United States. 2. Hispanic Americans–Education–United States. I. Téllez, Kip.
II. Moschkovich, Judit N. III. Civil, Marta.
   QA13.L3725 2011
   510.71–dc22

                                                      2011010620

Printed in the United States of America

CONTENTS

FOREWORD

Luis C. Moll
University of Arizona

This volume is the result of several years of research on mathematics and education produced by the NSF-sponsored Center for the Mathematics Education of Latino Students (CEMELA). From its beginnings, as conceptualized by Marta Civil of The University of Arizona, the goal of CEMELA was to undertake research on this crucial research topic in a variety of social settings and conditions found in different regions of the country, and with a special focus on Latino students, given the great demographic growth of this population. The work thus required not only the collaboration of colleagues from four different universities, and of administrators, teachers, families and students at many schools, but also broad agreement on a general framework for the work that the group came to depict as a sociocultural approach.

The great challenge offered by any sociocultural approach is that of bringing to life the study of human learning and development. As Alexander Luria (1982) famously suggested, the key is to locate the study of human thinking not in the "recesses of the human brain or in the depths of the sprit" but "... in the external processes of social life, in the social and historical forms of human existence" (p. 25). This volume seeks to meet this challenge, and does so admirably, through a range of studies of mathematics and education situated in a variety of conditions for learning.

Latina/os and Mathematics Education, pages vii–viii

The emphasis of the work presented herein, however, is not only on understanding the social configuration of circumstances for teaching and learning mathematics, or on whether broader social forces constrain or enable these activities. The emphasis is also on identifying the resources available to enhance or otherwise mediate or transform those immediate circumstances within which we ask students to learn mathematics. In brief, a central characteristic of the work is on turning diversity into a pedagogical asset.

There are, to be sure, no prescriptions offered here, no facile ways of bringing theory directly to practice, there never are; but there is a strong orientation to teaching and learning as socially accomplished, and to indentifying and gaining access to the cultural resources that can serve to facilitate a challenge, and perhaps even a transformation, of the disturbing status quo of education for Latino students. In the chapters that follow, therefore, the reader will come to appreciate, among many other themes, the power of social relations in teachers engaging students in learning; the value of bilingualism in expanding the teachers and students' discourses for learning; and the importance of helping children discuss and understand the relevance of mathematics to their learning and development in and out of classrooms.

I commend my colleagues for their valuable contributions to this volume, and for taking up the challenge inherent in understanding student learning in connection to the actual relationships that constitute their realities. As L. S. Vygotsky (1926/1997) wrote many years ago:

> Ultimately, only life educates, and the deeper that life, the real world, burrows into the school, the more dynamic and the more robust will be the educational process. That the school has been locked away and walled in as if by a tall fence from life itself has been its greatest failing. Education is just as meaningless outside the real world as is a fire without oxygen, or as is breathing in a vacuum. (p. 345)

PREFACE

This volume is intended for an audience of researchers, mathematics educators, and policymakers who are interested in the intersection of Latina/os and mathematics education. As we point out in the initial chapter of the book, the ongoing underperformance in mathematics of Latina/os in U.S. schools is unacceptable, and we hope that this book will serve as both a resource and motivation to make the necessary changes to transform this woeful condition.

We intended for the volume to be an interdisciplinary collection. While all the authors are scholars in the field of education research, several bring expertise in fields other than mathematics education. This mingling of expertise was a purposeful choice because we believe that improving the mathematical learning of Latina/os is a challenge that requires a wide range of voices and perspectives.

As readers will notice, many of the chapters acknowledge the support of a National Science Foundation Center for Learning and Teaching, the Center for the Mathematics Education of Latina/os (CEMELA). This is no coincidence. As the editors of this volume, we were among the principal investigators for CEMELA, and many, though not all, of the authors throughout the book were affiliated with CEMELA. As a collaborative consortium involving four universities (University of Arizona, University of Illinois at Chicago, University of New Mexico, and University of California, Santa Cruz), dozens of schools and school districts, and several community/after-school projects, CEMELA brought together researchers from several disciplinary backgrounds: language specialists with an interest in mathematics, mathematics education researchers, mathematics educators with an interest

Latinos/as and Mathematics Education, pages ix–x
Copyright © 2011 by Information Age Publishing
All rights of reproduction in any form reserved.

in culture and language, and cultural specialists with an interest in mathematics education. CEMELA offered faculty, doctoral students, and postdoctoral researchers a space to consider the ways in which research could inform what we know and need to know about improving the mathematics education for Latino/a children and youth. Collaborations across institutions included summer institutes, research symposia, and presentations at national and international conferences. Several of the chapters here are the result of these very fruitful collaborations, across disciplines and now across space.

Although CEMELA was a galvanizing organization for many of the authors in the volume, we are confident that the research and attention to improving Latino/a performance in mathematics will continue. If this volume motivates other researchers to join in the effort, then it will have been a great success.

We would like to thank the authors in this volume for their commitment and patience and the series editors for their support. We would also like to thank Hersh Waxman and Yolanda Padron for their series' editorship. Esperanza Zamora assisted whenever we needed her. We are also indebted to Nancy Rosenbaum, whose skillful and careful proofing and formatting contributed much to the accuracy and coherence of the book.

Last, but never least, we would like to thank our families for their continued support.

—**Kip Téllez**
Judit Moschkovich
Marta Civil

CHAPTER 1

LATINOS/AS AND MATHEMATICS EDUCATION

Why This Book Now?

Kip Téllez
UC Santa Cruz

Judit Moschkovich
UC Santa Cruz

Marta Civil
University of Arizona

As the title of this volume suggests, we have chosen to compile a book that addresses the mathematics education of Latinos/as, a specific cultural group. But why would researchers focus a volume on the mathematics learning and teaching on any single group, and specifically one defined by ethnicity? The rich history of research on girls' and women's experiences in mathematics offers one example (e.g., Walkerdine, 1998), but gender is clearly something different than culture. After all, is not mathematics a largely culture-free discipline, in which language plays but a minor role?

Latinos/as and Mathematics Education, pages 1–19
Copyright © 2011 by Information Age Publishing
All rights of reproduction in any form reserved.

1

We argue that this misguided view is, in fact, partly responsible for the mathematics underperformance of Latinos. And it is this underperformance that provides our first compelling reason for a focus on Latinos/as. Like other "minority" groups in the U.S., Latinos/as score well below their dominant culture counterparts in mathematics. We point to data from National Center on Educational Statistics showing that Latinos generally score about a standard deviation lower on tests of mathematics achievement than their white counterparts (Jencks & Phillips, 1998; Rumberger & Gándara, 2004). Overall, 4th and 8th grade scores on the National Assessment of Educational Progress (NAEP) mathematics assessment increased in 2009; however, Latinos continued to score among the lowest, and from 1990 to 2009 the gap in the scores for whites and Latinos did not change significantly (http://nationsreportcard.gov/math_2009/). The 2009 NAEP results show 44% at or above proficient for white students compared to 17% for "Hispanic" in 8th grade mathematics; for that same grade level, 17% white and 43% Hispanic are below basic (Aud, Fox, & KewalRamani, 2010). In spite of the overall consistency in scores, the achievement gap is particularly acute for mathematics achievement at the secondary level, where the white–Hispanic mathematics score difference for 17-year-olds has increased substantially since 1990 (Perie et al., 2005). This puzzling finding has educators and researchers asking more questions about the persistent underachievement of Latinos, the nation's largest "minority" group at 12% of the total population, a figure that increases to over 25% when we count only those under age 25 (Therrien & Ramirez, 2000), and has generated a call to action at several governmental levels. Moreover, we want to point out that Latinos are the least educated among the nation's major racial and ethnic groups. More than 27% of Latinos, compared to just over 4% of whites, have less than a ninth-grade education (Snyder & Dillow, 2010). The dropout rate for Hispanics is twice the average for whites, 6.0 and 2.8, respectively (Stillwell, 2010), although these dropout figures are disputed. For instance, (Gándara & Contreras, 2009) estimate that over 50% of Latino youth do not receive a diploma after four years of high school. Another aspect of concern is parental level of education: About 40% of Latino children ages 6 to 18 have a parent with less than a high school education, compared to about 6% for white children (Aud et al., 2010).

The consequences of Latino underperformance in mathematics is made clear in more than just test score and dropout data: Latinos are awarded only a small fraction of all science and engineering degrees, earning 7.1, 4.1, and 4.3% of bachelor's, master's, and doctoral degrees, respectively (Chapa & De La Rosa, 2006). Relative to other ethnic groups, these figures are unacceptably low and reveal the real-life consequences of an education system that is failing Latino/a students in mathematics and the sciences.

Among the reasons we might count as encouraging a focus on Latinos/as is that the student population is growing rapidly and therefore presents a *prima facie* reason for concern. While it is true that Latinos/as are indeed a large and growing sector of the U.S. population and an increasing number of school age children in the U.S. are from this population, we must be very cautious in allowing population shifts alone to drive research and policy interests. Nevertheless, the data paint a compelling picture of the future. Latino/a population in the U.S. in 2006 was reported to total approximately 44 million or 14.8% of the total U.S. population (Passell & Cohn, 2008). This is an increase from 12.5% in 2000 (Therrien & Ramirez, 2000) and 14% in 2005 (Passel & Cohn, 2008). Projections for 2050 estimate that Latinos/as will then make up about 29% of the U.S. population. Latinos/as also represent a large portion of the foreign-born population at 44.6% (Passel & Cohn, 2008). Latino/a children are a significant and growing student population in K–12 classrooms. In 2005–2006 Latinos/as accounted for approximately 19.8 % of all public school students, a 55% increase from 12.7% in 1993–1994 (Fry, 2007). Latino/a students in 2001 constituted the majority in virtually all the major urban school districts in the country (Young, 2002). It is reasonable to expect that as the Latino/a population grows and extends to other areas and regions in the U.S., many public school teachers in this country will be teaching Latino/a children. Finally demographic data also show that the great majority of the Latino population is low-income or working class: Over a quarter (28%) of Latino children (under 18 years) live below the poverty level, a condition that is clearly affecting their preparation for and nature of their schooling (Lee & Burkam, 2002; Moll & Ruiz, 2002).

We do not dispute the demographic forecasts predicting the growth in the number of U.S. Latinos but find this argumentation troubling because it sometimes promotes, often inadvertently, a panic among non-Latinos, especially whites, who see a growing Latino/a population as a threat to "established" cultures in the U.S. Gimenez (1997) points out the dangers of media portrayals of this growth when she writes,

> The mass media and politicians exploit data about the youth, higher fertility, and growth rates of the "Hispanic" population in ways that, ultimately, intensify racist fears among those worried about low white fertility, increase the likelihood of conflict with blacks (who see their communities competing for scarce resources with an ever-growing "minority" group), and strengthen stereotypes about "Hispanic" cultural traits. (1997, p. 227)

Similarly, López (2008) writes:

> There is a growing anti-Latino sentiment percolating across the nation. Although Latinos represent over 14% of the U.S. population, dominant dis-

courses frame us as a threat to the social and moral fabric of the United States, as well as a drain to social services. These national discourses...and representations of Latino immigrants are important because they represent racist racial projects that shape the allocation of resources. (p. 45)

To our minds, Latino underachievement in mathematics should be of the utmost concern to educators, policymakers, and the community, regardless of demographic trends, and we should never allow demographic data to cause panic among educators and policymakers. To employ the "shocking" growth in the Latino/a population argument as reason alone for concern strikes us as needless rhetoric.

If mathematics education has something to learn from research specifically on Latinos/as, then we have an obligation to describe, in the most useful manner, who Latinos/as are. Thus far in this chapter we have been using the term Latino/a as a general descriptor for a population, but this term can obfuscate important differences among groups of people, even those who all may self-identify as Latino/a. Important differences such as the length of residence in the United States, language proficiency in English, language proficiency in Spanish, prior school experience, living in an urban or rural region, and socio-economic status are all important distinction among Latinos/as when considering instructional programs. These differences suggest that the needs of Latino/a students are both diverse and specific to individual students. Consider, for example, two 14-year-old Latina students, one of whom is a recent arrival from the state of Jalisco, Mexico, who has already missed three years of school, who is fluent in Spanish orally but is not yet proficient in writing or reading. This student will have very different needs in the mathematics classroom when compared to a student who, although also a recent arrival, has not missed any school in her native Monterrey, Mexico, completed a year of college-track algebra in Spanish and is highly literate in Spanish and close to oral proficiency in English. These two immigrant Latina students may have very different schooling experiences than, say, a second generation student whose parents immigrated from Michoacan, Mexico 20 year ago. She has been to school only in the US, speaks Spanish at home, and is, of course, literate and fluent in English. In spite of these differences, all three students would be identified—and likely self-identify—as Latinas.

Taking a wider look at the term Latino/a, we recognize that culture is a complex phenomenon and that attempts at generalizations often lead to dangerous stereotypes (González, 1995). Nevertheless, we do recognize an obligation to provide some provisional commonalities. The foremost manner to learn what makes a Latino/a a Latino/a is to become connected to a community of people who identify as such. Direct experience has no peer when it comes to cultural learning/acquisition (Téllez, 2010). On the other hand, Latino/a scholars such as Rúa (2005) have developed the notion of "latinidad" as a representative identity rooted in a history of European colonialism, U.S. imperialism, and a stigmatization by the dominant ruling classes in the Americas. These collective experiences emerge as cultural "expressions" in observable behavior such as religion. Rúa suggests that the Latino/a solidarity found during the civic marches of May 2006, when Latinas of various national ties came together to protest the draconian Border Protection, Antiterrorism, and Illegal Immigration Control Act of 2005, offers clear evidence of latinidad. Still, she is careful to point out that a broad cultural identifier such as latinidad can be used to over-generalize and thus erode Latino/a identity as easily as it can empower.

We have used the term Latino/a in this chapter (partly to recognize the importance of gender in marginalized communities), but we want to make clear that the research in this volume is not intended to be a representative sample of all Latino/a learners or communities. Based on the physical locations of the universities connected via the CEMELA project, the majority of the studies herein focus on Latino/a communities whose national heritage is primarily Mexican. We fully recognize that research in immigrant communities and those of color is highly contextualized and rough generalizing can result in a morass from which even the most thoughtful researcher cannot escape. It is our hope that this volume may inspire additional mathematics education researchers to conduct research in a wide array of Latino/a communities.

A BRIEF REVIEW OF THE RESEARCH ON LATINAS/OS AND MATHEMATICS EDUCATION

Among the most important reasons for studying Latinos/as specifically, and perhaps the most important reason for researchers, is that few empirical studies have focused on mathematics learning or teaching among Latinos/as, and the extant research is quite narrow in scope and theoretical orientation. For instance, early studies of Latino, bilingual students leaning mathematics framed the "problem" as one entirely owing to linguistic challenges: solving word problems, understanding individual vocabulary terms, or translating from English to mathematical symbols (Cocking & Mestre, 1988; Cuevas, 1983; Cuevas, Mann, & McClung, 1986; Mestre, 1981; Spanos & Crandall, 1990; Spanos, Rhodes, Dale, & Crandall, 1988). Although we value these foundational studies for directing our attention to the role of language in the learning of mathematics, the research corpus has largely failed to address the role of bilingualism as a linguistic resource—instead of a challenge to be overcome—as well as divorcing language from its cultural roots. In the following paragraphs, we devote attention to these early studies, primarily because they provide a window into the history of the research and offer a portent of the research featured in this volume.

Early research with Latino/a learners focused primarily on arithmetic computing and solving traditional word problems (see Moschkovich, 2007b, 2007d, for reviews of early research). One paradigmatic set of studies (several with adults and several with elementary students) focused on arithmetic calculation. Several studies explored adults' preferred language during computation and compared monolinguals and bilinguals in terms of response times. These studies were typically concerned with individual students calculating one, two, or three-step problems using the four arithmetic operations. A second paradigmatic set of studies focused on word problems. Several studies examined how students translated traditional word problems from English to mathematical symbols.

While many early studies used narrow conceptions of mathematical activity and focused on quick performance on arithmetic computation, a few early studies with young children used Piagetian tasks (see work by De Avila, 1988, for examples). Later studies developed a broader view of mathematical activity, examining not only responses to arithmetic computation but also reasoning and problem solving (e.g., Mestre & Gerace, 1986), detailed protocols of students solving word problems (e.g., Spanos et al., 1988), the strategies children used to solve arithmetic word problems (Secada, 1991), and student conceptions of two digit quantities (Fuson, Smith, & Lo Cicero, 1997). This progression is not surprising since the fields of cognitive psychology and mathematics research moved in a similar direction in framing mathematical activity.

The majority of studies involved two paradigmatic scenarios, carrying out arithmetic computation and solving word problems. Therefore, conclusions could only be limited to these two mathematical topics. It is not possible to generalize from studies on arithmetic computation and algebra word problems to other topics in mathematics such as geometry, measurement, probability, or proportional reasoning. Most of the early studies used narrow conceptions of arithmetic or algebra. Studies focusing on response time during arithmetic computation tell us little about strategies or conceptions participants use to carry out these computations. Studies that focused on translating word problems to algebraic equations tell us little about participants' algebraic thinking.

Narrow conceptions of mathematics that focus on arithmetic computation or word problem translation while ignoring strategies, reasoning, and conceptual understanding constrain mathematical activity to lower-order cognitive skills and limit our views of what constitutes mathematical proficiency. Since much of the early research for this student population focused on lower-order cognitive skills, and only a few studies went beyond computation and translating word problems, it is not possible to reach conclusions for Latino/a students regarding higher-order mathematical thinking or other aspects of mathematical proficiency such as conceptual understanding.

Research studies are needed for this student population that include broader notions of mathematical activity. This can be accomplished by expanding mathematical topics beyond arithmetic and algebra, considering conceptual understanding as well as procedural fluency, or examining how students use and connect multiple mathematical representations. The chapters in this volume expand the research base for this population by using broader notions of mathematical activity in precisely these ways.

We also need more research on Latino/a populations that uses current views of mathematical activity using, for example, perspectives that move beyond seeing mathematics learning only as an individual cognitive phenomenon. Recent research in mathematics education provides a view of mathematical activity as developing socio-mathematical norms (Cobb, Wood, & Yackel, 1993), presenting mathematical arguments (Forman, 1996), participating in mathematical discussions (Lampert, 1990), and participating in mathematical discourse practices (Moschkovich, 2007b). Situated perspectives of cognition (Brown, Collins, & Duguid, 1989; Greeno, 1994; Lave & Wenger, 1991) present a view of learning mathematics as learning to mathematize situations, communicate about these situations, and use resources for mathematizing and communicating (Greeno, 1994). These perspectives assume that learning is inherently social and cultural "whether or not it occurs in an overtly social context" (Forman, 1996, p. 117), that participants bring multiple views to a situation, that representations have multiple meanings for participants, and that these multiple meanings for representations and inscriptions are negotiated.

Although focusing on arithmetic computation and word problems may have been sufficient in the past, this emphasis does not include current views of mathematical activity or instructional practices in many classrooms. The research presented in this volume demonstrates a next step in the research on Latino/a mathematics learning by integrating sociocultural perspectives and studying more complex forms of mathematical activity, such as working on projects and using multiple mathematical representations.

EXPECTATIONS AND PREVIEWS

We believe that the most important contribution of this volume is that each and every chapter assumes that mathematics instruction for Latinos/as can be based on the resources to be found in culture and language. By inverting the deficit perspective, we believe this volume redresses the shortcomings found in some of the previous literature. The authors frame language (i.e., bilingualism) not as an obstacle, but as a resource for mathematical reasoning. Several address the notion of cultural variation not as a liability but as a resource. In this view, educators reframe culture as a focus on resources (i.e., those practices, objects, inscriptions, or people that connect mathematical concepts to student thinking and experiences, both in and out of school).

Section on Latino/a Students, Learners, and Mathematics Education

The chapters in this section address the need to focus on students and learners in order to better understand their experiences, learning, and language use in mathematics classrooms. This section begins to address questions about Latino/a students' experiences in classrooms: how they relate to curricular models, express resistance, and use language.

Nancy O'Rode's chapter, "Latino/a Students' Understanding of Equivalence: Use of Two Standards-Based Curricula in Eighth Grade Algebra" describes the resources Latino/a students used to make sense of mathematics. The study examines how Latino/a students used resources related to two standards-based curricula to develop understanding of equivalence, a fundamental concept in algebra. The study focuses on the concept of equivalence and examines how students used two types of resources, language and curricular models, to solve problems involving equivalence. This study documents how students from two algebra classrooms used resources to solve equivalence problems during interview tasks. The Latino/a students in this study engaged with standards-based curricular materials that encourage communication, reasoning, and problem solving and were in a classroom environment that provided many opportunities for students to engage in conversations about mathematics.

The chapter by Zahner and Moschkovich, "Bilingual Students Using Two Languages During Peer Mathematics Discussions: ¿Qué Significa? Estudiantes Bilingües Usando Dos Idiomas en sus Discusiones Matemáticas: What Does it Mean?" uses classroom data to consider several competing hypotheses about why student codeswitch during mathematical discussions. The chapter extends Moschkovich's (2007b) work by showing how the use of two (or more) languages by bilingual (or multilingual) students provides a set of linguistic resources for managing the social and cognitive demands of mathematical discussions. The analysis considers the possible functions of using two languages during mathematical discussions in light of alternative theories about language in general and bilingualism in particular. The chapter addresses competing hypotheses about students' use of two or more languages in mathematical discussions using theory, previous research findings, and examples from the two excerpts to consider the merits of each of these hypotheses in turn.

Heather Cavell's chapter examines the resistance by four fifth-grade Latino/a students in response to the classroom environment and teacher practices. The study was framed using Solórzano and Bernal (2001), Yosso (2000). Solórzano and Bernal (2001) place resistance into several inter-related themes: reactionary behavior, self-defeating, conformist, transformational, and resiliency. Resistance provides students with a means to gain control and connection to educational spaces. Resistance can also be seen as a threat by educators and is often considered an attribute of student failure. The analysis considers the forms of resistance to the classroom norms, teacher, and mathematics that students used and explores the experiences prompted students to use these forms of resistance. The case studies showed that communication between the teacher and students was critical to providing quality instruction while not suppressing cultural values.

Section on Latino/a Community, Parents, and Mathematics Education

Research focused on working-class, minoritized communities highlights the power issues that characterize parents-schools relationships (Henry, 1996; Lareau, 2000; Reay, 1998; Vincent, 1996). Minoritized parents' voices are often not heard (or listened to) in school settings. Within mathematics education, the work of Civil and colleagues argue for the need for schools to recognize the experiences and backgrounds of families as resources towards their children's schooling (Civil & Andrade, 2003; Civil & Bernier, 2006; Civil, Bratton, & Quintos, 2005; Civil & Menéndez (2011); Civil & Planas, 2010; Civil & Quintos, 2009; Quintos, Bratton, & Civil, 2005). Their research centers on a non-deficit view of working-class Latino/a parents and on the need to establish a dialogue between communities (parents) and schools (teachers and administrators) in which different views about teaching and learning of mathematics are shared towards the goal of improving the mathematics education of Latino/a children. This body of work informs us of Latino/a parents' perceptions about the teaching and learning of mathematics underscores the concept of valorization of knowledge, by which parents (as everybody else) often have well-established beliefs about content and pedagogical approaches in mathematics. However, as Quintos, Bratton, and Civil (2005) write, "Alternative approaches are often not treated equally.... In this context, the parents' or home method is not given the same value as the teacher's or textbook method. Historical relations of power at the schools can not only be reproduced but also exacerbated through mathematics education" (p. 1189).

The chapters in this section address the continued need for a stronger and meaningful communication between schools and Latino/a parents. This communication should encompass the varied views about the teaching and learning of mathematics that the different participants (in particular, parents and teachers) may have, as well as considerations for the role of language in mathematics education, in particular in contexts where English is the dominant language in the school while Spanish is the main language in the home.

The chapter by Morales, Vomvoridi-Ivanović, and Khisty gives an example of the potential of multi-generational setting to generate rich mathematical engagement for Latino/a students. Situated in the context of an after-school project, the chapter illustrates the use of cultural and linguistic (English and Spanish) resources in a mathematical environment around probability and arithmetic based games. The participants include elementary school-age children, the mothers of some of them, and undergraduate and graduate students. The chapter focuses on the case of one student and his mother and highlights the connections between school mathematics (through the child) and home mathematics (through the mother's knowledge). It also adds to our understanding of issues related to students' language choice when doing mathematics.

In his chapter, Domínguez underscores the need to develop spaces for parents to engage in dialogues about problem solving with other parents, with students, and with teachers. Working with a group of seven Latina mothers, Domínguez analyzes the dialogue of these mothers as they talk about their experiences with mathematics, reflect on their children's mathematics education, and suggest ideas for practice to one teacher. Using Belenky, Clinchy, Goldberger, and Tarule's (1986) framework for women's ways of knowing, Domínguez characterizes the dialogue of this group of mothers among themselves as representing primarily "silence" and "constructed knowledge." In their interactions with three students, Dominguez hints at a possible gender aspect in how the mothers interacted with male and female students, promoting more independent thinking in the boys while using a more prescriptive (reproduction of specific methods) with the girl. These findings are tentative given the small sample, but may be worth pursuing given their own experiences as women in mathematics. Their dialogue with the teacher points to a possible difference of opinion between the mothers and the teacher in that the mothers suggest ideas that could be used to enrich the mathematical learning in the classroom, while the teacher seems to indicate that not everything is learned in the classroom and appears to separate the two contexts (in and out of the classroom). Domínguez highlights the lack of appropriation of each other's (teacher–mothers) dialogue. As he writes, "the need for a dialogic interspace between parents and teachers has been identified and requires further research."

Acosta-Iriqui, Civil, Díez-Palomar, Marshall, and Quintos-Alonso discuss the impact of two different language policies on Latino/a parental engagement in mathematics education. While the New Mexico Constitution endorses bilingual education, Arizona severely restricted bilingual education in 2000 with the passing of Proposition 203 (based on Proposition 227 passed in 1998 in California). Both CEMELA sites (Albuquerque and Tucson) had parents' groups with whom the authors conducted in-depth interviews, focus groups, and mathematics classroom observations and debriefings. The chapter discusses the situated nature of parental engagement and then centers on the effects of the different language policies on the engagement of Spanish-dominant parents in their children's mathematics education. The findings reveal the crucial role of context within mathematics education, which includes the historicity of the communities and the impact of the different educational policies. Parents in both contexts are aware of the benefits and limitations that bilingual education or English-only policies create for them and their children. In particular, in the case of the Arizona parents, they express their frustration at not being able to feel as connected with their children's mathematics education (e.g., homework) as they wished due to the language barrier. While the New Mexico parents seemed optimistic about their children's educational future, some of the Arizona parents were concerned about the dropout risk for their children. Overall, parents were in favor of bilingual education as the way to keep the connection with the family's linguistic and cultural background. This chapter points to the need to consider the role of language policies in the mathematics education of Latino/a students.

Turner, Varley Gutiérrez, and Díez-Palomar study students' experiences in an after-school mathematics club that focused on "mathematizing" activities in various local community settings (a donut shop/baker, a custom auto shop that specialized in low-riders, a store that sold candies and piñatas, and a neighborhood park that had recently burned down). A central notion in this chapter is community mathematization, which refers to the ways in which participants use mathematics to make sense of their worlds. The participants included 18 third- through sixth-grade Latino/a children, most of them bilingual English–Spanish. Working in small groups (facilitated by undergraduate research assistants and by CEMELA researchers), students analyzed the practices of each community setting with an eye on the mathematics in those practices. Students then posed an authentic problem that emerged from their understanding of the mathematical practices and developed a digital story to illustrate their learning. The chapter presents findings related to the students' mathematizing activity and to their problem-posing work. In particular they discuss the mathematization in the context of the auto shop setting. One of the practices involves enlarging a design. The authors illustrate how the children explored this topic through their interview with the auto shop owner. The mathematics embedded in the practice centers on scaling, an activity that was further explored in the after-school club. The chapter adds to the existing research on tensions in mathematizing unfamiliar practices. Many of the problems posed involved computation or measurement as these may be activities that are more easily identified as being part of the mathematics in these practices. The authors discuss the presence of other factors that often make some forms of mathematics less obvious in some practices, thus adding to the tension of implicit–explicit mathematics. The chapter also addresses how students used their understanding of the real world to make sense of the practices and of the mathematics. As the authors write, "We emphasize that students drew upon real-world considerations not only because the integration of real-world understandings and mathematical understandings was central to the practice of community mathematization, but also to highlight the various ways that real-world considerations impacted and shaped the mathematics that occurred." This chapter underscores the potential of engaging students in mathematizing activities in the community.

Section on Latinos/as, Teacher Education, and Mathematics Education

Decades of research in educational reform have confirmed what should have always been obvious: teachers, what they know and what they do, are chief to any academic reform or enhancement (Darling-Hammond & McLaughlin, 1995). Therefore, any thoughtful effort to improve the mathematics achievement of Latinos must account for teachers' knowledge and skills. This section of the volume shares three "thickly" described studies of teachers working to better understand their own practices and engage in those strategies and pedagogical stances that better serve Latino/a learners. These chapters on teaching help us to make sense of the complex connections between teacher knowledge, beliefs, and behavior and student performance.

In the research reported by Anhalt and Ondrus, we learn that teachers' content knowledge grows when they are confronted with the prospect of teaching students who do not share their native language. Using algebra blocks to represent challenging mathematical concepts, the teachers in this study came to realize the power of multiple representations as a tool for promoting both complex thinking and mathematical conversations. This case study research underscores the power of the use of multiple representations in assisting mathematical understanding. While this finding has been corroborated many times in the research literature, Anhalt and Ondrus point out the importance of the *teacher's* understanding of the value of multiple representations. Their candid assessment of the professional development program they developed offers all teacher educators several pieces of very good advice; specifically, the integration of mathematics, language, and pedagogy appears to have been a crucial piece of their work.

In the Musanti, Marshall, Ceballos, and Celedón-Pattichis chapter, we are able to follow the growing mathematical and linguistic knowledge and skills of both teacher and researchers, illustrating, once again, the power of collaboration in advancing pedagogical knowledge. The teacher's own admission of her weakness in understanding mathematical concepts is shared openly. The researchers themselves admit to gaps in their practical understanding of Cognitively Guided Instruction (CGI). Together, however, their progress in creating a rich mathematical environment in a bilingual primary classroom—an educational context rarely explored in mathematics education—offers both researchers and educators a thoughtful way forward. Most important, perhaps, is the teacher's report on the confidence and mathematics her students gained as a consequence of CGI, mathematics instruction in Spanish, and the reliance on their prior ambient understanding of mathematics (e.g., shopping at the Flea Market, selling tamales). This study therefore offers indisputable and practical evidence that working class Latino English learners can engage in complex mathematical understanding.

The research by Quintos, Civil, and Torres demonstrates that teaching in non-dominant communities requires a vision of social justice. By following the work of an expert teacher (Torres), this chapter underscores the importance of studying mathematics education from a critical and situated perspective that foregrounds the historical and socio-cultural, as well as demonstrating what a single teacher can do for her students even as the larger structural forces are weighed against critical engagement. Their study confirms that a deep knowledge of students' identities is crucial for truly critical teaching. But the research also notes the time and dedication such knowledge requires. There is no shortcut when teachers take seriously the rights of students and their own capacity for meaning making.

Section on Latinos/as, Assessment, and Mathematics Education

Although the chapters in this section reflect perhaps a broader focus than the others, the issues surrounding assessment are crucial if we are to accurately measure progress in improving the achievement of Latinos/as in mathematics. As the country enters the second decade of the accountability era, tests and other assessments continue to be misused in the evaluation of Latinos/as, especially those who are EL. These chapters, taken together, suggest new, thoughtful, and valid assessment practices at the classroom, school, and national level.

Castellón, Burr, and Kitchen use an interactive interview research protocol to assess Latino/a ELs' knowledge of fractions. The idea behind the use of this interactive interview protocol is not only to assess ELs' understanding of fractions but also to foster their understanding. This protocol promotes a focus on the resources that ELs bring to the discussion of problems, rather than a deficit approach. Their findings suggest that the interactive interview protocol created a supportive environment in which students' language capacity would not determine their understanding of mathematical concepts and allowed students to explain their thinking using methods that also represent competent mathematical communication (Moschkovich, 2007a). In sum, this chapter contributes to the area of research on understanding of fractions, through an in-depth study with four middle-school EL students. Some of the examples from the data show how knowledge is socially constructed through the interviewing process. The interaction between each student and the two interviewers allowed for rich communication of mathematical ideas, beyond an emphasis on using only academic language, thus positioning the students as competent problem solvers.

The chapter by Solano-Flores reminds us that we must always be on the lookout for systematic bias in all tests and assessment. As Solano-Flores points out, cultural differences and limited proficiency in the language influence the performance of students on tests, and that testing practices for these students have not changed significantly. He points out in careful detail, that the complexity of language, the multiple linguistic features of mathematics test items, and the linguistic heterogeneity of EL populations, testing for Latino/a EL should be based on a deep and abiding understanding of the relationship between language variation and score variation. He also discusses the process of development large-scale assessment and examines the limitations of current practice in the testing of ELs that result from not properly incorporating a view of language as a process. This important chapter fills in some serious gaps in our knowledge of how ill-conceived testing schemes can work against the proper placement of Latino EL.

Next, Mosqeda's work offers a compelling examination of several variables long discussed in the mathematics achievement of Latinos but rarely explored for their complex relationships. Using the 2002 Educational Longitudinal Study, Mosqueda explores whether academic tracking and math teachers' content knowledge and teaching preparation influences the mathematics performance of Latino secondary students, both native and non-native English speakers. After analyzing the data using multilevel models, his analysis confirms that Latino ELs are indeed placed in lower track mathematics classes, a practice that appears to be based solely on English capacity and not on mathematical knowledge. Not surprisingly, this type of tracking results in lower performance for Latino ELs. The analysis also revealed some interesting findings regarding teacher qualifications: Having a teacher with a mathematics degree was associated with higher achievement whereas credential status was not. Mosqueda is cautious in interpreting this finding, but it nevertheless suggests additional study on the preparation of teachers for Latino EL mathematics learners is warranted. Most importantly, the study reveals that some of the patterns of underperformance by Latino ELs are a consequence of poor policy decisions often made at the local level, which, unlike large bureaucracies, can be easily modified.

FINAL THOUGHTS

We are confident that the research in this volume will inspire additional researchers to conduct investigations that will yield new practices and policies to improve the mathematics education of Latinos/as. But we would remind readers that research and its careful application takes time. Latino underperformance in mathematics, while an urgent issue, cannot be guided by panic. Researchers are beholden to a systematic process of discovery, a set of rules for the generalization of findings, and thoughtful guidelines for the application of research findings to the practice setting. Unfortunately, misguided accountability schemes, such as No Child Left Behind, encourage schools and school systems to seek the "quick fix," employing untested curricula and methods not because they necessarily believe they will benefit students but rather to provide policymakers with evidence that they are doing *something* to improve test scores. By contrast, the chapters in this volume all demonstrate that improving the mathematics education of Latinos/as cannot be achieved with a simple curricular grafting or an afternoon of teacher "training."

It is striking that any educator or educationalist might imagine that it is otherwise. After all, improving mathematics instruction for Latinos/as intersects at two of our most complex human systems: culture and language. And it is our hope that this book has served to complicate these two issues regarding the teaching and learning of mathematics, especially when we are considering students who represent a cultural group whose background differs from the vast majority of those in charge of the schooling system itself. We have chosen to explore Latino/a learners and teachers in U.S. schools and communities to examine these issues in great detail, and have thus selected studies that examined systematically studied the role of language, culture, or both for its influence on the mathematical experiences of Latinos/as, both in and out of school. We are confident that each chapter in this book provides evidence that mathematics educators who choose to ignore language or culture in their pedagogy risk shortchanging their Latino/a students.

REFERENCES

Aud, S., Fox, M.A., & KewalRamani, A. (2010). *Status and trends in the education of racial and ethnic groups*. Washington, DC: National Center for Education Statistics.

Belenky, M. F., Clinchy, B. M., Goldberger, N. R., & Tarule, J. M. (1986). *Women's ways of knowing: The development of self, voice, and mind*. New York: Basic Books.

Brown, J. S., Collins, A., & Duguid, P. (1989). Situated cognition and the culture of learning. *Educational Researcher, 18* (1), 32–42.

Chapa, J. & De La Rosa, B. (2006). The problematic pipeline: Demographic trends and Latino participation in graduate science, technology, engineering, and mathematics programs. *Journal of Hispanic Higher Education, 5*(3), 203.

Civil, M., & Andrade, R. (2003). Collaborative practice with parents: The role of the researcher as mediator. In A. Peter-Koop, V. Santos-Wagner, C. Breen, & A. Begg (Eds.), *Collaboration in teacher education: Examples from the context of mathematics education* (pp. 153–168). Boston, MA: Kluwer.

Civil, M., & Bernier, E. (2006). Exploring images of parental participation in mathematics education: Challenges and possibilities. *Mathematical Thinking and Learning, 8*(3), 309–330.

Civil, M., Bratton, J., & Quintos, B. (2005). Parents and mathematics education in a Latino community: Redefining parental participation. *Multicultural Education Journal, 13*(2), 60–64.

Civil, M., & Menéndez, J. M. (2011). Impressions of Mexican immigrant families on their early experiences with school mathematics in Arizona. In R. Kitchen & M. Civil (Eds.), *Transnational and borderland studies in mathematics education* (pp. 47–68). New York, NY: Routledge.

Civil, M., & Planas, N. (2010). Latino/a immigrant parents' voices in mathematics education. In E. Grigorenko & R. Takanishi (Eds.), *Immigration, diversity, and education* (pp. 130–150). New York, NY: Routledge.

Civil, M., & Quintos, B. (2009). Latina mothers' perceptions about the teaching and learning of mathematics: Implications for parental participation. In B. Greer, S. Mukhopadhyay, S. Nelson-Barber, & A. Powell (Eds.), *Culturally responsive mathematics education* (pp. 321–343). New York, NY: Routledge.

Cobb, P., Wood, T., & Yackel, E. (1993). Discourse, mathematical thinking, and classroom practice. In E. Forman, N. Minick, & C. A. Stone (Eds.), *Contexts for learning: Sociocultural dynamics in children's development* (pp. 91–119). New York: Oxford University Press.

Cocking, R. R., & Mestre, J. P. (1988). *Linguistic and cultural influences on learning mathematics*. Mahwah, NJ: Lawrence Erlbaum.

Cuevas, G. (1983). Language proficiency and the development of mathematical concepts in Hispanic primary school students. In T. H. Escobedo (Ed.), *Early childhood bilingual education: A Hispanic perspective* (pp. 148–163). New York: Teachers College Press.

Cuevas, G. J., Mann, P. H., & McClung, R. M. (1986). *The effects of a language process approach program on the mathematics achievement of first, third, and fifth graders.* Paper presented at the annual meeting of the American Educational Research Association, San Francisco, CA.

Darling-Hammond, L., & McLaughlin, M. W. (1995). Policies that support professional development in an era of reform. *Phi Delta Kappan, 76*(8), 597–604.

De Avila, E. (1988). Bilingualism, cognitive function, and language minority group membership. In R. Cocking & J. Mestre (Eds.), *Linguistic and cultural influences on learning mathematics* (pp. 101–121). Hillsdale, NJ: Lawrence Erlbaum.

Forman, E. (1996). Learning mathematics as participation in classroom practice: Implications of sociocultural theory for educational reform. In L. Steffe, P. Nesher, P. Cobb, G. Goldin, & B. Greer (Eds.), *Theories of mathematical learning* (pp. 115–130). Hillsdale, NJ: Erlbaum.

Fry, R. (2007). *The changing racial and ethnic composition of U.S. public schools.* Washington, DC: Pew Hispanic Center.

Fuson, K., Smith, S., & Lo Cicero, A. (1997). Supporting Latino first graders' ten-structured thinking in urban classrooms. *Journal for Research in Mathematics, 28*(6), 738–766.

Gándara, P., & Contreras, F. (2009). *The Latino education crisis: The consequences of failed social policies.* Cambridge, MA: Harvard University Press.

Gimenez, M.E. (1997) Latino/Hispanic—Who needs a name?: The case against a standardized terminology. In A. Darder, R. D. Torres, & H. Gutiérrez (Eds.), *Latinos in education: A critical reader* (pp. 225–239). New York: Routledge.

González, N. (1995). Processual approaches to multicultural education. *Journal of Applied Behavioral Science, 31*(2), 234–244.

Greeno, J. (1994, August). *The situativity of learning: Prospects for syntheses in theory, practice, and research.* Paper presented at the American Psychological Association, Los Angeles, CA.

Henry, M. (1996). *Parent–school collaboration: Feminist organizational structures and school leadership.* Albany, NY: SUNY.

Jencks, C., & Phillips, M. (1998). The Black–White test score gap: Why it persists and what can be done. *Brookings Review, 16*(2).

Lampert, M. (1990). When the problem is not the question and the solution is not the answer: Mathematical knowing and teaching. *American Educational Research Journal, 27*(1), 29–64.

Lareau, A. (2000). *Home advantage: Social class and parental intervention in elementary education* (Updated ed.). Lanham, MD: Rowman & Littlefield.

Lave, J., & Wenger, E. (1991). *Situated learning: Legitimate peripheral participation.* New York: Cambridge University Press.

Lee, V. E., & Burkam, D. T. (2002). *Inequality at the starting gate: Social background differences in achievement as children begin school.* Washington D.C.: The Economic Policy Institute.

López, N. (2008). Antiracist pedagogy and empowerment in a bilingual classroom in the U.S., circa 2006. *Theory Into Practice, 47*, 43–50.

Mestre, J. P. (1981). Predicting academic achievement among bilingual Hispanic college technical students. *Educational and Psychological Measurement, 41,* 1255–1264.

Mestre, J. & Gerace, W. (1986). A study of the algebra acquisition of Hispanic and Anglo ninth graders: Research findings relevant to teacher training and classroom practice. *NABE Journal, 10,* 137–167.

Moschkovich, J. N. (1999). Understanding the needs of Latino students in reform-oriented mathematics classrooms. In L. Ortiz-Franco, N. Hernandez, & Y. De La Cruz (Eds.), *Changing the faces of mathematics: Perspectives on Latinos* (vol. 4, pp. 5–12). Reston, VA: NCTM.

Moschkovich, J. N. (2000). Learning mathematics in two languages: Moving from obstacles to resources. In W. Secada (Ed.), *Changing faces of mathematics (Vol. 1): Perspectives on multiculturalism and gender equity* (pp. 85–93). Reston, VA: NCTM.

Moschkovich, J. N. (2002). A situated and sociocultural perspective on bilingual mathematics learners. *Mathematical Thinking and Learning,* Special issue on Diversity, Equity, and Mathematical Learning, N. Nasir & P. Cobb (Eds.), *4*(2&3), 189–212.

Moschkovich, J. N. (2007a). Beyond words to mathematical content: Assessing English learners in the mathematics classroom. In A. Schoenfeld (Ed.), *Assessing Mathematical Proficiency* (pp. 345–352). New York: Cambridge University Press.

Moschkovich, J. N. (2007b). Bilingual mathematics learners: How views of language, bilingual learners, and mathematical communication impact instruction. In N. Nasir & P. Cobb (Eds.), *Diversity, equity, and access to mathematical ideas* (pp. 89–104). New York: Teachers College Press.

Moschkovich, J. N. (2007c). Examining mathematical discourse practices. *For The Learning of Mathematics, 27*(1), 24–30.

Moschkovich, J. N. (2007d). Using two languages while learning mathematics. *Educational Studies in Mathematics, 64*(2), 121–144.

National Clearinghouse for Bilingual Education. (1983). *Information on technical assistance needs of Title VII demonstration projects: Validation and evaluation.* Washington, DC: Office of Bilingual Education and Minority Language Affairs.

Passel, J., & Cohn, D. (2008). *Trends in unauthorized immigration: Undocumented inflow now trails legal inflow.* Washington, DC: Pew Hispanic Center.

Perie, M., Grigg, W., & Dion, G. (2005). *The nation's report card: Mathematics 2005.* Washington, DC: US Government Printing Office.

Quintos, B., Bratton, J., & Civil, M., (2005). Engaging with parents on a critical dialogue about mathematics education. In M. Bosch (Ed.), *Proceedings of the Fourth Congress of the European Society for Research in Mathematics Education* (pp. 1182–1192). Sant Feliu de Guíxols, Spain: FUNDEMI IQS, Universitat Ramon Llull.

Reay, D. (1998). Cultural reproduction: Mothers involvement in their children's primary schooling. In M. Grenfell & D. James (Eds.), *Bourdieu and education: Acts of practical theory* (pp. 55–71). Bristol, PA: Falmer.

Rúa, M. M. (2005). Latinidades. In S. Oboler and D.J. González (Eds.), *The Oxford Encyclopedia of Latinos and Latinas in the United States,* (pp. 505–507). New York: Oxford University Press.

Rumberger, R. W., & Gándara, P. (2004). Seeking equity in the education of California's English learners. *Teachers College Record, 106*(10), 2032–2056.

Secada, W. (1991). Degree of bilingualism and arithmetic problem solving in Hispanic first graders. *Elementary School Journal, 92*(2), 213–231.

Snyder, T. D., & Dillow, S. A. (2010). *Digest of Education Statistics, 2009.* NCES 2010-013. National Center for Education Statistics, 732.

Solorzano, D. G., & Bernal, D. D. (2001). Examining transformational resistance through a critical race and LatCrit theory framework. *Urban Education, 36*(3), 308.

Spanos, G., & Crandall, J. (1990). Language and problem solving: Some examples from math and science. In A. M. Padilla, H. H. Fairchild, & C. M. Valadez (Eds.), *Bilingual education: Issues and strategies* (pp. 157–170). Beverly Hill, CA: Sage.

Spanos, G., Rhodes, N. C., Dale, T. C., & Crandall, J. (1988). Linguistic features of mathematical problem solving: Insights and applications. In R. Cocking & J. Mestre (Eds.), *Linguistic and cultural influences on learning mathematics* (pp. 221–240). Hillsdale, NJ: Lawrence Erlbaum.

Stillwell, R. (2010). *Public School Graduates and Dropouts From the Common Core of Data: School Year 2007–08* (NCES 2010-341). National Center for Education Statistics, Institute of Education Sciences, U.S. Department of Education. Washington, DC. Retrieved from http://nces.ed.gov/pubsearch/pubsinfo.asp?pubid=2010341

Téllez, K. (2010). *Teaching English language learners: Fostering language and the democratic experience.* Boulder, CO: Paradigm Publishers.

Therrien, M. & Ramirez, R. (2000). *The Hispanic population in the United States: March 2000.* Washington, DC: U.S. Census Bureau.

Vincent, C. (1996). *Parents and teachers: Power and participation.* Bristol, PA: Falmer Press.

Walkerdine, V. (1998). *Counting girls out: Girls and mathematics.* New York: Routledge.

Yosso, T. (2000). *A critical race and LatCrit approach to media literacy: Chicana/o resistance to visual microagressions.* Unpublished doctoral dissertation, University of California, Los Angeles.

Young, B. (2002). *Characteristics of the 100 largest public elementary and secondary school districts in the United States: 2000-01*, NCES 2002-351. Washington, DC: U.S. Department of Education, NCES.

CHAPTER 2

LATINO/A STUDENTS' UNDERSTANDING OF EQUIVALENCE

Use of Two Standards-Based Curricula in Eighth-Grade Algebra

Nancy O'Rode, Ph.D.
Department of Elementary Education
California State University, Northridge

INTRODUCTION

Mandates across the United States calling for algebra in the eighth grade heighten the demand for curricula that support all students in learning algebra. Few published studies consider curricular influences on mathematics learning, and researchers (e.g., Stein, Remillard, & Smith, 2007) have called for more research devoted to influences of curricula on student learning. If we are to improve the teaching and learning of algebra for all students, it is imperative that we examine in detail how curriculum influences learning for Latino/a students.

Latinos/as and Mathematics Education, pages 19–36

This chapter documents a study that examined how Latino/a students used the resources related to two standards-based curricula to develop understanding of a fundamental idea in algebra. The study focused on the concept of equivalence and examines how students used two types of resources, language and curricular models, to solve problems involving equivalence.

STUDENTS' USE OF RESOURCES
FOR UNDERSTANDING EQUIVALENCE

This study examined how students from two algebra classrooms used resources to solve equivalence problems during interview tasks. The Latino/a students in this study were using standards-based curricular materials that encourage communication, reasoning, and problem solving, and were in a classroom environment that provided many opportunities for students to engage in conversations about mathematics. The analysis explores the resources that the students brought to the mathematical conversations, especially the resources that contributed to their knowledge and understanding of algebra.

To frame the study, I draw on Moschkovich's (2000) suggestion to focus on the resources students use, rather than the obstacles they face. I also draw on Khisty's (1995) suggestions that we understand learners on their own terms and that we view the process that enculturates students into the mathematical world as having many components. In trying to understand how these Latino/a students thought about solving equations and what ideas they brought to the process, the analysis considered the learners on their own terms, as Khisty suggested, and looked at the resources they brought to their sense making, as Moschkovich proposed.

Brenner's (1994, 1998) studies contrasted types of mathematical communication that took place in language minority classrooms and asked whether language minority students benefit equally from language-intensive standards-based curricula. Brenner's studies found that when English language learners (ELLs) were engaged in mathematical discussions in these algebra classes, they did benefit equally from the standards-based curricula (Brenner et al., 1997).

Equivalence is a worthy topic for study. The National Council of Teachers of Mathematics (NCTM, 2000) suggested that students in middle grades need experience with equivalence relationships before they are exposed to transforming and solving linear equations. Researchers have addressed the topic of equivalence, and Kieran (1988) saw it as a key feature for 13-year-olds in the successful transition from elementary school mathematics to algebra. Previous research suggested that lack of understanding of equivalence as a relationship is a major stumbling block for students in algebra classrooms (Falkner, Levi, & Carpenter, 1999; Filloy & Rojano, 1989; Kieran, 1984, 1988, 2007; Steinberg, Sleeman, & Ktorza, 1990). Much of the literature in the 1980s and 1990s that focused on recognizing and maintaining equivalence for equations provided quantitative analyses of student mistakes, but failed to show what students understood about the concept. This study explored what students understood about equivalence and how curricula supported or failed to support students' sense making. The central research question was how the enacted curriculum, with its language-rich, equitable, standards-based environment, influenced Latino/a students' learning and understanding of algebra and the concept of equivalence. In particular, the study documents how students used language and curricular models to solve problems involving equivalence.

THE TEACHER, CURRICULA, AND CLASSROOM

In 2000, California mandated that all eighth graders enroll in algebra. Oakes, Joseph, and Muir (2003) have shown that, in California, although many eighth-grade algebra courses had been created, only a few encompassed the full year of high school algebra, thus reenacting the unequal opportunities for many eighth graders that the mandate was meant to overcome. In the midst of this curricular upheaval in California stood Mr. H, a teacher of six junior high mathematics classes, who had to decide what curricular supports would help him effectively teach algebra to all of his eighth-grade students. His decisions were a microcosm of the thousands of similar decisions being made across the state at that time to determine how to provide all eighth graders equitable opportunities to learn algebra and comply with the mandate.

The study was carried out in a large K–8 school district in southern California that served over 16,000 students. In the junior high school (grades 7–8) in which the study took place, the population of 1,025 students was comprised primarily of Latino/a students (94%) with African American, European American, Filipino, and Pacific Islanders comprising the remaining 6%. Approximately 62% of the junior high school students were classified as ELLs. Of the school's total student population, 80% qualified for the free and reduced-price lunch program. This junior high school was selected as the research site for several reasons. The school district was interested in using standards-based curricula throughout grades K–8, due in part to the district's participation in the 1990s' NSF-funded Local Systemic Change Initiative. Mr. H was a well-respected teacher who had won district and county teaching awards, as well as leadership awards for advocating for educational opportunities for his students. Furthermore, implementation of two standards-based algebra curricula by the same teacher in the same year created a unique situation for study.

Mr. H taught mathematics to six classes of eighth-grade students per day, as is customary in many U.S. junior high schools. The classes ranged in size from 28 to 36 students. He decided to use the Interactive Mathematics Program (IMP) (Fendel, Resek, Alper, & Fraser, 1998a, 1998b) for the first three classes of the day and use the College Preparatory Mathematics (CPM) program curriculum (Sallee, Kysh, Kasimatis, & Hoey, 2000) for the last three classes of the day. The decision to use two different standards-based curricula was based, in part, upon his leadership experience in mathematics at the district and county level; Mr. H's desire to be a part of the new initiative at the junior high level, which would result in more students enrolling in advanced high school mathematics; and his desire to find a curriculum that provided the best support for his students.

As Mr. H reported in interviews, his guiding teaching principle was equity: He sought a safe learning environment that provided eighth graders with the tools and tasks that nurtured mathematical learning. As a participant observer in the classroom, I observed a classroom culture that can be described as a standards-based learning environment (Stein et al., 2007), a setting in which students are asked to find multiple strategies for problems posed, to make conjectures and justify their reasoning, and to communicate their thinking—in short, a setting in which mathematical thinking was at the core of each lesson.

The IMP and the CPM program were developed in California, just as the NCTM (1989) called for innovative curricula to match the new standards. Both the IMP and the CPM program are standards-based curricula and deemed exemplary by the U.S. Department of Education (Mathematics and Science Expert Panel, 1999). Curricula for both the IMP and CPM indicated that the programs were intended for both college-bound students and students entering the job market after secondary school. The design of both curricula incorporated problem-based and collaborative approaches to instruction. Mr. H's eighth-grade students were headed to large high schools where a choice between IMP and CPM or a traditional curriculum was offered, and thus, with the emphases in California on having all eighth graders take the first year of algebra, and his inclination to give the eighth graders an introduction to high school mathematics, Mr. H decided to use the beginning units of the IMP and CPM curricula. This study focused on the IMP unit entitled *Solve It!* and the CPM unit entitled *Choosing a Phone Plan*.

THE STUDENTS

I was interested in seeing how the curricula supported, or failed to support, Latino/a students as they wrestled with the concept of equivalence. Data from semistructured interviews of 32 student pairs of eighth graders in Mr. H's classes were collected to ensure a large sample of students' ideas. Approximately one month before the end of the school year, I interviewed student pairs to capture mathematical communication between peers, and to discover the influence each curriculum may have had on students' understanding of equivalence. The sample of 16 student pairs from the IMP and 16 student pairs from the CPM were matched on language proficiency, mathematics grades, district computation test scores, and SAT-9 scores from the seventh-grade year. The school district annually assesses students whose primary language is not English to determine the level of English proficiency by administering the California English Language Development Test. ELLs were assessed each year until they were classified as fluent English proficient. Each set of 16 student pairs was comprised of four pairs of Latino/a students labeled by the district as English only, eight pairs with one student labeled limited English proficient and one student labeled English only, and four pairs of students, each of whom were labeled limited English proficient. The interviews were videotaped and transcribed.

THE MONEY TASK

During one school year, students were observed working in cooperative groups and talking about equations and equivalence. Student comments and questions in the classroom setting on variables and operations with variables led to the creation of the four interview tasks. The first interview task, the money task, did not involve the use of symbols or equations, and pertained to a quasi-realistic situation, which, I hoped, might elicit students' thinking through physical movements captured on videotape. This task used foreign currency, which set up the pretense of buying identical items from a shopkeeper in a foreign country. As there were no familiar numbers to read on the bank notes or on the coins, students could not use a number referent to solve the problem.

I gave each student an identical bank note and they used the bank note to buy an item from a shopkeeper. Each student received change in the form of coins. One student received three large coins and four small coins in change, and the other student received one large coin and 18 small coins in change. After the students agreed to the equivalence of the value of the change they had received, they were told to work together to find out "how many small coins were the same as one large coin." I probed for student thinking about equivalence by referring to what the student pair did with the coins and asking them to justify their steps. The students talked together as they worked out the solution to the problem, and I recorded their problem-solving talk. The solution to the money task could be described symbolically by the linear equation $3x + 4 = 1x + 18$ (see Appendix for Money Task and other interview protocols).

Most student pairs took one large coin from each pile and then took four small coins from each pile. Students usually organized their workspace to visibly demonstrate that similar amounts and sizes of coins were removed from each pile. This activity left two large coins in one pile and 14 small coins in the other. At this stage, most student pairs divided up the 14 coins in two piles and announced, "One large coin is the same as seven small coins." As the students completed the money task, I probed their thinking by asking questions such as, "*I saw that you both removed one large coin from each pile of coins. How did you know how to do that?*" and "*What would have happened if one of you removed four small coins and the other person did not?*"

METHODS

The study examined two aspects of the student interviews: how students used language and how they used curricular models to solve problems. Language use during the money task offers clues about how the students conceptualized equivalence and whether they used any curricular models. Difficulties in speaking about equivalence were exemplified in the difficulty I had in creating the tasks and carefully monitoring my language to avoid certain words and influencing students' language. For example, I was careful not to say "equal" in the interview, and substituted the phrase "the same as" to refer to equivalence.

To investigate how the curricula supported Latino/a eighth graders' understanding of equivalence, I analyzed the interviews from 32 pairs of students on the money task and three other tasks, which used think-aloud protocols. The talk, gestures, and actions captured on the videotapes were transcribed. Two coding schemes were employed to analyze student responses to the tasks. Segments of the money task were coded as, for example, problem setup, agreement of equal worth, probing questions, explanation to partner, coin manipulation discussion, connections to algebra class, and so on. By coding the interviews in this manner, episodes in which student pairs discussed equivalence and justified their solutions were identified. Descriptive matrices using direct-quote raw data were compiled from specific episodes, such as the partner explanation segment or algebra class connections (Miles & Huberman, 1984). A constant comparative method of analysis of the data (Strauss & Corbin, 1994) from the matrices was completed to identify language and gestures used by students when solving the tasks.

In addition, a content analysis (Marshall & Rossman, 1995; Patton, 1990) was conducted on the IMP and CPM integrated mathematics curricula for representations, strategies, and language used to teach concepts of equivalence found in student texts, teacher guides, and assessments for each unit. This analysis documented several curricular models. *Curricular models* are devices found in curricula to help students understand a concept. These models, which include pictures, objects, illustrations, manipulatives, activities, demonstrations, role-playing situations, and representations, are employed by curriculum writers as a means to illustrate a concept such as equivalence relationships between terms, expressions, or equations (Lesh, Post, & Behr, 1987). The IMP curriculum, for example, used a tug-of-war game to demonstrate the result of adding equal terms to both sides of an equation. To model solving equations, the CPM curriculum used cups and number tiles, whereas the IMP curriculum provided a contextual story about the weight of mysterious bags of gold on the pan balance. Both IMP and CPM provided curricular models for students; this study investigated which of these models supported students as they communicated their understanding of algebraic concepts.

STUDENTS' CONNECTIONS TO CURRICULAR MODELS

When students were finished with the first task, I asked whether they could make any connections between this completed task and their algebra class. Specifically, I asked, "While you were working on the problem, did anything come to mind that reminded you of Mr. H's algebra class?" The responses by student pairs on the connections they made between algebra class and the money task they had just completed are presented in Table 2.1. The interviews were conducted at the end of the eighth-grade year and thus the student pairs were recalling features of their algebra class and the unit on solving equations taught 6 to 7 months earlier.

As presented in Table 2.1, the consistent responses from IMP students regarding the connections they made to the IMP curriculum indicate that

TABLE 2.1 Connections to Curriculum Made by Student Pairs During Interview

IMP curriculum connection	# pairs	CPM curriculum connection	# pairs
Pan balance	11	Algebraic equations	4
No connection made	2	Cups and tiles	2
Fractions	1	Hot and cold cubes	2
		Fish populations	2
		Pan balance	2
		Tug-of-war	2

Note: The question was not administered to two student pairs from each curriculum.

many students recalled the balance model, and that this model may have been a salient feature for many students. The other IMP students named no other curricular model. In contrast, the CPM student pair responses were varied and distributed evenly between six options so that no one curricular model emerged as a favored resource for making sense of equivalence concepts.

An analysis of how students used models from each curriculum provides some explanation for the different responses by the IMP and CPM students. In CPM, the major model used for equivalence was cups and tiles, which was used early for a period of two days during the 11-day unit. The name, cups and tiles, refers to the use of manipulatives: paper cups to simulate variables and tiles marked with positive and negative signs to simulate integers. One page in the student text is allotted for an example of the modeling process in which cups, shown as circles, and tiles, shown as squares, are used to illustrate the equal subtraction and division operations needed to maintain equivalence when solving equations. Teacher involvement is necessary for the cups and tiles modeling process to explain that the cups stand for variables in the equation, tiles are integers, the same amount of tiles must be in each cup, and the object is to determine how many tiles should be in each cup to solve the problem. The CPM unit also used the undoing model, which was a problem-solving strategy of working backward by undoing operations on the variable (Sallee et al., 2000).

More CPM students named algebraic equations than the cups and tiles, although there was no model in CPM explicitly labeled by that name. The focus for the CPM unit was solving algebraic equations symbolically, and as approximately half of the work assigned in CPM directed students to solve equations, the response of "algebraic equations" is understandable. Although it was not part of the CPM curriculum, the teacher demonstrated the balance model three times during the CPM unit. Two CPM student pairs connected the balance with the interview task, which gives some indication of the power that this simple demonstration may have on students. Similarly, the short and simple in-class tug-of-war demonstration by Mr. H, in which he used a thick rope and three students on each side pulled the rope to win the contest, was mentioned by two pairs of CPM students. Although the CPM students spent more than one class period using the cups and tiles manipulatives, it is curious that more students did not connect the physical aspects of the cups and tiles manipulatives to the coin manipulations in the money task.

The IMP curriculum used more varied representations for equivalence than did the CPM curriculum. The IMP featured a balance metaphor throughout the unit, along with five other types of models using area, repeated addition, and substitution to show equivalence. The IMP used a wide variety of curricular models to represent equivalence such as students in a tug of war, a student looking into a mirror with an equivalent equation reflected back on his shirt, as well as many pictures of a pan balance. The IMP introduced the mystery bags game as a model for solving equations: Mystery bags are each filled with the same amount of gold and can be balanced with a combination of lead weights on a pan balance.

Overall, these responses indicate that the balance model (presumably taken from the IMP program, curricular models of which incorporated mystery bags on a pan balance for 10 days of the 15-day unit) may have been a salient feature for the IMP students. In contrast, the CPM students' varied responses may reflect a curricular model of short-lived duration. The consistent responses of the IMP group probably reflect the long-term, repeated use of the balance model in the IMP unit.

STUDENTS' USE OF CURRICULAR MODELS AND LANGUAGE

To explore whether the curricular models supported students as they communicated their understanding of equivalence, an analysis of student talk in response to the algebra class connection prompts was carried out. In this analysis, language related to equivalence, transforming equivalent equations, or equal relationships was noted along with any curricular model students used.

If we examine more closely the responses from the students connecting the curricular model to the algebra classroom, the students' language indicates that when students chose the balance or tug of war, they also used the response as a vehicle to support additional sense making about the money task. This connection was true for student pairs from both the CPM and the IMP curricula who chose the balance or tug-of-war models. Students explained why the balance worked and incorporated the ideas into the physical model or suggested operations on equations that maintained equivalence. In contrast, other discourse patterns emerged that described the end product, focusing upon variables or the value of the variable x, but not the means to find the solution for x by transforming equivalent equations.

Student responses about curricular models in which students elaborated on equivalence and in which students did not elaborate on equivalence are presented in Table 2.2 and Table 2.3, respectively. The data in Table 2.2 provide evidence for the differences in how curricular models appear to have supported students' understanding of equivalence. As presented in Table 2.2, when the CPM students reported a curricular connection with the balance or tug-of-war model, they also included explanations and elaborations on the model connecting it with equivalence. In contrast, when CPM students responded with the cups and tiles or algebraic equations cur-

TABLE 2.2   Eighth-Grade Student Pairs' Interview Responses Elaborating on Equivalence

Curriculum	Curriculum connection	Responses elaborating on equivalence
IMP	Balance	"Taking away the same, equal"; "Yeah, both sides"; "He took away from both sides and cancelled one side and then the rest"
IMP	Balance	"The scale—what we do to one side we have to do to the other."
IMP	Balance	"The little balance, we have to do the same thing to the other side"; "so it can be even" [uses hand gestures to show up and down motion]
CPM	Balance	"About [Mr. H's] scale, he put some objects on one side and made the other side equal."
CPM	Tug of war	"You take away one and you take away one over there...to make it equal." [uses hand gestures to show up and down motion] To make it equal, on the sides, yeah."
CPM	Tug of war	"If I added one and then my friend added one then it would be equal."
CPM	Cups and tiles	"You have to take the same amount from each side, every time you take it away."

TABLE 2.3   Eighth-Grade Student Pairs' Interview Responses Not Elaborating on Equivalence

Curriculum	Curricular connection	Responses not elaborating on equivalence
CPM	Cup and tiles	"Like those problems we did with the cups and that we had to figure out, like um, solve for x and those kinds of problems."
CPM	Algebra equations	"The equations where you have to know what x equals to."
IMP	Fractions	"Anything like pizzas or anything,...like taking portions out of it. It always has to do with x, if you are doing an x-y table, it always has to do with x."

riculum models, they did not elaborate on the models or connect them to equivalence.

An example of how two students described the cups and tiles model is presented below. The excerpt is from an interview in which the students explicitly expressed their opinions of this model.

> **Teresa:** I probably want to say those cups and tiles things but I got confused when he was talking about those.
>
> **Evelia:** That whole balancing equations things.

Teresa: I guess these [four coins] would be the tile things but I never got that whole lesson.
Interviewer: Was the cups and tiles thing different than balancing equations?
Teresa: I don't know.
Evelia: I think it was the same thing.
Teresa: I think these [coins] are like the tiles, like you had to even it out.
Teresa: But those were negative and positive, weren't they?

Teresa and Evelia connected the cups and tiles model to the interview task but seemed confused about the purpose of the model and tentative about any connection to equivalent equations.

One conjecture about the cups and tiles model is that students in the CPM curriculum did not make connections with this model because of its complexity, especially the processing load that the manipulatives and the two-dimensional representations of the manipulatives required of students. This theory seems plausible, given that researchers warn that complex manipulatives may hinder concept formation rather than help because of the processing load that the manipulatives demand (Boulton-Lewis , Cooper, Atweh, Pillay, Wilss, & Mutch, 1997; MacGregor & Stacey, 1997; Vlassis, 2002).

Students' Use of Words, Phrases, and Gestures

Use of "Equal"

During the interviews, student pairs were asked to justify their reasoning about the equivalence situation in the money task. As the students explored their understanding about equivalence in conversation, they used the term *equal.* For example, one student pair explained, "We still just have to equal them out." Although this syntax is not the usual or formal way to use this term, the meaning behind this usage is clear and seems appropriate for a discussion of equivalence and for describing how to make two values equal. The students used the term equal in several ways, as demonstrated in these examples: "We are supposed to equal two of the same thing," "We need to find out how many equals into it," and "Two of these large coins should equal up to seven of these small ones." Students also used the term equal to describe a relationship between two terms, as in, "So that means these four coins are equal to this one large coin."

There were times when student pairs applied the term equal in the usual sense and then in the next utterance used the term in inventive ways. For example, consider this interaction:

Ricardo: Well, we're trying to group it to see which one works.
Edmundo: Nothing else equals 18 except for 9 times 2.
Ricardo: We can equal the value to this then.

The exchange between Ricardo and Edmundo illustrates how students used the term equal in two different ways to communicate their reasoning: one way to show that number values are the same and another way to communicate that the solution will involve an equal relationship. Students were trying to make sense of these mathematical ideas and thus were using language that carried meaning for them, rather than formal mathematical language. I reviewed the data to explore whether these inventive ways to express equivalence were related to English proficiency levels and found no connection to English language proficiency. These findings suggest that providing opportunities to discuss the ideas related to equivalence may be profitable for all students, regardless of English proficiency.

Use of Gestures

As students described situations of equivalence, they repeatedly used nonverbal communication to show evenness in very similar ways. The gesture began with students holding out their hands in front of them with palms up and level with each other and then moved the palms up and down, eventually settling them even to each other (see Figure 2.1). The gesture was a simple one that was repeated with uncanny similarity as students groped for words to describe equivalence.

The limited number of words used to describe equality (e.g., just, even, the same as) may add to the difficulty of explaining how equivalence is maintained. In every instance of using the gestures, the students were de-

Figure 2.1   Gestures suggesting the movement of a balance used by many students.

scribing the process of balancing two parts and making them equal. This usage, especially with many ELLs who used the gestures, indicates that students with limited English language skills are able to communicate their ideas in social situations to describe equivalence.

Use of the Phrase "Whatever you do . . ."

As students discussed their thinking throughout the four interview tasks, the use of the catchphrase "Whatever you do to one side of the equation, you do to the other side" was pervasive. When students were asked to justify transforming an equation into another equivalent equation, almost all student pairs cited some form of the catchphrase, "Whatever you do to one side, you have to do to the other." Neither curriculum used this catchphrase in the student text, but the idea was discussed in both of the teacher's editions. In the classroom, the catchphrase was commonplace as students worked at the board or in groups on problems, and during teacher demonstrations. Thus, the catchphrase "Whatever you do . . ." seemed to be a part of the curricula, intended or not.

During the money task and the three other tasks, I probed students for their understanding of the "whatever you do . . ." catchphrase. For approximately half of the student pairs, the catchphrase came to mean either "use only subtraction to simplify an equation" or "getting rid of" nuisance variables to make simplifying the problem easier (O'Rode, 2002). The vagueness of this catchphrase may result in algebra learners devising their own meaning for the term, such as demonstrated in the exchange among Antonio, Jaime, and the interviewer, below, in which a pair of students explained how to simplify an equation:

> **Antonio:** Because whatever you do to one side, you have to do to the other.
>
> **Interviewer:** Could you add half an x to the right and half an x to the left side of the equation?
>
> **Jaime:** I don't think so . . . aren't you supposed to subtract all the time?
>
> **Antonio:** I think that you couldn't do that [adding] . . . you need to subtract it.

For these students, the meaning behind the catchphrase may have become a restricted treatment of equivalence, where the operations for transforming equations are limited to subtraction of terms.

Another excerpt illustrates how students interpreted the catchphrase as doing whatever is needed to solve the equation $6x = -x + 7$, including "getting rid of the x" in whatever manner is available.

Teo: Cause *x* doesn't really have a value.

Gerardo: You have to figure it out.

Teo: But you have to move it around.

Gerardo: What you do to one side, you have to do to another side to figure out how you get the answer. . . .

Interviewer: Could you add an *x* to one side and add an *x* to the other side?

Teo: No. You have to put a negative *x* here [points to side with 6*x*] and put a positive *x* there [points to side with −*x* + 7].

Interviewer: You'd make this a negative *x* and this a positive *x* and why would you do that?

Teo: Because this is positive [points to 6*x*] and this is a negative [points to −*x*] and you have to do the same thing to both sides, get rid of the *x*.

Gerardo: Yeah.

For Teo and Gerardo, doing the same thing to both sides meant subtracting an *x* on the left and adding an *x* on the right.

These two examples and other similar responses from the interview pairs provide evidence that the catchphrase may have been misleading for students. Overall, only half of the student pairs used the catchphrase as it was intended, to explain how equivalence is maintained when transforming equations (O'Rode, 2002). The imprecise "Whatever you do . . ." catchphrase may limit students' choices of operations or, conversely, may expand students' choices to include canceling and other operations that were not intended.

The catchphrase "Whatever you do . . ." may have been unclear to students because the phrase is limited and vague—limited to stressing an operation with its *do* command and vague in its lack of specificity of number, amount, or object with its *whatever* beginning. The catchphrase may be meaningful to those who already understand equivalence—that equations transformed by similar operations on equal amounts will maintain equivalence. However, to young learners, the catchphrase may not make much sense. If the concept of equivalence is not already understood, then the phrase should be explicitly and carefully explained so that all students can uncover the meaning behind it.

CONCLUSIONS

This study documented how two aspects of the curricula—models and language use—had an impact on Latino/a students' understanding of algebraic equivalence. The analyses revealed the following findings:

- Six months after the equations-solving unit in the IMP was taught, most IMP students connected the pan balance curricular model to an equivalence task during semi-structured interviews.

- CPM students did not favor any one curricular model used in the CPM program.
- Student interview data suggest that curricular models that were used repeatedly and throughout the unit, such as the balance and tug of war, were more likely to be invoked by students and used as a resource during problem solving.
- When students described the balance or tug-of-war curricular models, they often elaborated on their understanding of equivalence.
- Students often used gestures as a support for communicating their ideas about simplifying equations.
- Students used the catchphrase "Whatever you do to one side, you do to the other" with several different meanings. Many student pairs used it to describe maintaining equivalence when transforming equations. Other student pairs used it to refer to a principle allowing only subtraction of terms, and still other students used the catchphrase to cancel terms without regard to maintaining equivalence.

These findings have several implications for instruction. Teachers should support students as they try out invented, creative, or unconventional ways to communicate about equivalence. As students grapple with both the algebraic ideas and the language for describing equivalence situations, they may not use formal language. By allowing students to use their own phrases, meanings, and approximations of mathematical language, teachers can have access to student thinking. Once student thinking is made public, teachers can provide opportunities for students to describe equivalence using more formal language. Teachers can scaffold student communication by using formal vocabulary terms that students can then later use to describe their thinking.

Students in the study appear to have been influenced by a number of curricular models. A curricular model such as the balance, which was used for a long period of time and supported in the text with illustrations, stories, problems, or assessments, seems to have supported student understanding and problem solving. The balance model in IMP, which was used throughout the 15-day unit, was recalled by over three quarters of the student pairs in interviews that took place six months later.

It may be surprising to learn that beginning algebra students used the catchphrase "Whatever you do to one side of the equation, you do to the other side" to justify both correct and incorrect ways to transform equations. Teachers may need to be more explicit when using this catchphrase and explain the operations used to transform equations. When using this catchphrase, it may be important to relate it to the concept of equivalence and to use language that makes sense to students.

APPENDIX: INTERVIEW PROTOCOL

Task 1: The Money Task

Money Problem Setup:

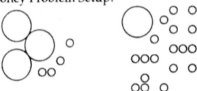

Question: How many small coins are the same as one large coin?

No Symbolic Equation (i.e., $3x + 4 = x + 18$) used.

Connections to algebra: "Did anything come to mind that reminded you of algebra class?"

Task 2: The Three Choices Task

Interview Question:
Three students were shown this equation and were asked, "What can you tell me about this step?"

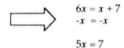

$$6x = x + 7$$
$$-x = -x$$
$$5x = 7$$

The first student said, "You can't do that because you don't know what x is."
OR
The second student said, "You can sometimes do that, but not all the time. It depends upon x."
OR
The third students said, "You can always do that, no matter what x is."

Think about these students' answers and decide which one you think gave the best answer.

Task 3: Messing Up Equations Task

$x = 3$	Start
$2 \cdot x = 3 \cdot 2$	Multiply by a number.
$2x = 6$	Add a number.
$2x + 5 = 6 + 5$	
$2x + 5 = 11$	What is the answer?
	Can you add x^2 to both sides?
$x^2 + 2x + 5 = 11 + x^2$	What is the answer now?

Task 4: Video Clip Task

Make
A 2 minute Video for
Next Year's Class.
On

"How to Solve Equations"

Manipulatives to Use:
Cups and Tiles
Stationary Balance
Algebra Tiles
x-tiles
Mystery Bags
Match boxes
Weights

REFERENCES

Boulton-Lewis, G., Cooper, T., Atweh, B., Pillay, H., Wilss, L., & Mutch, S. (1997). Processing load and the use of concrete representations and strategies for solving linear equations. *Journal of Mathematical Behavior, 16*(4), 379–397. doi: 10.1016/S0732-3123(97)90014-6

Brenner, M. E. (1994). A communication framework for mathematics: Exemplary instruction for culturally and linguistically diverse students. In B. McLeod (Ed.), *Language and learning: Educating linguistically diverse students* (pp. 233–267). Albany: State University of New York Press.

Brenner, M. E. (1998). Development of mathematical communication in problem solving groups by language minority students. *Bilingual Research Journal, 22,* 149–174. Retrieved from http://www.tandfco.uk/journals/ubrj

Brenner, M. E., Mayer, R. E., Moseley, B., Brar, T., Durán, R., Smith Reed, B., & Webb, D. (1997). Learning by understanding: The role of multiple representations in learning algebra. *American Educational Research Journal, 34*(4), 663–689. doi: 10.3102/00028312034004663

Falkner, K. P., Levi, L., & Carpenter, T. P. (1999). Children's understanding of equality: A foundation for algebra. *Teaching Children Mathematics, 6(4),* 232–236. Retrieved from http:// www.nctm.org/

Fendel, D., Resek, D., Alper, L., & Fraser, S. (1998a). *Interactive mathematics program: Integrated high school mathematics: Year 2.* Berkeley, CA: Key Curriculum Press.

Fendel, D., Resek, D., Alper, L., & Fraser, S. (1998b). *Solve it!: Interactive mathematics program: Year 2.* Berkeley, CA: Key Curriculum Press.

Filloy, E. & Rojano, T. (1989). Solving equations: The transition from arithmetic to algebra. *For the Learning of Mathematics, 9(*2), 19–25. Retrieved from http:// flm.educ/ualberta.ca

Khisty, L. L. (1995). Making inequality: Issues of language and meanings in mathematics teaching with Hispanic students. In W. G. Secada, E Fennema, & L. B. Adajian (Eds.), *New directions for equity in mathematics education* (pp. 279–297). Cambridge, UK: Cambridge University.

Kieran, C. (1984). A comparison between novice and more-expert algebra students on tasks dealing with the equivalence of equations. In J. M. Moser (Ed.), *Proceedings of the Sixth Annual Meeting of the North American Chapter of the International Group for the Psychology of Mathematics Education* (pp. 83–91). Madison: University of Wisconsin Center for Education Research.

Kieran, C. (1988). Two different approaches among algebra learners. In A. F. Coxford & A. P. Shulte (Eds.), *The ideas of algebra, K–12* (pp. 91–96). Reston, VA: National Council on Teachers of Mathematics.

Kieran, C. (2007). Learning and teaching algebra at the middle school through college levels: Building meaning for symbols and their manipulation. In F. K. Lester, Jr. (Ed.), *Second handbook of research on mathematics teaching and learning* (pp. 707–762). Reston, VA: National Council on Teachers of Mathematics.

Lesh, R. A., Post, T. R., & Behr, M. J. (1987). Representations and translations among representations in mathematics learning and problem solving. In C. Janvier (Ed.), *Problems of representation in the teaching and learning of mathematics* (pp. 33–40). Hillsdale, NJ: Erlbaum.

MacGregor, M., & Stacey, K. (1997). Students' understanding of algebraic notation: 11–15. *Educational Studies in Mathematics, 33*(1), 1–19. doi: 10.1023/A:1002970913563

Marshall, C. & Rossman, G. B. (1995). *Designing qualitative research* (2nd ed.). Thousand Oaks, CA: Sage.

Mathematics and Science Expert Panel. (1999). *Exemplary and promising mathematics programs.* Washington, DC: U.S. Department of Education. Available from http://www.enc.org/

Miles, M. B. & Huberman, A. M. (1984). *Qualitative data analysis: A sourcebook of new methods.* Beverly Hills, CA: Sage.

Moschkovich, J. (2000). Learning mathematics in two languages: Moving from obstacles to resources. In W. G. Secada (Ed.), *Changing the faces of mathematics: Perspectives on multiculturalism and gender equity* (pp. 85–93). Reston, VA: National Council of Teachers of Mathematics.

National Council of Teachers of Mathematics (NCTM). (1989). *Curriculum and evaluation standards for school mathematics.* Reston, VA: Author.

National Council of Teachers of Mathematics (NCTM). (2000). *Principles and standards for school mathematics.* Reston, VA: Author.

Oakes, J., Joseph, R., & Muir, K. (2003). Access and achievement in mathematics and science: Inequalities that endure and change. In J. A. Banks & C. A. M. Banks, (Eds.), *Handbook of research on multicultural education* (2nd ed., pp. 69–90). San Francisco, CA: Jossey-Bass.

O'Rode, N. (2002). Supporting Latino students' learning in eighth-grade algebra: Usage of language, resources, and models for understanding equivalence by students using two reform-based curricula. *Dissertation Abstracts International, 63* (09A), 274. (UMI No. 3064752)

Patton, M. Q. (1990). *Qualitative evaluation and research methods* (3rd ed.). Newbury Park, CA: Sage.

Sallee, T., Kysh, J., Kasimatis, E., & Hoey, B. (2000). *College preparatory mathematics 1: Algebra 1* (2nd ed.). Sacramento, CA: CPM Educational Program.

Stein, M. K., Remillard, J., & Smith, M. S. (2007). How curriculum influences student learning. In F. K. Lester, Jr. (Ed.), *Second handbook of research on mathematics teaching and learning* (pp. 319–370). Reston, VA: National Council of Teachers of Mathematics.

Steinberg, R. M., Sleeman, D. H., & Ktorza, D. (1990). Algebra students' knowledge of equivalence of equations. *Journal for Research in Mathematics Education, 22*(2), 112–121. doi: 10.2307/749588

Strauss, A., & Corbin, J. (1994). Grounded theory methodology: An overview. In N. K. Denzin & Y. S. Lincoln (Eds.), *The Sage handbook of qualitative research* (pp. 273–285). Thousand Oaks, CA: Sage.

Vlassis, J. (2002). The balance model: Hindrance or support for the solving of linear equations with one unknown. *Educational Studies in Mathematics, 49*(3), 341–359. doi: 10.1023/A:1020229023965

CHAPTER 3

BILINGUAL STUDENTS USING TWO LANGUAGES DURING PEER MATHEMATICS DISCUSSIONS

¿Qué Significa? Estudiantes Bilingües Usando Dos Idiomas en sus Discusiones Matemáticas: What Does it Mean?

William Zahner
Judit Moschkovich
Department of Education
University of California, Santa Cruz

INTRODUCTION

On a typical Wednesday morning in Ms. B's sixth-grade mathematics class in a dual-immersion bilingual school located in California,[1] a group of six students were sitting at their table and working on percentage problems from a worksheet. Claudia, Amber, and Francisco disagreed over their answer to the exercise (see Figure 3.1), and they asked Ms. B for help. Claudia

Latinos/as and Mathematics Education, pages 37–62
Copyright © 2011 by Information Age Publishing
37

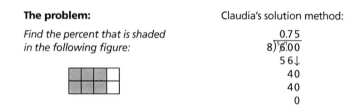

Figure 3.1   The problem discussed in Excerpt 3.1.

thought the answer should be 75%, while Amber and Francisco thought it was 33%. Claudia ultimately prevailed in the debate when the teacher verified her answer. Francisco was still not sure how his group-mates had obtained 75% from the fraction $\frac{6}{8}$, and he asked for more help. The group's discussion is presented in Excerpt 3.1.

Excerpt 3.1. [Wednesday class, session 1, 25:20–25:55][2]

1 **Francisco:** "Ah—why six over eight— seventy five percent?"
2 **Claudia:** ((bobbing head slowly)) "Divide it."
3   **Amber:** "OK watch. Six goes inside divide by eight [*xxx*" =
4 **Claudia:**   ["*Por eso 'ira*"
                                                   (("that's why, look."))

5   **Amber:** = "And [that."
6 **Claudia:**   ["Goes in the *casita*, you take out eight you put a
                        decimal *porque no se puede* [[put a decim—you put a
                        zero"=
                        (("goes in the little house, you take out eight , you
                        put a decimal because you cannot put a decim—
                        you put a zero."))=
7   **Amber:**   [["Uh-huh."
8 **Claudia:** = "*Ocho por siete*, put a seven here, it's fifty-six."
              (("eight times seven , put a seven here, it's fifty-six."))
10 **Dennis:** "Four." =
11 **Francisco:** = "(And that's) four."
12 **Dennis:** [["Four."
13 **Claudia:** [["Five, it's ten is four."
14 **Francisco:** "Oh yeah, seventy five percent."
15 **Claudia:** "*Y (luego)* [*xxx* zero."
              (("And (then) zero."))
16 **Dennis:** ["Zero, then five."
17 **Claudia:** "*Y luego es* seventy-five percent."
              (("And then it is seventy-five percent."))

These students attended a dual immersion bilingual school where classes were taught in both Spanish and English, and bilingualism was both encouraged and valued. All of the students in this group were bilingual, although some reported a preference for speaking Spanish and others preferred speaking English both inside and outside of school. Given that all of the students in the group were able to talk about this exercise in both Spanish and English, why did Claudia mix both Spanish and English in her explanations? What social and mathematical functions were served by her use of two languages? The purpose of this chapter is to explore these questions in more depth using examples from bilingual students' mathematical discussions to understand explanations for why bilingual students use multiple languages during mathematical discussions.

We think that a chapter about using multiple languages during mathematical discussions is especially relevant in the current U.S. context, where bi/multilingualism is increasingly becoming the norm. According to the U.S. Census Bureau (2008), a language other than English is spoken in 40% of all California households. In some areas of the state (such as Los Angeles and the San Francisco Bay area), the concentration of bilingual households is significantly higher. At the same time that demographic trends show an increase in societal bilingualism, restrictive language policies in schools have led to mandated English-only schooling in several states, including California (Gándara & Contreras, 2009). In the midst of a social and political shift, few mathematics educators have looked carefully at the function of using multiple languages in mathematical discussions.

In this chapter we follow up on Moschkovich's (2007b) analysis of bilingual students' use of two languages while doing mathematics. In our analysis, we confirm and corroborate Moschkovich's previous findings about one of the functions of using two languages during mathematical discussions. We extend Moschkovich's work by showing how the use of two (or more) languages by bilingual (or multilingual) students provides a set of linguistic resources for managing the social and cognitive demands of a group mathematics discussion. Finally, we consider the possible functions of using two languages during mathematical discussions in light of alternative theories about language in general and bilingualism in particular. In the discussion, we argue that future research relating language(s) to students' mathematical reasoning must carefully align theory, data, methods, and conclusions.

Our analysis is organized in a format that reflects our own path of inquiry as mathematics education researchers working with a research group. We begin with an overall conceptual framework for the analysis of students' mathematical discussions. Next, we provide a brief overview of the data that we used in Excerpt 3.1 and in Excerpt 3.2 (see Appendix B). Then we consider several competing hypotheses to explain students' use of two languages in mathematical discussions. As we consider various hypotheses about students' use of two or more languages in mathematical discussions, we use theory, previous research findings, and examples from the two excerpts to consider the merits of each of these hypotheses in turn. Finally, we conclude with a discussion of themes that emerge from this work.

CONCEPTUAL FRAMEWORK

Our perspective on learning mathematics and learning languages draws on assumptions from the sociocultural tradition. Learning is signaled by changing patterns of participation in a community (Newman, Griffin, & Cole, 1989; Rogoff, 2003; Vygotsky, 1978), and we specifically assume that learning mathematics is mediated by the use of multiple semiotic tools such as spoken and written words, specialized mathematical symbols, graphs, gestures, and mathematical discourse practices (Forman, 1996; Lemke, 2003; Moschkovich, 2007a; Radford, 2001, 2003). In mathematics classrooms, learning mathematics is inextricably bound to participating in mathematical discourse practices that are related to both the discipline of mathematics as well as the unique forms of mathematics found in schools (Forman, 1996; Moschkovich, 2002, 2004). In our analysis of language, we draw on theories and methods of sociolinguistics, focusing on the social uses of language rather than grammatical structures and prescriptive rules for usage (Drew & Heritage, 1992; Sacks, Schegloff, & Jefferson, 1974; Zentella, 1997).

Our approach to research is also grounded in K. D. Gutiérrez and Rogoff's (2003) recommendations for describing learners and communities. We treat culture as a set of practices, as something that people do, rather than as a static attribute of individuals or groups of people. Following K. D. Gutiérrez and Rogoff, we describe children's bilingualism in terms of how they participated in bilingual discussions rather than treating bilingualism as an individual attribute, as something they have acquired, or a school program category. K. D. Gutiérrez and Rogoff also emphasized that individuals participate in "constellations" of multiple cultural practices and that people's practices are constantly changing, so we use the past tense to describe what these students did in this setting at the time of data collection, rather than writing as if our observations generalize to all bilingual students across time and settings. Despite our local orientation, we believe that insights from our analysis will be useful for mathematics education research and teacher education in other settings.

Defining language is beyond the scope of this chapter, but we use our understanding of Spanish and English as speakers of these two languages to attend to when an utterance is all in Spanish (e.g., Excerpt 3.2, line 21: "*No porque Claudia quatro por seis es veinticuatro*"), all in English (e.g., Excerpt 3.1, line 1: "Ah—why six over eight, seventy five percent?"), or a mixture of both (e.g., Excerpt 3.1, line 6: "Goes in the *casita*, you take out eight, you put a decimal, *porque no se puede* put a decim—you put a zero"). Previous researchers have used a wide variety of terms to describe the practice of using two or more languages during one unit of discourse, and linguists make a number of subtle distinctions in regard to this practice, including whether switches involve single words, using loan words, and whether switches occur at the start, in the middle, or at the end of a unit of discourse (Moschkovich, 2007b; Sánchez, 1994). These disparate practices have been called, among many terms, code mixing, borrowing, or code switching. While we acknowledge that many of these distinctions are important for linguists, for mathematics education, we think the most relevant issue is how the use of two languages facilitates (or not) students' participation in mathematical discourse practices. In this chapter, we follow Moschkovich (2007b) and refer to the use of two languages during a continuous mathematical discussion as code switching.

DATA, SETTING, AND METHODS

The student discussions we use in this chapter were recorded during classroom observations by the primary author. These observations were part of a study of sixth-graders' peer interactions during mathematics group work. The overarching research questions for the project were the following:

1. In what mathematical discourse practices did students engage during peer mathematics discussions?
2. What were the rules of these discussions?
3. How did intellectual authority mediate these discussions?

In this chapter, we focus on part of the first and second questions.

Setting and Participants

The participating students were sixth graders (age 11–12) in a K–8 dual-immersion bilingual school in a rural town in central California. Over 90% of the students in this school identified as Latino/a, and all students were bilingual in Spanish and English. The sixth-grade students in this school took two math classes, one taught in Spanish and the other class taught in English. The two sixth-grade teachers divided the sixth-grade mathematics curriculum; Ms. B taught her sections in English while the other sixth-grade teacher taught his sections in Spanish. All of the sixth graders had both teachers for mathematics, so they studied half of the sixth grade mathematics curriculum in English and the other half of the curriculum in Spanish. Both teachers used the same English-language mathematics text although, in earlier grades, students used Spanish-language mathematics texts. All observations for this study took place in the English-language mathematics class. Although Ms. B lectured and conducted whole-class discussions in English, she was bilingual.

Data and Methods

In collaboration with Ms. B, we selected one focal group of students from the classroom for this study. Ms. B's class had a total of 28 students sitting in four tables made of seven desks each. Ms. B. selected students to sit at the focal group (near our video camera) by choosing typical students who she thought would be likely to engage in lively discussions. We videotaped all interactions of the focal group during the students' mathematics class for one week. Adopting a naturalistic (Moschkovich & Brenner, 2000) and ethnomethodological (Garfinkel, 1967; Heritage, 1984; Mehan, 1979) approach, we chose to record the students' peer mathematics discussions in the class; we allowed the teacher to structure the groups and decide on the mathematical activities on which the class would work. Between four and seven students sat at the table at which the focal group worked. All seven students were bilingual, and, in a language preference survey, four of them reported speaking primarily Spanish outside of school while two reported speaking primarily English outside of school (the seventh student did not complete the survey).

We videotaped a total of five hours of the focal students' in-class interactions, and we selected excerpts from the data when the students engaged in sustained mathematical discussions for analysis. We used Pirie and Schwartzenberger's (1988) definition of a mathematical discussion: "purposeful talk on a mathematical subject in which there are genuine pupil contributions and interaction" (p. 461). Based on our selection criteria, we transcribed a total of 56 minutes of the students' interactions using a modified version of Jefferson's transcription conventions (Schiffrin, 1994). Our analysis included two phases. During the first phase, we focused on the students' mathematical discourse practices and we attended to the content frame (Barnes & Todd, 1995) of the students' discussions. We analyzed how the students used the peer discussion to accomplish their mathematical goals. During the second phase of the analysis, we used methods from conversation analysis (Drew & Heritage, 1992; Schiffrin, 1994) to understand the implicit rules of these students' peer discussions, specifically attending to the rules for turn taking (Sacks et al., 1974), the function of questions as a signal of authority (Linde, 1988), and details such as overlapping speech and ignored propositions (Barron, 2003). This chapter represents a third phase of this project in which we make connections between the interactional norms, the mathematical reasoning, and the two languages used in these discussions.

FINDINGS AND NEW QUESTIONS RAISED BY THE STUDY

There are two overarching findings from this study. First, these students primarily engaged in "calculational" discussions (Thompson, Philipp, Thompson, & Boyd, 1994, p. 79). Although their discussions involved hybrid discourse practices (K. D. Gutiérrez, Baquedano-López, & Tejeda, 1999), including mixing everyday, school, and academic mathematical discourse practices, their discussions were principally oriented towards calculations rather than concepts. Second, intellectual (or mathematical) authority mediated the conversational rules of the students' peer discussions. However, intellectual authority did not necessarily align with who students thought was best at mathematics in the group (according to their responses to a survey question) or who had the correct answer to the exercise under discussion.

We observed that during their peer mathematics discussions, these students frequently alternated between using Spanish and English (which may be thought of as a hybrid discourse practice). The students' use of two languages, while not surprising, led to questions about how the two languages functioned in these peer discussions. In our initial analysis, we did not focus on this practice because numerous writers have already addressed this issue (see Moschkovich, 2007b, for more details). However, one of the fundamental assumptions of conversation analysis (and ethnomethodology in general) is that the microlevel details of interaction can reveal information about people's interpretations of the social worlds they inhabit and discursively create. Therefore, no details of interaction can be dismissed a priori (Schiffrin, 1994). This assumption, together with questions from numerous audiences of our presentations and readers of our manuscripts, has led us to this analysis focusing on the students' use of Spanish and English in more detail.

OVERVIEW OF EXCERPTS 3.1 AND 3.2

To ground our discussion of code switching in examples of students' mathematical discussions, we start with a summary of two excerpts from our study of students' mathematical discussions in peer groups. Here we summarize the mathematical ideas that the students were discussing and provide our summary of the students' interaction patterns in both excerpts. We briefly introduced Excerpt 3.1 at the start of this chapter. A second, more extended discussion by the same group of students is presented in Excerpt 3.2 (see Appendix B).

In Excerpt 3.1, the group was solving the shaded area exercise represented in Figure 3.1. Prior to the start of the interaction captured in Excerpt 3.1, Claudia argued that the answer was 75%, reasoning that "six over eight" is 75%. Amber and Francisco initially disagreed with Claudia, claiming that the answer should be 33%. After asking the teacher for help, the students appeared to agree that the answer was 75%. Excerpt 3.1 began when Francisco asked a question to the group for clarification about how they got 75% from "six over eight." Both Amber and Claudia began to answer his question. The overlapping talk in lines 3–7 indicates that Amber and Claudia struggled for control of the conversational floor.

By line 7, Amber ceded the floor to Claudia, marked by her back-channeling agreement with Claudia ("uh-huh"). Claudia then proceeded to talk through all steps for computing $6 \div 8$ using a long division algorithm (all of the steps are shown in Figure 3.1). In line 13, Claudia vocalized the "borrow" step necessary to compute $60 - 56$, which is significant because Francisco and Dennis had both already said "four" in the preceding lines. Likewise, in line 14, Francisco said "Oh yeah, seventy-five percent," indicating that he was satisfied with the answer. Nonetheless, Claudia persisted in her explanation until line 17.

Excerpt 3.2 (see Appendix B) is a lengthier discussion from the same group of students. The exercise the students discussed in Excerpt 3.2 was $6/25 = \_\_\_\_\%$ (Problem 8 on their worksheet). The transcript starts when Claudia told Amber her solution for the exercise. In the ensuing discussion, the students debated how to use the long division algorithm they had learned to find the percentage by taking the quotient $6 \div 25$. Francisco appeared to be confused about when to add a decimal in the long division algorithm when the divisor is greater than the dividend. In contrast with the fairly linear discussion in Excerpt 3.1, Excerpt 3.2 includes competing ideas, more disputes for the conversational floor, and nested/overlapping sequences of initiations and responses.

Claudia initiated the discussion by giving her answer to Problem 8 on the worksheet, and then starting in line 28, she demonstrated how to set up and do the long division $25\overline{)6}$. From lines 17 to 60, Francisco tried to convince the group that the answer should be 2.4% and he argued that each time a zero is added to the dividend in long division, a decimal is added in the quotient (this is not correct; in the standard algorithm, a decimal is added to the quotient only once, the first time a zero is added to the dividend). Joaquin and Dennis played a minor role in this discussion, but in lines 29 and 32, Joaquin appeared to respond with a correct proposition to Francisco's argument about when to add the decimal in the quotient. Amber appeared to shift between initially disagreeing with Claudia and then, by the end of the excerpt, she appeared to agree with Claudia and disagree with Francisco. For example, in lines 16, 18, and 21 Amber either disagreed with Claudia's answer or with Claudia's agreement with Francisco (it is not precisely clear):

16   **Amber:** "No, you could go." =

17 **Francisco:** "It has to be [two point."

18   **Amber:**   [="It's six times four is forty, *t* is twenty-four."

19 **Francisco:** "It has to be like two point something. It can't be twenty-four, Claudia." ((watching as Claudia approaches table))

20   **Claudia:** "Yes."

21   **Amber:** ["*No: porque Claudia quatro por seis es veinticua:tro.*"
             ["No, because Claudia, four times six is twenty-four."]

The confusing part of line 21 is that Amber named Claudia as her addressee, but her initial "no" was apparently a response to Francisco's suggestion that the answer was "two point something." Amber may have been suggesting an alternative way to get the solution without using long division: "*Quatro por seis es veintiquatro*" represents one possible way to reach the answer to this question

$$\frac{6}{25} \cdot \frac{4}{4} = \frac{24}{100} = 24\%.$$

Despite this point of ambiguity, Amber appeared to align with Claudia for the majority of this discussion and she ended her contribution by helping Claudia complete the computations in the long division method of finding the solution.

These students used the long division algorithm to solve the percent problems. Given the students' focus on using the algorithm correctly (rather than on explaining why this was the best solution method), we describe these discussions as reflecting a calculational orientation.3

COMPETING HYPOTHESES ABOUT CODE SWITCHING

In this section, we consider five hypotheses about students' use of two languages during mathematical discussions. Some of these hypotheses relate to code switching in general, while others are specific to code switching during a mathematics discussion. In response to each hypothesis, we consider relevant theory and use examples from excerpts 3.1 and 3.2 to analyze how code switching between Spanish and English functioned.

Hypothesis 1: *Students use two languages due to a linguistic or cognitive deficit; children use their first language for words they do not remember*

This hypothesis about the reason for code switching has the advantage of being intuitive. Those of us who have tried to learn a new language can imagine forgetting a word. Unfortunately, this hypothesis has the liability of being wrong, at least in this bilingual setting. Moschkovich (2007b) noted that the "missing word" (p. 139) explanation for code switching reflects a deficit view of children's linguistic or mathematical proficiency. To avoid making deficit-based assumptions about the students' knowledge of mathematical vocabulary, a more nuanced interpretation of this use of language starts with the observation that code switching is different in bilingual communities than in settings in which people are learning a second language. With that caveat in mind, we think it is also important to recognize that in bilingual communities in which schooling is conducted exclusively in a language different from the language used outside of school (a common arrangement for students in former colonies and some communities in the United States), then children are likely to develop technical, academic vocabulary in the language of instruction, but not in their home language. For example, antibilingual education initiatives have resulted in many California schools systematically denying access to content instruction in students' home language (Gándara & Contreras, 2009). In such contexts, the missing word interpretation of code switching may be more valid.

However, the data in this study is from a dual-immersion bilingual school in California,3 where the children learned mathematics in both Spanish and English. Given this unique setting, we did not see the children systematically using English or Spanish for technical mathematical language. For example, in excerpts 3.1 and 3.2, the students used both the Spanish and English words for the mathematical concepts and operations they were discussing: percent/*porciento*, divided/*entre*, times/*por*, *punto*/decimal/point. One instance of a word that was only said in Spanish is "*primerito*," which was part of Joaquin's suggestion in lines 29 and 32 of Excerpt 3.2 of when to add a decimal in long division. Joaquin's use of the diminutive form may indicate he was intentionally playing with words or condescending to Francisco (which is consistent with Joaquin and Francisco's other interactions). We think it is likely that Joaquin knew how to express this idea in English as well as Spanish although, in this excerpt, we do not have direct evidence of Joaquin using technical vocabulary in both languages. We are more interested in investigating his language choice and the effect that it had, rather than speculating about Joaquin's English skills.

We end with two final notes about the missing word hypothesis to explain code switching. First, assuming a bilingual person is completely balanced in their two languages is unrealistic; a person who participates in multiple language communities will not develop the same fluency in both languages (Grosjean, 2001; MacSwan, 2000; Moschkovich, 2007b; Zentella, 1997). Languages are learned and used in specific situations and often for specific functions. The second major point about the missing word hypothesis is that even when children do use their first language to fill in vocabulary they do not know in the language of instruction, there is no indication that doing so is necessarily detrimental for learning mathematics. Rowland's (2000) conclusions about the utility of using pronouns for making mathematical generalizations seem relevant here. In his study of language and mathematics (in monolingual English settings), Rowland noted that students, as well as expert mathematicians, used hedges, estimators, and ambiguous words like "it" or "you" to talk about mathematical objects they could not yet define precisely. Rowland argued that using vague language facilitated, rather than hindered, making mathematical generalizations (he also noted that the context matters—using vague language serves an important role during the learning process, but vague language is not generally allowed in completed, formal mathematical generalizations). In terms of using two languages, as long as students also have opportunities to use and learn the meaning of words in both languages, then we argue that using a word from Spanish or English in the middle of mathematical discussions could even facilitate learning the corresponding word in the other language. If bilingualism is the goal (rather than English acquisition), then using primary language vocabulary may be an effective way to facilitate vocabulary development in a new language, assuming that children have the opportunities to learn and use both languages.

Hypothesis 2: *Children use their primary language to do computations*

That people tend to recall bits of information such as addition and multiplication facts in the language in which they memorized those facts appears to be true. Moschkovich (2007b) reviewed several studies of computation time in bilingual students and adults (Marsh & Maki, 1976; McClain & Huang, 1982; Secada, 1991; Tamamaki, 1993). The major points made in those studies were (1) bilingual participants appeared to recall arithmetic facts in the language in which they had learned those facts; and (2) despite the very small time lag in carrying out arithmetic computations, bilingualism had no significant effects on computational accuracy. Although this phenomenon is interesting, doing computations in one language or another is not likely to have profound effects on the ability of bilingual students to reason and communicate mathematically. Mathematical communication involves far more than doing computations (Pimm, 1987), and this hypothesis has little to say about other practices associated with mathematical reasoning such as conjecturing, proving assertions, and imagining (Moschkovich, 2007a).

Some of the students in these examples expressed computations in both Spanish and English, while others appeared to rely on one language for computation. Amber and Claudia provide us with contrasting cases of language use in their computational private speech (Zahner & Moschkovich, 2010). In both excerpts 3.1 and 3.2, the numbers in Amber's computational private speech were all uttered in English (line 3 of Excerpt 3.1 and lines 8, 40, 44, 53, and 59 of Excerpt 3.2). However, Amber used Spanish for numbers when she was explicitly communicating with other group members (e.g., in line 21: "*no porque Claudia quarto por seis es veinticuatro*"). Claudia, on the other hand, appeared to carry out and voice computations in both languages. In lines 30, 39, and 42 of Excerpt 3.2, she set up the long division $25 \overline{)6}$ while speaking English. Then, in lines 47, 50, and 54 of Excerpt 3.2, she talked through the steps of that same computation in Spanish. In line 57, she used both the Spanish and English forms of the word for the digit 0 in rapid succession.

These students' language choice for verbalizing computation and for communication with group-mates seems intimately tied to the communicative function of each utterance. Both Amber and Claudia used number words from both languages in their computations and in the group discussions. Amber vocalized computational private speech in English, but sometimes switched to Spanish when addressing her group-mates. Claudia appeared more fluid in her language choice while voicing computations, sometimes expressing them in Spanish, and at other times expressing the same computation in English. Rather than systematically switching languages for arithmetic recall, the communicative function of each utterance appears far more important in terms of language choice. Generally, when the children wanted to get the speaking floor, they used both languages (or switched between languages) to command attention (we consider this phenomenon further in Hypothesis 4, below).

Hypothesis 3: *Bilingualism allows for cognitive flexibility and children switch languages when they encounter cognitive roadblocks*

Vygotsky's (1978, 1986) genetic theory of human development gave a primary role to language and culturally shared sign systems as mediators of thinking. Cognitive psychologists (Bialystok, 2001) and, to a lesser extent, cultural psychologists (John-Steiner, 1991) have used Vygotsky's focus on language as a mediator of thought to investigate the impact of bi/multilingualism on thought. Early research in this area attempted to show the detrimental effects of bilingualism on intelligence although, for many of these researchers, their biases against bilingual immigrants permeated the studies (Bialystok, 2001). Since Peal and Lambert (1962) showed a bilingual advantage on nonverbal intelligence tests, more recent research based on cognitive theories has shown mixed results for the hypothesis that bilingualism has significant effects on cognition. In her review of cognitive research of nonlinguistic effects of bilingualism, Bialystok (2001) concluded that, in general, there are no differences between bilingual and monolingual problem solvers although, on some tasks, bilingual children were able to ignore misleading clues more effectively than their monolingual peers. This has led some researchers to hypothesize that bi/multilingualism allows for greater cognitive flexibility.

One question arising from the cognitive flexibility hypothesis is whether the students in our study switched languages when they got stuck on a problem or when they experienced other difficulties. If the children systematically switched from English to Spanish (or vice versa) at moments of confusion, then we might see some indirect evidence for bilingualism allowing for cognitive flexibility. However, we do not see evidence of this practice in our data—in fact, even specifying which language the students spoke is difficult because the children frequently used both Spanish and English in the same utterance. One example is Claudia's statement in lines 52–57 in Excerpt 3.2: "*Y luego 'ira son dos son cincuenta por ciento.* You take one, and that's zero. Zero bring down the zero, *es cero, cien.*" (She appears to be doing the intermediary steps $2 \times 25 = 50$ and $60 - 50 = 10$ for the long division $25\overline{)6}$.) Claudia's fluid use of Spanish and English echoes the use of languages in Zentella's (1997) study among Puerto Rican children in New York. For the children in this group, the norm is speaking both Spanish and English at the same time.

Hypothesis 4: *Using two languages facilitates interactions, specifically management of the conversational floor and face saving*

This hypothesis appears to focus on the social, rather than cognitive, functions of code switching. However, we argue that because cognition is socially distributed (Cole & Engeström, 1993; Hutchins, 1996), making a clear distinction between the social elements and the cognitive elements of a mathematical discussion is a false dichotomy. The social functions of code switching facilitate mathematical reasoning during group discussions. Our analysis focuses on two primary issues: the management of "face" during a mathematical discussion and the issue of turn taking. In both instances, students used code switching as a resource.

Rowland's (2000) study of vagueness in mathematical discourse noted that mathematical discussions are especially face-threatening events. Drawing on Lakoff's (1973) framework for politeness and the management of face in conversations (Brown & Levinson, 1987), Rowland argued that the perception that there are right and wrong answers in mathematics and the potential for publicly being identified as incorrect leads to the frequent use of estimators, hedges, and vague pronouns in mathematical discussions. One linguistic resource these students drew upon for managing face was code switching—which was also one of the functions of code switching identified by Sánchez (1994). For example, in lines 18 and 21 of Excerpt 3.2, Amber appears to contradict first Francisco and then Claudia's apparent agreement with Francisco. In lines 16–18, Amber disagreed with Franscico's proposition that the answer was 2.4: "No, you could go, it's six times four is forty, *t* is twenty-four." After Claudia apparently agreed with Francisco in line 20, Amber said "*No, porque Claudia quarto por seis is veinticuatro.*" Amber essentially repeated the same message in both Spanish and English.

In Excerpt 3.2, there are at least two more examples of students switching between Spanish and English in potentially face-threatening moments. In line 33, Amber contradicted Claudia's "Six" from line 30 with "no, six *no vale.*" While this utterance is difficult to interpret mathematically, by adding the tag "*no vale*" in Spanish, Amber was skillfully using her languages to navigate a disagreement with Claudia and Francisco. With the Spanish phrase "*no vale,*" Amber softened the effect of her direct contradiction of Claudia (Sánchez, 1994). Claudia repeated this same pattern in lines 52–57 when she used both languages in her direct contradiction of Francisco's assertion that the answer should be 2.4%.

Besides management of face, other relevant conversational issues evident in these discussions were managing turn taking and controlling the conversational floor (Sacks et al., 1974). Management of the floor is an important issue in mathematical discussions. For example, Barron (2003) studied group discussions among 16 triads of monolingual middle school students in the southeastern United States, and she observed that management of turn-taking was one issue that led to breakdowns in group coordination. While we do not claim that these discussions show perfect coordination, we do see evidence in these excerpts that the students used Spanish and English in their bids to gain and control the conversational floor. Claudia's use of Spanish in Excerpt 3.1 is an example of such a bid. Francisco started the discussion with a question in English (line 1), and Claudia's initial response was also in English, reflecting the bilingual pattern of responding in the language of initiation (Sánchez, 1994). In line 3, Amber attempted to take the floor after a short pause by Claudia, but Claudia did not cede the floor. In lines 4 and 6, Claudia talked in Spanish over Amber to take back control of the conversational floor. We are not claiming that Claudia's use of Spanish was the only reason Amber ceded the floor (recall that prior to Excerpt 3.1, Claudia had corrected Amber on this exercise), but we note how Claudia used Spanish as a resource for gaining control of the floor in this discussion.

Related to managing turn-taking is the issue of getting one's propositions heard and acknowledged by the group during a mathematical discussion (Barron, 2000, 2003). Moschkovich (2007b) identified that code switching is one resource for politely repeating a proposition: "[C]ode switching has been documented as a resource for elaborating on a point that is repeated, without repeating the initial utterance word for word" (p. 138). In Excerpt 3.2, there are several instances in which students used both Spanish and English to repeat themselves as they attempted to gain the floor. For example, in lines 18 and 21 of Excerpt 3.2, Amber repeated her assertion that "six times four is twenty-four" in both languages. Likewise in lines 43, 46, 48, and 51, Francisco made his argument that the answer should be 2.4 in Spanish, and then repeated himself in English.

One idea that was not repeated in both languages was Joaquin's assertion that the decimal is inserted in the quotient only the first time a zero is added (see Excerpt 3.2, lines 29 and 32). This idea was not taken up by any of the group members. This is one example of a correct proposition that was not taken up by the group (Barron, 2003), and it raises the question of how Joaquin's language choice was related to the group's lack of uptake of his idea because Joaquin did not repeat his idea in English. However, when interpreting this interaction, we must be cautious because Joaquin also spent much of the time during mathematics group work engaging in behaviors that appeared "off task" and he did not regularly contribute to the group's mathematical discussions. Thus, it is difficult to know whether Francisco's lack of uptake of Joaquin's suggestion was due to Joaquin's language choice, his use of the diminutive form (which may be interpreted as condescending), or a general pattern of interaction between Joaquin and his group-mates.

Gaining and holding the floor during the discussion in Excerpt 3.2 appeared to be difficult. The three main participants in this conversation each appeared to have his or her own idea of how to solve the problem. In this midst of each student's contested bids for the conversational floor, one resource Claudia used to make a bid for the floor was the use of the word "*mira*"/"*'ira*" ("look" or "watch"). Claudia repeatedly used this word to focus her group-mates' attention on how she solved the problem. For example, in lines 28, 30, and 34 of Excerpt 3.2, Claudia started her computation verbalized in English with "*Miren.*" Later in lines 52–57, Claudia explained the final steps of the division by saying, "*Y luego 'ira son dos son cincuenta por ciento* (.) you take one, and that's zero. Zero, bring down the zero, *es cero, cien.*" Claudia also used this bid in line 4 of Excerpt 3.1. Bilingual speakers from this discourse community reported that this construction (*Mira* + utterance in English or Spanish) is common in the children's community. The ubiquity of this construction leads us to interpret this practice as one way of making a bid for the floor by using a common bidding device.

In noting that these students used two languages to manage the interactional flow of their mathematical discussions, we are not implying that students in monolingual settings lack such resources. Numerous studies of peer discussions in monolingual settings have shown that monolingual children manage issues such as preserving face and regulating turn taking (Barron, 2000, 2003; Jurow, 2005; Pirie, 1991). Our analysis simply shows that when students are in a bilingual setting, the use of code switching is one additional resource that children can use for these purposes during mathematical discussions.

Hypothesis 5: *Use of nondominant language(s) is a way to position self or others vis-à-vis larger social power structures*

Many theorists have studied and written about the intimate relationship between language(s) and power. For example, Fairclough's (2001) critical language studies focused on how mundane details of texts and spoken language (such as using active or passive voice) position readers and authors in specific ways that reinforce social power relations. Gee's (1996) discourse analysis took a broader perspective on language, and he distinguished between the lowercase discourse as a unit of text, and the initial-cap Discourse as socially meaningful ways of using language, other symbolic tools, and artifacts to define identities. Gee argued that Discourses are necessarily related to ideologies and relations of power. At the broadest level, Bourdieu (1991) used economic metaphors to explain how the use of official languages and dialects is a practice that reinforces and reproduces inequitable relations of power. In one salient example, Bourdieu showed how a politician in a rural area of France skillfully used the local dialect in an effort to align himself with the local population when giving a speech, but used the official language in other settings to align with the larger political power structure. While broad-based theories of language and power add a great deal to our understanding of the relationship between using particular languages (or Discourses) and power, can we use these theories to interpret students' use of two languages in their peer mathematics discussions in the context of our study?

Previous studies in mathematics education have documented how language policies about the use of Spanish and English at the classroom level have an impact on Latino/a students' participation in school mathematics (R. Gutiérrez, 2002; Gutstein, Lipman, Hernández, & de los Reyes, 1997; Khisty, 1995; Khisty & Viego, 1999; Moschkovich, 1999). For example, Rochelle Gutiérrez (2002) studied successful high school mathematics teachers in an urban school with a large number of Latino/a students where the students varied in terms of their use of Spanish and English. She noted that many of the monolingual English-speaking mathematics teachers allowed their students to use both Spanish and English during class, and she related such policies (along with several other factors) to the teachers' relative success in teaching high-level mathematics to Latino/a students (R. Gutiérrez, 2002). López-Leiva and Khisty (2009) have observed how children and their teacher's use of Spanish or English in a bilingual after-school program signaled the creation of social positions for participants in mathematical discussions. In López-Leiva and Khisty's study, using Spanish was generally associated with a lower social positioning.

These mixed findings about the use of Spanish and English in mathematics classrooms point to the complexities of interpreting language practices and policies in the United States, especially in relation to how Spanish and English are used in schools or informal educational settings. Making an ideological claim requires careful documentation of participants' language practices, as well as a deep understanding of the local context. For example, Sánchez (1994) started her analysis of code switching among Chicanos in the U.S. Southwest with an extensive review of the historical and economic relationship between Mexico and the United States. Then, grounding her analysis of everyday dialogues in the broader social and historical setting allowed Sánchez to make ideological observations about the functions of code switching. For example, Sánchez noted how some bilingual Chicanos systematically switched to English during disputes in a bid to align with power structures.

In terms of this study, making an ideological interpretation of these children's use of Spanish and English in the classroom depends on the social and institutional context of the discussions. Given that the school in which excerpts 3.1 and 3.2 were recorded was a dual-immersion bilingual school—a school in which bilingualism was actively valued and encouraged—assigning ideological meaning to the students' language choices seems dangerous. In California post-Proposition 227, the use of Spanish by students in a classroom might be viewed as resistance against a subtractive school system (Gándara & Contreras, 2009; Valenzuela, 1997). Although it is tempting to make such an interpretation of these students' language choices during their mathematical discussions, we also need to recall that this school valued and actively promoted bilingualism. Thus, this interpretation may be a step too far for this situation, especially given the type of data and our ethnomethodological orientation. Making claims about the students' use of Spanish or English as it relates to ideology would require the incorporation of more ethnographic observational data on language attitudes and practices in the community, at this school, and in this classroom. In future work, we could pursue such questions more explicitly, documenting how historical and institutional factors are related to social norms and microlevel interactions within organizational/institutional settings (Ogawa, Crain, Loomis, & Ball, 2008). Language policies are certainly an important part of shaping children's mathematical interactions in schools, and we think investigating the interaction between language policies and students' mathematical reasoning is a fruitful area for future research.

CONCLUSIONS

In this chapter, we have analyzed excerpts from a mathematical discussion among one group of bilingual sixth-grade students to better understand the functions of their code-switching practices. Our analysis has focused on how the students' use of multiple languages facilitated their mathematical reasoning, and we have used samples of students' discussions to evaluate five common hypotheses to explain why bilingual students code switch during mathematical discussions.

Our analysis of one group of students' code switching during a mathematical discussion in a bilingual middle school classroom gives us comparative power and helps us extend Moschkovich's (2007b) earlier findings about the function of code switching in children's mathematical discussions. As Moschkovich proposed, one function of using two languages in a bilingual mathematics discussion is to elaborate on a point or to repeat a proposition. Here we have corroborated this finding and extended this idea by showing that code switching also functioned as a face-saving tool during the students' discussions. We then related this finding to earlier studies of how students use language to manage face (Rowland, 2000) and bid for the floor during mathematical discussions (Barron, 2000, 2003). We also considered other common hypotheses about the role of code switching during students' mathematical discussions, but we did not see sufficient evidence to support these hypotheses in our data. Although we did not see evidence for four of the five hypotheses we considered, our conclusions must be interpreted in light of the bilingual school context and the type of data we presented here.

The importance of aligning theory, research questions, methods, data, and conclusions is often the first lesson of social science research methods. It is also a lesson worth repeating, especially when studying something as deceptively simple as language practices. To carefully analyze students' code switching during bilingual/multilingual mathematical discussions, we needed to step back from common-sense notions of language or our personal experiences of learning languages to approach students' interactions and use of language through a systematic scholarly perspective. By adopting systematic methods and relying on scholarly perspectives, we have shown that the missing word/cognitive deficit hypothesis did not explain code switching in these students' mathematical discussions. Likewise, there was no evidence to support the hypothesis that the students switched languages while doing computations or during moments that required some kind of mental flexibility. What we do see in the data is that students used words and expressions from both languages to describe mathematical operations and concepts. Furthermore, their switches in language did not systematically align with shifts from informal to formal or from everyday to mathematical registers.

Overall, the data do not support the first three hypotheses about code switching that we considered. In terms of the fifth hypothesis, we do not have sufficient ethnographic observations of the students' language practices in school and out of school that would allow us to make statements about the sociopolitical implications of these students' use of Spanish. Our data and methods seem best suited to support the fourth hypothesis that code switching functioned as a way for the students to manage the social/interactional demands of their mathematical discussions. In the future, we hope to investigate how the skillful management of social interactions facilitates the students' mathematical reasoning.

ACKNOWLEDGMENT

This manuscript is based upon work supported in part by the National Science Foundation under Grant No. 0424983 to the Center for the Mathematics Education of Latinos/Latinas (CEMELA). Any opinions, findings, and conclusions or recommendations expressed in this material are those of the author(s) and do not necessarily reflect the views of the National Science Foundation. We would like to thank the participating students and the classroom teacher.

NOTES

1. We think it is important to note that the school's survival after Proposition 227 depended on a significant amount of community support and political efforts to maintain the school in a policy environment hostile to bilingual education.
2. Transcript conventions are based on Jefferson's conventions (Schiffrin, 1994). A key to transcription symbols is given in Appendix A. For utterances where several words are in Spanish, an English gloss of the utterance (our translation) appears directly below the uttered words, in [paired square brackets]. Also, some lines are omitted because they were part of side conversations in parallel to the main discussion.
3. We were intrigued by Amber's suggestion in line 21 of Excerpt 3.2, "*Quatro por seis es veinticuatro,*" because this suggestion represents an alternative solution to the percent problem. However, Amber did not follow up on this idea with her group and it is possible the 4 was from doing $25 \div 6$ rather than $6 \div 25$.

APPENDIX A
TRANSCRIPT CONVENTIONS

(.) short pause
(#) pause of # seconds
[start of overlapping speech mid-utterance
[[two utterances starting simultaneously or two consecutive overlapping turns
italics Spanish utterance or part of an utterance
((text)) Translation of Spanish utterance or part of an utterance
? rising intonation
. stop with falling intonation
: elongated syllable
= latched phrases
(uncertain transcription)
((transcriber comments or relevant student gestures))

APPENDIX B
EXCERPT 3.2

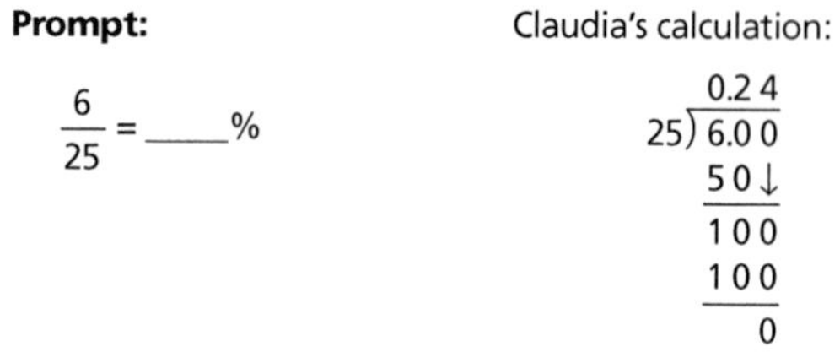

Prompt:

$$\frac{6}{25} = \underline{\quad}\%$$

Claudia's calculation:

$$25\overline{)6.00} \quad 0.24$$
$$50\downarrow$$
$$100$$
$$100$$
$$0$$

Figure 3.2 The exercise discussed in Excerpt 3.2 and our reconstruction of Claudia's computation.

Excerpt 3.2. [Wednesday Session 1 31:39 – 33:50]

1 **Claudia:** "It's twenty-four [percent." ((looks up at Amber))
2 **Joaquin:** ["*xxxx.*" ((looking off camera))
3 **Claudia:** "It's twenty-four percent ((erases paper)). Amber, it's twenty-four percent."
4 **Dennis:** "What?"
5 **Amber:** "*Qué?*"
    (("*What?*"))
6 **Claudia:** "The number eight is twenty-four percent."
7 **Francisco:** "Twenty-four?"
8 **Amber:** "My bad, twenty-fi:ve, six, that's three, no, times four, is *t-* twenty-four, that's *xxx* [zero." = ((Claudia walks away from

group, the second half of this utterance appears to be Amber thinking aloud))

10 **Amber:** = "That goes in (.) [two." ((Still thinking aloud))

11 **Francisco:** ["Oh yeah, twenty-four percent."

14 **Amber:** "How is it twenty-four?"

15 **Francisco:** "OK, 'cause look, OK, *xxx* when you put the decimal there, then with that, it will be two, ten, that'll be fifty, then you have to bring down, then you have—wait—what the heck?"

16 **Amber:** "No, you could go."=

17 **Francisco:** "It has to be [two point."

18 **Amber:** [= "It's six times four is forty, *t*- is twenty-four."

19 **Francisco:** "It has to be like two point something. It can't be twenty-four, Claudia." ((watching as Claudia approaches table))

20 **Claudia:** "Yes."

21 **Amber:** ["*No: porque Claudia quatro por seis es veinticua:tro.*"
(("No, because Claudia four times six is twenty-four."))

23 **Claudia:** "*Miren.*"
(("Look."))

24 **?:** "Claudia."

25 **Francisco:** "But you have to put the decimal in the middle of two." =

27 **Francisco:** "= After two, you have to put a [decimal"

28 **Claudia:** ["*Miren.*"
(("Look."))

29 **Joaquin:** "*Desde de primerito* [*no?*"
(("From the very first little one, right?"))

30 **Claudia:** ["Six."

31 **Francisco:** ["*xxx* (put a) decimal right after two."

32 **Joaquin:** = "(On the) *primerita nueva.*"=
(("(On the) first new little one."))

33 **Amber:** ["No, six (*no vale*)."
(("No, six isn't good."))

34 **Claudia:** ["Divided (but then)."

35 **Joaquin:** ="This is the way."

36 **Dennis:** "This is the way [*vale.*"
(("This is the way, OK."))

37 **Amber:** ["Oh, then."

39 **Claudia:** "Twenty-five."

40 **Amber:** "Point six."

42 **Claudia:** "You put a decimal."

43 **Francisco:** "That, see it's like two point four percent, two point four percent."

44 **Amber:** "Twenty-five."

45   **Claudia:** *"Porque 'ira."*
        (("Because look."))
46 **Francisco:** *"Dos punto cuatro por ciento."*
        (("Two point four percent."))
47   **Claudia:** *"Dos (.)"*
        (("Two."))
48 **Francisco:** *"Punto cuatro."*
        (("Point four."))
50   **Claudia:** *"No como como va el seis como va el seis [entre veinte y cinco."*
        (("No, how how six goes into twenty-five?"))
51 **Francisco:**   ["In *t-* in the last zero,
        when you're doing that, you put a point. Oh my go-"
52   **Claudia:** *"Y luego 'ira."*=
        (("And then look."))
53   **Amber:** "Ten."
54   **Claudia:** ="*Son dos son cincuenta por ciento* (.) you take one, and [that's
        zero."
        (("It's two, it's fifty percent."))
57   **Claudia:** "Zero, bring down the zero, *es cero,* [*cien.*"
                          (("it's zero, one hundred."))
58 **Francisco:**   ["(But) when you bring
        down the zero, you put a decimal."
59   **Amber:** "No you do:n't."
60 **Francisco:** "You have to." ((quietly))
61   **Amber:** "No, you just add another zero."
62 **Francisco:** "Oh my god."
63   **Amber:** "And the:n tha:t is (by) four."
64   **Joaquin:** "Yoo::" ((looking away from group))
65 **Francisco:** "Point twenty-four percent."
66   **Amber:** "Yes." ((nods head))
67   **Claudia:** "Yes."

REFERENCES

Barnes, D. R. & Todd, F. (1995). *Communication and learning revisited: Meaning making through talk.* Portsmouth, NH: Boynton/Cook.

Barron, B. (2000). Achieving coordination in collaborative problem-solving groups. The *Journal of the Learning Sciences, 9*(4), 403–436. doi: 10.1207/S15327809JLS0904_2

Barron, B. (2003). When smart groups fail. *Journal of the Learning Sciences, 12*(3), 307–359. doi: 10.1207/S15327809JLS1203_1

Bialystok, E. (2001). *Bilingualism in development: Language, literacy, and cognition.* Cambridge, England: Cambridge University Press.

Bourdieu, P. (1991). *Language and symbolic power.* Cambridge, MA: Harvard University Press.

Brown, P. & Levinson, S. C. (1987). *Politeness: Some universals in language usage.* Cambridge, UK: Cambridge University Press.

Cole, M. & Engeström, Y. (1993). A cultural-historical approach to distributed cognition. In G. Salomon (Ed.), *Distributed cognitions: Psychological and educational considerations* (pp. 1–48). Cambridge, England: Cambridge University Press.

Drew, P. & Heritage, J. (1992). Analyzing talk at work: An introduction. In P. Drew & J. Heritage (Eds.), *Talk at work: Interaction in institutional settings* (pp. 3–65). Cambridge, UK: Cambridge University Press.

Fairclough, N. (2001). *Language and power* (2nd ed.). New York, NY: Longman.

Forman, E. (1996). Learning mathematics as participation in classroom practice: Implications of sociocultural theory for educational reform. In L. P. Steffe, P. Nesher, P. Cobb, G. A. Goldin, & B. Greer (Eds.), *Theories of mathematics learning* (pp. 115–130). Mahwah, NJ: Erlbaum.

Gándara, P. & Contreras, F. (2009). *The Latino education crisis: The consequences of failed social policies.* Cambridge, MA: Harvard University Press.

Garfinkel, H. (1967). *Studies in ethnomethodology.* Englewood Cliffs, NJ: Prentice-Hall.

Gee, J. P. (1996). *Social linguistics and literacies: Ideology in discourses* (2nd ed.). Bristol, PA: Taylor & Francis.

Grosjean, F. (2001). The bilingual's language modes. In J. L. Nicol (Ed.), *One mind, two languages: Bilingual language processing* (pp. 1–22). Malden, MA: Blackwell.

Gutiérrez, K. D., Baquedano-López, P., & Tejeda, C. (1999). Rethinking diversity: Hybridity and hybrid language practices in the third space. *Mind Culture and Activity, 6*(4), 286–303. doi: 10.1080/10749039909524733

Gutiérrez, K. D. & Rogoff, B. (2003). Cultural ways of learning: Individual traits or repertoires of practice. *Educational Researcher, 32*(5), 19–25. doi: 10.3102/0013189X032005019

Gutiérrez, R. (2002). Beyond essentialism: The complexity of language in teaching mathematics to Latina/o students. *American Educational Research Journal, 39*(4), 1047–1088. doi: 10.3102/000283120390041047

Gutstein, E., Lipman, P., Hernández, P., & de los Reyes, R. (1997). Culturally relevant mathematics teaching in a Mexican American context. *Journal for Research in Mathemaics Education, 28*(6), 709–737. doi: 10.2307/749639

Heritage, J. (1984). *Garfinkel and ethnomethodology.* Cambridge, UK: Polity Press.

Hutchins, E. (1996). *Cognition in the wild.* Cambridge, MA: MIT Press.

John-Steiner, V. (1991). Cognitive pluralism: A Whorfian analysis. In R. L. Cooper & B. Spolsky (Eds.), *The influence of language on culture and thought* (pp. 61–74). Berlin, Germany: Mouton de Gruyter.

Jurow, A. S. (2005). Shifting engagements in figured worlds: Middle school mathematics students' participation in an architectural design project. *The Journal of the Learning Sciences, 14*(1), 35–67. doi: 10.1207/s15327809jls1401_3

Khisty, L. L. (1995). Making inequality: Issues of language and meanings in mathematics teaching with Hispanic students. In W. G. Secada, E. Fennema, & L. B. Adajian (Eds.), *New directions for equity in mathematics education* (pp. 279–297). Cambridge, UK: Cambridge University Press.

Khisty, L. L. & Viego, G. (1999). Challenging the conventional wisdom: A case study. In W. G. Secada (Ed.), *Changing the faces of mathematics: Perspectives on Latinos* (pp. 71–80). Reston, VA: National Council of Teachers of Mathematics.

Lakoff, R. T. (1973). The logic of politeness; or minding your P's and Q's. In C. Corum, T. Cedric Smith-Stark, & A. Weiser (Eds.), *Papers from the 9th Regional Meeting of the Chicago Linguistic Society* (pp. 292–305). Chicago, IL: University of Chicago Press.

Lemke, J. (2003). Mathematics in the middle: Measure, picture, gesture, sign, and word. In M. Anderson, A. Sáenz-Ludlow, S. Zellweger, & V. V. Cifarelli (Eds.), *Educational perspectives on mathematics as semiosis: From thinking to interpreting to knowing* (pp. 215–234). Brooklyn, NY: Legas.

Linde, C. (1988). Who's in charge here?: Cooperative work and authority negotiation in police helicopter missions. *Proceedings of the 1988 ACM Conference on Computer-supported Cooperative Work, Portland, Oregon*, 52-64. doi: 10.1145/62266.62271

López-Leiva, C. A. & Khisty, L. L. (2009, May). *"Drawing us apart from within our village": Appropriation of exclusionary practices in the mathematics education of Latinas/os.* Paper presented at the 3rd Annual Conference of Critical Race Studies in Education, "Reclaiming the Village," Tucson, AZ.

MacSwan, J. (2000). The threshold hypothesis, semilingualism, and other contributions to a deficit view of linguistic minorities. *Hispanic Journal of Behavioral Sciences, 22*(1), 3–45. doi: 10.1177/0739986300221001

Marsh, L. G. & Maki, R. H. (1976). Efficiency of arithmetic operations in bilinguals as a function of language. *Memory & Cognition, 4*(4), 459–464. Retrieved from http://www.psychonomic.org

McClain, L. & Huang, J. Y. S. (1982). Speed of simple arithmetic in bilinguals. *Memory & Cognition, 10*(6), 591–596. Retrieved from http://www.psychonomic.org

Mehan, H. (1979). *Learning lessons: Social organization in the classroom.* Cambridge, MA: Harvard University Press.

Moschkovich, J. N. (1999). Understanding the needs of Latino students in reform-oriented mathematics classrooms. In L. Ortiz-Franco, N. G. Hernández, & Y. de la Cruz (Eds.), *Changing the faces of mathematics: Perspectives on Latinos* (pp. 5–12). Reston, VA: National Council of Teachers of Mathematics.

Moschkovich, J. N. (2002). A situated and sociocultural perspective on bilingual mathematics learners. *Mathematical Thinking and Learning, 4*(2 & 3), 189–212. doi: 10.1207/S15327833MTL04023_5

Moschkovich, J. N. (2004). Appropriating mathematical practices: A case study of learning to use and explore functions through interactions with a tutor. *Educational Studies in Mathematics, 55*(1–3), 49–80. doi: 10.1023/B:EDUC.0000017691.13428.b9

Moschkovich, J. N. (2007a). Examining mathematical discourse practices. *For the Learning of Mathematics, 27*(1), 24–30. Retrieved from http://flm.educ.ualberta.ca

Moschkovich, J. N. (2007b). Using two languages when learning mathematics. *Educational Studies in Mathematics, 64*(2), 121–144. doi: 10.1007/s10649-005-9005-1

Moschkovich, J. N., & Brenner, M. E. (2000). Integrating a naturalistic paradigm into research on mathematics and science cognition and learning. In A. E.

Kelly & R. A. Lesh (Eds.), *Handbook of research design in mathematics and science education* (pp. 457–486). Mahwah, NJ: Erlbaum.

Newman, D., Griffin, P., & Cole, M. (1989). *The construction zone: Working for cognitive change in school.* Cambridge, UK: Cambridge University Press.

Ogawa, R. T., Crain, R., Loomis, M., & Ball, T. (2008). CHAT-IT: Toward conceptualizing learning in the context of formal organizations. *Educational Researcher, 37*(2), 83–95. doi: 10.3102/0013189X08316207

Peal, E. & Lambert, W. E. (1962). The relation of bilingualism to intelligence. *Psychological Monographs: General and Applied, 76*(27), 1–23. Retrieved from http://www.apa.org

Pimm, D. (1987). *Speaking mathematically: Communication in mathematics classrooms.* New York: Routledge.

Pirie, S. E. (1991). Peer discussion in the context of mathematical problem solving. In K. Durkin & B. Shire (Eds.), *Language in mathematical education: Research and practice* (pp. 143–161). Philadelphia: Open University Press.

Pirie, S. E., & Schwarzenberger, R. L. (1988). Mathematical discussion and mathematical understanding. *Educational Studies in Mathematics, 19*(4), 459–470. doi: 10.1007/BF00578694

Radford, L. (2001). Signs and meanings in students' emergent algebraic thinking: A semiotic analysis. *Educational Studies in Mathematics, 42*(3), 237–268. doi: 10.1023/A:1017530828058

Radford, L. (2003). On culture and mind: A post-Vygotskian semiotic perspective with an example from Greek mathematical thought. In M. Anderson, A. Sáenz-Ludlow, S. Zellweger, & V. V. Cifarelli (Eds.), *Educational perspectives on mathematics as semiosis: From thinking to interpreting to knowing* (pp. 49–80). Brooklyn, NY: Legas.

Rogoff, B. (2003). *The cultural nature of human development.* New York: Oxford University Press.

Rowland, T. (2000). *The pragmatics of mathematics education: Vagueness in mathematical discourse.* London: Falmer.

Sacks, H., Schegloff, E. A., & Jefferson, G. (1974). A simplest systematics of the organization of turn-taking in conversation. *Language, 50*(4), 696–735. doi: 10.2307/412243

Sánchez, R. (1994). *Chicano discourse: Socio-historic perspectives.* Houston, TX: Arte Público Press.

Schiffrin, D. (1994). *Approaches to discourse.* Malden, MA: Blackwell.

Secada, W. G. (1991). Degree of bilingualism and arithmetic problem solving in Hispanic first graders. *The Elementary School Journal, 92*(2), 213–231. doi: 10.1086/461689

Tamamaki, K. (1993). Language dominance in bilinguals' arithmetic operations according to their language use. *Language and Learning, 43*(2), 239–261. doi: 10.1111/j.1467-1770.1992.tb00716.x

Thompson, A. G., Philipp, R. A., Thompson, P. W., & Boyd, B. A. (1994). Calculational and conceptual orientations in teaching mathematics. In A. Coxford (Ed.), *1994 Yearbook of the NCTM* (pp. 79–92). Reston, VA: National Council of Teachers of Mathematics.

U.S. Census Bureau. (2008). *American FactFinder: California.* Retrieved from http://factfinder.census.gov/home/saff/main.html?_lang=en

Valenzuela, A. (1997). Mexican-American youth and the politics of caring. In E. Long (Ed.), *From sociology to cultural studies: New perspectives* (pp. 322–350). Malden, MA: Blackwell.

Vygotsky, L. S. (1978). *Mind in society: The development of higher psychological processes.* Cambridge, MA: Harvard University Press.

Vygotsky, L. S. (1986). *Thought and language.* Cambridge, MA: MIT Press.

Zahner, W., & Moschkovich, J. N. (2010). Talking while computing in groups: The not-so-private functions of computational private speech in mathematical discussions. *Mind, Culture, and Activity, 17*(3), 265–283. doi: 10.1080/10749030903515213

Zentella, A. C. (1997). *Growing up bilingual: Puerto Rican children in New York.* Malden, MA: Blackwell.

CHAPTER 4

STUDENT RESISTANCE IN A FIFTH-GRADE MATHEMATICS CLASS

Heather Cavell
Department of Mathematics
The University of Arizona

INTRODUCTION

Mathematical spaces in classrooms in the United States often confine young people to activities that are devoid of connections to their real social worlds. Relationships between students and teachers are developed from adult-centric views that frame learning as an approximation to adult experience (Andrade, 1994; Cahan, Mechling, Sutton-Smith, & White, 1993). A lack of attention to children's lives can create spaces that suppress student learning. Students of minority or low socioeconomic status are especially vulnerable because they are in educational spaces for extended periods of time with little or no connection to their communities (Trueba, 1998). In an effort to maintain engagement, some students create resistant behavioral forms (Giroux, 1992). The purpose of this study was to observe and analyze how one group of fifth-grade students used resistance in a mathematics classroom.

Latinos/as and Mathematics Education, pages 63–87
Copyright © 2011 by Information Age Publishing

This study was conducted in conjunction with work through the Center for the Mathematics Education of Latinos (CEMELA). In keeping with the goals of the center, this study used a sociocultural perspective as its guiding conceptual framework. Use of this perspective necessitated several assumptions. First, we assumed that creating a supportive environment for learning is both a social and cultural process. In this process, knowledge is constructed from personal experience gained in classroom activity that incorporates mental reflection. Sociocultural theorists perceive learning as a function of social interaction during classroom activities. The social structure of the classroom and classroom norms serve as the catalysts for student acceptance or resistance to their teacher, peers, and academic learning.

Latino students in the U.S. school system are often described as not meeting educational goals because of their dropout rates, grade repetition, and overrepresentation in special education programs. It becomes critical to understand how students interact within educational spaces where they struggle and where they succeed. A growing numbers of studies have shown that miseducation of Latino children may be the norm (McNeil & Valenzuela, 1998; Reyes, 1995; Valencia, 2000). This norm suggests that many educational spaces may not meet Latino/a students' needs and thereby influence failure rates. Results from one study indicated Latino students have the

> highest annual high school dropout rate of any ethnic group (7.1%, nearly double that of non-Hispanic Caucasian students). Additionally, the percentage of Latino adults age 18–24 who are no longer enrolled in school and who have not completed high school (34%) is more than double that of any other ethnic group as measured by the census. (Jamieson, Curry, & Martinez, 2001, p. 525)

Resistance provides students with a means to gain control and connection to educational spaces. Resistance can also be seen as a threat by educators and is often considered an attribute of student failure. It is important for educators and researchers to understand why and how students use resistance.

The goal of this study was to describe the resistance strategies used by elementary Latino/a students in a mathematics classroom. The guiding research questions were as follows:

1. What forms of resistance to the classroom norms, teacher, and mathematics did students use?
2. What experiences prompted students to use these forms of resistance?
3. Why did students select these forms of resistance?

The chapter begins by providing a brief summary of research literature relevant to student resistance. The analysis of the data is provided in two parts. The first part summarizes four case study narratives. These case studies are followed by a description of students' passive and aggressive resistance. Lastly, a discussion of the teachers' approaches to dealing with resistant behavior is offered.

RESISTANCE IN CLASSROOMS

In her ethnographic work with Mexican youth, Valenzuela (1999) described the situation for many Latino/a students in school:

> All people share a basic need to be understood, appreciated, and respected. Among many acculturated, U.S.-born, Mexican American youth at Seguin [a school], however, these basic needs go unmet during the hours at which they are at school. The students' culturally assimilated status only exacerbates the problems inherent in an institutional relationship that defines them as in need of continuing socialization. (p. 108)

Valenzuela (1999) found that the subtractive school experience increased the disassociation students felt due to their lack of control of their education. She described how students engaged in resistance as they "posture and pose, mentally absent themselves, physically absent themselves, or attend and participate only in those classes that interest them" (p. 109).

Resistance behaviors range over a broad spectrum. On one end are "students who are simply acting out in class without any critique of the social conditions that may contribute to their disruptive behavior" (Solórzano & Bernal, 2001, p. 316). On the other end are students who may provide "strong critiques of their oppressive social conditions but who ultimately help re-create these conditions through their own self-defeating resistant behavior" (Solórzano & Bernal, 2001, p. 316). Resistance is not always self-defeating. It can also include hiding a library book amongst textbooks and reading from the library book instead of the textbook, speaking Spanish in a non-Spanish language class, avoiding English immersion programs that restrict students to dead-end education tracks, or going beyond the standard set forth in one's curriculum and learning content beyond what is provided in class.

Resistance theories differ from many forms of sociocultural reproduction and stereotype threat theories because the concept of resisting emphasizes that the individuals are not simply acted on by societal structures (Solórzano & Bernal, 2001). Instead, individuals are described as involved in negotiations and struggles with these societal structures when creating their own meaning from interactions. Resistance theory acknowledges that individuals have agency within educational spaces. *Human agency* is the ability for individuals to make their own choices and to impose those choices on their world. Agency is affected by the social, cultural, and economic conditions in which an individual is placed and the individual's motivation to participate in the correction of social wrongdoings.

Solórzano and Bernal (2001) place resistance into several interrelated themes: reactionary behavior, self-defeating, conformist, transformational, and resiliency. *Reactionary behavior* refers to students who lack a critique of the oppressive conditions in which they are placed and are not motivated to act to correct these conditions. For example, reactionary students may challenge their teacher or act out just for the fun of doing it. They offer no reason for their behavior in relation to their educational setting. *Self-defeating resistance* describes students who have an opinion on the oppressive social conditions but have no motivation to participate in the correction of these conditions. Although this form of resistance acknowledges human agency, it is limited because students' behaviors can be destructive to themselves or others. *Conformist resistance* describes students who are motivated to participate in social justice struggles, but have no opinion of the systems that are acting to oppress them. For example, this term would be applied to students who may develop a tutoring program to help peers at risk of dropping out of school but who do not challenge the institutional and social programs that lead to students being categorized as at risk. *Transformational resistance* refers to students who are motivated to participate in social justice movements and who offer their own critique of the oppressive situation. For students with a deeper level of understanding of social justice, transformational resistance provides the strongest possibility for creating change.

METHODS

Site and Participants

This study was conducted at Agave Elementary School,[1] a public K–6 school in a primarily Latino neighborhood of the southwestern United States. The neighborhood maintains many characteristics of Mexico, such as the small bungalow-style houses, signs in Spanish, and local businesses selling Mexican products, reflecting the history of the area as being a part of Mexico (González, 2001). Agave serves a 90% Hispanic student body of 272 students with an estimated 95% of the student body qualifying for free or reduced-price lunch, and 38.4% of the students are classified as English language learners (ELLs) with 92% reporting that they speak Spanish at home (Greatschools.net, n.d.). The percentage of students eligible for the federal free and reduced-price lunch program is one indication of the low student economic level (or family income level) of the families the school serves. The school makeup is a reflection of the surrounding community of low-income families of predominantly Latino heritage. At Agave, due to changes in Arizona's educational policies and legislation concerning bilingual education, all ELLs are placed into structured English immersion classrooms rather than bilingual classrooms. The goal of structured English immersion is for students to be immersed into the English language if they test below a certain level on an English language test.

The classroom selected for study was one of two fifth-grade classes headed by veteran teacher Cynthia P.[2] Ms. P grew up in a small northwestern town. She was raised in a working-class family and decided at an early age that she would become a teacher. She pursued education in college and finished her bachelor's degree in education after relocating to the southwest. She earned her master's degree in education and she continued to take courses through her district and local university. At the time of the study, Ms. P had taught at Agave for several years, moving between third grade and fifth grade. She participated regularly in professional development opportunities and after-school activities with her students. The fifth-grade class was composed of 30 students: 14 boys and 16 girls.

Students were arranged in cooperative working groups throughout the duration of mathematics lessons. Peer activities and groups were essential to Ms. P's instructional practice. Ms. P used mixed-ability groups and believed that high-level students support the learning of low-level students. Rules, norms, and expectations were posted throughout the room and reinforced the school's policies overall. Sometimes group work conflicted with her classroom management. As in many classrooms, moments of instability were caused by daily conflicts among groups of students and lesson transitions between academic subjects.

Observations and interviews with students indicated that there were many environmental levels to this classroom. On the content level, students were separated by intellectual or mathematical ability. On the social level, students were constrained by their intellectual marks and seemed to position themselves relative to their more advanced peers. Advanced students displayed some authority and status. The teacher expected the advanced students to provide support, resources, and a high academic standard for their peers. The students stayed in social cliques, leaving many students socially isolated. To combat this isolation and ensure that certain groups were distributed (and thus to decrease conflict), the teacher established a seating pattern using five to six desks arranged to form tables and to allow students to face one another.

Three individual desks were separated from the six group tables (see Figure 4.1 for a representation of the classroom layout). These three desks were usually occupied by students who had lost their privilege to work in groups, had been absent and needed more focused attention, elected to not sit with others, or needed to focus on a task different from the activity

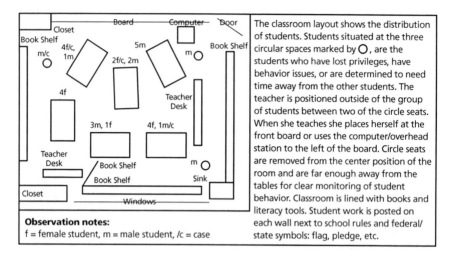

The classroom layout shows the distribution of students. Students situated at the three circular spaces marked by ◯, are the students who have lost privileges, have behavior issues, or are determined to need time away from the other students. The teacher is positioned outside of the group of students between two of the circle seats. When she teaches she places herself at the front board or uses the computer/overhead station to the left of the board. Circle seats are removed from the center position of the room and are far enough away from the tables for clear monitoring of student behavior. Classroom is lined with books and literacy tools. Student work is posted on each wall next to school rules and federal/state symbols: flag, pledge, etc.

Observation notes:
f = female student, m = male student, /c = case

Figure 4.1 Ms. P's classroom layout (remained constant throughout the year).

taking place at that time. There were three to four students who routinely filled these seats, while the other students were organized into new working groups weekly. Three of these students usually had lost their privilege to work with others or elected to sit by themselves; it was always the same three students with a potential fourth one who varied from among the other members of the class.

The classroom space, as set up by Ms. P, was difficult to navigate. It was crowded and the grouping of desks and chairs limited movement. Students had difficulty walking to classroom resources without bumping into each other or tables. Banners covered the windows and almost all walls. Grouping of tables had students facing in many different angles, many away from the board or teacher's desk. Transitions between lessons were difficult because of the physical space limitations; lessons often required rearrangement of chairs, teaching materials, and children. The front board was covered with school flyers, content posters, performance objectives, and detention lists. These adornments reduced the amount of board space available for writing to an area approximately 2' × 3'. Desks were cluttered with name tags, books, papers, writing materials, and folders. Overall, there was a strong atmosphere of confinement in this classroom.

Data Collection

The timeline for this study was nine months (one academic year for the elementary school). Data were collected from interviews, field observations, and student work. Formal and informal interviews were conducted separately with Ms. P and the students. Interviews with Ms. P were conducted as informal meetings consisting of semi-structured and open-ended questions. Guiding questions were determined prior to the initial interview. There were two purposes for conducting the teacher interviews. First, the teacher interviews allowed a rapport to be established with Ms. P and a baseline understanding to be developed with regard to her classroom philosophies, student perspectives, and ideology of learning mathematics, general classroom structure, and routines. The second purpose of the interviews was to promote more specific discussion about her perspectives on the issue of resistance and how she, as an educator, defined, interpreted, and addressed resistance.

Four students (two girls and two boys) were selected as case studies and were informally interviewed individually. The reason for interviewing and selecting four cases was to understand the variation in the classroom, provide the students an opportunity to interact and ask questions of the researcher, and obtain a baseline for comparison. Student interviews were conducted during designated student work times or during lunch and lasted approximately 10 to 15 minutes. Observations were conducted prior to the first interviews to establish background and rapport with students. Case study students were selected based on teacher feedback, student performance, and student participation in classroom activities during initial observations.

Observations were conducted twice a week during the mathematics block, an instructional period lasting approximately 75 minutes every Tuesday and Thursday. Field notes were taken at each observation and interview. The purpose of these classroom observations was to look for instances of student resistance as they occur during mathematical tasks. Observations were also conducted on Thursdays during the designated lunch period for fifth graders. The lunch period offered an opportunity for the researcher and students to interact with one another outside of the academic activities as a means to triangulate classroom behaviors with interactions in other settings. These lunch period observations also provided data on how the teacher and students interacted during unstructured time. Lunch time offered students an opportunity to engage in school clubs, sports, and group projects. For example, students participating in the fifth-grade chorus often practice with the music teacher during lunch or use the time to coordinate after-school activities.

Student work was collected throughout the study for predetermined lessons to gauge which activities maintained student interest and those that did not. Students kept journals for each academic subject and were allowed to write reflections on activities, concerns, and thoughts about content and personal reflections. Reflections allowed students to elaborate on their feelings about activities or other issues that might affect their classroom behavior or content learning. Student work and reflections provide the data for a detailed picture of the classroom.

Data Analysis

Data collected in field notes, focal interview transcripts, and student work were analyzed using an ethnographic and constant comparative method to develop both descriptive and categorical themes and relationships. In keeping with the constant-comparative foundations of grounded theory, alternate phases of data collection and analysis were utilized (Glaser, 1992; Glaser & Strauss, 1967; Merriam, 1998; Strauss, 1987). New data collected from observation, interview, and discussion were constantly compared to information collected to continually refine and guide observations, interviews, and activities.

Two levels of analysis were carried out: The first was a description account and the second was category construction. The descriptive account provided the narrative meaning of the phenomenon under investigation, and the categorical construction allowed for the development of themes and patterns across the various types of data (Merriam, 1998). The unit of analysis for this study was considered to be "any meaningful (or potentially meaningful) segment of data" (Merriam, 1998, p. 179); in this study, the unit of analysis was as small as a single word, phrase, or utterance and as large as an interview segment or page of student work. The development of categories or themes began by reading through the data and identifying important or striking pieces of information. These pieces of information were tracked using Microsoft Excel spreadsheets. Once these pieces of information were isolated, the data were reviewed again to identify supporting data and links between sets of data. Once links were established, arguments for their presence were developed to help provide explanation for that particular piece and its place in the larger context of the study. Once all of these arguments were developed, preliminary hypotheses could be developed and models built to explain the data as a means to answering research question. The process is represented in Table 4.1.

Coding was conducted at two levels following the constant-comparative method. The process began with open coding and involved all individual pieces of data and culmination of data in the case study format. Once this coding was established, axial coding was performed around several categories or themes that arose from the data. Codes were also created using research study questions, theoretical frameworks, and categories that developed out of open coding to address all possible interpretations.

TABLE 4.1 General Phases and Examples of Data Collection

Phases

1: Identify units of data	2: Category development (using data from Phase 1)	3: Linkages (using information from phases 1 and 2)	4: Models/theories (using information from phases 1–3)	5: Answers to research questions (using information from phase 1–4)

Examples of Data Collection

1	2	3	4	5
Positive or negative comment about a mathematical algorithm or mathematical experience	Student peer relationships, teacher-student relationships, mathematical reasoning, student compliance behavior	Students relate learning to positive experiences; home learning to academic performance; and student behavior to overall mathematical experiences	Students' behavior complies with classroom rules when their academic interests are met; students perform higher on content tests when provided time for exploration and reflection.	Students resist classroom spaces that do not utilize first language

Examples of Data Forms/Other

1	2	3	4	5
Student work, interview transcripts	Multiple utterances, uses of a type of algorithm, incidences of a type of behavior	Connection of multiple utterances to student preference toward content, incidences of behavior to relationships with peers	Students are more engaged when they are interested in the mathematical task, students placed in cooperative groups that do not include their friends tend to perform better.	Student interviews and questionnaires show that academic learning is more significant to students when it utilizes their home language.

Note: Adapted from *Qualitative Research and Case Study Applications in Education,* by S. B. Merriam, 2001, p. 178–197. Copyright 2001 by Jossey-Bass.

To analyze students' mathematical work, the sociocultural approach recommended by Campbell, Adams, and Davis (2007) was followed to determine the cognitive demands of mathematical tasks for ELLs. It was more important to the goals of this study to focus on understanding the underlying issues related to student perceptions toward mathematics than on whether student responses were right or wrong. The approach by Campbell and colleagues provides a holistic look at all of the factors that have an impact on students' problem-solving abilities. The framework (see Figure 4.2) has four components: "(a) mathematical content; (b) mathematical and cognitive processes; (c) mathematical and contextual language; and (d) cultural/life experiences" (Campbell et al., 2007, p. 20), and these components correspond to the contents of Table 4.2. Together, these components describe the key questions and themes coded for when analyzing student work.

Student responses to mathematics tasks assigned in the classroom were logged in a Microsoft Excel spreadsheet along with the responses to questions in the framework. Any comments made by students during interviews or classroom observations in reference to their work were also noted. After student work and tasks were analyzed within this framework, the work and tasks were compared to findings for all other forms of data and then re-coded for connecting themes, trends, or patterns.

Each of the four case studies began with a descriptive narrative of the student; this narrative included data from qualitative sources such as observations, interviews, and student work. The focus of each case was the student as an academic learner and member of the mathematics classroom.

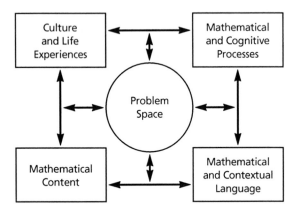

Figure 4.2 Meta-reflective interactions in the problem space. *Note*: Adapted from "Cognitive Demands and Second-language Learners: A Framework for Analyzing Mathematical Instructional Contexts," by A. E. Campbell, V. M. Adams, and G. E. Davis, 2007, *Mathematical Thinking and Learning, 9,* p. 20. © 2007 by Taylor & Francis.

TABLE 4.2   Framework for Planning and Reflection on Mathematics Instruction

Framework component

A: Academic content	B: Mathematical and cognitive processes	C: Mathematical and contextual language	D: Cultural/life experiences
Focus questions			
How experienced were students with mathematics concepts and procedures? With concepts from other content areas (e.g., science and social studies) that are required?	What mathematical processes were needed and how experienced are students at using them? What cognitive processing skills were needed/ employed? What mathematical issues occurred?	Did the students' prior experiences include development of mathematical language and the reflective and command functions of natural language in learning of mathematics? Does language used in problem statement or instruction correspond to level of English language development of ESL students? Are words used that have specialized/ different meanings in mathematics and natural language?	What knowledge of cultural or life experiences was needed to understand problem statement? What connections needed to be made between classroom mathematics and student experience?

Note: Adapted from "Cognitive Demands and Second-Language Learners: A Framework for Analyzing Mathematical Instructional Contexts," by A. E. Campbell, V. M. Adams, and G. E. Davis, 2007, *Mathematical Thinking and Learning, 9,* 18–23. Copyright 2007 by Taylor & Francis.

Once the narrative was written, the four phases of the framework were completed to uncover patterns across case studies. Patterns were entered into a Microsoft Excel spreadsheet as Word tables and tally tables constructed to highlight connections between cases and multiple forms of data (Stake, 2006; Yin, 1984, 1994a, 1994b, 1997).

FINDINGS

This section has two parts: the narrative for the case studies and the multi-case study analysis. Part 1 provides the descriptive narratives for four case studies. Each student narrative describes the students' behavior in the classroom; student reflections on their feelings; attitudes toward their teacher, school, and peers; and their own thoughts about their learning. Case study students' academic abilities ranged from low-average learners Penny and Alberto to high-level learners Carmen and Luis. Part 2 describes the themes and relationships that came out of the cross-case analysis of the case study students and other study data.

Part 1: Descriptive Narratives

Penny

Penny was an average student (as determined by her teacher using Arizona's Instrument to Measure Standards [AIMS] scores and classroom performance) who spent much of her free time taking care of her younger brother. Penny reported in an interview that she enjoyed school and often participated in after-school activities, such as a math club. She was observed to be quiet during structured time but seemed happy and energetic during group activities and free time. In the interviews, she commented that she liked school and that mathematics was a chance to be creative and active in learning. She reported that mathematics was a challenge for her, but a challenge she liked. The after-school researchers perceived Penny to be an insightful student who seemed to view mathematics as a time to be both creative and active. Penny was observed in the after-school mathematics club participating more actively in the social justice mathematics projects that involved analyzing issues in her community than she did in her classroom-based mathematics tasks. A portion of an interview with Penny during which she described her time in the after-school math club is presented in Excerpt 4.1.

Excerpt 4.1. Penny interview

Researcher: "So how is your mathematics class different from your math club?"

Penny: "It's easy because the math club shows you more math and here [in class], it shows you a little bit of mathematics."

Researcher: "You learn more mathematics in math club?"

Penny: "But in here [class], they show you the same way you do, but in the math club it shows you different."

Researcher: "How do you feel about math now?"

Penny: "It's fun."

Researcher: "Yeah."

Penny: "It's good . . . the way of showing you're learning . . . it's the way to show people how you learn and you care to take away."

Although Penny seemed to be aware of the differences between the types of teaching provided in her classroom and in the after-school setting, she did not feel comfortable asking for changes to be made in her classroom. In school, Penny maintained a respectful attitude and stated that "in the classroom the teacher is in control and you have to give her your attention; you have to be respectful" (personal communication, October 17, 2006).

Luis

Luis spent the majority of his class time reading while he waited for his classmates to finish mathematical tasks that he had completed in mere minutes. Luis was a bilingual participant in the Tucson school district's gifted and talented education program, and Ms. P considered him to be an excellent student. Ms. P was often observed placing him in leadership roles and seeking his help to aid other students. He appeared to enjoy being called on and explaining his reasoning in detail. During group projects, he took charge to make sure things were done to his standards. This behavior sometimes appeared to cause conflicts with his fellow group members. In one of our interviews, Luis reported that he had many friends and enjoyed competing with fellow classmate Carmen when doing academic tasks. He was occasionally observed passing notes and playing coding games on small pieces of paper that could be covered when Ms. P walked nearby. Luis sometimes read from the children's comedy joke books he kept in his desk rather than read the assigned text. Luis's explanation of these classroom behaviors is presented in Excerpt 4.2.

Excerpt 4.2. Luis interview

Researcher: "Luis, tell me about your everyday mathematics class."

Luis: "It is not fair, we have to do the same work and some can't keep up. I am bored, so I find other ways to spend my time so I can move on. I don't say much so I don't get in trouble, and I get my work done."

Researcher: "Why are you bored?"

Luis: "Most of what we do is review. It helps some students but I don't get to do harder problems unless I look for other ways to do things."

Researcher: "What do you mean by other ways to do things?"

Luis: "I just look for other patterns or different ways to solve problems."

Researcher: "Do you ask your teacher for harder problems?"

Luis: "No, she gives them to me sometimes, though."

Researcher: "What are the other ways you spend your time?"

Luis: "I read, play games or puzzles. I like puzzles."

Researcher: "How often do you get to do puzzles?"

> **Luis:** "Almost every day. Ms. P doesn't know I do them most of the time. She is busy with the others."
> **Researcher:** "Do you do the puzzles with other students, too?"
> **Luis:** "Sometimes, but if we get caught, then we have to go back to their work."

He remarked that he was able to do puzzles most of the time because the teacher was busy with other students. Luis seemed to recognize that when his teacher was helping students, her time was divided unequally because of the variation in students' skill levels.

Alberto

Alberto was one of a handful of students who seemed to look forward to their transition to middle school. He lived with his mother and spent most weekends with his father. Alberto appeared to spend most of his time during the mathematics block sitting at one of the single desks set outside the group tables. He seemed to choose to sit alone but would speak with whoever was closest to him at his convenience. As an example of one such incident, Alberto was working alone at his assigned seat (at a single desk behind a table of six other students). He had skipped some assigned worksheet problems and was working on a word problem that required him to order a set of events based on the times given in the corresponding clock faces. As he worked on Problem 7, another student asked him whether he could borrow a pencil. Alberto responded, "No," and then proceeded to tell him about his new pen.

Alberto quickly extracted a bright red pen from his backpack. The other student took Alberto's pen and wrote a note on Alberto's paper, and they both started laughing. Ms. P responded by telling the other student to turn around and get to work. Alberto replied to the teacher, "He is just looking at my new pen." Ms. P responded, "Not right now, you have work to do, get started." Alberto then said, "I have started." Ms. P ignored this retort and turned to answer another student's question. Alberto then retrieved the pen from his classmate and wrote all over his paper. He spent the rest of the class period (10 minutes) drawing on his name-tag with his new pen. At the lunch bell, Ms. P asked the students to turn in their work. Alberto crumbled his paper and tossed it in his desk. A student working at the computers behind him said to Alberto, "You are going to lose points." Alberto responded, "I don't care."

In this example, Alberto showed signs of self-defeating behavior. He had chosen to not complete his assignment and instead, drew on it. It appears that his dislike of the teacher's redirection sparked this particular behavior. He did not like what he was told to do and sought Ms. Ps's acknowledgement that he was working, even though he was not on task when the teacher came around to check progress.

Alberto often shouted in the hallways to friends and teachers. His work generally appeared to be left incomplete or completed with as little effort as possible. In a dialogue with a classmate, he stated, "I can't wait until I am dead so I can be a shadow" (personal communication, October 17, 2006). He went on to describe how being a shadow would allow him to participate without others infringing on him.

Alberto appeared to enjoy helping students who had trouble with mathematics tasks. He challenged them to beat his time to complete a problem or helped them with concepts about which they were uncertain. An example of how Alberto challenged another student who seemed to have difficulty with a fractions task is offered in Excerpt 4.3. This student often did not do assignments or homework. He appeared to be both withdrawn from and often intimidating to other students. He often told Alberto that he was frustrated with not understanding the assignments and that he was afraid to ask for help.

Excerpt 4.3. Alberto and Student A

Student A: "Alberto, let's play basketball at lunch."

Alberto: "Yeah, we can get Carmen to play."

Ms. P: "Student A and Alberto, get to work."

Student A: "I'm done ."

Ms. P: "Then bring it to me."

Student A: "No."

Ms. P: (Ms. P stands and walks to the student's desk) "You have not even started, Student A. You need to sit down and get to work."

Student A: "I don't want to do this. This is stupid."

Ms. P: "Get started or you are going next door."

Student A: "Fine with me."

Alberto: "Student A, just sit down."

Ms. P: "Alberto, get to work. Student A, what is it going to be?"

Student A: (Sits down) "Fine, I will do it."
(Teacher returns to her desk)

Alberto: (moves from his desk and sits next to Student A) "Just finish it and we will compare answers."

Student A: "I don't get this."

Alberto: "Ok, look. You just need to look at the denominators. See this one (pointing to ½), if you multiply the bottom by 2, what do you get?"

Student A: "Four."

Alberto: "Where do you see 4?"

Student A: "Right there." (pointing to 2/4)

Alberto: "Okay, so does the top work too?"

Student A: "Yeah, 2 times 1 is 2."

Alberto: "See that is all it is. Let's see who finished first."

Student A: "I'm going to beat you!"

Alberto: "No you're not, I'm almost done" (The two students work on the paper, continuing to challenge one anther verbally, until Student A gets stuck and Alberto helps him again. This activity continues until they finish and compare answers. Student A and Alberto both seem pleased with their papers.)

In this incident, Student A appeared to be frustrated. When Student A refused to do his mathematics assignment, the teacher told him that he would have to leave the class. Alberto stepped in to keep him from having to leave class. Alberto made the task a game, a race to see who could correctly answer the worksheet problems the fastest. Alberto commented later in an interview that the rules were unfair in the class and school. He explained that his friend was always getting in trouble for things others could get away with and that his friend was picked on because everyone thought of him as a troublemaker. When I asked Alberto why he did not let Ms. P know that Student A was having trouble or that he thought the class was unfair, he responded "I don't want to get in trouble. They [adults] don't listen to us any way. I just want to get out of here."

Carmen

Carmen appeared to be an outgoing student who enjoyed being in the spotlight. Based on her teacher-reported grades and state test cores, she was a high-achieving student. She participated in sports, chorus, and a variety of other activities, and took on leadership roles in both academic tasks and social networks. She described herself as feeling pride in completing her work before her classmates. The teacher often gave her alternative tasks to do when the rest of the class was working. Unlike Luis, who seemed to prefer to read or play a quiet game, she spent the majority of her lunchtime in the classroom doing tasks for Ms. P or organizing activities for herself and her friends. Carmen often stated that she preferred academics to be a competition in the classroom and in the social settings associated with it.

Although Carmen thought of herself as popular, she encountered conflicts with her classmates when she attempted to show off. She was an advanced student and this advantage seemed to provide her with benefits in the classroom. For example, she was allowed to use the computers to type her papers. She also seemed to be treated more favorably by the teacher. Carmen was observed to be exempted from certain tasks by arguing with the teacher. When other students attempted the same behavior, they seemed to receive harsher responses.

Carmen was often observed participating in group activities. An example of an exchange during participation in a group activity is presented in Excerpt 4.4.

Excerpt 4.4. Carmen, Student B, and Ms. P

> **Carmen:** "Hey, hey..." (to Student B at adjacent table)
> **Student B:** (Female student) "What, Carmen? We are trying to work."
> **Carmen:** "So? We are already done."
> **Student B:** "So?"
> **Carmen:** "Look, look at these."
> **Student B:** "What are they?"
> **Carmen:** "My ribbons, they are all first place."
> **Student B:** "So, let us work."
> **Carmen:** "Fine. Ms. P, Ms. P, look!"
> **Ms. P:** "Carmen, you need to keep working."
> **Carmen:** "I am done. Look at these, Ms. P."
> **Ms. P:** "Those are nice, good job. Why don't you and your partner play the game again and see if anything changes."
> **Carmen:** "But I already know this. You said I could work on my paper today."
> **Ms. P:** "After this, Carmen."

Carmen was observed several times as she argued her way out of doing a task or even changing the requirements of a task, as demonstrated in Excerpt 4.5. Although this dialogue took place between Ms. P and Carmen, like many observed instances, it took place in front of the whole class. Carmen was witnessed aggressively arguing her way out of the task. By giving in to Carmen, probably because the teacher had to turn her attention to the students who needed her help, the teacher confirmed Carmen's different status in this classroom.

Excerpt 4.5. Carmen and Ms. P

> **Carmen:** "Ms. P, I did this activity last year."
> **Ms. P:** "Yes, I know but this is review for the AIMS."
> **Carmen:** "Yeah, but you know I know how to do this. Do I really have to do the questions? I have the data and made the graph."
> **Ms. P:** "Yes, Carmen you need to be able to do this."

> **Carmen:** "I already can, you know that. Here, look, this is the outlier (pointing to her plot), the mean, and median. See? I already know this."
>
> **Ms. P:** "We are almost done, Carmen, just work on the questions."
>
> **Carmen:** "No, can't I just sharpen the pencils until they're [the class] done?"
>
> **Ms. P:** "Fine, just do it quietly in the back of the class."

The exchange presented in Excerpt 4.5 exemplifies Carmen's talent for restructuring tasks during group activities by arguing with Ms. P over instructions, task procedures, or final task products.

An exchange that occurred as part of another event, one in which Carmen included her friends in getting her way, is presented in Excerpt 4.6. In this excerpt, four girls left the classroom to talk to another teacher without obtaining permission from Ms. P and returned in time for the lunch bell. They let Ms. P know that the other teacher was on her way to help them practice. Ms. P acknowledged this with a nod and told them to stay in the classroom and wait for the other teacher while she took the rest of the class to the lunchroom. When Ms. P returned, she said nothing about their leaving.

Excerpt 4.6. Carmen and choir practice
(Carmen and her group members are working at one of the
classroom computers typing up their findings. Ms. P walks over to
check their progress.)

> **Carmen:** "Ms. P, we are finished."
>
> **Ms. P:** "Let me see (she reads over their findings). You haven't touched on all of the discussion questions."
>
> **Carmen:** "But you said just to talk about what we thought."
>
> **Ms. P:** "I told you to answer the discussion questions and use them to guide your findings."
>
> **Carmen:** "But you said we did not have to."
>
> **Students C and D (girls in group):** "Yeah Ms. P."
>
> **Carmen:** "Yeah, and you said we could go practice for choir while the others finished."
>
> **Ms. P:** "I said you could practice at lunch."
>
> **Carmen:** "But we need to organize and ask Ms. (Choir teacher) to come here for lunch."
>
> **Ms. P:** "You will have to do that at lunch."
>
> **Carmen:** "We won't have time. We need to do it now."
>
> **Ms. P:** "You need to finish this."
>
> **Carmen:** "We are finished, this is what we have. We don't have anything else to add. This is what you said."

> **Ms. P:** "You need to be ready to present tomorrow."
> **Carmen:** "We are. This is the only time we have to practice."
> **Students C and D:** "Yeah, Ms. P."
> **Ms. P:** "Carmen, you can go ask but you two need to keep practicing for your presentation."
> (Ms. P leaves to check on other groups)
> **Carmen:** "Okay let's go, Student E, come with us."
> **Student E (Another female student):** "I can't, I have to finish."
> **Carmen:** "Finish when we get back. You're with me. She won't say nothing."

In contrast to other students, Carmen seemed to get what she wanted with little to no consequences from the teacher. Ms. P seemed to carefully choose her battles with Carmen, selecting when to be more or less assertive with her.

Part 2: Cross-Case Analysis

For these four case study students, both passive and aggressive behaviors were observed. These students were observed using common passive forms of resistance such as sitting quietly and not paying attention, ignoring the task, or writing notes to a friend. This behavior occurred routinely during the mathematics class, especially during worksheet-driven activities. Students seemed most engaged during discovery learning activities, but this teaching method was not often used. Students were also observed using more aggressive forms of resistance, such as verbally confronting peers or the teacher, walking out of class, shouting, or voicing their dislike for a task. As presented in Excerpt 4.7, Luis is observed to display passive resistance and his teacher's response to his behavior. Luis had spent his mathematics time playing a game with a nearby student. When he was caught, he was not punished; instead, the teacher asked him to finish the worksheet. He completed the worksheet in just a few moments and then continued the puzzle, instead of completing a reading assignment.

Excerpt 4.7. Luis and his puzzle
(While students work on their mathematics worksheet, Luis
appears to work quietly, reading his language arts book.)

> **Ms. P:** "Luis, you need to finish your math."
> **Luis:** "I'm done."
> **Ms. P:** "You are."
> **Luis:** "Yeah, I am just reading the next story."
> **Ms. P:** "Okay."

> **Ms. P:** "Luis, you have done nothing."
> (Luis begins scribbling in his book and then pulls a small piece of paper out of the text and passes it to nearby Student S. Student S selects the box he wants and passes it back. This exchange occurs repeatedly until Ms. P walks over to check the group's progress.)
> **Ms. P:** "Please finish your worksheet and then you can keep reading."
> (Luis smiles at her and she looks at the puzzle in the middle of his book, then looks at Student S.)
> **Ms. P:** "Get to work."

As noted in Excerpt 4.7, Ms. P responded to Luis's passive behavior by smiling at him and redirecting him. In contrast, her response to Student S was more direct: "Get to work."

The teacher's responses to Luis are in sharp contrast to her responses to Alberto. Alberto displayed more aggressive behaviors, which were also met with more direct responses from the teacher. For example, during a mathematics lesson in which students were asked to break different-sized square grids into equal pieces, Alberto was observed transitioning from using active resistance to passive resistance when faced with the consequence of detention. The class was asked to divide the area of a grid into eight equal sections. Alberto came up with a solution of breaking the grid into triangles, the areas of which were equal. He was the only student to picture the grid this way and he seemed sure his method was valid. He presented his solution to Ms. P, who told him his solution was not what she was looking for, that there was a specific process she was trying to highlight in the lesson.

Ms. P said that she wanted him to use the process of the lesson and she asked him to try again. He became upset and remarked to her in front of the class that she was wrong. He seemed very sure that his method was equally valid. He became loud and continued to try to convince the teacher for several minutes that he was correct by describing the area within the triangles as equal. Ms. P instructed him to return to his seat or he would face detention. He returned to his seat upset and sat quietly, staring at the computers stationed near him. As the class moved on to the writing lesson, Alberto erased his solution to the problem and then copied his classmates' answer.

In the example of the square grids, Alberto backed down when he was threatened with detention. It appeared that the nonvalidation of his solution upset him. He had found a novel solution and appeared to be quite proud of himself. When his novel solution was not confirmed, even though it was correct, he first reacted strongly, using active resistance, and then later appeared to use more passive resistance by changing his answer.

During interviews, Ms. P reported that she was keenly aware of these resistance patterns and I observed her catching many incidences before they began. Ms. P stated that she identified the "problem students" in the classroom at the beginning of the year and directed much of her attention to making sure they were on task and separated from each other. Alberto, for example, was often placed at the solitary desks, as described in Methods.

Passive behaviors such as Luis's puzzles were safe avenues for students to negotiate their educational space with little fear of punishment. During these instances, Ms. P paid less attention to the passive student, a move that left them to understand the task through interactions with advanced students such as Luis. When, in the course of a personal interview with Ms. P, this lack of attention was pointed out to her, she dismissed the matter as an oversight on the observer's part (personal communication, November 15, 2006). In the rush of the lesson and school day, teachers like Ms. P do their best to ensure all students receive the help and attention they need, but it is inevitable that a student's question or concern will not be addressed.

The two examples described here in Part 2 demonstrate Luis's awareness of the different academic levels of the students in this classroom. The cooperative grouping used in the class offered students opportunities to talk about mathematics and to hear how other students were solving tasks. If the students had questions, they just asked their classmates. Advanced students seemed largely unchallenged by the tasks; they resisted both passively and aggressively. In general, low-achieving students were more aggressive resisters, seemed afraid to ask questions, and reported feeling out of place in the classroom.

DISCUSSION

Many of the students in this study reported an awareness of the difficulty in negotiating the sociocultural norms of the classroom. However, students also stated that they preferred to maintain these norms to avoid punishment from the teacher or ridicule from their peers. The teacher seemed to select students who entered this classroom with prior labels, such as disruptive or at risk, and worked to ensure they conformed to classroom procedures. The types of resistance students used were closely related to their academic levels. Students found alternative methods of engagement that were met with different levels of consequences administered by the teacher. This conclusion supports the theories of resistance described by Solórzano and Bernal (2001), that students, especially self-defeaters, acted as agents in the recreation of the conditions needed to perpetuate their resistant behavior.

Ms. P and the students created a classroom environment that identified aggressive resisters in different ways. Sometimes students were identified as problems, like Alberto, and other times, they were identified as advanced students, like Carmen. Advanced students were able to negotiate and challenge the teacher with few, if any, consequences. Students labeled as problems appeared to have a more difficult time challenging the teacher. The teacher provided consequences that seemed to stifle students' aggressive resistance.

The teacher seemed to spend more time with students who were more aggressive resisters, and this distinction may have had an impact on other students. Luis, for example, noticed that Ms. P spent more time with students who acted out. He remarked that this left students who were afraid to speak up with unanswered questions. Students who were labeled as more academically advanced, in this case Luis and Carmen, appeared to be treated differently by the teacher and by their peers. Their misbehaviors did not receive the same stern responses from the teacher as their peers received. Thus, differences between how the teacher responded to more and less aggressive resisters had an impact on the experiences of all the students in this classroom.

CONCLUSIONS

This study investigated fifth-grade students' experiences with resistance and described two types of resistance, passive and aggressive, that were witnessed in interactions in a fifth-grade classroom. The teacher established her classroom norms and teaching methods to monitor aggressive resisters and provide them with consequences for perceived wrongdoings. The teacher perceived these behaviors as negative.

Advanced passive resisters like Luis appeared to have more control of their time than other students did. For example, as an advanced student, Luis could finish his work quickly and correctly, leaving him with more free time. On-level students and remedial students who were passive seemed to have difficulty getting questions answered because they were afraid to ask their peers or teacher, they were overshadowed by aggressive students taking the teacher's time and attention, or were overlooked because their silence was interpreted as an understanding of the task.

Advanced aggressive resisters like Carmen were observed redirecting the teacher's time for their own purpose. As seen in excerpts 4.5 and 4.6, Carmen acted as an authority figure by stating her high test scores and her knowledge of the content to get what she wanted. In contrast, other aggressive resisters were considered problem students and chose to sit at desks away from their peers.

Labels based on academic achievement appeared to be a strong part of the classroom context. Although being an advanced student seemed to provide an advantage in students' negotiation and direction of their classroom time, being labeled as a regular or remedial student did not appear to warrant the same benefits. For example, Carmen knew she was labeled as advanced and she used that label and knowledge to build a case in her arguments. She argued that she should receive certain benefits because she already knew what was required of her. She brought her first-place ribbons, announced her high AIMS scores, and solved problems quickly. Her peers seemed to acknowledge Carmen as a high-achieving student. Students also acknowledged Alberto as a high-achieving student because of his location in the class, his behavior, and the consequences he received or averted.

When managing resistance in classrooms, it is worth noting the demands placed on teachers by both the realities of the school context and the students. Resistance needs to be considered in terms of situated phenomena within the context of the classroom space. As these case study students and their classmates leave Agave to move into middle school settings, it is unclear how their transition will evolve or how their resistance techniques will factor into their academic successes or failures.

More research is needed to understand how teachers can learn to respond to students' resistance. Like Ms. P, many teachers elect to provide consequences to resistant behaviors but they may not provide students with alternatives. This dilemma may often not be by choice but rather the result of the demands and constraints teachers face within classrooms. A longitudinal study of students over the course of their elementary experience would be ideal for understanding the impact of resistance and acceptance in relation to classroom norms. By studying a group of students over time, a better picture of how different teachers respond to student resistance would emerge.

ACKNOWLEDGMENT

This manuscript is based upon work supported in part by the National Science Foundation under Grant No. 0424983 to the Center for the Mathematics Education of Latinos/Latinas (CEMELA). Any opinions, findings, and conclusions or recommendations expressed in this material are those of the author(s) and do not necessarily reflect the views of the National Science Foundation.

NOTES

1. The school, teacher and student names are all pseudonyms.

2. Ms. P is a leader at this school and it should be noted that although this paper highlights resistance, Ms. P is a caring professional who takes both her students' learning and educational success very seriously.

REFERENCES

Andrade, R. (1994). *Children's constructive social worlds: Existential lives in the balance.* Unpublished doctoral dissertationm, University of Arizona, Tucson.

Cahan, E., Mechling, J., Sutton-Smith, B., & White, S. H. (1993). The elusive historical child: Ways of knowing the child of history and psychology. In G. H. Elder, J. Modell, & R. D. Parke (Eds.), *Children in time and place: Developmental and historical insights* (pp. 192–223). Cambridge, UK: Cambridge University Press.

Campbell, A. E., Adams, V. M., & Davis, G. E. (2007). Cognitive demands and second-language learners: A framework for analyzing mathematical instructional contexts. *Mathematical Thinking and Learning, 9*(1), 3–30. doi: 10.1207/s15327833mtl0901_2

Center for the Mathematics Education of Latinos/as (CEMELA). (n.d.). *CEMELA's theoretical framework.* Retrieved from http://cemela.math.arizona.edu/english/principles/rationale.php

Giroux, H. A. (1992). *Border crossings: Cultural workers and the politics of education.* New York: Routledge.

Glaser, B. G. (1992). *Basics of grounded theory analysis: Emergence vs. forcing.* Mill Valley, CA: Sociology Press.

Glaser, B. G. & Strauss, A. L. (1967). *The discovery of grounded theory: Strategies for qualitative research.* Chicago: Aldine.

González, N. (2001). *I am my language: Discourses of women and children in the borderlands.* Tucson, AZ: University of Arizona Press.

Greatschools.net. (n.d.). *Agave elementary school.* Retrieved from http://www.greatschools.net/cgi-bin/az/

Jamieson, A., Curry, A., & Martinez, G. M. (2001). *School enrollment in the United States: Social and economic characteristics of students* (pp. 520–533). Washington, DC: U.S. Department of Commerce, Bureau of the Census.

McNeil, L. M. & Valenzuela, A. (1998). *The harmful impact of the TAAS system of testing in Texas: Beneath the accountability rhetoric.* Cambridge, MA: Harvard University Civil Rights Project.

Merriam, S. B. (1998). *Qualitative research and case study applications in education.* San Francisco: Jossey-Bass.

Reyes, P. (1995). Educational policy and the growing Latino student population: Problems and prospects. In A. M. Padilla (Ed.), *Hispanic psychology: Critical issues in theory and* research (pp. 303–325). Thousand Oaks, CA: Sage.

Solórzano, D. G., & Bernal, D. D. (2001). Examining transformational resistance through a critical race and Latcrit theory framework: Chicana and Chicano students in an urban context. *Urban Education, 36*(3), 308–342. doi: 10.1177/0042085901363002

Stake, R. E. (2006). *Multiple case study analysis.* New York: Guilford Press.

Strauss, A. L. (1987). *Qualitative analysis for social scientists.* Cambridge, England: Cambridge University Press.

Trueba, H. (1998). The education of Mexican immigrant children. In M. M. Suárez-Orozco (Ed.), *Crossings: Mexican immigration in interdisciplinary perspectives* (pp. 251–275). Cambridge, MA: Harvard University Press and the David Rockefeller Center for Latin American Studies.

Valencia, R. R. (2000). Inequalities and the schooling of minority students in Texas: Historical and contemporary conditions. *Hispanic Journal of Behavioral Sciences, 22*(4), 445–459. doi: 10.1177/0739986300224005

Valenzuela, A. (1999). *Subtractive schooling: U.S.-Mexican youth and the politics of caring.* Albany: State University of New York Press.

Yin, R. K. (1984). *Case study research: Design and methods* (2nd ed.). Newbury Park, CA: Sage.

Yin, R. K. (1994a). Discovering the future of case study method in evaluation research. *Evaluation Practice, 15*(3), 283–290. doi: 10.1016/0886-1633(94)90023-X

Yin, R. K. (1994b). Evaluation: A singular craft. In C. S. Reichardt & S. F. Rallis (Eds.), *The qualitative-quantitative debate: New perspectives, Vol. 61* (pp. 71–84). San Francisco, CA: Jossey-Bass.

Yin, R. K. (1997). Case study evaluations: A decade of progress? *New Directions for Evaluation, 1997*(76), 69–78. doi: 10.1002/ev.1088

SITUATING MEXICAN MOTHERS' DIALOGUES IN THE PROXIMITIES OF CONTEXTS OF MATHEMATICAL PRACTICE

Higinio Domínguez
Department of Curriculum and Instruction
Texas State University, College of Education

Las mujeres pobres tienen pocas ocasiones de estar con otras conversando y haciendo cosas importantes
[Poor women have few opportunities to be with others conversing and doing important things]
—Serrano, 2008, p. 55

INTRODUCTION

This chapter explores the dialogues of Mexican mothers with themselves, with students, and with a teacher on the topic of problem solving. The problem that motivated this report—students' low performance in school-based problem solving, as reported by teachers—served to reveal another

Latinos/as and Mathematics Education, pages 89–123
Copyright © 2011 by Information Age Publishing
All rights of reproduction in any form reserved.

problem: teachers' resistance to appropriating mothers' voices and ideas about problem solving in teachers' mathematics education agenda. According to situated-learning theorists, problem-solving performance differs across problem-solving contexts—school-based versus real-life contexts, in this case (Lave & Wegner, 1991; Young, 1993). This differential and disconnect inspired the focus of this chapter: *la aproximación de diálogos*, or the bringing together of different dialogues.

The chapter approaches dialogues about problem solving by following ethnomethodology's central tenet: People's methods for solving problems create a social order (Garfinkel & Rawls, 2002, 2006) that could be described as "this is how we do things here." Although this tenet explains why people do things the way they do, it does not suggest how to disconnect the dialogues from how people do things the way they do and begin to make people reflect on how they do problem solving, which is a way of relearning problem solving and relearning about one's problem-solving identity. An ad hoc theory for this purpose is Bakhtin's (1981) notion of dialogue. Dialogue is more revealing and intense not when it is located within well-defined contexts—where it tends to become unchallenged and authoritative—but rather when it is situated in the proximities of contexts that include, as in the case of this study, mathematical practices (e.g., school-based mathematics and everyday mathematics, children's mathematics and mothers' mathematics, teachers' mathematics and mothers' mathematics). These proximities are *interspaces* that create and are created by dialogue. The main argument presented in this chapter is that people's *ethnomethodologies*—their dispositions to getting things done in certain ways—can undergo transformations when the dialogue of others is transformed and appropriated in these proximities of practice.

In this study, the dialogue of a group of seven mothersis the focus of an analysis based on Bakhtin's (1981) theory of dialogue, as well as on the metaphor of voice from Belenky, Clinchy, Goldberger, and Tarule's (1986) framework for women's ways of knowing. The dialogue of mothers is crucial for understanding issues of power and identity for various reasons: (1) mothers' dialogue is hardly heard in well-defined contexts such as schooling; (2) mothers have inhabited most of these contexts (e.g., home and school); and (3) mothers have an interest in children's mathematics education that is proximal to that of the teachers.

RESEARCH QUESTION

The study focuses on investigating the following question: When mothers' dialogues about problem solving are positioned in proximity among themselves, with students, and with teachers, to what extent are their dialogues appropriated by other mothers, by students, and by teachers?

CONCEPTUAL FRAMEWORK

The first main idea in this conceptual framework is that mothers, students, and teachers are accustomed to engaging in problem solving in certain ways; these ways are their ethnomethods. The problem, however, is not so much getting used to one's own methods for solving problems (Garfinkel & Rawls, 2002, 2006), but more a matter of these ethnomethods—and the practices that include them—becoming so well established as cultural practices (Cobb, 2007) that participants often do not look elsewhere to improve their practice. Thus, the practices remain disconnected. It is a problem because student learning of problem solving does not stop at the school doors but it extends into their everyday lives. Therefore, students' school-based problem solving could benefit from an understanding of how students solve problems, for instance, with mothers in their everyday lives. Similarly, teachers could benefit by learning about how mothers and students solve problems in their own lives. These were the interspaces under investigation in this study.

The second main idea in this conceptual framework is that to understand how these disconnected ways of engaging in problem solving become established cultural practices (Cobb, 2007), one must listen to participants' voices in dialogue to appreciate their ways of doing things. The metaphor of voice (Belenky et al., 1986) to investigate participants' dialogues about mathematical problem solving is useful for this purpose. Mothers' voices about how they relate to mathematical problem solving, as presented in Table 5.1, ranged from an absence of a voice to a rich collaboration in bringing multiple voices to construct mathematical understanding.

This continuum of voices was used in the study to illustrate a fundamental phenomenon: Appropriating dialogue is a matter of degree, and these proximities are expected to illuminate how this degree of appropriation occurs. Bakhtin (1981) argued in relation to dialogue that

> [l]anguage lies on the borderline between oneself and the other. The word in language is half someone else's. It becomes "one's own" only when the speaker populates it with his own intention, his own accent, when he appropriates the word, adapting it to his own semantic and expressive intention. . . . It exists in other people's mouths, in other people's contexts, serving other people's intentions: it is from there that one must take the word and make it one's own . . . many words stubbornly resist, others remain alien, sound foreign in the mouths of the one who appropriated them and who now speaks them: they cannot be assimilated into his context and fall out of it. . . . Expropriating it [the word], forcing it to submit to one's own intentions and accents, is a difficult and complicated process. (pp. 293–294)

TABLE 5.1   Mothers' Voices About Problem Solving

Knowledge	Voice	Others	Learning
Silence	No voice	Excluded	"I cannot learn math; it is not for me. Feeling 'dumb' or 'not good at math', therefore withdrawing from participation ('why bother?' kind of attitude); marginalized learner. An extreme in denial of self.
Received knowledge	Voice of authority	Included as authority	"I can learn math, but only if it 'comes' from some recognized external authority (e.g., textbooks, teachers); then I can follow rules."
Subjective knowledge	Private voice	Comes from within, emerging	"I can learn math by listening to my private voice, but still that voice tells me that there is always a right or wrong answer in math."
Separate knowledge	Separate voice	Not affecting own ways of knowing	"I can learn math independently of how others learn math."
Constructed knowledge	Multiple voices	Helping me construct my own knowledge	"I can learn math by reasoning about how mathematical knowledge is constructed, by understanding my own methods and locate them within a constellation of other approaches"

In this study, participants demonstrated a range of dialogue appropriation. The analysis of dialogues in proximity supports the difficult process of dialogue appropriation identified by Bakhtin (1981).

PARTICIPANTS: WHO ARE THESE MOTHERS, STUDENTS, AND TEACHER?

Bianca, Constanza, Mirna, Judith, Bety, Daría, and Maura are seven Mexican mothers who participated in these problem-solving conversations. Mirna did not join in these conversations until the fourth session because she was recovering from surgery. All of these women emigrated from Mexico, where they had completed various levels of mathematics education. Bianca and Mirna finished elementary school, whereas Maura finished middle school. Bety finished high school and was accepted to the Universidad Nacional Autónoma de México, where she completed one semester. Unfortunately, family-imposed responsibilities truncated her university experience. In a dialogue among themselves at the beginning of the project, Bety recalled her family's unfavorable views toward her education: "...y más que *en ese tiempo se decía, ¡ay que la escuela no es para las mujeres!"* ["... and what's more, back in the day, the prevalent belief was, 'Oh no, school is not for women!'"] Judith, who finished elementary school, echoed Bety's recollection: *"Sí porque también a mis hermanos les dieron, hasta la secundaria."* ["Yes, because my brothers were sent even to middle school."] Expanding on her remembrances, she said,

> *Yo tenía muchas ganas de ir a la secundaria, pero como una prima mía salió embarazada en la secundaria, desde entonces empezó, no, que, que, las mujeres no son para la escuela, nomás los hombres. Que luego las muchachitas se van a la escuela, luego, luego salen con su panza.*

> [I had great desire to go to middle school, but my cousin got pregnant in middle school, and since then, it was like, no, no, women are not for school, only men. Then those little girls, as soon as they go to school, they end up pregnant.]

Constanza finished high school and went on to become a registered nurse. Similarly, Daría finished high school and worked first as a nurse's aid, and then completed on-the-job training until she became a registered nurse. She recounted, with an emotionally charged voice, her experience trying to obtain an education:

> *Eso es bien triste, a mí eso me pasó, hubo quien me regalara mi carrera de medicina, y mi mamá y mi papá no me dejaron seguir. (golpea la mesa) Yo me escondí como seis años, y yo no quería ni salir de la casa de puro coraje y sentimiento. Y nadie lo supo más que yo. (ríe) Fue algo horrible.*

> [That's so sad, this happened to me, there was someone who offered to pay for my education, but my dad and my mom didn't allow me to continue. (taps on table) I hid like for six years, and I didn't want to even get out of the house because I was extremely angry and sad. And no one but me knew what that meant. (laughs) It was horrible.]

At the time this study was conducted, these mothers' children, all born in the United States, were in grade five in an urban school in Chicago, with 98% of the student population identified as Latino, 98.5% as low-income students, and 52.8% English language learners (Chicago Public Schools, n.d.). The teacher who participated in these conversations with mothers, Mr. T, had 11 years of teaching experience with similar student populations. He was using *Investigations in Number, Data, and Space* (Technical Education Research Centers, 1995–1998) as the base curriculum for teaching mathematics. Mr. T used Spanish in his mathematics teaching, a practice that was supported by the school's endorsement of bilingual education.

METHODS

Setting

The researchers organized six open-dialogue sessions with the seven mothers, one session per week. Concurrent with these dialogue sessions, the mothers' children attended an after-school mathematics program designed and implemented by the Center for the Mathematics Education of Latinos/as (CEMELA). The program, with approximately 20 participant students and five undergraduate facilitators, was designed to offer students an informal space to learn and often relearn important mathematics concepts through challenging mathematical activities, tasks, and games. Prior to these conversation sessions, mothers had been participating in their children's education in rather peripheral ways that did not have an impact on the after-school program. For example, they had been learning how to use a computer and how to type on a computer keyboard.

Data Collection

When data collection on the problem-solving conversations began, participant students were in the third year in the after-school program and the researcher was in his second year in a postdoctoral research position with CEMELA. Following a discussion between the researcher and the principal investigator about redesigning mothers' participation in the after-school program to reflect the view of parents as intellectual resources (Civil & Bernier, 2006), the researcher planned the dialogue sessions. The dialogue sessions were planned so that each of the three interspaces was dedicated to mothers' dialogues among themselves, with students, and with teachers, with minimal researcher intervention. The mothers were only prompted to start dialogue in each interspace and were guided from one interspace to the next by the researcher.

The first interspace consisted of three sessions (approximately 5 hours total). In these sessions I, in my role as a researcher, asked the mothers to identify problems in their everyday lives and to talk among themselves about how they solved these problems, including what it took to solve a problem, who was involved, and whose problem was being solved. Mothers identified various problems including school-related problems (e.g., children carrying backpacks too heavy for them), community-related problems (e.g., neighbors who did not remove snow from sidewalks), learning experience problems (e.g., learning English), household-related problems (e.g., helping husbands replace a floor), and work-related problems (e.g., inventorying produce at work or helping husbands process work orders). As part of these conversations, we moved on to discussing similarities and differences between everyday problems and school-based problems. These sessions generated the data used to answer the first part of the research question: When mothers' dialogues are positioned among themselves, to what extent are those dialogues appropriated by other mothers?

Next, the mothers and I invited some students from the after-school program as participants in two of the mother–student problem-solving sessions (approximately 3 hours total). The objective of these sessions was to create an interspace in which mothers' dialogue and students' dialogue about problem solving could come together. Concurrent with these mother–student sessions, the researcher asked mothers to spend time at home working with their children on coauthoring problems that reflected experiences that matter to the family and to the student. The mothers brought these problems to our sessions and used the problems in instructional interactions with the students we invited from the after-school program. These problem-solving sessions between mothers and students generated the data used to answer the second part of the research question: When mothers' dialogue is positioned in proximity with students' dialogue, to what extent is that dialogue appropriated by students?

After reflecting among themselves and doing problem writing and problem solving with after-school students, mothers expressed the desire to position their dialogue in a new proximity. This time, they requested a meeting with the two teachers of the after-school students. The invitation was extended to the two teachers, and one was able to attend this meeting. Not being familiar with this interspace, mothers were unsure about how to best approach the teacher. They asked for the researcher's advice. Aware of the delicate nature of this interspace, I suggested to simply share with the teacher what they had learned in the previous interspaces among themselves and with the students. In this seminal meeting (approximately 1.5 hours), mothers invited the teacher to hear their voices to expand their collective reasoning and to learn together about the importance of (1) recontextualizing problems to reflect what really matters to students, (2) retooling problem solvers with neglected tools such as bilingualism and everyday experiences (Domínguez, 2008), and (3) reimagining school-based problem solving to bring about students' invented strategies (Carpenter, Franke, Jacobs, Fennema, & Empson, 1998), sense making, collaboration, and responsibility for demonstrating and sharing understanding. This session generated the data used to answer the third part of the research question: When mothers' dialogue is positioned in proximity with a teacher, to what extent is that dialogue appropriated by the teacher?

FINDINGS

The findings are organized in three sections. The first section includes the mothers' dialogues among themselves are presented. The second section includes the dialogues between the mothers and a group of CEMELA after-school students as they worked on solving mathematics problems. The third and final section includes mothers' dialogues in proximity with the voice of a teacher. Together, these three sections provide a complex picture of what mothers know and believe about problem solving, and how this knowledge mediates their relationships among themselves, with their children, with their families, and with the teacher of their children. The analysis of dialogues in proximity can help us understand how participants (mothers, students, and the teacher) practice problem solving and to what extent and under what conditions these dialogues are a catalyst for appropriating other ways of doing problem solving.

Mothers' Dialogues Among Themselves

Two of the voices in the conversations that mothers had among themselves were particularly salient: silence and constructed knowledge (see Table 5.2). In the next sections, examples of how these voices emerged as mothers intimated about their knowledge about problem solving are provided.

Silence, or "I don't know math, math is not for me ..."
When talking among themselves about situations involving mathematics, mothers' dialogues were imprinted with a sense of voicelessness or *silence.* This silence appeared in relation to major events in their lives that ranged from their own childhood experiences learning mathematics to their present lives and contact with mathematics in situations such as their own work, their husbands' jobs, and their children's mathematics.

Of the 50 occurrences of silence (see Table 5.2), nine were related to their perception of their own experience learning mathematics as children, including lack of parental support or teacher support. For example, when

TABLE 5.2   Mothers' Dialogue with Themselves

Voice	Frequency
Silence	50
Received knowledge	11
Subjective knowledge	8
Constructed knowledge	47

mothers brought to the dialogue sessions the problems they created with children at home, they decided to work on Bianca's problem about sharing a $300 rent among seven people. Prior to the interaction represented in Excerpt 5.1, Bety had explained to the group how she had successfully used division to solve the problem. Their dialogue acquires a sense of silence (lines 1, 2, and 4).

Excerpt 5.1   Silence and School Mathematics Experiences

1   **Daría (a Constanza):** "*La verdad, no sé dividir.*"
    ["Honestly, I don't know how to divide."]

2   **Judith:** "*Yo tampoco sé dividir pero voy a tratar de hacerlo.*"
    ["I don't either, but I will try."]

3   **Bianca:** "*Vamos a recordarlo entonces, OK, vamos a recordarlo.*"
    ["Let's remember then, OK, let's try to remember it."]

4   **Daría:** "*Yo nunca fui buena para dividir, yo no, me declaro...*"
    ["I was never good at dividing, me? No, I declare my-self..."]

Within this consensus of silence, there was an initiative to start appropriating Bety's division method when Judith started a new line of dialogue, as she declared that she will try division (line 2). This line was picked up by Bianca, who encouraged the entire group to try to remember the division method (line 3). In other words, they were using dialogue to constitute an interspace from which they could challenge their learned silence and, in turn, transform their own dialogue. This attempt at appropriating Bety's method illustrates appropriating dialogue, or Bety's "word," in Bakhtin's (1981) terms, and making it their own.

Mothers also expressed a concern about how they perceived their children were learning mathematics in less than optimal ways (eight such instances). Fear that in time the children themselves may learn to suppress their voices characterized the dialogue in Excerpt 5.2.

Excerpt 5.2   Silence and School Teachers

1   **Judith:** "*Yo creo que también por eso los niños se sienten así, porque si el maestro no les ayuda, porque ellos apenas están aprendiendo los problemas de matemáticas, y el maestro les diga, lo tienes que hacer bien, entonces como que no les está dando confianza.*"
    ["I believe that's also why kids feel that way, because if the teacher doesn't help them, because they are barely learning the math problems, and to have the teacher telling them you have to do it right, it's like the teacher is not trusting them."]

2   **Bety:** "*Y hay muchos niños que prefieren quedarse con la duda.*"
      ["And many kids prefer to keep their doubts to them-
      selves."]
3   **Daría:** "*No preguntan.*"
      ["They don't ask."]
4   **Bety:** "*No, porque se molesta el maestro, porque, dice 'ya expliqué, ya
      ese es tu problema, no el mío,' (mira a la cámara) porque sí hay
      maestros así.*"
      ["No because the teacher gets upset, because the teacher
      says, 'I already explained, now that's your problem, not
      mine,' (looks at camera) some teachers are like that."]
5   **Maura:** "*Si porque si a mi hijo tú le gritas, o regañas o así, no te pre-
      gunta, puesto que yo lo he hecho. Le digo, '¡dime!' y si le grito más
      menos, me lo va a decir.*"
      ["Yes because if you raise your voice to my son, or rep-
      rimand him, he won't ask you, because I've done that. I
      go, 'Tell me!' and if the more I scream at him, the less he
      would respond."]
6   **Constanza:** "*Se queda callado.*"
      ["He stays quiet."]

This interaction exemplifies Bakhtin's (1981) idea that people appropriate dialogue "when the speaker populates it with his [her] own intention,
his [her] own accent" (p. 293). Note how mothers added details (see Excerpt 5.2, lines 3 and 6) to the argument about students developing a sense
of silence and also provided their own examples of lived experiences (see
line 5) to support the argument. This appropriation of dialogue creates a
robust argument that, in the end, belongs to all of the mothers.

The most frequent expression of voicelessness, with 21 instances, occurred as mothers expressed their inability to do their own mathematical
work. These comments emerged spontaneously as mothers were invited to
talk about past or present jobs (see Excerpt 5.3).

Excerpt 5.3   Silence and Mothers' Mathematics

1   **Judith:** "*Pues también por ejemplo donde yo trabajo se hace un inventario
      y hay que contar hileras de naranjas o cebollas o lo que sea, pero
      a mi a veces se me hace un poco trabajoso porque a veces la hilera
      trae de 7 y tengo que contar de 7 en 7 hasta (mira hacia arriba,
      pensando) 5 ó 6...*"
      ["Well, for example, where I work, an inventory is made
      and rows of oranges or onions or whatever have to be
      counted, but sometimes this is kind of hard for me because

each row sometimes comes with seven and I have to skip
count by seven until (looks up, thinking) five or six..."]

2 **Daría:** "*¿Y por qué no lo multiplicas?*"
   ["And how come you don't multiply?"]

3 **Judith:** "*Sí por eso, o sea, como, soy un poco mala para las matemáticas,
pues tengo que 1, 2, 3, 4, son 7, y 7 son, 14 y después ya irle
este...*"
   ["Yes, exactly, I mean, since I am a little bad for mathematics, I have to one, two, three, four, it's seven, and seven, it's
fourteen, and then I just keep, I mean..."]

Judith, the only one who worked at a job outside her home at the time
of the data collection, when questioned about not using multiplication to
speed up her repeated addition of sevens (see Excerpt 5.3, line 2), blamed
herself for this inability, calling herself "bad for math" (line 3). In fact, in
an earlier conversation, Judith also blamed herself for not memorizing the
multiplication tables:

1 **Judith:** "*Pero sabe qué, yo era mala para eso, que yo no me las aprendí
(tablas de multiplicación).*"
   ["But you know what? I was bad for that, I did not learn
them (multiplication tables)."]

But the most common case of this voiceless position emerged in relation
to their inability to execute mathematical procedures, specifically the standard division algorithm. This perceived need for dividing emerged in connection to the problem that Bianca and her child created at home about
sharing $300 among seven people (see Excerpt 5.4).

Excerpt 5.4 Silence and Mathematical Procedures

1 **Bety:** "*¿Todavía está multiplicando, Constanza?*"
   ["Are you still multiplying, Constanza?"]

2 **Constanza:** "*Yeah, pero no me sale.*"
   ["Yeah, but I don't get it."]

3 **Bety:** "*Es dividir.*"
   ["It's divide."]

4 **Constanza:** "*Es dividir, pero a mí se me hace más difícil dividir que multiplicar.*"
   ["It's divide, but for me dividing is harder than multiplying."]

5 **Judith:** "*Yo también no sé dividir.*"
   ["I don't know how to divide either."]

In this interaction, Bety's suggestion to Constanza to divide instead of multiply (lines 1 and 3) was acknowledged by Constanza (line 4), but it also raised her own and Judith's awareness of their inability to execute division (lines 4 and 5). In another conversation in which they were contextualizing the problem 36 ÷ 3 (presented by the researcher), Daría's voicelessness resurfaced:

1   **Bety:** *"Puede ser 3 dólares, $3 entre 36 personas."*
           ["It could be three dollars, three dollars among thirty-six people."]

2   **Daría:** *"3 entre 36, 3, yo soy tan tonta que voy, (cuenta con los dedos) 3, 6, 9, 12, como los niños."*
           ["Three among thirty-six, three, I am so dumb that I am going like (finger counts) three, six, nine, twelve, like the little kids."]

Although they changed the relationship between 36 and 3 (from 36 ÷ 3 to 3 ÷ 36), the researcher did not intervene so as to capture the process of recontextualization rather than the correct interpretation of this relationship. Furthermore, although Bety proposed this changed relationship (line 1), Daría's strategy of skip counting by three (line 2) suggests that they may be misspeaking about the original relationship of 36 divided by 3; the strategy of skip counting seemed aligned with an interpretation of 36 divided by 3 as a measurement division, not with 3 divided by 36. Also, Bety did not question Daría's strategy as inconsistent with how she spoke about 36 divided by 3. More important for this analysis is that, although Daría's strategy made sense, she evaluated her own mathematical ability rather negatively based on this strategy.

Finally, a sense of silence was expressed in relation to family interactions in which the mothers drastically reduced their voices and transferred them to family members, usually their husbands. For example, Daría and Judith described interactions with their husbands:

1   **Daría:** *"Yo lo que me fijo es con mi esposo cuando le ayudo a veces, no mucho porque no soy tan buena para las matemáticas, pero a veces le ponen cierta cantidad de cosas y le dicen vas a llevar cierta cajas. Entonces dice, caben tantas en cada caja, échame tantas para acá. O sea que de volada las saca en la mente, entonces, échame tantas para acá, yo ya nomás se las arrimo y él las empaqueta."*
           ["What I have noticed is that sometimes when I help my husband, not too often, because I am not that good at math, but he sometimes has a number of things to do and

is asked to carry a certain amount of boxes. So then he says, 'A box can hold this many, give that many over here.' I mean, in no time he figures that out in his mind, so then he goes, 'Give me that many,' and I just bring them near him and he packages them."]

2   **Judith:** "*Mi esposo sí sabe mucho de matemáticas. Porque como este, uh, en la casa que tenemos, estaba un poco destruido el primer piso. El puso el piso y luego le puso la madera que va en las (apunta a las paredes) paredes, y todo yo veo que medía, mide con una escuadra que tiene, y cuántos milímetros y cuántos centímetros, y pulgadas (ceño) y no sé qué tanto (niega con la cabeza), pero pues yo nomás miro.*" ["My husband does know a lot about mathematics. Because like I mean, uh, in the home we have, the first floor was a little damaged. He installed the floor and then he installed the wood that goes along the (points to the walls) walls, and in all that I saw that he was measuring, he measures with an angle ruler, like how many millimeters and how many centimeters, and inches (frowns) and I have no clue (shakes head), but oh well, I just look."]

In this exchange, the two mothers described themselves as spectators of their husbands' mathematical abilities (lines 1 and 2), with no indication that they were invited to "populate" the husbands' words with their own understandings.

Constructed knowledge, or "I can learn math by constructing knowledge with others"

Another frequent voice in the mothers' conversations among themselves was that of *constructed knowledge*, that is, the disposition to learn mathematics by understanding their own methods and locate them within a constellation of other approaches. Mothers adopted this voice in various situations. For example, in a session in which the researcher brought the problem about finding the average for 15, 20, and 10 that Nasir, Hand, and Taylor (2008) used with students who were basketball players, they collectively struggled to remember the concept of average (see Excerpt 5.5).

Excerpt 5.5   Constructed Knowledge and School Mathematics

1   **Daría:** "*Ni sabemos que es promedio.*" (*ríe*).
     ["We don't even know what average is." (laughs)]

2   **Bety:** "*No, sí, sí, yo sabía, yo sabía hacer eso... o sea que, es lo máximo, ¿no?*"
     ["No, yes, yes, I used to know, I used to know how to do that... I mean, it's the maximum, no?"]

3   **Daría:** "*¿Lo más alto?*"
        ["The highest?"]

4   **Bety:** "*Lo más alto.*" (*repite con Daría*)
        ["The highest." (echoes Daría)]

5   **HD:** "*La fórmula para hallar el promedio es suma uno, en este caso
        15+20+10* (Bety: "*Uh-huh.*") *y lo divide entre 3* (Bety: "*Entre
        3.*") *porque son 3 juegos.*"
        ["The formula to find the average is, one adds, in this case,
        fifteen plus twenty plus ten (Bety: "Uh-huh.") and divide
        that by three (Bety: "By 3.") because there are 3 games."]

6   **Bety:** "*Uh-huh, entonces serían 15.*"
        ["Uh-huh, so it would be fifteen."]

7   **Bianca:** (*reflexiona*) "*15 es el promedio.*"
        [(reflectively) "Fifteen is the average."]

8   **Daría:** (*después de reflexionar*) "*El promedio es todas... partes... igua-
        les (pone ambas manos a la misma altura). Todas las partes
        iguales.*"
        [(after reflecting) "The average is all the... parts... made
        the same (puts both hands at same height). All the parts
        equal."]

9   **Bianca:** "*Como dividirlo entre qué, entre juego, entre juego, no...*"
        ["Like dividing it by what, by games, by games, no..."]

10   **Judith:** "*O sea que tenemos que dividirlo entre 3 (muestra 3 dedos) para
        que todos salgan igual.*"
        ["So we have to divide it by three (shows three fingers), so
        all (scores) came out the same."]

11   **Bety:** "*Para que queden iguales.*" (*expresa acuerdo con Judith*)
        ["So all (scores) become the same." (agrees with Judith)]

In this interaction, Daría characterized all members of the group as collectively lacking knowledge of the concept of average (line 1). Bety immediately excluded herself from this collective characterization (line 2), thus reframing the dialogue from "we don't know" to "some of us do know." This
reframed dialogue offered members of the group the opportunity to realign
with reconstructing the concept of average. This new realignment and ensuing dialogue was powerful enough to cause the researcher, in his role as
a participant observer, to contribute a working formula, not the concept,
of average (line 5). More importantly, this transformed dialogue seemed to
benefit Daría, who was able to construct (or perhaps reconstruct) her own
definition of the concept of average as making all parts equal (line 8). This
reconstruction of an important concept in mathematics was appropriated
first by Judith (line 10) and then by Bety (line 11). When the researcher
asked them to think about the benefit of doing problem solving collabora-

tively, their voices again aligned with a constructed knowledge perspective as captured in Excerpt 5.6.

Excerpt 5.6   Constructed Knowledge and Collaborative Problem Solving

1   **Daría:** "*Pues que aprendemos unas de otras, pues para mí eso.*"
         ["Well, that we learn from one another, well, for me that's it."]

2 **Constanza:** "*Que cada quien tiene una idea diferente.*"
         ["That we each have a different idea."]

3   **Bety:** "*Y llegamos a lo mismo, el mismo resultado.*"
         ["And we reach the same, the same result."]

4   **Maura:** "*Y que por si no le entiendo, ya me sacan de la duda.*" (*ríe*).
         ["And in case I don't understand, all of you can get me out the doubting moment." (laughs)]

5   **Daría:** "*Pues sí, porque,*" (*mira a las demás*) "*algunas sabemos más que otras.*"
         ["Well yes, because," (looks at them) "some of us know more than others."]

This episode resonates with Bakhtin's (1981) idea of a person catching up the word of another and making it their own. The cycle started and ended with Daría (lines 1 and 5) and in between, mothers extended a line one at a time (lines 2, 3, and 4), creating a common argument that belonged to all of them. Each mother populated this growing argument with her own meanings.

Hearing other mothers' ideas for creating interesting mathematical problems made some mothers go back to the drawing board and create more problems with their children, an opportunity for them to co-construct knowledge (see Excerpt 5.7).

Excerpt 5.7   Co-constructing Knowledge

1   **Judith:** "*Maestro ¿yo puedo cambiar el mío, o tiene que ser el mismo?*"
         ["Teacher, can I change mine, or does it have to be this one?"]

2   **HD:** "*No, lo puede cambiar.*"
         ["No, you can change it."]

3   **Judith:** "*Porque estoy pensando en algo.*" (*mira a las demás*)
         ["Because I'm thinking about something." (looks at the other moms)]

In the session following this, Judith brought a new problem about how many chairs can be arranged around a table with given dimensions. This showed how mothers extended this interspace into their homes by taking some ideas back home and co-constructing new problems with their children.

Finally, mothers co-constructed knowledge by recontextualizing each other's problems to make sense of each other's reasoning. For example, Daría and her daughter created a problem about buying 22 cakes at $25 each, cutting each cake into 6 slices, and then selling each slice at $3.00 (see Excerpt 5.8).

Excerpt 5.8 *Co-constructing Problem Contexts*

1   **Bianca:** "*$3, y sale a 6 × 3, 18, y luego 18 por veinti-...*"
    ["$3, and it comes to 6 × 3, 18, and then 18 times twent-..."]

2   **Bety:** "*Pero ahí salió nomás, si el pastel les costó 25 dólares...*"
    ["But right there it came out only, if the cake cost 25 dollars..."]

3   **Judith:** "*Les va a salir más barato, ¿no?*"
    ["It's going to come out as cheaper, no?" (means the earnings are less than the costs)]

4   **Bety:** "*Y ahí están perdiendo.*"
    ["And there you are losing."]

5   **Judith:** "*Sí.*"
    ["Yes"]

6   **HD:** "*No van a hacer negocio.*"
    ["You're not going to stay in business."]

7   **Judith:** "*¡No!*" (Todas ríen) "*Porque si el pastel les costó $25...*"
    ["No." (they all laugh) "Because if the cake cost twenty-five dollars..."]

8   **Bety:** "*Y van a salir, y lo van a vender y van a sacar $18.*"
    ["And you'll get, and they're going to sell it and you'll get eighteen dollars."]

9   **HD:** "*Van a sacar 18 si lo venden en rebanadas.*"
    ["You'll get eighteen if you sell it by the slice."]

10 **Bety:** "*Rebanadas.*"
    ["By the slice."]

11 **Judith:** "*En 6, en 6.*" (*ademanes para rebanadas*)
    ["In six, in six." (hand gestures slices)]

12 **Bety:** "*Ahí la pregunta es cuánto perdieron.*" (*ríe*)
    ["So there the question is how much they lost." (laughs)]

13 **Daría:** "*Cuánto perdimos.*"
    ["How much we lost."]

14 **Bianca:** "*Está interesante nomás es de acomodarlo, acomodarlo bien.*"
    ["It's interesting, it's just a matter of rearranging it, arranging it well."]

Using sense of humor as denoted by their friendly laughs (lines 7 and 12), mothers helped Daría realized that her problem required reframing. One of them, Bianca, broaches the interaction in a manner that credits Daría for an interesting situation that only required some arranging of the parameters (line 14). This move, along with the remarks and sense of humor, maintained Daría in close proximity with the argument. Note how Daría stayed in the argument by echoing the comments that the others offered (line 13).

Summary 1: To what extent did mothers appropriate each other's dialogue?

Mothers' dialogue with themselves was characterized primarily by two kinds of voices: silence and constructed knowledge. By sharing dialogue, mothers created an interspace and hence an opportunity for themselves to transform this dialogue. This transformation, however, did not occur automatically but instead was facilitated by powerful examples given by mothers. For example, in the interactions in which they expressed silence, mothers' dialogue converged toward trying to remember division after listening to Bianca's explanation of how she used division. Other times, mothers appropriated dialogue instead of transforming it by contributing their own examples and evidence from lived experiences, such as when they discussed the concern that their children might develop a sense of voicelessness.

Mothers also used their dialogic interspace to (re)construct knowledge together. For example, it was through reframing dialogue that they were able to realign themselves as being able to reconstruct and reappropriate the concept of average. Similarly, as they recontextualized each other's problems, they created a common space in which all could participate. The occasions on which their dialogue remained unaltered (neither transformed nor appropriated) occurred when they were told by others what to do, as when they were performing lengthy additions or multiplications instead of division. This indicates that transformative dialogue requires proximity, that is, dialogue must be structured in such a way as to allow participants to see something in the others' dialogue that resonates with what they are doing and how they are doing it.

Mothers' Dialogues with Students

All mothers worked with their children at home constructing mathematics problems around everyday situations in which students participated. Bianca and Daría noticed how their children expressed interest in constructing and solving problems at home. For example, Bianca told us:

Yo ví que a Cornelio le interesó más esto (problema sobre compartir entre siete personas la renta de un puesto) que el del juego (otro problema)...y hasta le dibujó, ¿eh? Y hasta lo coloreó (muestra el dibujo que Cornelio hizo para ilustrar la situación representada en el problema). En éste, como que le gustó más dibujar y colorear.

[I noticed that Cornelio got more interested in this one (problem about sharing a booth's rent among seven people) than the one about the game (another problem)...and he even drew it, huh? And he even colored it (shows Cornelio's drawing illustrating the problem's situation). In this one, it was like he enjoyed more drawing and coloring.]

Daría also shared her experience with her daughter:

Me puso un ejemplo y me ponía otro, má vamos haciendo éste, y rápido, (chasquea los dedos) pero rápido así ponía uno y ponía otro, y no mami es así, pero te sale más fácil así, me quedé corta con mi niña porque yo no me había puesto a aprend-, a así hacer algo con ella, nomás 'M'hija la tarea, que les falta para hacer su tarea,' sí, pero que me sentara con ella, no, hasta anoche y nos quedamos casi hasta las 2 de la mañana, las dos ahí, y yo me sorprendí mucho de mi niña. Rápido se inventan y rápido sacan, pero si, me dio gusto.

[She would give me example after example, "Ma, let's do this one, and fast," (snaps fingers) but really fast. She would put one and then another one, and "No mommy, it's like this, you can do it easier like this." I was astonished by my girl because I had not learned with her, like that, doing something with her, I was just, "My daughter, your homework, what else do you need to do your homework." Yeah, but sitting with her, no, until last night and we stayed until almost two in the morning, the two of us there, and I was surprised a lot by my girl. They invent things so fast, and they get results fast, but yeah, I was pleased.]

To follow up on what mothers had noticed of their children, the researcher suggested bringing Bianca's and Daría's children from the CEME-LA after-school program to work with all the mothers on problem solving. The researcher sought to have these children participate with mothers because they had created interesting problems at home. Along with these students, we invited a student who had demonstrated consistent disengaged in mathematics. The objective was to offer mothers not just an opportunity to showcase their own children's mathematical ability, but also to learn something about how to best support students who struggled with learning mathematics.

The analysis of mothers dialoguing with these three students revealed two contrasting patterns of mothers' voices (see Table 5.3). These patterns must be interpreted cautiously given that two students were these mothers' children. In addition, interactions with only three of the 18 students in the CEMELA program did not allow for a description of these patterns

TABLE 5.3   Mothers' Voices with Students

Voice	Male students	Female students
Silence	1	5
Received knowledge	2	27
Subjective knowledge	4	2
Constructed knowledge	16	5

beyond emerging, and generalization would require interactions with all 18 students. However, what was found was that mothers used the dialogues with the two male students to create an interspace filled with invitations for students to invent their own solution strategies and therefore demonstrate mathematical understanding in ways that mothers were not expecting. In contrast, mothers' dialogues with the female student forged an interspace characterized by invitations to reproduce certain solution methods, showing concern for the student to demonstrate mathematical understanding in rather expected ways.

For example, the interaction between mothers and a male student solving the problem about sharing $300 among seven people proceeded as presented in Excerpt 5.9.

Excerpt 5.9   Mother and Male Student

1   **Bianca:** *"Si quieres, como quieras. Dividiendo, o multiplicando, como tú creas. ¿Cómo sacarías una cuentita así? Como tú creas, ¿cómo crees que, que sería?"*
["If you want, whichever way you want. Dividing, or multiplying, the way you believe. How would you do your calculations? The way you think, how do you think that, that it would be?"]

2   **Daría:** *"Cuánto pagaría cada persona."*
["How much would each person pay?"]

3   **Bianca:** *"Cada persona."*
["Each person."]
. . .

4   **Bianca:** *"O como se te haga más fácil a ti. Como se te haría otra idea; pero saca tus cuentas. Sacando tú tus cuentas."*
["Or the way you think it's easier for you. If you can think of another idea; but you get your calculations. By doing your calculations."]

First, Bianca encouraged the student to solve the problem in his own way (line 1). Daría only restated the problem's question, challenging the student to think for himself (line 2), while Bianca continued to encourage student to come up with his own way of solving the problem (line 3).

Later in this interaction (see Excerpt 5.10), mothers saw the student struggling to understand the problem context. Expertly, one mother decided to recontextualize the problem in multiple ways, a practice deemed effective in mathematics education research (Roth, 1995).

Excerpt 5.10   Mothers' Voices with Male Student: Recontextualizing Problem

1   **Bianca:** *"O sea, si ya pues (palmea al estudiante en el hombro, él la mira con atención), si no habláramos ya de las siete, si tú fueras y era tu negocio, si tuvieras, amigos, que te ayuden, se turnan los días, un día cada quien. Pero vendes todo, pero además tendrías que sacar para tu renta. Vas a tener que sacar de ellos, para pagar los (busca la cantidad en la hoja) los 280 dólares por semana, o sea van a pagar 280 dólares entre las siete personas, puede ser tú y tus amigos."*
["I mean, if instead (pats student on shoulder, he looks at her attentively), if we were not talking about those seven, if it was you and it was your business, if you had friends who could help you, you take turns on those days, one day for each one. But you sell everything, but you also would have to get enough for your rent. You will have to get some from them, to pay for the (looks up for amount on paper) the two hundred eighty dollars per week, in other words, you all are going to pay two hundred eighty among the seven people, it could be you and your friends."]
. . .

2   **Bianca:** *"Bueno, haz de cuenta que no son billetes, que voy a repartir tortillas pa' la comida, y tengo 3 hijos, y nada más tengo tres tortillas. ¿Cuánto le doy a cada uno?"*
["Alright, pretend that it's not about dollars, let's say that I am going to distribute tortillas for the lunch, and I have three children, and I only have three tortillas. How many do I give to each?"]

3   **Student:** *"Una."*
["One."]

4   **Bianca:** *"Es lo mismo, papi, mira, dice, es lo mismo nomás que con dinero, pero, tú figúrate, si yo tengo tres tortillas y tengo 3 hijos, ¿de a cómo le toca a cada uno?"*
["It's the same, son, look, it says, it's the same only with money, but, you imagine, if I have three tortillas and I have three children, how many does each one get?"]

5   **Student:** *"Una."*
["One."]

6   **Bianca:** "*¿Verdad? Que le toca una.*"
            ["Right? They each get one."]

First, Bianca animated the student by including him and his friends as characters in the story (line 1). Noticing that the student was still experiencing difficulty, Bianca changed the context to a more familiar one, one in which she animated herself as distributing tortillas to her three children (line 2). This storyline produced a response by the student (line 3), which Bianca used to refer back to the original context (line 4). Interestingly, nowhere in this dialogue did Bianca communicate to the student that she expected him to solve the problem in a certain way. Finally, when the student left the room, mothers reflected on what they did to help this student (see Excerpt 5.11).

Excerpt 5.11   Mothers' Voices with Male Students: Reflections

1   **Bianca:** "*Sí, no, es como, algo que le motive, porque vio que le cambié el tema a tortillas y él si captó (HD: ¡Exacto!) luego, luego. Vio que yo le dije, o sea, él no captaba con el dinero.*" (HD: "*Inmediatamente agarró la onda.*") "*¿Verdad? Luego, luego dijo, a no, pues son 3 tortillas. O sea que a lo mejor se motiva, más con otra cosa, como dice, todo es, de hallarles a ellos, la manera de motivarlos para que saques sus*" (*se toca la cabeza*) "*... sus buenas ideas.*"
            ["Yes, I mean, it's like, something that motivates him, because you saw that I changed the topic and he got it," (HD: "Exactly!") "right away. You saw what I was telling him, I mean, he wasn't getting it with the money." (HD: "He immediately was in the loop.") "Right? Right away he said, oh no, it's got to be three tortillas. In other words, maybe he got motivated, better, with other stuff, I mean, it's all about finding the right way, the way to motivate them so they can use their" (touches head) "... their good ideas."]
2   **HD:** "*Para que saquen sus buenas ideas, eso se me hizo muy interesante, el cambio de...*"
            ["So they can use their good ideas, I thought that was interesting, the change of..."]
3 **Constanza:** "*De idea.*" (HD: "*De situación.*") "*... sí, cambió.*"
            ["Of idea." (HD: "Of situation") "... yes, he changed."]

After working with the two male students, the researcher suggested the mothers work with a female student. Daría volunteered to bring her daughter Viviana from the CEMELA after-school program. Unlike the interaction with male students, in this interaction, mothers were concerned with the student performing in accordance with an expected way of solving problems. This expected way positioned the student as a receiver of mothers' ideas and strategies for solving a problem:

1 **Daría:** "*Vas a dividir los 300 entre seis.*" (*está viendo el problema que tiene en sus manos*) (*la estudiante escribe 300 ÷ 6, en forma vertical*).
["You are going to divide the three hundred by six." (is looking at problem in her hands) (student writes 300 ÷ 6, in vertical format)]

First, Daría told the student what operation to use in the problem about sharing $300 among seven people (line 1). Here, Daría referred to six people because she was focusing only on the numbers that were explicit in the text of the problem, although represented in the problem was a situation in which seven people, Cornelio's aunt and her six friends, shared a $300 rent. Noticing that the student was not getting anywhere with the instructions she was expected to execute, other mothers started giving her additional instructions:

1 **Bety:** "*Puedes hacer, digamos sumar siete veces por ejemplo si tú crees que $20, sumar siete veces los 20 e ir aumentándole e ir aumentándole, hasta que...*"
["You can do, let's say add seven times. For example, if you think its $20, add twenty seven times and keep increasing it and increasing it, until you..."]
2 **Daría:** "*Mira, son siete personas, entonces agarra los 300 y haz las partes parejas entre esas personas. Puede ser de a 30, de a 40, de a veinti-algo, o sea tú vas a dividirlo, esos 300 a cada cual le tiene que tocarle igual.*"
["Look, there are seven people, so get the three hundred and make equal parts among those seven, it could be thirty each, or forty, or twenty-something, I mean, you are going to divide it, those three hundred, each has to get the same."]

Although Bety animated Viviana as the owner of a strategy of guessing ("if you think it's twenty," line 1) the strategy did not belong to Viviana. She was only listening to this dialogue and was not appropriating it. Next, Daría showed a concern for Viviana to solve the problem in an expected manner, as she told Viviana to divide (line 2). At this point, one mother recalled how one of the male students decided to solve the problem, and this prompted mothers to continue reminding the student to solve the problem according to their expectations (see Excerpt 5.12).

Excerpt 5.12   Mothers' Voices with Female Student: Directing

1 **Constanza:** "*A Cornelio, yo lo hice con Cornelio y Cornelio lo fue sumando, primero se fue de 30 y después fue aumentando de 35 y luego lo hizo de 40 y hasta que le dio.*"
["For Cornelio, I worked it out with Cornelio, and Cornelio was adding, first he went for thirty and then he kept increasing it to thirty-five and then to forty until he got it."]

2 **Bety:** "*O puedes dividir, o multiplicar.*"
["Or you can divide, or multiply."]

3 **Daría:** "*Yo pienso que, que dividir, los 300 entre las siete personas dijo ¿verdad?*" (Bianca: "*Uh-huh.*") "*De esos 300 tiene que, sacar...*"
["I think that, that divide, the three hundred by the seven people you said, right?" (Bianca: "Uh-huh.") "From those three hundred, she has to get..."]

4 **Bianca:** "*Uh-huh, a ver divide hija, los 300.*"
["Uh-huh, let's see daughter, go on and divide the three hundred."]

5 **Daría:** "*Divide 300 entre siete hija.*"
["Divide three hundred by seven, daughter."]

6 **Bety:** "*¿Sabes hacer la división, Viviana? ¿Sí sabes hacer la división?*" *(no responde)*
["Do you know how to do the division, Viviana? Do you know how to do the division?" (she does not respond)]

7 **Bianca:** "*Haz la división, hija. Tú hazla, te va a salir. Nomás es que, que te concentres.*"
["Do the division, daughter. You do it, you'll get it. It's a matter of, that you get focused."]

Interestingly, although Bety offered Viviana at least two options, divide or multiply (line 2), Daría, who declared silence for executing the division, insisted that the student use this operation to solve the problem (lines 3 and 5) and Bianca joined in making the same request (lines 4 and 7). Bety began to notice that Viviana was not fulfilling their expected way of solving the problem, so she directly asked her if she knew how to divide, but she received no confirmation from Viviana (line 6). However, Bety continued inquiring, thus creating a turning point in the interaction (see Excerpt 5.13).

Excerpt 5.13   Mothers' Voices with Female Student: Inquiring about Student's Space

1 **Bety:** "*Viviana, ¿no sabes hacer la división, m'hija? Como la hace, uh,*" (Daría: "*Repartir 300 dólares entre siete.*") "*300 entre siete,*" *(escribe la notación del algoritmo y la muestra a la estudiante)* "*¿no sabes cómo hacer la división?*"

["You don't know how to do the division, my daughter? Like it's done, uh," (Daría: "Distribute three hundred dollars among seven.") "three hundred by seven," (writes algorithm notation and shows it to student) "you don't know how to do the division?"]

2   **Viviana:** (*niega con la cabeza*) "*Uh-uh.*"
       [(shakes head) "Uh-uh."]

3   **Bety:** "*¿No te han enseñado a ti eso?*"
       ["They haven't taught you that?"]

4   **Viviana:** "*Sí, pero no le entiendo.*"
       ["Yes, but I don't understand it."]

5   **Bety:** "*¿No has entendido como hacer la división?*"
       ["You haven't understood how to do the division?"]

6   **Viviana:** (*niega con la cabeza*) "*No mucho.*"
       [(shakes head) "Not much."]

Here, in the dialogue captured in Excerpt 5.13, Bety realized that Viviana was not going to be able to solve the problem in the way they expected. Note how Viviana acknowledged that the division algorithm had been taught to her (line 4), but she also declared that she did not understand this method (lines 4 and 6). This admission illustrates that Viviana had only heard this dialogue about division, possibly in classrooms, but had not been able to reinvent it and ultimately appropriate it. Bety's line of inquiry marks an important interruption in the mothers' expected ways of Viviana's performance. It is a dialogic interruption that raised a possibility for mothers to restructure this mothers–student interspace in a way similar to that created for the male students. Mothers began to explore this possibility, as the student arrived at an approximate answer by repeated addition of quantities that she heard from the mothers (see Excerpt 5.14).

Excerpt 5.14 Mothers' Voices with Female Student: Restructuring Interspace

1   **Bety:** "*¿En cuánto te salió, m'hija?*"
       ["What did you get, daughter?"]

2   **Viviana:** "*319.*"
       ["Three hundred nineteen."]

3   **Daría:** "*Te pasaste. Tiene que ser menos.*"
       ["You went past it. It has to be less."]

4   **Bety:** "*¿Pero de a cómo tocó, de a 43?*"
       ["But how much did each one get? Forty-three?"]

5   **Viviana:** "*Uh-huh.*"
       ["Uh-huh."]

6   **Daría:** "*No tiene que existir el 19, tienes que irte para atrás. Son trescientos nomás los que vas a repartir.*"

           ["The nineteen (from three hundred nineteen) shouldn't
be there, you have to go back. It's only three hundred,
what you are going to distribute."]

7   **Bety:** *"No, m'hija porque si tenías los, si tenías los 380, cómo te salió,
este,"* (Daría: *"¿Cómo le aumentó?"*) *"¿cómo te salió 319, m'hija,
si tenías 280?"*

           ["No, my daughter because if you had the, if you had the
three hundred eighty, how did you get, uh," (Daría: "How
did she get more?") "how did you get three hundred nine-
teen, my daughter, if you had two hundred eighty?"]

8   **HD:** *"¿Quieres seguir intentándolo Viviana o quieres regresar a tu
clase?"*

           ["Do you want to keep trying or do you want to go back to
class?"]

9   **Viviana:** "I want to go back to class." (the researcher agreed and
walked her back to her class.)

First, Daría reminded Viviana that her tentative answer needed to be
reconsidered according to problem parameters (line 3). Bety seemed intrigued and therefore tried to find out more about Viviana's answer (line 4).
Daría continued trying to realign Viviana's answer to the given amounts in
the problem (line 6), while Bety continued challenging her answer (line 7).
Noticing that Viviana was becoming uncomfortable, the researcher gave
her the opportunity to continue or to stop her work (line 8). Viviana decided to end the interaction (line 9).

Summary 2: To what degree did students and mothers appropriate each other's dialogue?

Mothers used dialogues with students in contrasting ways. By encouraging male students to develop their own problem-solving methods while supporting their reasoning with multiple recontextualizations of the problem,
mothers established dialogues that helped them investigate ways of supporting the students and, at the same time, positioned students as inventing
their own problem-solving methods. In other words, the mothers withheld
any expectations regarding how students should solve problems. In contrast, by suggesting that the female student solve the problem using division
without investigating whether the student had previous understanding of
this method, mothers may have reproduced a kind of dialogue that the
student had not been able to appropriate.

The student's failure to fulfill the mothers' expected way of solving the
problem created frustration for the mothers. Not being able to fulfill the
mothers' expected way of solving the problem seemed to have created a
sense of silence for the student. Interestingly, silence was the prevailing

voice when mothers described their interactions with their husbands (e.g., "... *pero pues yo nomás miro*" ["... but, oh well, I just look"]) and when recalling past experiences with mathematics (e.g., "... *yo nunca fui buena para eso*" ["... I was never good for that"]). The researcher suggests the need for more mothers–students interactions to qualify these patterns as more than tentative. Even so, it seemed that mothers' dialogue may be communicating different expectations to male and female students. These expectations, as enacted in mother–student interspaces, may have mediated the process of dialogic appropriation.

Mothers' Dialogue with Teacher

The dialogues between the mothers and the teacher who agreed to these conversations suggest a polarization of voices, as indicated by the distribution of the two most salient voices, separate knowledge and constructed knowledge (see Table 5.4). In other words, while mothers managed to express their views about helping students construct their own mathematical knowledge, Mr. T responded with what Belenky et al. (1986) referred to as *separate knowledge,* a position in which a person listens to what others have to say about what they know and how they know it, but maintains his or her knowledge unaffected and separate.

For example, Bianca shared with Mr. T the benefits she saw in her child's learning by contextualizing problems with experiences that matter to the students:

1   **Bianca:** "*Bueno, o sea, [lo mío es] una sugerencia, porque o sea, yo sé que ustedes tienen su plan, sus, sus guías, o sus notas, o sus, ¿verdad? Sugiriendo, pero un poco más como involucrarse el niño también a, a, a motivarlo o, a crear tipos de problemas así, que se involucren con su vida este, cotidiana o personal, eh, basado, basado a la matemática. Porque si, ya ve que todo, realmente todo si lo vemos este casi todo es, de matemáticas si, en la vida, también en la vida de nosotros, como por decir, este tengo tanta*

TABLE 5.4   Mothers' Dialogue with Teacher

Voice	Frequency
Silence	5
Received knowledge	2
Separate knowledge	16 (Mr. T)
Constructed knowledge	10 (mainly mothers)

familia tengo que comprar esto, estas libras de carne, o así, o este,
tortillas, y en realidad también para los niños, ¿sabes qué? Este,
tienes tantos uniformes, o este, de la semana, es siempre de así,
casi viendo uno, uno saca sus cuentas. Por eso digo yo que, yo
le tomé, yo vi que mi niño si avanzó un poquito, o sea avanzó,
poniendo atención avanzó más en, o sea como en este, estilo o
que se puede decir, o esta, operación o sea, no sé, no sé las demás
mamás qué opinan también de sus niños pues porque yo si vi que
él le tomó más sabor así."

["Well, I mean [this is] one suggestion, because I mean, I
know that you have your plan, your, your guides, or your
notes, or your, right? I am only suggesting, but a little
more like involving the child, too, to, to, to motivate the
child, to create types of problems like these, that have
to do with their lives, uh, daily or personal lives, uh, but
based on mathematics. Because you know that everything,
really everything if we see it, almost everything is, mathematics, in life, also in our lives, like for example, uh, I have
these many people in my family and I have to buy this,
these pounds of meat, or like that, or, uh, tortillas, and
really also for the children, you know what? Uh, you have
these many uniforms, or, the weekdays, it's almost something like that, when we see that, we can do our calculations. That's why I say that, I got, I saw that my child did
progress a little more, I mean he progressed, by paying
attention he progressed more in, like, in this style or how
can we call it, I don't know, or in this, operation I mean, I
don't know, I don't know what the other moms have to say
about their children because I did see that my child got
the flavor of it like this."]

This interaction was the breakthrough of mothers' voices (about mathematics instruction) into the teacher's dialogical space. Bianca was tactfully
offering her suggestions to enrich students' understanding with meaningful contexts (line 1). While she displayed respect and recognition for the
teachers' work, she also demonstrated agency by taking the initiative to be
the first one to directly talk with the teacher about mathematics instruction. As she noticed that the teacher was only listening, she invited other
mothers to lend strength to the case she was trying to make. Bety accepted
the invitation by adding specificity to Bianca's argument in the form of the
kinds of mathematical difficulties experienced by students:

1   **Bety:** *"Porque muchos, la mayoría, eh, tuvieron problemas en la división. Porque no supieron este, como llegar a, como dividir. Llegaban al resultado pero unos sumando, otros multiplicando, o así, con trabajos, pero llegaban a, a su resultado, pero era a veces más fácil dándoles nombre a ellos, que ellos conocieran, que ellos estuvieran familiarizados."*
["Because many, the majority, uh, had a hard time with division. Because they didn't know uh, how to get to, how to divide. They would get to the result but some did so by adding, others by multiplying, or like that, with a lot of work, but they did get to, to their result, but sometimes it was easier for them to give names to the, that they knew, that they were familiar with."]

Although Bety's idea was quite simple—to name something in the problem that the students knew about (line 1)—her idea is well recognized in the everyday mathematics research tradition (see Carraher, 2008, for a discussion of manipulation of quantities and manipulation of symbols). In this interaction, Bety's contribution served to push Bianca's voice into the teacher's dialogic space even further. In contrast, when the researcher asked Mr. T what he thought of the mothers' ideas about how they saw possibilities to improve problem solving in the classroom, his response was polite, yet it indicated a clear separation between classroom learning and out-of-school learning.

1   **Mr. T:** *"Ah, pues, todo tiene uh, este, mucho sentido lo que están diciendo, creo que es lo primero."* (mira hacia arriba) *"A mí me interesa mucho escuchar este* (mira hacia arriba) *o ver que han descubierto algunas cosas muy este, muy"* (además) *"que les puede ayudar a sus niños, en clase. Poder, ver la importancia de, no nada más de pensar, de pensar que van a aprender todo esto en, en el salón, pero que también el aprendizaje continúa afuera del salón."*
["Ah, well, everything makes uh, uh, a lot of sense, what you're saying, I think that's my first comment." (looks up) "I am very interested in hearing uh," (looks up) "or seeing that you have discovered some very interesting things, very," (hand gesture) "that it can help your children, in the classroom. To be able, to see the importance of, not just to think, to think that they are going to learn all of this in, in the classroom, but that learning also continues outside the classroom."]

Here, the teacher seemed extremely cautious about responding to and establishing proximity with the mothers' dialogue, as shown by his looking up twice and his multiple false-start expressions (line 1). While he acknowledged what mothers have discovered that may be helpful for the students' learning in the classroom, he picked up a different line as he declared that not everything will be learned in the classroom. This observation created a polarization in that the mothers' dialogues were about enriching classroom learning with everyday practices, while the teacher's dialogue was about establishing limits on how much students can learn in the classroom. Clearly, these were two different dialogues, and neither was transformed nor appropriated by participants.

The teacher also talked about the relationship between school and nonschool learning as starting in school and then moving out of school in the form of application of school knowledge in the everyday world. Mothers, on the other hand, were concerned mainly about improving learning in the classroom by using relevant contexts in problems:

1   **Mr. T:** "*Y yo creo que, por la mayor parte, todo lo que, están aprendiendo en el salón, cuando salen de la escuela, se sup-...y ya viendo que es cierto, uh, lo importante es que lo apliquen en una situación real porque de eso se trata, poder utilizar la información que estamos aprendiendo en el salón y ponerlo en una situación real.*"
["I think that, overall, all that, all that they are, they are learning in the classroom, when they get out of school, and it's supposed—...and seeing that it's true, uh, what's important is that they apply this in a real situation because that's what it's all about, to be able to use the information that we're learning in the classroom and to put it out in a real situation."]

Again, the teacher's dialogue continued the polarizing of dialogues. First, there was a suggestion that school learning was not about what is real ("...*cuando salen de la escuela...y ya viendo que es cierto*" ["...when they get out of school...and seeing that it's true"] (line 1). Having established these boundaries, then the value of school knowledge was in its applicability in real situations (line 1). The mothers' view, as expressed through their collective voices, was about enriching school learning with everyday situations.

Mr. T framed his talk as an eloquent recognition of what mothers do for their children:

1   **Mr. T:** "*Uh, lo importante en este caso, uh, con ustedes, es que ustedes entienden la importancia, la importancia de matemáticas, por,*

simplemente por estar aquí, y ustedes están dando esa informac-, están dando ese ejemplo a sus hijos, y cuando sus hijos ven que ustedes están hablando de matemáticas, ellos tamb-, o sea, les están dando más apoyo, les están dando un buen ejemplo."
["Uh, what's important in this case, uh, with you, is that you understand the importance, the importance of mathematics, by, simply by being here, and you are giving that informat-, you are giving that example to your children, and when your children see that you are talking about mathematics, they also, I mean, you are supporting them, you are giving them a good example."]

Absent in the teacher's recognition of mothers' work was an indication of wanting to connect what mothers do with what teachers do. The teacher maintained this disconnection by strictly talking *to* the mothers about their involvement. Although the teacher was careful to not impose his views, his dialogic space was well protected by resisting talking *with* the mothers. The end result was that neither mothers nor the teacher appropriated the other's dialogue. Instead, they became listeners or spectators of the other's dialogue.

In one of the final interactions between Mr. T and the group of mothers, one mother expressed to the teacher her desire to help her daughter with mathematics and her concern that she did not understand the school's way of teaching mathematics. The teacher trivialized the seriousness of this issue, making the mother's child responsible for not being able to explain to the mother (see Excerpt 5.15).

Excerpt 5.15   Mothers' Voices with Teachers: Unappropriated Dialogues

1   **Mirna:** *"Sí pero, como, este, a veces uno como, bueno, a mi me ha tocado que la niña mía a veces lleva problemas, y como dice ella."*
(*apunta hacia Constanza*)
["Yes but, like, uh, sometimes one like, well, I have seen that my girl sometimes brings problems, and like she says." (points toward Constanza)]

2   **Mr. T:** *"Uh-huh."*
["Uh-huh."]

3   **Mirna:** *"Nos los enseñaron diferentes, así es de que como si yo le quiero ayudar a mi niña a hacer las tareas, uh, ni ella me entiende a mí ni yo le entiendo a ella, y, o sea yo le quiero ayudar pero no puedo . . ."*
["We were taught the problems differently, so it's like if I want to help my girl to do the homework, uh, neither she understand me nor do I understand her, and, I mean, I do want to help her but I can't . . ."]

4   **Mr. T:** "*Sí, sí.*"
        ["Yes, yes."]
5   **Mirna:** "*Y, y ella lo quiere hacer como ella sabe pero yo no le entiendo. Ese es el problema también. Sí le puede ayudar uno, pero necesita ella entenderme y yo entenderle a ella para poder, yo también ayudarle.*"
        ["And, and she wants to do it the way she knows but I don't understand it. That's also the problem. I can help her, but she needs to understand me and I need to understand her so I can, so I can help her."]
6   **Mr. T:** "*Sí, eh, yo no creo que debería de ser un problema. Eso no debería de ser un problema. Tal vez es un problema porque, la manera que, que su niño se esté explicando.*"
        ["Yes, uh, I don't think that should be a problem. That should not be a problem. Maybe it is a problem because, the manner that, that your child is explaining herself."]

Mirna not only recognized her desire to help her daughter with mathematics (line 3) but also declares her ability to do so (line 5). Her impediment was the lack of understanding of the daughter's methods (line 5). Again, the teacher picked up a new line in this dialogue by locating the problem in the quality of the student's explanation (line 6). This new line reduced the proximity between the mothers' and the teacher's dialogue.

Summary 3: To what degree did the teacher and mothers appropriate each other's dialogues?

Of the three interspaces, the teacher–mothers dialogue showed the greatest resistance for appropriating or transforming each other's dialogues. This resistance was achieved by a separation of dialogues that the teacher managed to establish in various ways: (1) by picking up divergent lines in the conversation; (2) by listening and respecting the mothers' ideas while maintaining his ideas separated; and (3) by reframing dialogues in a manner that reified the methods, practices, and ways of talking that prevail in schools.

The teacher's separation of dialogues was not contested by the mothers' dialogues. This acquiescence was not surprising given that this interspace was the most unexplored of the three. That is, because mothers interacted with students at home daily, the dialogic interspace between them at school most likely used patterns of interaction brought from home. The same inference could be made about the interspace of the mothers talking with each other. However, the interaction between mothers and teachers around problem solving is an unexplored interspace that has almost no history for either mothers or teachers. In other forms of interaction, such as teacher–parent conferences or school open houses, mothers do not bring dialogue about problem solving in the way they did in the interspace with the teacher. Civil and Bernier (2006) explored parent–teacher relationships in schools. Their purpose for bringing together parents, teachers, and administrators in a parent leadership project in mathematics was "to work toward establishing a dialogue that would allow us to break the traditional power structures that are in place in schools" (Civil & Bernier, 2006, p. 311). The need for a dialogic interspace between parents and teachers has been identified and requires further research.

CONCLUSIONS

In this study, the metaphors of voice and dialogic interspace provided a framework to understand the extent to which mothers' dialogue about problem solving penetrated the dialogic spaces of other mothers, students, and teachers. Findings reveal that mothers' dialogues are more easily appropriated and transformed when they share their voices with other mothers. For example, when mothers' dialogues were positioned in proximity with themselves, their dialogues generated a collective voice that valued the construction of knowledge while acknowledging that they did not always have this opportunity in their histories of learning mathematics in school. In fact, they expressed a strong sense of silence or voicelessness when recalling their mathematical past, which included many truncated opportunities to continue learning mathematics. As they talked about their children's mathematics education, they clearly articulated a desire to help them develop a voice in mathematics, because they have experienced being voiceless and their mathematical lives as adults have been affected by these experiences.

When positioned in mothers–students interspaces, mothers' dialogues were used in contrasting ways. Interactions with male students were characterized by encouragement and support to make sense of problems in personally meaningful ways, whereas those with a female student were characterized by an expectation of the student to solve a problem in a given way. The limited number of these interactions makes results in this particular interspace only tentative.

Finally, when positioned in mothers–teacher interspace, mothers' dialogues resisted appropriation. In this interspace, participants' dialogues about problem solving were acknowledged but remained disconnected. In this conversation, mothers' voices converged towards the view of constructed knowledge as the most beneficial form of learning mathematics for their children. They substantiated this view with examples of their work with students on problem solving both at home and at school. In response, the teacher remained at a distance from these epistemic views. While not invalidating the mothers' views, the teacher decided to highlight a different kind of dialogue, one that prevails in most schools.

Informed by research that questions the subtraction of parents' voices in their involvement in schools (Civil & Bernier, 2006; Henry, 1996; Lareau & Horvat, 1999; Leistyna, 2002; Reay, 1998), as well as women's perceptions of mathematics (Civil & Andrade, 2002), the study presented in this chapter uses a dialogic approach to understand mothers' voices about learning mathematics, always in relation to how these voices can exert a transformative effect through the connecting of dialogues, first on the mothers themselves, but also on significant others like students and teachers. As Brew (2003) suggested, "there is a direct relationship between one's epistemological perspective toward knowledge and the role that significant others (identified as teacher and peers) play in learning" (pp. 70–71). Findings suggest the need for more of these interspaces in which participants can transform and appropriate their own and others' dialogues around problem solving. These dialogic transformations are essential for rethinking our views about everyday mathematics, school mathematics, and the role of parents in mathematics education.

ACKNOWLEDGMENT

This manuscript is based upon work supported in part by the National Science Foundation under Grant No. 0424983 to the Center for the Mathematics Education of Latinos/Latinas (CEMELA). Any opinions, findings, and conclusions or recommendations expressed in this material are those of the author(s) and do not necessarily reflect the views of the National Science Foundation.

REFERENCES

Bakhtin, M. M. (1981). *The dialogic imagination: Four essays.* C. Emerson & M. Holquist (Trans.). Austin: The University of Texas Press.

Belenky, M. F., Clinchy, B. M., Goldberger, N. R., & Tarule, J. M. (1986). *Women's ways of knowing: The development of self, voice, and mind.* New York: Basic Books.

Brew, C. (2003). Mothers returning to study mathematics: The development of mathematical authority through evolving relationships with their children. In L. Burton (Ed.), *Which way social justice in mathematics education?* (pp. 65–100). Westport, CT: Praeger.

Carpenter, T. P., Franke, M. L., Jacobs, V. R., Fennema, E., & Empson, S. B. (1998). A longitudinal study of invention and understanding in children's multidigit addition and subtraction. *Journal for Research in Mathematics Education, 29*(1), 3–20. doi: 10.2307/749715

Carraher, D. W. (2008). Beyond 'blaming the victim' and 'standing in awe of noble savages': A response to "Revisiting Lave's 'cognition in practice.'" *Educational Studies in Mathematics, 69*(1), 23–32. doi: 10.1007/s10649-008-9126-4

Chicago Public Schools. (n.d.). *Unidentified Elementary School profile*. Retrieved from www.cps.edu/Schools/

Civil, M., & Andrade, R. (2002). Transitions between home and school mathematics: Rays of hope amidst the passing clouds. In G. de Abreu, A. J. Bishop, & N. C. Presmeg (Eds.), *Transitions between contexts of mathematical practices* (pp. 149–169). Dordrecht, The Netherlands: Kluwer Academic.

Civil, M., & Bernier, E. (2006). Exploring images of parental participation in mathematics education: Challenges and possibilities. *Mathematical Thinking and Learning, 8*(3), 309–330. doi: 10.1207/s15327833mtl0803_6

Cobb, P. (2007). Putting philosophy to work: Coping with multiple theoretical perspectives. In F. K. Lester, Jr. (Ed.), *Second handbook of research on mathematics teaching and learning*. Charlotte, NC: National Council of Teachers of Mathematics.

Domínguez, H. (2008). *The discourse of mathematization: Bilingual students reinventing mathematics and themselves as mathematical thinkers*. Unpublished doctoral dissertation, University of Texas. Retrieved from http://repositories.lib.utexas.edu/

Garfinkel, H., & Rawls, A. W. (Ed.). (2002). *Ethnomethodology's program: Working out Durkheim's aphorism*. New York, NY: Rowman & Littlefield.

Garfinkel, H., & Rawls, A. W. (Eds.). (2006). *Seeing sociologically: The routine grounds of social action*. Boulder, CO: Paradigm.

Henry, M. E. (1996). *Parent–school collaboration: Feminist organizational structures and school leadership*. Albany: State University of New York Press.

Lareau A., & Horvat, E. M. (1999). Moments of social inclusion and exclusion: Race, class, and cultural capital in family-school relationships. *Sociology of Education, 72*(1), 37–53. doi: 10.2307/2673185

Lave, J., & Wegner, E. (1991). *Situated learning: Legitimate peripheral participation*. Cambridge, UK: Cambridge University Press.

Leistyna, P. (2002). Extending the possibilities of multicultural community partnerships in urban public schools. *The Urban Review, 34*(1), 1–23. doi: 10.1023/A:1014417010771

Nasir, N. S., Hand, V., & Taylor, E. V. (2008). Culture and mathematics in school: Boundaries between "cultural" and "domain" knowledge in the mathematics classroom and beyond. *Review of Research in Education, 32*(1), 187–240. doi: 10.3102/0091732X07308962

Reay, D. (1998). Cultural reproduction: Mothers involvement in their children's primary schooling. In M. Grenfell & D. James (Eds.), *Bourdieu and education: Acts of practical theory* (pp. 55–71). London: Falmer.

Roth, W.-M. (1995). *Authentic school science: Knowing and learning in open-inquiry science laboratories*. Dordrecht, The Netherlands: Kluwer Academic.

Serrano, M. (2008). *La Llorona.* Miami, FL: Planeta.

Technical Education Research Centers. (1995–1998). *Investigations in number, data, and space (grades K–5).* Menlo Park, CA: Dale Seymour.

Young, M. F. (1993). Instructional design for situated learning. *Educational Technology, Research, and Development, 41*(1), 43–58. doi: 10.1007/BF02297091

CHAPTER 6

CONVERSATIONS AROUND MATHEMATICS EDUCATION WITH LATINO PARENTS IN TWO BORDERLAND COMMUNITIES

The Influence of Two Contrasting Language Policies

Jesús M. Acosta-Iriqui
Marta Civil
The University of Arizona

Javier Díez-Palomar
Universitat Autònoma de Barcelona

Mary E. Marshall
The University of New Mexico

Beatriz Quintos
University of Maryland

Latinos/as and Mathematics Education, pages 125–147
Copyright © 2011 by Information Age Publishing
All rights of reproduction in any form reserved.

INTRODUCTION

The work presented in this chapter was part of the research agenda for the Center for the Mathematics Education of Latinos/as (CEMELA), which aims to understand the interplay of mathematics education and language, social, cultural, and political issues that affect Latino communities. The research discussed in this article is a collaboration between two CEMELA partner sites—the University of Arizona and the University of New Mexico. An argument is made for the need to examine mathematics education opportunities or the lack thereof for Latinos, expanding what takes place at school and in the classroom context. Families' voices have often been excluded from the conversations that concern their children's mathematics education. In this study, we look into factors that support or impede Mexican-American or Mexican-immigrant families' school involvement regarding mathematics. In so doing, we engage in a conversation that opens a space to counter negative views and myths in the collaboration with Latino families (Valencia, 2002). To help us understand this issue, we explore the following question: How do the different language policies in the two settings (Arizona, where bilingual education is severely constrained, and New Mexico, where the state's constitution endorses it) affect the engagement of Spanish-dominant parents in their children's mathematics education?

THEORETICAL FRAMEWORK

Our work is grounded on the assumption that students' communities and families are essential to reversing the challenging trends of low achievement and persistence rates in mathematics among Latino students (Civil & Bernier, 2006). The concept of funds of knowledge is key to our research. This theoretical concept highlights the interaction between the community background and knowledge in the learning process (González, Moll, & Amanti, 2005; Moll, Amanti, Neff, & González, 1992; Moll & Ruiz, 2002). This approach assumes that community knowledge and, more specifically, the knowledge of the household members can provide strategic resources for classroom practices. The concept of funds of knowledge in the context of mathematics education and Latino families has been the focus of research (Civil & Andrade, 2002; Civil & Bernier, 2006; Civil, Planas, & Quintos, 2005).

The concepts of social and cultural capital, in particular as they have been applied to research with working-class families, are applicable to our work. It has been asserted that everyone has social and cultural capital (Horvat, Weininger, & Lareau, 2003; Lareau & Horvat, 1999), but the value of this capital is not equal in all fields. Its value depends on the context and the power relationships within this context. Our research with parents was influenced by Flecha's (2000) work with adult learners following a dialogical learning approach that encourages an egalitarian perspective to value all contributions (not only "scholarly" ones) in the construction of knowledge.

Lave and Wenger (1991) provided a framework to assess the dynamics of knowledge and learning as situated processes that are affected by cultural, social, and linguistic dimensions. The linguistic dimension is of particular interest in the research presented here because we focus on the influence of language policies on issues related to parents' engagement in their children's mathematics education. There is a large body of research on the role of language in the learning and teaching of mathematics, and of particular interest to us in this study was the research on language and mathematics with English language learners (ELLs) (Celedón-Pattichis, 2004; Khisty, 2006; Khisty & Chval, 2002; Moschkovich, 1999, 2002, 2007). Many mathematics classrooms emphasize discourse and communication with the expectation that students will talk and write about their mathematical thinking and solutions. Several of the reform curricula in mathematics are language rich. Our concern is, how do these language-rich environments for mathematics instruction and language policies have an impact on parental engagement, especially when parents are not proficient in English?

CONTEXT

In 2005, the Latino population in Arizona was 28.5% of the total state population, and in New Mexico, it was 43.4% (U.S. Census, n.d.a, n.d.b). The study reported in this chapter focused on Spanish-dominant, mostly immigrant Latino parents who often navigate between two educational systems, one in the United States and one in Mexico. Prior research has documented immigrant parents' perceptions on the differences between the two educational systems (Bratton, Quintos, & Civil, 2004; Civil, Bratton, & Quintos, 2005; Civil, Planas, & Quintos, 2005, Civil & Quintos, 2006; Civil & Planas, 2010). In this study, our focus was on the two different school language policies in place in Arizona and New Mexico.

In November 2000, Arizona voters passed an anti-bilingual ballot initiative (Proposition 203) that severely restricted the ability of school districts to implement bilingual education programs and of parents to place their children in such programs.[1] The new law replaced bilingual education with structured English immersion (SEI) classes in which instruction is offered in English only, although teachers are allowed to use a minimal amount of the child's native language for clarification. The law also specified that SEI would be provided "during a temporary transition period not normally intended to exceed one year," after which time English learners would be transferred to "English language mainstream classes" (ARS, 15-752; Combs, Evans, Fletcher, Parra, & Jiménez, 2005).

On the other end of the language spectrum, New Mexico actively promotes bilingual education. The history of bilingual education in the state is one of continuous improvement of the program; as of 2010, the program also includes Native American language considerations. Legislation in 2004 actively endorses parents' choices of bilingual programs for their children and provides funding for parent advisory committees in schools. Article 23 of the Bilingual Multicultural Education Act of 2004 states the following:

> Due to its unique history, New Mexico is a leader among the states in providing multilingual and multicultural curricula. The *Constitution of the State of New Mexico*, adopted in 1911, reflects the intent to protect the languages and cultures of the state's peoples. Article XII, Section 10 of the Constitution states that children of Spanish descent shall never be denied the right to attend public school nor will they be educated in separate schools. Additionally, Section 8 calls for the Legislature to provide for training of teachers to become proficient in both the English and Spanish languages. (p. vi)

We argue that it is important to understand how these different language policies have an impact on immigrant parents' engagement in their children's education—in the case of this study, mathematics education. Our research indicates that Latino parents may be discouraged to attend school events when they perceive the language as a barrier. An example of this phenomenon was Verónica, a mother who participated in a previous research project (Bratton et al., 2004). When her child was placed in an English-only classroom, she stopped going to her child's classroom because she did not think she could help him there; she believed she did not understand English well enough.

Verónica [AZ]: *"A mí lo que me gustaba era que si mientras estuvieran en un programa bilingüe, yo podía estar involucrada. . . . Como cuando estaba en el kinder, pues muy fácil, recortar, pasarles trabajitos a los niños, recogérselos, hasta me traía trabajo para la casa para llevárselo a la maestra otro día. En primero igual, me iba con él y como ella hablaba español, pues me daba para calificarle y cosas así, pero ya me veía ahí mi niño, ya oía, yo ya miraba ahí, al estar ahí sentada, yo estoy mirando, me estoy dando cuenta. Y ya cuando David, ya puro segundo fue, a puro inglés y con el maestro que hablaba puro inglés, pues ya no, ya no fui."*
["I liked it while they were in a bilingual program; I could be involved. . . . When he was in kindergarten, it was easy to cut out things, pass out the projects to the kids, gather them up. I even brought work home to take it to the

teacher the next day. In first grade, it was the same thing, I went with him and because the teacher spoke Spanish, she gave me things to grade and other jobs like that. My son saw me there, I could listen to him, I watched him. By being there watching, I realize many things. And then when David went to second grade into English-only and with a teacher that only spoke English, then I didn't go. I didn't go."]

On the basis of the frames discussed in Theoretical Framework and previous studies such as the one by Bratton and colleagues (2004), we point out the equity implications of English-only instruction and challenge the compatibility of restrictive language policies with the 21st-century push for parental engagement.

METHOD

Setting and Participants

Our overarching research goal is to gain a better understanding of Latino parents' perceptions about their children's mathematics education. This overall goal leads to several subgoals, one of which is the primary focus of this chapter: What is the impact of different language policies in Arizona and in New Mexico on a group of immigrant parents' perceptions and the effect of these policies on their engagement as reported by the parents? To this end, we conducted audiotaped interviews with 14 mothers from two different schools in Tucson, Arizona, and with three mothers and one father from two different schools in New Mexico, one urban, one rural. All parents were Spanish language dominant. In addition to these interviews with parents, we conducted three classroom observations, two in Tucson and one in Albuquerque. Four mothers participated in one school in Tucson and one mother participated in the other school in Tucson. At the elementary school in Albuquerque, nine mothers participated.

Data Collection

We have developed a systematic approach to these classroom observations in prior research (Civil & Quintos, 2006, 2009). In these visits, one to three researchers and a small group of three to six parents observed a mathematics lesson and then met to debrief the experience. We have found this approach to be a powerful way to engage with parents in a dialogue based on a common experience, that of having observed a class together. These debriefings were audio- and/or videotaped.

Both the interviews and the classroom observation debriefings were transcribed and then analyzed from the grounded theory perspective (Glaser & Strauss, 1967), coding them for emerging themes. Through these in-depth interviews and classroom observations, we documented Latino parents' views and beliefs on their own engagement (Barton, Drake, Perez, St. Louis, & George, 2004) with their children's mathematics education. Our methodological approach is also grounded on phenomenology (Van Manen, 1990), which relies heavily on participants' contributions to the experience. This methodology strives to triangulate the data collected through multiple experiences and sources. The lived experience of each parent is considered central to our own understanding. This methodology is also consistent with a critical-communicative approach (Flecha & Gómez, 2004), which incorporates parents' voices into the scientific discourse from an egalitarian point of view.

In the Arizona case, we had an additional source of data: All the mothers were regularly attending the *Tertulias Matemáticas* [mathematical circles]. These programs were modeled after earlier work (Quintos, Bratton, & Civil, 2005) and consist of a series of six to eight sessions in which parents engage in mathematical explorations as well as in conversations about issues related to the teaching and learning of mathematics and, in particular, their children's schooling.

FINDINGS

In the next two sections, we present our findings in relation to parental engagement in their children's mathematics education. We begin with an overview of the nature of this engagement to underscore, as other researchers have done, the importance that working-class Latino parents give to their children's education. We then turn to the main focus of this article, which is the impact of language policies on such engagement.

Nature of Parents' Engagement in Their Children's Mathematics Education and Beliefs Regarding this Engagement

Our findings highlight parents' forms of engagement as congruent with the broader concept of the Spanish term "*educación*," which goes beyond "education" to encompass also "behavior" (Goldenberg & Gallimore, 1995) and the impact on their children's achievement. To support parents' engagement in mathematics education requires the schools to create new spaces that offer more opportunities for parents to participate in their children's schooling, and to revise the power imbalances that parents face, which prevent them from collaborating as they want—on an equal basis, as participants, as our studies have noted.

All parents in our study mentioned that their motivation to participate in the mathematical circles or in the research was primarily to be able to help their children with mathematics homework or related tasks. For example, in Selena's case, she was concerned with acquiring the skills needed to help her children attending elementary school, and even her daughter in high school. The following excerpt was taken from one of the two interviews conducted with her:

> **Selena [AZ]:** "*No le entran mucho, es la que te dije que tenía problemas con álgebra, que yo quería aprender para ayudarle, porque ella me decía, "mamá, me puedes ayudar," pero yo no sé álgebra.*"
> ["They are not easy for her, she is the one I told you that had problems with algebra, that I wanted to learn to help her, because she used to tell me, 'Mom, can you help me?' but I don't know algebra."]

In the case of Arizona, because of the format of the parents' group, mothers attended the *Tertulias Matemáticas* (mathematical circles) with the idea of learning the mathematic concepts and skills their children were doing in school, which in most cases were different from what these parents had experienced as part of their own education in their home country. Parents in New Mexico also expressed their willingness to help their children and gave examples of their involvement in school-related tasks. Brenda, for example, reported that when it was possible, she took time from work to attend school to be informed about her child's progress. An example of this dedication was expressed in the following excerpt from the interview with her:

> **Brenda [NM]:** "*Pues, por ejemplo, yo pienso, la oportunidad como la que hubo hoy es buena oportunidad para asistir... Yo soy quien trabaja, yo soy quien provee todo en la casa, pues regularmente no, no tengo el tiempo porque son en las mañanas, porque es a las once de la mañana, o a las doce, y yo estoy en mi trabajo desde las nueve, diez de la mañana, hasta las seis de la tarde. Entonces solamente, por ejemplo, como hoy, miércoles, que es cuando tuve que pedir un tiempo para esto.*"
> ["For example, I think, the opportunity like the one today, is a good opportunity to attend... I am the one who works,

I'm the one providing everything at home, the truth is that regularly I don't, I don't have the time because they are in the mornings, because it is at 11:00 a.m. or at 12:00 p.m., and I am at work since 9, 9 in the morning until 6 in the afternoon. Then only, like today, Wednesday, for example, I have asked [for] some time at work to do this."]

We are aware that the parents in our study were a selected sample and may not have been representative of all parents in these schools. But we want to stress the deep commitment that these parents had towards their children's education, thus challenging a perception that Latino parents do not care about education (see Valencia, 2002). In most cases, when parents stopped attending the mathematical circles, it was related to logistic issues such as work, transportation, day care, schedules, and so on.

Our data support that our participants' involvement goes beyond attending the workshops, picking up their children, attending school events, and the like. When parents were asked in the interview what they did if they were not able to help their children with homework or school tasks, a common theme emerged among all different responses; all parents stated that if they did not know how to help with homework, the first person they often went to was the teacher, first to find out how their children were doing in the different subjects and second to ask how they could help them. Other people to whom they turned for help were other school personnel, their own relatives or their neighbors, as well as other community resources. An example of this pursuit for help is provided in the following excerpt from Laura's interview:

> **Javier:** "*Y si hay problemas en los que tú no las puedes ayudar, ¿qué hacen ellas?*"
> ["What about if there are problems in which you cannot help them, what do they do?"]
> **Laura[AZ]:** "*Pues ahí buscan ayuda con mi esposo, por ejemplo, y si no entiende él tampoco, pues entonces andamos buscando, y le pido ayuda por ejemplo aquí a Alicia (PTO), o a algún maestro.*"
> ["So they ask for my husband's help, for example, and if he doesn't understand either, well then, we keep looking, and I ask for help, for example here to Alicia (PTO), or to a teacher."]

Certainly, it is difficult to measure how much parents are involved in the education of their children. Our previous and current work with Latino families tells us that parental involvement is not as many teachers and schools perceive it. Civil and Andrade (2003) pointed out that, particularly in working-class communities, the expectations for parental involvement are often tied to tasks such as helping out in the cafeteria or in the playground, and seldom to parents contributing their knowledge and experiences in the classroom teaching.

Another finding regarding the nature of this engagement is the importance parents give to the affective support they show towards their children as they are learning mathematics. In both settings, Arizona and New Mexico, some comments during the debriefing of the classroom observation pointed to this matter. Quotes captured of Angela (NM) and Lucrecia (AZ) talking about the importance for them to be in school and the feelings of their children knowing that they are around school underscore parents' commitment.

Angela [NM]: *"Yo pienso que ya lo sabían, lo importante para ellos es sentir la presencia de los padres o alguien que les estaba acompañando. No tanto lo que aprendieron, sino que alguien, que mi mamá, o mi prima, o mi abuelita... que me está viendo."*
["I think they knew it, it is important for them to feel the presence of the parents or someone who was accompanying them. It is not just what they learned, but that someone, my mom, or my cousin, or my grandmother...she is with me."]

In the case of Lucrecia, who arrived from Mexico shortly before our study began, mathematics was not a problem for her children but her support for them impelled her to constantly ask her children's teachers questions about their achievement because they were separated to take English classes.

Lucrecia [AZ]: *"Les dan en ciertas hora inglés, los separan para darles inglés, y a la niña también, a la niña también. Pero ahí como le digo, en el salón cuando se trata de matemáticas el Mr. S dice que el niño está bien, dice, 'Es muy listo para las matemáticas," pero ya cuando se trata de que están hablando otra cosa, que no sea matemáticas y que es puro inglés ahí sí se le papalotea pa' todos lados... entonces yo por eso estoy, a cada rato voy con él a preguntarle, y preguntarle para pues, es una manera de que el niño sepa que estoy allí."*
["They teach them English at a certain time; they separate them to give them English classes, my daughter also. But as I tell you, in the classroom when it is about mathematics, Mr. S says my son is doing well, he says, 'He is very smart in mathematics,' but if [it] is about discussing something else that is not mathematics, and it is all English, it is there

> where he goes in all directions . . . and that is the reason why I am, I go to him often to ask, and to ask him so, it is one way my son knows that I'm there."]

In both cases and in both settings, Angela and Lucrecia talked about the emotional support their presence represents for their children. This behavior goes beyond the concept of parental involvement they experienced in their home country that, in most cases, was limited to what they could do at home to help their children.

Parents' Perceptions About the Impacts of Language Practices on Their Children's Learning

Parents' perceptions about their children's schooling are shaped by their children's experiences. Even though they do not know specifics about policies in education, their children's work and behavior reflect the school practices. Combs and colleagues (2005) discussed the effects of Proposition 203 on a school with a student population very similar to the schools in our study (low-income Mexican American). The implementation of this initiative brought consequences to the entire school community, including school administrators, teachers, and students. This initiative affected the engagement of parents by restricting bilingual education. Parents expressed how this legislation is damaging their children and their concerns for future schooling:

> Parents were shaken by the effect of the SEI experience on their children. . . .
> [T]he change was so abrupt and dramatic that parents were taken aback.
> Some children who had happily attended a bilingual education classroom the
> previous year now pleaded for their parents to let them stay home. Twelve of
> the 15 parents having children in SEI classes either in the current or previous
> school year described their children's despondency, self-loathing, and bursts
> of anger. (Combs et al., 2005, p. 711)

Since the passage of Proposition 203 in 2000, Latino parents in Arizona have been limited in the kind of school-related activities in which they participate with their children. Not only bilingual children and teachers are affected. Parents also find themselves caught in the middle of a debate that is taking away the instruction in their native languages (Stritikus & Garcia, 2005). Cummins (2000) argued that bilingual education is not and never has been a process that is neutral. He also mentioned that the education of minority students is part of larger immigration issues, distribution of wealth and power, and the empowerment of students.

English-Only: Barriers and challenges for parents

English-only instruction raises barriers that are difficult for parents to cross. Parents are challenged to understand the teaching methods their children are experiencing, and also to make sense of the curriculum in a language other than their own.

Seven mothers in Arizona (Dorotea, Candida, Jacinta, Veronica, Elena, Lucrecia, and Selena) mentioned that the exclusive instruction in English affected their participation in helping with homework because all instructions and problem descriptions were in English, making it difficult for them to help their children understand and solve the problems. The issue of translation was raised by all of these mothers when they were asked how they worked with their children. In the cases of Selena and Jacinta, they tried to find extra time to attend English classes to be able to translate or understand what their children were being asked to do. With regard to this challenge, Selena had much to say:

> **Selena [AZ]:** "*O sea, porque hay cosas que él dice "mami, yo voy a hacer lo que yo, lo que yo entiendo"; hay cosas que me las, me dice "mami yo te voy a leer aquí a ver dime tú," y él me lo traduce en español, hay veces que le entiendo lo que me está diciendo en inglés, hay veces que definitivamente no le entiendo nada, por eso yo estoy yendo a clases de inglés, entonces, este, hay cosas, que le digo yo, "mi'jo, no pues no le entiendo aquí."*
>
> ["Like, because there are things that he, he says, 'Mommy, I will do what I, what I understand.' There are things he, he says to me, 'Mommy I will read to you, you tell me,' he translates to me in Spanish. Sometimes I understand what he is saying to me in English, sometimes I definitely, I do not understand anything. That is why I am studying English, but there are things that I have to tell him, 'Son, no, I just do not understand this.'"]

The parents in our study mentioned learning English as a challenge that was not easy to overcome because they had limited time to attend English classes. So, to help their children with homework, these mothers used a dictionary or turned to one of their older children who knew English. There was also the case of mothers like Jacinta and Selena, who took time from other obligations to take English classes and be more able to involve themselves in their children's school work.

The interviews with the parents in New Mexico did not reveal English as a barrier. Because of the bilingual education opportunity for these children, the parents in New Mexico were able to visit the classroom comfortably, observe the instructional strategies of the teacher, and read homework instructions and problem descriptions. One mother of a fifth-grade student talked about how she helped with homework, illustrating the power of parental engagement when there is a common language that connects home and school.

> **Bianca [NM]:** *"No, yo trato de ayudarle,* (inaudible), *cuál es la respuesta de la, le hago preguntas al mismo tiempo para que ella vaya relacionando el problema y sólo cuando de plano ya ella no entiende la forma pues yo le pongo fácil el problema para que ella ponga la respuesta. Un ejemplo nada más yo se lo hago y luego le ayudo a comprobarlo y ya que ella siga haciendo el resto. O sea, yo nada le digo cómo y ya después yo le checo los resultados."*
>
> ["No, I try to help her (inaudible), what is the answer of the ... I ask her questions at the same time so she can make connections to the problem and only when she doesn't understand, I make it easier so she can put the answer. I give her just one example and then I help her check this and then she does the rest. I only tell her how and then I check the answers."]

In Bianca's case, language was not a barrier because homework is done in both Spanish and English. As noted in the previous quote, she provided us with an example of the interaction when helping her daughter with mathematics homework.

English-Only: A major barrier for children whose first language is not English

Children of immigrant parents face many challenges in the adaptation process when they arrive in the United States. Not knowing English may be one of their biggest challenges. English-only instruction raises a number of issues for students: silent period, affective filter, bicultural ambivalence, and so on. Krashen's (1981) theory of silent period refers to new students learning a second language (English, in the case of the U.S.) and not speaking it or showing any competence for a period of up to six months after they enter school. Affective filter (Krashen, 1981) has to do more with anxiety, lack of self-confidence, and not being motivated to speak the new language. Cummins's theory of bicultural ambivalence, on the other hand, refers to a child being ashamed of his or her first language and hostile towards the second one (Crawford, 2004).

The interviews conducted in Arizona provided evidence of the emotional issues experienced by these children following the implementation of Proposition 203. Five out of 14 mothers expressed sentiments about the negative impact they perceived in their children's emotions. The fact that their children cried every day and wanted to go back to Mexico had a strong impact on Jacinta, who felt that she had to do something to help her children overcome that barrier. The following excerpt describes her feelings about her children's experience:

Jacinta [AZ]: "*No, primero estaban todos en inglés, y ya yo empecé a menearme y, dije, no, pues, pobrecitos, porque estaban bien traumados. Ya no querían ir a la escuela, se querían regresar para México, y era de todos los días, que lloraban . . . desesperados. Hasta ahora, dice la maestra que después de dos años, dice, "estoy muy contenta con Ramón porque ya se ríe". ¿Después de dos años se ríe? Le dije a la miss. "Yo no le conocía su risa". Y ahora está más contento en la escuela... Pero tuvieron que pasar dos años. Se me hace que es tiempo que se perdió.*"

["No, first they were all in English, and then I started being proactive and, I said, no, poor children, because they were traumatized. They didn't want to go to school anymore, they wanted to go back to Mexico, and it was every day that they cried . . . desperate. Until now, the teacher says that after two years, she says, 'I am very happy because Ramon is laughing.' After two years he is laughing? I replied to the [teacher], 'I didn't know his laughter.' And now he is much happier at school. But it was [not] until two years had passed. I think that it is time that was wasted."]

The frustration of Jacinta seeing her children struggling in school due to the language of instruction pushed her to advocate for them. She went beyond what engagement means for many school stakeholders; she knew that her children needed another kind of assistance and, in the end, managed to get them into a bilingual program that, for her, was the best solution. In addition to limited comprehension and wasted time, some parents are aware that communication with their children is reduced if they are not able to participate in school activities or if they do not speak the school's language of instruction.

We wonder about the potential loss in linguistic communication and its implications for the relationship between parents and children. Valenzuela (1999) wrote about subtractive schooling as encompassing "subtractive assimilationist policies and practices that are designed to divest Mexican students of their culture and language" (p. 20). As Worthy (2006) noted, "as linguistic connections with their families and roots fade, these children also face a loss of cultural knowledge, family values, personal nurturing, and academic support" (p. 140). On this topic, Olsen (2000) commented,

igrants are surprised and often discouraged by the contradictory pres-
es to become English speaking and the many roadblocks and barriers they
scover to developing that proficiency. They and their families are saddened
y the discovery, which comes too late, that becoming English fluent usually
is accompanied by a loss of home language use, fluency and development.
The longer immigrant students are in the United States, the greater is their
awareness of being caught in a power struggle over the use of English and
other languages. (p. 197)

Because of New Mexico's language policy in education, participants from
this state did not share the same frustration as the parents in Arizona. When
parents in New Mexico were asked how they would feel if their children
were in an English-only classroom, they expressed concern, relying on their
own experiences of not knowing English. Ana, one of the four interviewed
parents in New Mexico, offered this comment:

Ana [NM]: "*Radical, hubiera sido completamente, yo en mi experiencia,
como yo no hablo inglés, cuando me hablan en inglés yo me quedo*
(gestures shaking her head, with hands up to the sides,
expressing that she doesn't understand anything that is being said), '*No entiendo.*' *Y yo pienso que para mi hija sería muy,
muy, muy difícil porque su idioma es español. Ella no entendería,
imagino yo que ni 10 por ciento de las matemáticas.*"
["Radical, it would've been completely, I, in my own experience, because I do not speak English, when someone talks
to me in English I say (gestures shaking her head, with
hands upon to the side, expressing that she doesn't understand anything that is being said), 'I do not understand.' I
think that for my daughter, it would be very, very, very difficult because her language is Spanish. She wouldn't understand, I imagine that, not even 10% of the math."]

The risk of dropping out is another important issue attached to language educational policies such as the one implemented in Arizona. Our
interviews in Arizona with the two mothers who had children in high school
revealed how damaging English-only practices can be. Both Ruth and Selena, whose children had previously attended school in Mexico, seemed to
attribute their daughters' dropping out of school to the fact that they did
not fully understand English. The following brief exchange includes Ruth's
explanation:

Javier: "*Y con la más grande ¿Qué tal? ¿Cómo vivió el cambio desde allá?*"
["And, with the oldest one, how was her experience?"]

Ruth[AZ]: *"No, dice que le zumbaban hasta los oídos, y mejor se salió de la escuela, aparte que ella ya estaba en tercero en la prepa, y aquí si quería una carrera tenía que hacer sabe cuántos años de inglés, cuatro creo y la pusieron en primero."*

["No, she said that even her ears were ringing, and she decided to stop going to school. She was already in 11th grade, and if she wanted to go to college, she had to study who knows how many years of English, four I think. They put her in ninth grade."]

The first time we interviewed Selena, she expressed being concerned for not being able to help her daughter with her mathematics classes in high school. Although her daughter expressed having difficulties expressing or giving answers in English, Selena did not see it as a problem:

Javier: *"Y cuando ella pasó a estudiar aquí (from Mexico to Tucson), ella lo notó?"*

["And when she moved here (from Mexico to Tucson), did she notice the difference?"]

Selena [AZ]: *"No, ella sí batalló mucho... bastante batalló ella, pero le ha echado muchas ganas, ya con el favor de Dios el año que entra se gradúa... pero ella sí ha batallado bastante, mucho, mucho, ella... es que yo pienso que muchas veces es ya mas vergüenza porque ella entiende muy bien lo del inglés, pero muchas veces dice 'hay mamá no hallo como decirlo o dar la respuesta....'"*

["No, she struggled a lot... I struggle a lot with her, but she has put a lot of effort, thank God she is graduating next year... but she has struggled very much, a lot, a lot, she... but I think that many times is due to embarrassment because she understands very well English, but many times she says, 'Mom, I do not know how to say it or give the answer....'"]

By the time we conducted the second interview, almost three months later, Selena's daughter was working at a fast-food restaurant and had dropped out of school, but there was hope that her daughter would finish high school at another school. The fact that their children left school before graduating concerned Ruth and Selena. Ruth mentioned having conversations with her daughter and telling her that her life was going to be *"truncada"* (truncated) if she did not continue with school; her daughter thought it over and decided to take English classes. In the case of Selena, her daughter started to work in a fast-food restaurant with the idea to continue her courses at another school.

Bilingual Education: More Doors Open for Children

There is a large body of research that suggests that bilingual education programs in the United States are the most beneficial for children whose first language is not English. Thomas and Collier (2002) have conducted extensive longitudinal investigations with large populations of students in multiple settings. They stated without a doubt that it is bilingual education that gives Spanish-speaking children the best opportunity to be successful academically and make the successful transition to English. Parents in both settings (Arizona and New Mexico) reported their beliefs that bilingual education programs brought educational opportunities for their children, opening doors for their children to succeed in life. Even though many parents in Arizona did not experience bilingual education with their children, they shared the same opinion of those who did. Three of the four interviewed parents and one mother from the classroom observation debriefing in New Mexico talked about the impact of bilingual education in their children's learning:

> **Olivia [NM]:** "*Y ahora yo veo a mi niño (Kinder) y está en el mismo nivel tanto en español como en inglés. Que los dos idiomas, los habla bien. Y que los sistemas de las escuelas están super avanzados a comparación a cuando yo llegué [prepa]. Mi niño me sorprende porque digo, habla tanto en inglés como en español, tanto en matemáticas, y en la escuela. Tanto él entiende el problema en inglés como él entiende el problema en español.*"
> ["I now I see that my son [Kindergarten] is at the same level in Spanish as in English. That the two languages, he speaks both well, and that the system of schools is more advanced in comparison to when I came [high school]. My son surprises me because he speaks as much in English as in Spanish, in mathematics, and in the school. He understands as much of the problem in English as he understands the problem in Spanish."]

In the case of Arizona, except for Ruth, there were no parents whose children had previously experienced bilingual education because most mothers attending the workshops were recent immigrants. Ruth, whose older children had attended a bilingual school in California, expressed that it is good to be in mainstream classroom where the instruction is only in English, but only if they already know Spanish. The following excerpt captures this mother's thoughts about learning content in two languages:

Ruth [AZ]: *"Pues yo los tenía allá en un programa bilingüe, eh, pero decía que por ejemplo si ellos ya sabían bien correctamente el español..."*
["Well, there, I put them in a bilingual program, eh, but I said, for example, if they already knew well, the Spanish correctly..."]

Javier: *"Pero ¿Tú decidiste que estuvieran en programa bilingüe?"*
["But did you decide for them to be in a bilingual program?"]

Ruth: *"Sí, que fuera bilingüe y que, que, le hacen una prueba de transición se le llama de que si ya saben, le hacen la prueba en español que si ya sabe todo, todo lo de español va al inglés sólo inglés..."*
["Yes, that it would be bilingual and that, that, they give them a transition test [it] is called, if they already know, they test them in Spanish, if they already know everything in Spanish, they go to English, only English..."]

In the particular case of Ruth, her two older sons experienced bilingual education when they lived in California. At the time of our study, she had a daughter in first grade and a teenager who dropped out of school, citing language issues. It was clear to us that she supported bilingual education programs and believed they were good. She mentioned that children could move to English-only classrooms only if they had already mastered their first language—in her case, Spanish.

Bilingual education programs allow for a sustained connection with family and their linguistic and cultural background. Parents feel more comfortable helping their children if they understand what is being asked in the instructions for the homework. The fact that parents expressed a preference towards bilingual education programs was not because they did not want to learn English. Many of them said that it was difficult for them to learn English because of the diverse responsibilities around the house and their work schedules. As Worthy (2006) described, Latino parents in her study wanted to learn English but encountered many obstacles along the way. Some of these obstacles, Worthy pointed out, have to do with the structure of English instruction for adults. She wondered, "Is the current low priority placed on adult English learning, as opposed to the high priority for earlier immigrants, a (unintentional, unconscious) way to maintain the status quo in regard to the occupations and education of immigrants?" (p. 152).

DISCUSSION

Previous research suggests that there is a strong relation between parents' involvement in education and children's achievement at school (Elboj, Puigdellívol, Soler, & Carol, 2002). The parents in our study were committed to their children's success in school. Teachers and administrators often mention the need for parents to be involved in their children's education; the parents in our study wanted to be involved in their children's schooling and, by many measures, they were. But, particularly in the case of Arizona, the school language policy legislated in 2000 limited their opportunities to be involved.

In a language immersion approach, students first have to learn the official language of teaching and learning, and then they are allowed to learn subject material, including mathematics. In the approach adopted by Arizona, language becomes a barrier to academic success, forcing ELLs to lapse academically. It makes the effort to catch up almost impossible and makes the communication among children, parents, and schools much more difficult. Our findings indicate that parents from New Mexico were comfortable with their children's learning of mathematics and the fact that they were learning in both Spanish and English. They expressed a belief that they could help their children with homework, hence having further opportunities to engage with their children in talk about academic content. On the other hand, some parents in Arizona shared their frustration in trying to help their children who were receiving all instruction in English. This frustration affected not only the parents, but also their children.

Our overarching research goal was to document parents' perceptions about the teaching and learning of mathematics. As our findings show, parents' perceptions become cultural tools from a social and cultural perspective because parents use these tools as referents that mediate their response to their children's necessities in learning mathematics. When parents try to help their children, they often draw on their prior knowledge and experiences in mathematics (O'Toole & de Abreu, 2005). Civil and her colleagues have argued for the need for schools to recognize the experiences and backgrounds of families as resources towards their children's schooling (Civil & Andrade, 2002, 2003; Civil & Bernier, 2006; Civil & Quintos, 2009). These studies highlighted that education is not an individual process. Researchers and educators who believe that learning is an individual process have argued that ELLs have to learn English first, and then they will be ready to learn other school subjects. However, from our perspective, learning is a holistic process that involves not only individuals, but also their communities (Elboj et al., 2002; Flecha, 2000; Lave & Wenger, 1991; Moschkovich, 2006).

Our findings show that parents turn to their community to help their children with mathematics. Some of them try to make connections between mathematics and everyday situations. Others look at teachers as resources, and yet others look for resources in the community—for example, community centers. This search for outside assistance is especially the case in Arizona, where parents are often not familiar enough with the language of instruction. Further research should examine issues related to parents' access to networks of support or other resources in the community.

CONCLUSIONS

Latinos are now the largest minority group in the United States. Throughout their educational history to date, this group has faced discrimination— particularly Mexican and Mexican American students and their families. Language plays a role in this discrimination. As several authors have noted, low-income, minority students face a myriad of challenges in their schooling, including out-of-field teachers, schools without enough resources to address the needs of these students, and curricula or pedagogical approaches that reflect low expectations (Gutierrez, 2002; Ortiz-Franco & Flores, 2001; Peske & Haycock, 2006; Secada, Fennema, & Adajian, 1995; Tate, 1997).

In this chapter, we provided further evidence for the importance of language in the mathematics education of Latino students. States' language policies are a crucial factor that should be taken into account if we are to fight for a more inclusive education. Change does not happen overnight, but we think that it is our duty and responsibility to look for ways in which Latino parents can feel included as active members with the opportunities to help their children in their academic journey. As Civil (2002) pointed out in reflecting on her work with parents,

> I suggest that through an authentic two-way dialogue in which these different forms of discourses and knowledge (community knowledge, school knowledge) and their associated values are brought into the open for scrutiny, we may in fact have a route towards the transformation of the educational experience for all, but in particular of the groups that have consistently been left behind in the academic journey. (p. 146)

ACKNOWLEDGMENT

This research was supported in part by the National Science Foundation under Grant No. 0424983 to the Center for the Mathematics Education of Latinos/as (CEMELA). Any opinions, findings, and conclusions or recommendations expressed here are those of the authors and do not necessarily reflect the views of the National Science Foundation.

NOTES

1. The law allows bilingual education only for students who meet the following requirements: (1) they already know English, (2) they are over the age of 10, and (3) they have "special individual physical or psychological needs" (ARS 15-753, §B.3).

REFERENCES

Arizona Revised Statutes, Title 15, Article 3.1, §15-751-756 (ARS 15-75x). (2000).

Barton, A. C., Drake, C., Perez, J. G., St. Louis, K., & George, M. (2004). Ecologies of parental engagement in urban education. *Educational Researcher, 33*(4), 3–12. doi: 10.3102/0013189X033004003

Bilingual Multicultural Education Act of 2004, NMex. Stat. Ann. §§ 22 (1978 & Supp. 2010).

Bratton, J., Quintos, B., & Civil, M. (2004, March). *Collaboration between researchers and parents for the improvement of mathematics education.* Paper presented at the 1st Annual Binational Symposium of Education Researchers, Mexico City, Mexico.

Celedón-Pattichis, S. (2004). Research findings involving English-language learners and implications for mathematics teachers. In M. F. Chappell, J. F. Schielack, & S. Zagorski (Eds.), *Empowering the beginning teacher of mathematics in elementary school* (p. 45). Reston, VA: National Council of Teachers of Mathematics.

Civil, M. (2002). Culture and mathematics: A community approach. *Journal of Intercultural Studies, 23*(2), 133-148. doi: 10.1080/07256860220151050A

Civil, M. & Andrade, R. (2002). Transitions between home and school mathematics: Rays of hope amidst the passing clouds. In G. de Abreu, A. J. Bishop, & N.C. Presmeg (Eds.), *Transitions between contexts of mathematical practices* (pp. 149–169). Dordrecht, The Netherlands: Kluwer Academic.

Civil, M. & Andrade, R. (2003). Collaborative practice with parents: The role of the researcher as mediator. In A. Peter-Koop, V. Santos-Wagner, C. J. Breen, & A. Begg (Eds.), *Collaboration in teacher education: Examples from the context of mathematics education* (pp. 153–168). Dordrecht, The Netherlands: Kluwer Academic.

Civil, M. & Bernier, E. (2006). Exploring images of parental participation in mathematics education: Challenges and possibilities. *Mathematical Thinking and Learning, 8*(3), 309-330. doi: 10.1207/s15327833mtl0803_6

Civil, M., Bratton, J., & Quintos, B. (2005). Parents and mathematics education in a Latino community: Redefining parental participation. *Multicultural Education, 13*(2), 60–64. Retrieved from http://www.caddogap.com

Civil, M. & Planas, N. (2010). Latino/a immigrant parents' voices in mathematics education. In E. Grigorenko & R. Takanishi (Eds.), *Immigration, diversity, and education* (pp. 130–150). New York: Routledge.

Civil, M., Planas, N., & Quintos, B. (2005). Immigrant parents' perspectives on their children's mathematics. *Zentralblatt für Didaktik der Mathematik, 37*(2), 81–89. doi: 10.1007/BF02655717

Civil, M., & Quintos, B. (2006). Engaging families in children's mathematical learning: Classroom visits with Latina mothers. *New Horizons for Learning Online Journal, 12*(1). Retrieved from http://www.newhorizons.org/spneeds/ell/civil quintos.htm

Civil, M., & Quintos, B. (2009). Latina mothers' perceptions about the teaching and learning of mathematics: Implications for parental participation. In B. Greer, S. Mukhopadhyay, S. Nelson-Barber, & A. Powell (Eds.), *Culturally responsive mathematics education* (pp. 321–343). New York: Routledge.

Combs, M. C., Evans, C., Fletcher, T., Parra, E., & Jiménez, A. (2005). Bilingualism for the children: Implementing a dual-language program in an English-only state. *Educational Policy, 19*(5), 701–728. doi: 10.1177/0895904805278063

Crawford, J. (2004). *Education English learners: Language diversity in the classroom* (5th ed.). Los Angeles, CA: Bilingual Education Services.

Cummins, J. (2000). *Language, power and pedagogy: Bilingual children in the crossfire.* Clevedon, UK: Multilingual Matters.

Elboj, C., Puigdellívol, I., Soler, M., & Carol, R. V. (2002). *Comunidades de aprendizaje. Transformar la educación.* Barcelona: Graó.

Flecha, R. (2000). *Sharing words: Theory and practice of dialogic learning.* Lanham, MD: Rowman & Littlefield.

Flecha, R. & Gómez, J. (2004). Participatory paradigms: Researching "with" rather than "on." In M. Osborne, J. Gallacher, & B. Crossan, (Eds.), *Researching widening access: Issues and approaches in an international context* (pp. 129–140). London: Routledge.

Glaser, B. G. & Strauss, A. L. (1967). *The discovery of grounded theory: Strategies for qualitative research.* Chicago: Aldine.

Goldenberg, C. & Gallimore, R. (1995). Immigrant Latino parents' values and beliefs about their children's education: Continuities and discontinuities across cultures and generations. In P. R. Pintrich & M. L. Maehr (Eds.), *Advances in motivation and achievement* (Vol. 9, pp. 183–228). Greenwich, CT: JAI Press.

González, N., Moll, L. C., & Amanti, C. (Eds.). (2005). *Funds of knowledge: Theorizing practice in households, communities and classrooms.* Mahwah, NJ: Erlbaum.

Gutierrez, R. (2002). Beyond essentialism: The complexity of language in teaching mathematics to Latina/o students. *American Educational Research Journal, 39*(4), 1047–1088. doi: 10.3102/000283120390041047

Horvat, E. M., Weininger, E. B., & Lareau, A. (2003). From social ties to social capital: Class differences in the relations between schools and parent networks. *American Educational Research Journal, 40*(2), 319–351. doi: 10.3102/00028312040002319

Khisty, L. L. (2006). Language and mathematics: Toward social justice for linguistically diverse students. In J. Novotná, H. Moraová, M. Krátká, & N. Stehlíková

(Eds.), *Proceedings of the 30th Conference of the International Group for the Psychology of Mathematics Education* (Vol. 3, pp. 433–440). Prague: Charles University.

Khisty, L. L., & Chval, K. B. (2002). Pedagogic discourse and equity in mathematics: When teachers' talk matters. *Mathematics Education Research Journal, 14*(3), 154–168. Retrieved from http://www.merga.net.au/

Krashen, S. D. (1981). *Principles and practice in second language acquisition.* London: Prentice-Hall International.

Lareau, A. & Horvat, E. M. (1999). Moments of social inclusion and exclusion race, class, and cultural capital in family-school relationships. *Sociology of Education, 72*(1), 37–53. doi: 10.2307/2673185

Lave, J. & Wenger, E. (1991). *Situated learning: Legitimate peripheral participation.* Cambridge, UK: Cambridge University Press.

Moll, L. C., Amanti, C., Neff, D., & González, N. (1992). Funds of knowledge for teaching: Using a qualitative approach to connect homes and classrooms. *Theory Into Practice, 31*(2), 132–141. doi: 10.1080/00405849209543534

Moll, L. C. & Ruiz, R. (2002). The schooling of Latino children. In M. Suárez-Orozco & M. Páez (Eds.), *Latinos: Remaking America* (pp. 362–374). Berkeley: University of California Press.

Moschkovich, J. N. (1999). Understanding the needs of Latino students in reform-oriented mathematics classrooms. In L. Ortiz-Franco, N. G. Hernández, & Y. de la Cruz (Eds.), *Changing the faces of mathematics: Perspectives on Latinos* (pp. 5–12). Reston, VA: National Council of Teachers of Mathematics.

Moschkovich, J. N. (2002). A situated and sociocultural perspective on bilingual mathematics learners. *Mathematical Thinking and Learning, 4*(2-3), 189–212. doi: 10.1207/S15327833MTL04023_5

Moschkovich, J. N. (2004). Mathematics, language, and bilingual Latina/o learners: A review of the empirical research literature. Technical report for the National Center for Improving Student Learning and Achievement in Mathematics and Science (NCISLA), University of Wisconsin, Madison.

Moschkovich, J. N. (2007). Using two languages when learning mathematics. *Educational Studies in Mathematics, 64*(2), 121–144. doi: doi: 10.1007/s10649-005-9005-1

Olsen, L. (2000). Learning English and learning America: Immigrants in the center of a storm. *Theory Into Practice, 39*(4), 196–202. doi: 10.1207/s15430421tip3904_2

Ortiz-Franco, L. & Flores, W. V. (2001). Sociocultural considerations and Latino mathematics achievement: A critical review. In B. Atweh, H. Forgasz, & B. Nebres (Eds.), *Sociocultural research on mathematics education: An international perspective* (pp. 233–254). Mahwah, NJ: Erlbaum.

O'Toole, S. & de Abreu, G. (2005). Parents' past experiences as a mediational tool for understanding their child's current mathematical learning. *European Journal of Psychology of Education, 20*(1), 75–89. doi: 10.1007/BF03173212

Peske, H. G. & Haycock, K. (2006). *Teaching inequality: How poor and minority students are shortchanged on teacher quality.* Washington, DC: The Education Trust. Retrieved from http://www.edtrust.org/sites/edtrust.org/files/publications/files/TQReportJune2006.pdf

Quintos, B., Bratton, J., & Civil, M., (2005). Engaging with parents on a critical dialogue about mathematics education. In M. Bosch (Ed.), *Proceedings of the Fourth Congress of the European Society for Research in Mathematics Education* (pp. 1182–1192). Sant Feliu de Guíxols, Spain: Universitat Ram Llull.

Secada, W. G., Fennema, E., & Adajian, L. B. (Eds.). (1995). *New directions for equity in mathematics education.* Cambridge, UK: Cambridge University Press.

Stritikus, T. T. & Garcia, E. (2005). Revisiting the bilingual debate from the perspectives of parents: Policy, practice, and matches or mismatches. *Educational Policy, 19*(5), 729–744. doi: 10.1177/0895904805278068

Tate, W. F. (1997). Race-ethnicity, SES, gender, and language proficiency trends in mathematics achievement: An update. *Journal for Research in Mathematics Education, 28*(6), 652–679. doi: 10.2307/749636

Thomas, W. P. & Collier, V. P. (2002). *A national study of school effectiveness for language minority students' long-term academic achievement.* Santa Cruz, CA: Center for Research on Education, Diversity, and Excellence.

Valencia, R. R. (2002). "Mexican Americans don't value education!"—On the basis of the myth, mythmaking, and debunking. *Journal of Latinos and Education, 1*(2), 81–103. doi: 10.1207/S1532771XJLE0102_2

Valenzuela, A. (1999). *Subtractive schooling: U.S.-Mexican youth and the politics of caring.* Albany: State University of New York Press.

Van Manen, M. (1990). *Researching lived experience: Human science for an action sensitive pedagogy.* Albany: State University of New York Press.

U.S. Census Bureau. (n.d.a). *State and county quickfacts, Arizona.* Retrieved from http://quickfacts.census.gov/qfd/states/04000.html

U.S. Census Bureau. (n.d.b). *State and county quickfacts, New Mexico.* Retrieved from http://quickfacts.census.gov/qfd/states/35000.html

Worthy, J. (2006). Como si le Falta un Brazo: Latino immigrant parents and the costs of not knowing English. *Journal of Latinos and Education, 5*(2), 139–154. doi: 10.1207/s1532771xjle0502_5

CHAPTER 7

LATINO/A BILINGUAL ELEMENTARY STUDENTS POSE AND INVESTIGATE PROBLEMS GROUNDED IN COMMUNITY SETTINGS

Erin E. Turner, PhD
Maura Varley Gutiérrez, PhD
Department of Teaching, Learning & Sociocultural Studies,
The University of Arizona, College of Education

Javier Díez-Palomar
Departament de Didàctica de la Matemàtica i
de les Ciències Experimentals
Àrea de Didàctica de la Matemàtica
Universitat Autònoma de Barcelona

INTRODUCTION

Many young students experience the school curriculum as disconnected from their lives and experiences (Chazan, 2000; Moll & Ruiz, 2002; Nod-

Latinos/as and Mathematics Education, pages 149–174
Copyright © 2011 by Information Age Publishing
All rights of reproduction in any form reserved.

149

dings, 1993; Valenzuela, 1999). The largely abstract and decontextualized nature of school mathematics provides little indication of how students or their communities will benefit from the content they learn (Martin, 2000). This phenomenon is particularly true for low-income students of color, whose experiences, languages, and ways of knowing are marginalized by mainstream curricula (Ladson-Billings, 1998; Nieto, 1999; Tate, 1995).

In contrast to these findings, the student interview presented in Excerpt 7.1, captured during an interview (personal communication, May 22, 2007), describes one student's experience with mathematics in an after-school mathematics club. In the excerpt, Elías, a fourth-grade bilingual Latino student, reflected on his experiences participating in an after-school mathematics club. He commented on what he learned during a project that involved investigating a neighborhood custom auto shop.

> **Elías:** "Yeah, but uh, one thing—I thought, I really thought you were gonna like teach us, division, subtraction, and everything, but you guys teached me like the—you guys took me places and you teached me [how to measure] distance and told me what you can do when you are there."
>
> . . .
>
> **Maura:** "Ok. Um, what do you think you learned from doing [the auto shop] project? Think of some examples so you can tell me what you learned."
>
> **Elías:** "Um, how to measure things perfect. And how to measure—the distance, like how to [take a small drawing and] make it big."
>
> **Maura:** "What do you think helped you learn that stuff?"
>
> **Elías:** "Math, um, really everything. There's mostly math in everything."
>
> . . .
>
> **Maura:** "What makes you know that? Why do you think math is in everything? How do you know that?"
>
> **Elías:** "...all of—my whole family tells me. I just told them what I was doing [with the auto shop project] and they told me, 'Did you know that I [also] used to use math in something that I worked in?'"

This conversation illustrates the potential of mathematics learning experiences that draw upon community settings. These experiences not only supported this student's mathematical learning, but also his understanding of the relevance of mathematics in his life.

Research has also documented that students often separate their real-world knowledge and experience from classroom-based problem-solving activity (Gravemeijer, 1997; Reusser & Stebler, 1997; Verschaffel, de Corte, & Lasure, 1994). Unlike Elías, whose comments reflected a desire to connect his life experiences with the mathematics he learned in school, students often approach contextualized problems in a proceduralized manner, privileging efficiency and correct answers over sense making, and neglecting to consider the real-world viability of their solutions (Gravemeijer, 1997; Reusser & Stebler, 1997; Schoenfeld, 1991). Although students' actions make sense in settings that focus on contrived word problems, the tendency to exclude realistic considerations from problem-solving activity has limited value outside the classroom.

To address these issues, we agree with other researchers (Arcavi, 2002; Masingila, Davidenko, & Prus-Wisniowska, 1996) that *mathematization*, a practice involving the integration (rather than separation) of real-world understandings and mathematical understandings, needs to become a central part of school mathematics. In particular, we argue for mathematization that is rooted in real experiences and that serves personal as well as socially negotiated purposes, a practice we refer to as *community mathematization*. In this view of mathematization, participants (e.g., students, parents, community members, and/or researchers) contribute understandings and experiences as they collaboratively use mathematics as a tool to make sense of their worlds. We contend that the practice of community mathematization is uniquely positioned to support students' mathematical understanding because it simultaneously reinforces participants' membership in communities with often overlooked mathematically rich knowledge bases (Civil, 2002). Moreover, insofar as students mathematize contexts that are relevant to their lives, this practice has the potential to foster a greater connection to the discipline (Civil, 2002, 2007; Turner, 2003; Varley Gutiérrez, 2009b), which is important for students and communities whose experiences have been marginalized in Western mathematics classrooms (Gutiérrez, 2007).

In this chapter, we analyze the experiences of third- to fifth-grade Latino/a students ($n = 18$) as they mathematized activity occurring in local community settings during their participation in an after-school mathematics club. The authors, two postdoctoral researchers, and several undergraduate research assistants were the primary facilitators of the club. Our analysis focuses on the nature of the mathematical activity that occurred, with particular attention to (1) the kinds of questions and problems that were posed, (2) the role that realistic considerations played in posing and solving problems, and (3) the ways that facilitators and/or community members supported students' opportunities to learn mathematics. Additionally, we discuss tensions that emerged and how participants negotiated those tensions.

CONCEPTUAL FRAMEWORK:
COMMUNITY MATHEMATIZATION

In this section, we review literature that has informed our conceptualization and analysis of community mathematization in an after-school mathematics club. *Community mathematization* refers to activity in which participants collaboratively use mathematics to make sense of their worlds. This includes participants posing and solving problems, as well as investigating mathematical practices (their own and others') in familiar settings. The key features of community mathematization are as follows: mathematizing activity, authenticity, integration of community knowledge bases, opportunities to pose problems, and informal learning environments.

Mathematizing Activity

According to Treffers (1978) *mathematizing activity* involves both using mathematical tools to represent, organize, and solve real-world problems and situations (i.e., horizontal mathematization), as well as formalizing and generalizing one's approach (i.e., vertical mathematization). Freudenthal (1991) offered alternative explanations, noting that *horizontal mathematization* involves movement from real-world situations into the world of symbols, while *vertical mathematization* means operating within the world of mathematical symbols, concepts, and strategies. We see both levels of mathematization as important and agree that horizontal mathematization precedes vertical mathematization, "as a springboard from situations to their mathematical models—and no less important—as a way to legitimize and make explicit students' ad hoc strategies" (Arcavi, 2002, p. 21). For this reason, this analysis focuses on students' horizontal mathematizing activity.

Connecting mathematization to *authentic* settings in the school and local community is a second key feature of community mathematization. We use the term authentic to refer to activity "that takes as its starting point the interests, perspectives, desires, and needs of the students," and/or their communities (Buxton, 2006, p. 701; see also Barton, 1998; Eisenhart, 2001). For instance, students who are selecting a carnival game for a community fair might analyze the cost of running the game, the odds of winning, and the likely appeal to community members to inform their decision. Additionally, they may create mathematical models to predict the profit each game would generate. This behavior is in contrast to solving problems grounded in real-world contexts that, although realistic, may not be authentic from the standpoint of the learner (Moschkovich, 2002). That is, solving a contrived textbook problem that involves selecting the "best" (i.e., most profitable) game does not matter in the same way, nor require the same activation of tools and resources that selecting a game for an actual community carnival would. Although grounding mathematization in authentic problems may increase students' interest and engagement (Civil, 2002; Turner, 2003), we see its value as extending beyond motivation. In fact, research has shown that education grounded in authentic experiences has the potential to be transformative and enhance students' learning (Aubert, Duque, Fisas, & Valls, 2004; Civil, 2007; González, Moll, & Amanti, 2005; González, Moll, Tenery, Rendon, González, & Amanti, 1995; Skovsmose & Valero, 2001; Valenzuela, 1999, 2002).

A third key feature of community mathematization is that it enhances opportunities *to integrate community members and community knowledge bases.* For instance, Turner, Varley Gutiérrez, Simic-Muller, and Díez-Palomar (2009) found that when students redesigned a recently burned-down neighborhood park, their sensibilities related to the needs of community members had an impact on how they allocated the park space. A critical aspect of students' home and community-based knowledge is their experience with language (Gutiérrez, 2002; Gutstein, 2007). In the case of Latino/a students, many of whom live in bilingual communities and draw upon both English and Spanish to communicate and understand ideas (Moschkovich, 2002, 2005), situating mathematical activity in bilingual settings facilitates students' capacity to leverage both languages as resources.

Additionally, grounding mathematization in local situations allows students to investigate how members of their own communities use mathematics in their daily lives. Research has demonstrated that, in everyday practices, individuals engage mathematics in ways that are reasonable and reflect sense making (Carraher, Carraher, & Schliemann, 1985; Nuñez, Schliemann, & Carraher, 1993). They solve complex tasks in an efficient manner, pose their own problems, and invent procedures and solution strategies as needed (Lave, 1988). We contend that an important aspect of community mathematization is that it models how members of students' own communities use mathematics in ways that are strategic and purposeful (Simic-Muller, Turner, & Varley, 2009). In doing so, students' home and community-based knowledge is positioned as a resource to support learning, rather than a deficit to overcome (e.g., Civil, 1994, 1998, 2002, 2006; Flores, 1997; González, Andrade, Civil, & Moll, 2001; Gutiérrez, 2002; Khisty, 1997; Moschkovich, 1999, 2005).

A fourth key feature of community mathematization is that participants have *opportunities to pose their own problems.* Not only is problem posing central to the discipline of mathematics, but also it can increase students' engagement and motivation (Winograd, 1991) and facilitate productive orientations towards the discipline (Silver, 1994). That said, classroom-based research has found that when students pose problems, they often fail to attend to real-world considerations, and the problems they pose reflect a narrow range of mathematical ideas (i.e., single-step operations) (English, 1997; Silver, 1994; Silver & Burkett, 1994). One intervention that has supported students in posing a broader range of problems is the use of realistic contexts (English, 1997). Given that community mathematization is grounded in settings that are realistic and familiar, we propose that it has the potential to support students' problem-posing capacity.

A final feature of community mathematization is that it occurs in *informal learning environments*, such as after-school programs, community centers, and neighborhood locations. In general, informal learning environments are characterized by curricular flexibility (i.e., ability to engage in extended projects and use multiple languages). Additionally, these settings often involve collaborative activities that integrate community members' perspectives, a feature that was essential to our work (see also Vásquez, 2003; Vomvoridi-Ivanovic, Simic-Muller, Varley Gutiérrez, Morales, & Díez-Palomar, 2007). We recognize that the informal, collaborative nature of the after-school setting allows for a unique kind of learning environment, one that may help students shift their beliefs about the relevance of community-based, real-world knowledge (de Corte, Verschaffel, & Greer, 2000).

Tensions Related to Community Mathematization

Although we see community mathematization as a generative practice that positions students as members of communities with mathematically rich knowledge bases and fosters sense making and problem posing as valuable mathematical tools, we acknowledge that tensions may arise. Exploring these tensions and how they are negotiated is one of the aims of our work. For example, identifying the mathematics in everyday practices is challenging (González et al., 2001) and, due to the inherent complexity of real-world contexts, problems generated from these contexts often involve reductions of reality, which may undermine the authenticity of those problems (Gravemeijer, 1997; Reusser & Stebler, 1997). Additionally, repeated experiences solving contrived word problems lead many students to conclude that real-world considerations are irrelevant to doing and learning mathematics (Gravemeijer, 1997). Finally, research has documented that designing projects that build on community knowledge and at the same time address rigorous mathematical content is challenging (Civil, 2007). In this report, we focus on these tensions and others related to the mathematical activity that occurred as students engaged in community mathematization.

In the sections that follow, we describe our research setting and methods and then report findings related to (1) the kinds of questions and problems participants posed as students engaged in community mathematization, (2) the role that realistic considerations played in posing and solving problems, and (3) the ways that facilitators supported students' opportunities to learn mathematics. We conclude with a discussion of tensions and implications for the design and research of mathematics learning environments.

METHOD, SETTING, AND PARTICIPANTS

Method

Our research is based on an after-school mathematics club (math club) facilitated by CEMELA[1] researchers for three years. The math club took place at Agave Elementary School,[2] which is located in a primarily Mexican/Mexican American neighborhood of a southwestern U.S. border city. Many of the Latino/a residents of this neighborhood are recent immigrants from Mexico, while others have lived here for generations. The school's student population is predominantly Latino/a (91%), as are many of the teachers, staff, and administrators. At Agave, 98% of the students qualify for free or reduced-price lunch, and 26% are classified as English language learners (personal communication, school district personnel, September 18, 2007). Due to state legislation having virtually eliminated bilingual education (Proposition 2033 [Arizona Revised Statutes 15-751-755]),[3] English language learner students are placed in structured English immersion classrooms. The result is that students who are talented bilinguals or predominant Spanish speakers are being limited from drawing upon their home language as a resource in school.

Participants

The math club met twice a week and participants included approximately 18 third- through sixth-grade students, four undergraduate facilitators, and five participant researchers (who were also math club facilitators). Participants were recruited through a brief announcement in their classrooms, in which we emphasized that we were inviting any interested students, regardless of how they felt about mathematics. In addition, the classroom teachers encouraged students with multiple levels of mathematical experience to participate. Because of our recruitment procedure and because students came from third through sixth grade, participants' mathematical skills varied. Their beliefs about themselves as learners also varied: some were in the math club because they liked mathematics and others because they felt they needed to improve.[4] The students were all Latino/a (some part-Native American), mostly Spanish-English bilinguals with varying levels of proficiency in each language.

After-School Setting

Like many after-school programs that have proven successful for low-income students from nondominant communities (e.g., Rahm, Martel-Reny, & Moore, 2005; Vásquez, 2003), the program was nonremedial, centered in students' lived experiences, and characterized by curricular flexibility. Math club sessions involved small group activities such as games or cooperative puzzles and extended projects that stretched over 10 to 12 sessions, one of which is the focus of this chapter.

Project Background

In the project highlighted here, students selected and investigated familiar community settings including (1) a neighborhood *panadería* (donut shop/bakery), (2) a custom auto shop that converted standard vehicles to "low-riders," (3) a *dulcería* that sold candies and piñatas, and (4) a neighborhood park that had recently burned down. The aim of students' investigations, which they conducted in small groups facilitated by an adult, were threefold. First, students worked to *understand the routine practices* of each setting, specifically the mathematics involved. To support this aim, students made repeated visits to each location. They had opportunities to observe and interview community members who worked in each site, and to audio- and/or videotape their interactions.

Second, students leveraged their increasing familiarity with a setting to *pose and investigate an authentic problem*. In some instances, the problems students posed closely mirrored the problems that community members described as part of their daily work (e.g., how to enlarge a small artists' sketch to create a design that would fill the hood of a car, or how to calculate the profit earned from selling a piñata). In other cases, students' conversations with community members engendered related problems (e.g., how to design a case to effectively display a large number of donuts). Third, each group of students created a *multimedia digital story*[5] that highlighted what they learned through their visits and the problems that they posed.

DATA COLLECTION AND ANALYSIS

All after-school sessions were videotaped and selected clips fully transcribed. For the purposes of this analysis, clips were chosen because they evidenced (1) students making sense of the practices of a given community setting (i.e., asking community members in that site about their practices, enacting the practices themselves in the after-school math club, discussing what they observed in the site); (2) students posing and solving problems related to the site; or (3) tensions that emerged related to mathematical activity. Tensions were identified as instances in the data similar to those found in the literature, or when the mathematical activity was somehow an adaptation of the activity in the setting, as discussed in Setting and Participants. A total of 50 clips that spanned 18 separate math club sessions were selected for in-depth analysis. Clips represented an entire exchange related to a similar topic of conversation with an average length of six minutes.

Each of the 50 transcripts was coded using a computer-based qualitative research tool. Codes attended to issues such as the nature of the problems students posed, how students engaged the problems (i.e., mathematically, nonmathematically), and the actions of facilitators as they supported students' mathematization. To refine our coding scheme and establish interrater reliability, researchers worked in pairs to code subsets of the transcripts and then the group of five researchers met to discuss and resolve any discrepancies in how each pair applied the codes. Following this step, adjustments were made to our code list and relevant portions of all transcripts recoded. After inconsistencies in how various members of the research team coded the data were minimized, each of the remaining transcripts was coded by one researcher (all researchers participated in this final round of coding). Finally, we identified patterns within instances of a given code and relationships between different codes, which formed the themes reported in our findings (Erlandson, Harris, Skipper, & Allen, 1993).

FINDINGS

We begin this section with an overview of students' mathematizing activity, and then present findings related to (1) the problems students posed, (2) the role that realistic considerations played in posing and solving problems, and (3) how facilitators supported students' opportunities to learn.

Overview of Students' Mathematizing Activity

Following multiple opportunities to visit sites, interview employees, and observe employees' daily practices, students collaborated to pose and investigate an in-depth problem related to each site. For example, students who had visited the *panadería* (bakery/donut shop) decided to design a donut case that would allow customers to easily view a range of donuts. Students investigating the *dulcería* (candy store) made a piñata, which involved scaling down a flour paste recipe and calculating a fair price and potential profit based on labor and costs. A third group, presented in Example Project, posed problems related to the practices of artists at a neighborhood custom auto shop that specialized in converting standard automobiles to low-riders.

Example Project: Enlarging a Design to Fit the Hood of a Car

After an initial visit to the shop, students wanted to learn more about how airbrushed images were designed and then transferred to cars. In posing this problem, Elías alluded to the need for precision, asking, "How do they make the paintings are they sure . . . how are they sure is it big enough [to fit on a car]?" Another student, Giselle, posed similar questions about the process of enlarging and transferring designs during an interview with the auto shop owner.

> **Giselle:** "*¿Cuándo hacen el diseño en el papel, cómo saben de que tamaño va a ser en el carro?*"
> ["When they do the design on the paper, how do they know what size it will be on the car?"]
>
> **Dan:** "*Lo que hacemos es medimos la área donde va a estar el diseño y luego de las medidas esas, hacemos el diseño para que le queda al carro. Primero medimos el carro y que tan grande puede ser el diseño.*"
> ["What we do is we measure the area where the design will be and then from those measurements, we do the design so that it will fit on the car. First we measure the car and how big the design can be."]

In this exchange, Giselle articulated her question in Spanish, and thus her use of her home language supported her active participation in her group's investigation. In fact, in each of the sites, students and community members frequently communicated in both Spanish and English, a practice that validated students' home languages and expanded the resources they could draw upon to articulate their understandings and make sense of the situations. This use of both languages stood in stark contrast to the students' classroom-based experiences, which were characterized by few, if any, opportunities to draw upon languages other than English.

In a subsequent visit, students again asked about the process of transferring an image to a car. One artist explained that they often used tools such as copy machines to enlarge designs:

> It's actually really simple. They start sometimes with a small design and what they'll do is they'll blow it—they'll go to Kinko's . . . and Kinko's will do a lot of things for you, and they will blow it up as far as for artists when they're painting. . . . They'll blow up the whole image much, much bigger.

As the quote captured during the subsequent visit demonstrates, community members often did not articulate the mathematics involved in a practice beyond general descriptions such as "we measure the hood of the car" or "they'll go to Kinko's" (see also Civil, 2002). Sometimes, this omission was because the mathematical work was accomplished with tools such as a machine or a computer. However, both facilitators and community members recognized that scaling was an important part of the process and suggested that students design a small image and then enlarge it—without the assistance of a copy machine—to better understand the mathematics involved.

Students began by designing an image on an 8½ × 11-inch sheet of paper. Next, the students were asked to enlarge their designs so that the designs filled a sheet of poster paper that was comparable to the size of the hood of a car. In the dialogue presented in Excerpt 7.1, Elías began to make sense of how proportional reasoning might apply in this context.

Excerpt 7.1. Proportional reasoning

> **Elías:** "You know you have to measure."
> **Maura:** "Measure what?"
> **Elías:** "What's 7 plus 7?"
> **Maura:** "You know, don't you?"
> **Elías:** "14, so I need another ruler." (14 inches only reaches about 2/3 of the paper's width)
> **Maura:** "Show me what you are measuring?"
> **Elías:** "Check this out. What's 3 times 7?"
> **Maura:** "Why are you—what's—why are you asking about those numbers? Where do those numbers come from?"
> **Elías:** "Three times—what is 3 times 7? Just—Miss, what is it?"
> **Maura:** "Twenty-one."
> **Elías:** "It has to be 21." (lining up two rulers)
> **Maura:** "Oh, what was 7? Elías, did this measure 7 inches?" (pointing to the width of his drawing)
> **Elías:** "Yeah."
> **Maura:** "So you're doing—you're saying it's going to be 3 times bigger?"
> **Elías:** "Yup. So this is how long it's supposed to be." (Elías is visually estimating that making his design three times wider would almost fill the width of the poster paper.)

Despite the fact that Elías did not enlarge his design in exactly the same way that the artists did (e.g., relying on Kinko's), he reenacted the practice in a way that highlighted the mathematics involved. We defined this process as a *modified reenactment* because Elías was enacting a modified version of the artist's practices (i.e., enlarging a drawing with measurements rather than at Kinko's). Given the often implicit nature of mathematics in community members' practices, we found that *modified reenactments*, such as this one, were critical to supporting students' understanding of the mathematics. Following this example of one group's mathematizing activity, we next present the results of our analysis across all groups' investigations.

Types of Mathematical Problems Students Encountered

As students mathematized familiar community situations, participants posed a variety of problems. In this section, we report on the mathematical content of the problems posed by students, facilitators, and community members.

Mathematical Problems Posed by Facilitators or Community Members

Across the 50 episodes analyzed, facilitators posed a total of 68 mathematical problems for students to investigate. In some instances, facilitators posed multiple problems about the same context (e.g., "How many round, glazed donuts could you fit in one box?" "What about the rectangular-shaped donuts, how many could you fit in one box?"). The problems were often related, given that they each had the potential to elicit a solution, but we counted them separately.

Although the problems reflected a range of mathematical ideas, problems involving computation with whole numbers ($n = 24$, or 35% of total) or measurement ($n = 25$, or 36% of total) were most common (see Table 7.1). For instance, after visiting the *panadería*, the facilitator asked students whether it would be a better deal to purchase seven individual donuts (one for each member of the group) or a dozen donuts. A relatively small number of problems ($n = 10$, or 15% of the total problems) addressed more sophisticated mathematical concepts such as proportional reasoning, or the construction of mathematical models (i.e., equations that accounted for the relative impact of multiple factors). As an example of a proportional reasoning problem, students making a *piñata* scaled down a flour paste recipe from the *dulcería* that called for 3 cups of water for every 2 cups of flour. Because the students planned to make a smaller *piñata*, the facilitator asked the students to figure out how much water would be needed if only 1 cup of flour was used.

We suspect that the predominance of problems involving computation ($n = 24$) or measurement ($n = 28$) reflected the fact that it was easier for community members to articulate and/or for facilitators to identify how more basic mathematical ideas related to the practices of each site. Part of this tension could be that the facilitators were not familiar with the practices that occurred at the site, making it challenging for them to understand the more complex mathematics that was happening. Consistent with Civil's

TABLE 7.1 Mathematical Content of Problems Posed by Facilitators or Community Members

Mathematical content	Sample problem	# of problems[a]	% of total[b]
Single-step computation	If you want to put 4 trays on the shelf and it is 16 cm wide, *about* how wide should each tray be?	17	25%
Multistep computation	If you only wanted 7 donuts, would it be better to buy just the individual donuts or to buy the whole dozen?	7	10%
Geometry/ measurement: Linear	What are the dimensions of your design? How wide? How tall?	20	29%
Geometry/ measurement: Area, volume	If you stack the donuts on top of each other, how many would fit in this box? Would a dozen fit?	8	12%
Proportional reasoning	If you need 3 c of water for 2 c of flour, how much water do you need for 1 c of flour?	8	12%
Average	You each measured [the length] and got 3 different numbers. How can we average those numbers to come up with one group measurement?	3	4%
Construct a mathematical model	How much should you charge for a *piñata* to make a reasonable profit?	2	3%
Other	Problems addressed counting, rounding, estimation, factors, or divisibility.	6	9%
Total problems		68	

[a] Total exceeds 68 because several problems addressed more than one mathematical concept or procedure.
[b] All percents rounded to the nearest whole number.

(2007) research, despite the fact that some (but not all) facilitators had an extensive mathematics background, it was still a challenge to mathematize unfamiliar practices. The tendency to pose more basic problems may also have been related to assumptions about appropriate content for elementary age students.

Mathematical Problems Posed by Students

Students also posed a range of problems ($n = 28$) about the settings they investigated. As shown in Table 7.2, the majority (71%) of the problems involved basic mathematics, such as counting (39%) or single-step computation (32%). For example, students asked numerous questions about

TABLE 7.2   Mathematical Content of Problems Posed by Student

Mathematical content	Sample problem	# of problems[a]	% of total[b]
Counting/quantifying	How many trees are there in the park?	11	39%
Single-step vomputation	What if she had 10 dozen donuts, how many would that be?	9	32%
Multistep computation	I wanted to know how long it would take for 3 students to each have 3 turns on the slide?	5	18%
Measurement: Linear	If we measure the trays [width], we can see [how many] fit inside the case.	5	18%
Measurement: Area	I was thinking how many basketball courts could fit in the [open area at the park]?	1	4%
Total problems		28	

[a] Total exceeds 28 because several problems addressed more than one mathematical concept or procedure.
[b] All percents rounded to the nearest whole number.

the prices of items or the number of items in a store (e.g., "How many [donuts] are in there [the display case]?"). Although students also posed problems that involved multistep computation ($n = 5$), none involved more sophisticated mathematics such as proportional reasoning or constructing mathematical models. These findings are consistent with previous research that has documented the limited nature of young children's problem posing (English, 1997). That said, we contend that the quantity and range of problems posed, although narrow, reflects the power of community settings to generate problem-posing activity.

Questions with Mathematical Potential

In addition to the mathematical problems posed, we found that facilitators and students asked numerous questions aimed at better understanding the practices at each site. While these questions did not include specific problems to solve, they were coded as having "mathematical potential" because they aimed to generate information about the mathematics used in community settings, or to focus students' attention on mathematical aspects of a situation. For example, facilitators working with the auto shop group posed questions such as, "How do you choose what size drill to use?" and "How do you know how much paint to mix?" Because the questions reflected the potential of community settings to support mathematical activity, we incorporated them in our analysis, including whether or not they were taken up in ways that highlighted mathematical ideas or practices.

Across the 50 episodes analyzed, facilitators posed a total of 33 questions with mathematical potential, and students posed 35, most often directed to community members during their visits. Unlike the problems discussed in Mathematical Problems Posed by Students, these questions represented a broad range of mathematical ideas. For example, a relatively small percentage (21% for facilitators and 37% for students) addressed basic mathematics such as counting or single-step computation, while we identified 12 questions (18%) that related to factors that might be included in a mathematical model.

Our analysis also attended to whether questions were taken up in ways that made explicit reference to mathematical ideas. We found that almost half of the questions fell into this category, while the remaining elicited responses that either alluded to (but did not make explicit) mathematical ideas, or responses that were clearly nonmathematical. For example, when a bakery shop employee was asked about the donuts customers buy, she replied by quantifying a typical purchase, "People, they'll come and get dozens at a time, or usually they get at least a dozen. And then, some [will buy] a few here and there. But usually they'll buy the dozen." We interpreted this response as including an explicit reference to mathematical ideas (i.e., ideas related to quantity) and thereby supporting mathematical activity. For instance, students could use information about a typical purchase to solve problems they posed (e.g., "About how many donuts are sold in a day?").

Other questions posed to community members were taken up in ways that alluded to, but did not make explicit, mathematical ideas. This situation often occurred when questions related to practices where the mathematics was implicit, or even hidden (see also Civil, 2007). For example, when an auto shop employee was asked how the shop determined selling prices for low-rider cars, he alluded to factors that might have an impact on the sales price (e.g., "depends how rare it is" and "how much of a demand there is for it"), but refrained from articulating a specific mathematical model. We suspect that responses like this one, where community members mention factors that have an impact on their decision making but do not describe the relative importance of and/or relationship between those factors, reflect the fact that explicit mathematical models may not be an important part of the everyday practices. Determining the sales price for a custom vehicle is inherently complex and employees may need to attend to multiple factors (i.e., time, artwork, materials, and so on) but on a case-by-case basis or in ways that keeps the mathematics implicit.

In the sections that follow, we discuss additional findings related to the role of real-world considerations and facilitator moves that "pushed" the mathematics.

The Role of Realistic Considerations in Students' Mathematical Investigations

Across the 50 clips included in our analysis, we identified 14 episodes when students drew upon realistic, real-world consideration as they discussed, solved, or evaluated solutions for mathematical problems. We defined an episode to be a sustained interaction among students and sometimes facilitators about a specific problem. These episodes occurred at multiple sites (e.g., the bakery, the *dulcería*, the custom auto shop), and in all cases were supported by students' familiarity with each site. That is, students either leveraged knowledge they had gained by visiting the site and interviewing community members, or prior knowledge from family and community interactions. For example, as students estimated profits earned by selling *piñatas*, they drew on their own prior experiences making *piñatas* (i.e., they knew that *piñatas* needed to dry overnight before adding more layers of paper maché) as well as conversations with the *dulcería* owner about the supplies needed and the time involved, and used this information to inform their estimates.

In 11 of the 14 episodes, facilitators made explicit moves to encourage students to draw upon real-world considerations. In some instances, facilitators made the problems about students, their friends, and families, which may have facilitated students' capacity to leverage real-world considerations. As an example, when students who had visited the donut shop discussed whether it was a better deal to buy single donuts or a dozen, a facilitator posed the following questions: "OK, Let's say that you, we're gonna go in today. OK, and you had six friends. Tomás, so if you wanted to buy a donut for each friend, how many donuts would you need to buy?"

Another way in which facilitators supported students in integrating real-world considerations with their mathematical activity was to create opportunities for students to reenact practices from the site (e.g., creating a *piñata*, enlarging a drawing to fit the hood of a car). For instance, as students designed and built a model of a donut display case, they considered issues such as how to strategically place the donuts and trays so that a wide variety of donuts would be visible to customers. One student, Carlos, considered the importance of displaying as many donuts as possible, saying he would place the trays in a certain way, "so more of [the trays] could fit. More donuts [on display], more money." Considering the realities of a business, he realized that it would matter to the store owner to place the donuts so as to maximize profit. He decided to use a combination of small trays on the top shelves of the case, each with a different kind of donut, and then larger trays with extra donuts on the bottom shelves of the case (the purpose of these trays would be to restock the smaller trays). If he had not considered the realities of the setting, he might have simply said that all trays could be the same size, eliminating the need to consider how trays of various sizes could be interchanged in the same case.

Finally, the most common move facilitators used to encourage students to attend to realistic considerations was to pose a question or make a comment that directed students' attention to a particular factor in the problem. Continuing with the example of students who built a model donut display case, when students were determining how to construct shelves on their model, the facilitator encouraged students to think about whether angled or flat shelves would make it easier for customers to see the donuts: "Tell me how you would be able to see the donuts better. Will you be able to see them better if I put it like that [places paper tray flat] or like that [places paper tray slanted towards customer]?" By considering the need for a business to display goods, the students engaged in a rich discussion about the optimal angle for shelves in the case (optimal meaning that the shelf was tilted enough so that customers could see most if not all of the donuts, and yet flat enough that donuts did not slide into one another).

We emphasize that students drew upon real-world considerations not only because the integration of real-world understandings and mathematical understandings was central to the practice of community mathematization, but also to highlight the various ways in which that real-world considerations had an impact on and shaped the mathematics that occurred. We found that understandings about reality had an impact on how students approached problems, including the mathematical models they generated, as well as how they evaluated their own solutions and those of other students. For example, students who investigated the rebuilding of a neighborhood park created a model that described how long it would take a given number of children to each have a turn on the swings.

Various real-world understandings informed their model, such as knowledge of how many children visit the park on a typical weekend. Peers evaluating their model also drew on realistic considerations, such as variance in how long children swing and the fact that some children may want to swing "again and again and again," to shape their comments. Given that previous research has documented that students often separate real-world knowledge from problem-solving activity (Reusser & Stebler, 1997; Verschaffel et al., 1994), we see these as examples of the power of familiar, community-based situations to facilitate mathematization.

Role of the Facilitator in Pushing the Mathematics

To understand how facilitators supported students' opportunities to learn, we identified facilitator moves that were intended to highlight or push the mathematics. The most common move, and one that is widely supported in the research on teaching mathematics (Franke, Kazemi, & Battey, 2007), was to ask questions aimed at eliciting and/or clarifying students' mathematical thinking. For example, when Elías was enlarging his drawing for the hood of a car, the facilitator asked him to explain what each measurement represented. This request for clarification often occurred when students engaged in mathematics but implicitly, and presumably was aimed at helping students articulate the mathematics involved in solving a problem.

Other moves that facilitators used to push the mathematics included (1) restating and mathematically refining a problem a student posed; (2) asking students to attend to quantity and space in their observations (e.g., time, measurements, prices, amounts, and so on); (3) pushing students to represent real-world situations symbolically, and to connect their symbolic work with real-world referents; and (4) introducing factors or terms that made students' problems more mathematically complex. As an example of a facilitator move that encouraged students to attend to quantity and space in their observations, when students were investigating how many trays would fit on each shelf of their model case, the facilitator asked how measurement might help them to make trays that were equal-sized and equidistant from each other. One example of how facilitators introduced factors that increased the mathematical complexity of students' problems is an instance when a student posed a problem about how long it would take to convert a car to a low-rider. In response, the facilitator suggested that students consider a variety of factors, such as number of workers, the time required for each artistic process, the number of changes involved, and so on.

To understand the impact of these facilitator moves on students' mathematical activity, for each of the clips included in our analysis, we traced what occurred directly following the various facilitator moves (i.e., moves that were coded as facilitators attempting to push the mathematics in some way). About half of the time (i.e., in 56 out of 115 coded instances), these facilitator moves led to additional mathematical activity. Just as often, students seemed to ignore the facilitator and/or explicitly resisted more mathematical ways of engaging a problem. When the facilitator pushed students to measure trays for their display case, the student insisted the workers could just "put [trays] until it's all full." However, closer analysis revealed that students' resistance was often reasonable. They sometimes approached problems with pragmatic, everyday solutions that although imprecise, were sufficiently effective to solve the pragmatic problem.

Tension arose because the facilitator's response was typically to push students to be more mathematically exact, when precision may not have been necessary to solve the pragmatic problem. For example, as students mixed flour and water to make paper maché for the *piñata*, the facilitator pushed them to use proportional reasoning to scale down the recipe. As the facilitator repeatedly posed this problem, students resisted her request to calculate the proportions and simply observed the mixture and added water until it reached a desired consistency, a perfectly logical and practical approach to the problem of making the mixture. In this case, although proportional reasoning would have resulted in a more exact solution, it simply was not necessary (see also Lave, 1988; Schoenfeld, 1998). There is strategic value in knowing when one needs to be precise (e.g., use proportional reasoning or exact measurement) and when estimation is sufficient.

CONCLUSIONS

Our aim in this report was to analyze the mathematical activity that occurred as students investigated several community settings, with particular attention to (1) the questions and problems that were posed by students, facilitators, and community members; (2) the role that realistic considerations played in posing and solving problems; and (3) the ways in which facilitators supported students' opportunities to mathematize. We found that while facilitators and students posed mathematical problems on an ongoing basis, the content of the problems was mathematically limited, most often requiring basic mathematics such as single-step computation or linear measurement. This result is not surprising, given the overemphasis on this type of mathematics in elementary curricula, nor is the fact that the problems reflected a somewhat narrow view of the practices in each site. However, given that prior research has noted the limited nature of young children's problem posing (English, 1997), we find it significant that at least some problems addressed more advanced ideas such as mathematical modeling.

Equally important is that students asked questions that had the potential to generate a broad range of mathematical activity. These finding are worth noting because they reflect the often overlooked mathematical richness of Latino/a students' communities, and the often underestimated capacity of young students to mathematize their worlds. Moreover, they suggest that through community mathematization, students can become "producers of mathematical practices" (González et al., 2001, p. 130), contributing to the discipline and countering traditional patterns of marginalization (Gutiérrez, 2007).

That said, although some of these questions were taken up in ways that highlighted mathematical ideas, in many instances, the mathematical potential remained relatively unexplored. As previous research has noted, the mathematical ideas that shape familiar practices are often difficult to recognize (see also Civil, 2002; Díez-Palomar, 2004; González et al., 2001; Niss, 1995). In our work, there were instances when the mathematics was so implicit in the day-to-day practices (e.g., auto shop artists who sent drawings to a copy shop to be enlarged) that although there was a *potential* to generate rich mathematical activity, substantial work was required to make the mathematics more explicit. To address this tension, facilitators helped students reenact modified versions of community members' practices—versions that made the mathematics more explicit.

We also observed other tensions. Even when the mathematics involved in community practices was easily recognizable, there was no guarantee that it would be accessible to elementary-age students. For example, students' interest in understanding issues of hydraulics to understand wheel and rim choices on low-riders generated an authentic need for rigorous mathematics, but the mathematics that was needed (e.g., understanding the relationship between the size of the tires and the gear ratios) was beyond the mathematics instruction that students had received. When this situation was encountered, facilitators sometimes reduced the complexity of the real-world situation, which, although useful in terms of making the mathematics more accessible, compromised the authenticity of the problems (see also Varley Gutiérrez, 2009a).

Finally, as we analyzed the questions posed by students and the comments made by community members, we recognized that it was much easier to identify the mathematical potential in retrospect (Civil, 2002). In other words, the "in-the-momentness" of this work—visiting community sites and asking questions about practices and situations as they arose—made it challenging to anticipate potential mathematical connections and even more so, to be prepared to support students' understanding of those connections. Clearly, the facilitator played a critical role, and in numerous instances, was able to call students' attention to important mathematical ideas.

Despite these tensions, our analysis uncovered the power of community mathematization to engage students in collaborative learning experiences, draw on their interests and experiences, and in doing so, support mathematical activity. In particular, students and members of their community were positioned as experts who had unique experiences, understandings, and sensibilities to share. Unlike traditional school mathematics, which often marginalizes students' community-based experiences (Tate, 1995), in the projects discussed here, students' interests and intentions served as an entry point to mathematical activity. We contend that this level of authenticity could not have been achieved by simply including more realistic problems in the school curriculum. Classroom word problems, as realistic as they may be, are always reductions of reality, and as such, are prone to the separation of real-world understandings and mathematical understandings that so often characterizes mathematics learning in school (Gravemeijer, 1997).

Finally, we argue that mathematization grounded in relevant community settings has the potential to help students redefine their *understanding of* and *relationship to* the discipline and to better appreciate the relevance and value of mathematics in their lives. While systematically documenting students' orientations towards the discipline was not a focus of this research, informal interactions with students suggested that numerous math club participants shared Elías's perspective that "math is in everything." Future research could examine the sustained impact, if any, of community mathematization on students' beliefs about mathematics and its relation to their lives.

This work has a number of implications for educators and researchers in mathematics education. To begin, further research is needed to understand how these experiences could inform school-based mathematics learning. For example, what features of classroom instruction might help students to integrate real-world understandings and mathematical understandings as they solve problems? How can teachers create classroom learning environments that reflect the authentic, collaborative, and purposeful nature of mathematical activity in community settings (Civil, 2002)? Additionally, while our findings highlight the potentially generative nature of community mathematization, future work might more closely explore the tensions that arise, and how they are navigated. Finally, our work provides one model for connecting mathematics instruction to students' communities in meaningful ways, a model that can be shared with teachers who are preparing to teach our increasingly diverse student population.

ACKNOWLEDGMENT

This manuscript is an adaptation of a paper originally presented at the Annual Meeting of the American Educational Research Association, New York, New York, March 27, 2008.

This manuscript is based upon work supported in part by the National Science Foundation under Grant No. 0424983 to the Center for the Mathematics Education of Latinos/Latinas (CEMELA). Any opinions, findings, and conclusions or recommendations expressed in this material are those of the author(s) and do not necessarily reflect the views of the National Science Foundation.

NOTES

1. CEMELA, the Center for the Mathematics Education of Latinas/os, is an interdisciplinary, multi-university consortium focused on the teaching and learning of mathematics with Latinas/os in the United States.
2. School and all student names are pseudonyms.
3. Proposition 203 became Arizona Revised Statutes, Title 15, Article 3.1, §15-751-17.755 (2000).

4. Information about why participants were in the math club and about their language proficiency was self-reported in interviews conducted with all participants.
5. A digital story is a multimodal, multimedia movie that includes narrated voice recordings, photographs, video images, student work, and background music (Hull & Nelson, 2005).

REFERENCES

Arcavi, A. (2002). The everyday and the academic in mathematics. In M. E. Brenner & J. N. Moschkovich (Eds.), *Everyday and academic mathematics in the classroom* (pp. 12–29). Reston, VA: National Council of Teachers of Mathematics.

Arizona Revised Statutes, Title 15, Article 3.1, §15-751-17.755 (2000).

Aubert, A., Duque, E., Fisas, M., & Valls, R. (2004). *Dialogar y transformar: Pedagogía crítica del Siglo XXI*. Barcelona: Graó.

Barton, A. C. (1998). Teaching science with homeless children: Pedagogy, representation, and identity. *Journal of Research in Science Teaching, 35*(4), 379–394. doi: 10.1002/(SICI)1098-2736(199804)35:4<379::AID-TEA8>3.3.CO;2-1

Buxton, C. A. (2006). Creating contextually authentic science in a "low-performing" urban elementary school. *Journal of Research in Science Teaching, 43*(7), 695–721. doi: 10.1002/tea.20105

Carraher, T. N., Carraher, D. W., & Schliemann, A. D. (1985). Mathematics in the streets and in the school. *British Journal of Developmental Psychology, 3,* 21–29. Retrieved from http://www.bpsjournals.co.uk/journals/bjdp

Chazan, D. (2000). *Beyond formulas in mathematics teaching: Dynamics of the high school algebra classroom.* New York: Teachers College Press.

Civil, M. (1994, April). *Connecting the home and school: Funds of knowledge for mathematics teaching and learning.* Paper presented at the American Education Research Association, New Orleans, LA.

Civil, M. (1998, April). *Bridging in-school mathematics and out-of-school mathematics.* Paper presented at the Annual Meeting of the American Educational Research Association, San Diego, CA.

Civil, M. (2002). Culture and mathematics: A community approach. *Journal of Intercultural Studies, 23*(2), 133–148. doi: 10.1080/07256860220151050A

Civil, M. (2006, May). *Working towards reform in mathematics education: Parents', teachers', and students' views of "different."* Paper presented at the Third Annual Appalachian Collaborative Center for Learning, Assessment, and Instruction in Mathematics (ACCLAIM) Research Symposium, Cherry Valley Lodge, OH.

Civil, M. (2007). Building on community knowledge: An avenue to equity in mathematics education. In N. S. Nasir & P. Cobb (Eds.), *Improving access to mathematics: Diversity and equity in the classroom* (pp. 105–117). New York: Teachers College Press.

De Corte, E., Verschaffel, L., & Greer, B. (2000, November). *Connecting mathematics problem solving to the real world.* Paper presented at the International Conference on Mathematics Education into the 21st Century: Mathematics for Living, Amman, Jordan.

Díez-Palomar, J. (2004). Hacia unas matemáticas para todas las personas. Una reflexión sobre la alfabetización matemática básica desde la perspectiva dialógica. *Boletim GEPEM (Grupo de Pesquisa e Educaçâo Matemática), 44,* 63–93. Retrieved from http://www.gepem.ufrrj.br/

Eisenhart, M. (2001). Educational ethnography past, present, and future: Ideas to think with. *Educational Researcher, 30*(8), 16–27. doi: 10.3102/0013189X030008016

English, L. D. (1997). The development of fifth-grade children's problem-posing abilities. *Educational Studies in Mathematics, 34*(3), 183–217. doi: 10.1023/A:1002963618035

Erlandson, D. A., Harris, E. L., Skipper, B. L., & Allen, S. D. (1993). *Doing naturalistic inquiry: A guide to methods.* Newbury Park, CA: Sage.

Flores, A. (1997). *Sí se puede,* "It can be done": Quality mathematics in more than one language. In J. Trentacosta & M. J. Kenney (Eds.), *Multicultural and gender equity in the mathematics classroom: The gift of diversity* (pp. 81–91). Reston, VA: National Council of Teachers of Mathematics.

Franke, M. L., Kazemi, E., & Battey, D. (2007). Understanding teaching and classroom practice in mathematics. In F. K. Lester, Jr. (Ed.), *Second handbook of research on mathematics teaching and learning* (Vol. 15, pp. 225–256). Reston, VA: National Council of Teachers of Mathematics.

Freudenthal, H. (1991). *Revisiting mathematics education: China lectures.* Dordrecht, The Netherlands: Kluwer Academic.

González, N., Andrade, R., Civil, M., & Moll, L. C. (2001). Bridging funds of distributed knowledge: Creating zones of practices in mathematics. *Journal of Students Placed at Risk, 6*(1/2), 115–132. doi: 10.1207/S15327671ESPR0601-2_7

González, N., Moll, L. C., & Amanti, C. (Eds.). (2005). *Funds of knowledge: Theorizing practices in households, communities, and classrooms.* Mahwah, NJ: Erlbaum.

González, N., Moll, L. C., Tenery, M. G., Rendon, P., González, R., & Amanti, C. (1995). Funds of knowledge for teaching in Latino households. *Urban Education, 29*(4), 443–470. doi: 10.1177/0042085995029004005

Gravemeijer, K. (1997). Solving word problems: A case of modelling? [Commentary]. *Learning and Instruction, 7*(4), 389–397. doi: 10.1016/S0959-4752(97)00011-X

Gutiérrez, R. (2002). Beyond essentialism: The complexity of language in teaching mathematics to Latina/o students. *American Educational Research Journal, 39*(4), 1047-1088. doi: 10.3102/000283120390041047

Gutiérrez, R. (2007). (Re)defining equity: The importance of a critical perspective. In N. S. Nasir & P. Cobb (Eds.), *Improving access to mathematics: Diversity and equity in the classroom* (pp. 37–50). New York: Teachers College Press.

Gutstein, E. (2007). Multiple language use and mathematics: Politicizing the discussion. *Educational Studies in Mathematics, 64*(2), 243–246. doi: 10.1007/s10649-006-9063-z

Hull, G. A. & Nelson, M. E. (2005). Locating the semiotic power of multimodality. *Written Communication, 22*(2), 224–261. doi: 10.1177/0741088304274170

Khisty, L. L. (1997). Making mathematics accessible to Latino students: Rethinking instructional practices. In J. Trentacosta & M. J. Kenney (Eds.), *Multicultural and gender equity in the mathematics classroom: The gift of diversity* (National Council of Teachers of Mathematics 1997 Yearbook, pp. 92–101). Reston, VA: National Council of Teachers of Mathematics.

Ladson-Billings, G. (1998). Just what is critical race theory and what's it doing in a nice field like education? *International Journal of Qualitative Studies in Education, 11*(1), 7–24. doi: 10.1080/095183998236863

Lave, J. (1988). *Cognition in practice: Mind, mathematics, and culture in everyday life.* Cambridge, UK: Cambridge University Press.

Martin, D. B. (2000). *Mathematics success and failure among African-American youth: The roles of sociohistorical context, community forces, school influence, and individual agency.* Mahwah, NJ: Erlbaum.

Masingila, J. O., Davidenko, S., & Prus-Wisniowska, E. (1996). Mathematics learning and practice in and out of school: A framework for connecting these experiences. *Educational Studies in Mathematics, 31*(1/2), 175–200. doi: 10.1007/BF00143931

Moll, L. C., & Ruiz, R. (2002). The schooling of Latino children. In M. M. Suárez-Orozco & M. M. Páez (Eds.), *Latinos: Remaking America* (pp. 362–374). Berkeley: University of California Press.

Moschkovich, J. N. (1999). Supporting the participation of English language learners in mathematical discussions. *For the Learning of Mathematics, 19*(1), 11–19. Retrieved from http://flm.educ.ualberta.ca

Moschkovich, J. N. (2002). A situated and sociocultural perspective on bilingual mathematics learners. *Mathematical Thinking and Learning, 4*(2–3), 189–212. doi: 10.1207/S15327833MTL04023_5

Moschkovich, J. N. (2005). Using two languages when learning mathematics. *Educational Studies in Mathematics, 64*(2), 121-144. doi: 10.1007/s10649-005-9005-1

Nieto, S. (1999). *The light in their eyes: Creating multicultural learning communities* New York: Teachers College Press.

Niss, M. (1995). Las matemáticas en la sociedad. *UNO: Revista de Didáctica de las Matemáticas, 2*(6), 45–58.

Noddings, N. (1993). Politicizing the mathematics classroom. In S. Restivo, J. P. van Bendegem, & R. Fischer (Eds.), *Math worlds: Philosophical and social studies of mathematics and mathematics education* (pp. 150–161). Albany: State University of New York Press.

Nuñez, T., Schliemann, A. D., & Carraher, D. W. (1993). *Street mathematics and school mathematics.* Cambridge, UK: Cambridge University Press.

Rahm, J., Martel-Reny, M.-P., & Moore, J. C. (2005). The role of after-school and community science programs in the lives of urban youth. *School Science and Mathematics, 105*(6), 283–291. doi: 10.1111/j.1949-8594.2005.tb18129.x

Reusser, K. & Stebler, R. (1997). Every word problem has a solution: The social rationality of mathematical modeling in schools. *Learning and Instruction, 7*(4), 309–327. doi: 10.1016/S0959-4752(97)00014-5

Schoenfeld, A. H. (1991). On pure and applied research in mathematics education. *Journal of Mathematical Behavior, 10*(3). Retrieved from http://www.elsevier.com/wps/find/journaldescription.cws_home/620200/description#description

Schoenfeld, A. H. (1998). Making mathematics and making pasta: From cookbook procedures to really cooking. In J. G. Greeno & S. V. Goldman (Eds.), *Thinking practices in mathematics and science learning* (pp. 299–320). Mahwah, NJ: Erlbaum.

Silver, E. A. (1994). On mathematical problem posing. *For the Learning of Mathematics, 14*(1), 19–28. Retrieved from http://flm.edu.ualberta.ca

Silver, E. A., & Burkett, M. L. (1994, April). *The posing of division problems by preservice elementary teachers: Conceptual knowledge and contextual connections.* Paper presented at the Annual Meeting of the American Educational research Association, New Orleans, LA.

Simic-Muller, K., Turner, E. E., & Varley, M. C. (2009). Math club problem posing. *Teaching Children Mathematics, 16*(4), 206–212. Retrieved from http://www.nctm.org/

Skovsmose, O. & Valero, P. (2001). Breaking political neutrality: The critical engagement of mathematics education with democracy. In B. Atweh, H. Forgasz, & B. Nebres (Eds.), *Sociocultural research on mathematics education: An international perspective* (pp. 37–56). Mahwah, NJ: Erlbaum.

Tate, W. F. (1995). Returning to the root: A culturally relevant approach to mathematics pedagogy. *Theory Into Practice, 34*(3), 166–173. doi: 10.1080/00405849509543676

Treffers, A. (1978). *Three dimensions: A model of theory and goal description in mathematics instruction—the Wiscobas project.* Dordretch, The Netherlands: Kluwer Academic.

Turner, E. E. (2003). *Critical mathematical agency: Urban middle school students engage in mathematics to understand, critique, and act upon their world.* Unpublished doctoral dissertation, University of Texas, Austin.

Turner, E. E., Varley Gutiérrez, M. C., Simic-Muller, K., & Díez-Palomar, J. (2009). "Everything is math in the whole world": Integrating critical and community knowledge in authentic mathematical investigations with elementary Latina/o students. *Mathematical Thinking and Learning, 11*(3), 136–157. doi: 10.1080/10986060903013382

Valenzuela, A. (1999). *Subtractive schooling: U.S.-Mexican youth and the politics of caring.* Albany: State University of New York Press.

Valenzuela, A. (2002). Reflections on the subtractive underpinnings of education research and policy. *Journal of Teacher Education, 53*(3), 235–241. doi: 10.1177/0022487102053003007

Varley Gutiérrez, M. C. (2009a). "I thought this U.S. place was supposed to be about freedom": Young Latinas engage in mathematics and social change to save their school. *Rethinking Schools, 24*(2). Retrieved from http://www.rethinkingschools.org/restrict.asp?path=archive/24_02/24_02_freedom.shtml

Varley Gutiérrez, M. C. (2009b). *"I thought this U.S. place was supposed to be about freedom": Young Latinas speak to equity in mathematics education and society* (Doctoral dissertation, University of Arizona). Available from ProQuest Dissertations and Theses database. (UMI No. 3355940)

Vásquez, O. A. (2003). *La Clase Mágica: Imagining optimal possibilities in a bilingual community of learners.* Mahwah, NJ: Erlbaum.

Verschaffel, L., de Corte, E., & Lasure, S. (1994). Realistic considerations in mathematical modeling of school arithmetic word problems. *Learning and Instruction, 4*(4), 273–294. doi: 10.1016/0959-4752(94)90002-7

Vomvoridi-Ivanović, E., Simic-Muller, K., Varley Gutiérrez, M., Morales, H., Jr., & Díez-Palomar, J. (2007, April). *Cross-generational mathematics learning in an after-school setting: The interdependence of contexts, networks, and resources.* Paper presented at the Annual Meeting of the American Educational Research Association, Chicago, IL.

Winograd, K. (1991). Writing, solving and sharing original math story problems: Case studies in the cognitive behavior of fifth grade children (Doctoral dissertation). *Dissertation Abstracts International, 51*(10), 3324A.

CHAPTER 8

A CASE STUDY OF MULTIGENERATIONAL MATHEMATICS PARTICIPATION IN AN AFTER-SCHOOL SETTING

Capitalizing on Latinas/os Funds of Knowledge

Hector Morales, Jr.
DePaul University, Interdisciplinary Science and Technology Center

Eugenia Vomvoridi-Ivanović
University of South Florida, College of Education

Lena Licón Khisty
Department of Curriculum and Instruction, University of Illinois at Chicago

INTRODUCTION

Mathematics is a critical area of education for all students: It is a high-stakes testing subject area, a recognized gatekeeper for educational and

Latinos/as and Mathematics Education, pages 175–193
Copyright © 2011 by Information Age Publishing
All rights of reproduction in any form reserved.

professional pursuits (Stinson, 2004), and a subject that has undergone curriculum reforms that redefined what students should know and be able to do (National Council of Teachers of Mathematics, 2000). Latina/o students score poorly on national assessments in mathematics: Scores for this population's fourth- and eighth-grade mathematics assessment in 2007 were among the lowest in the nation (KewalRamani, Gilbertson, Fox, & Provasnik, 2007), a statistic that underscores the importance of this investigation. In spite of mathematics' role in education in general and in students' educational careers, little attention has been paid to the relationship among Latinas/os' language, cultural learning resources, and mathematics. Although research has acknowledged the importance of linguistically sensitive learning environments for Latinas/os in mathematics (e.g., Khisty, 1995; Moschkovich, 1999a, 1999b) and to practices teachers can use to facilitate bilingual students' content learning (e.g., Khisty & Viego, 1999; Walqui, 2000), there remains a question of how students' language, home, and community knowledge—and the learning capital inherently derived from these resources—interacts with the mathematics context.

The role of students' language in mathematics learning is particularly crucial because one of the key pillars of mathematics reform is student engagement in rich, sophisticated construction of content knowledge via all forms of communication. Research in mathematics education has addressed some of the issues and challenges faced by Latina/o students in constructing mathematical knowledge, negotiating meanings, and participating in mathematical communication in classrooms (e.g., Khisty & Chval, 2002; Morales, 2004; Moschkovich, 1999b). However, Latinas/os' language and culture tend to be discounted or overlooked, creating a distance between what Latina/o students and their parents know and classroom mathematics (Moschkovich, 1999b). School practices continue to marginalize Latinas/os, rather than value their linguistic and cultural learning capital (Moll & Ruiz, 2002).

This chapter reports on a project that encouraged and supported collaborative multigenerational participation among students, parents, and the university partner. The purpose of this project was to facilitate increased mathematical dialogue and meaning making related to nonremedial mathematics among all participants in an informal setting. We see these experiences as integral aspects of learning mathematics while bringing to the foreground the language and cultural learning capital of Latinas/os, their families, and their communities. In the next sections, we set forth our theoretical framework, provide some context to the larger study, and then focus our attention on a case study of a student's co-construction of mathematical meanings through the mutual shaping of influences and interactions within networks (or learning communities) of multiple and diverse participants.

THEORETICAL FRAMEWORK

The theoretical orientations that guided our research are those that place culture and interaction at the center of human learning and development (Blanton & Bremme, 2006). Learning is a social activity involving interaction within specific environmental contexts (Vygotsky & Cole, 1978). Collaboration is a process in which culturally, linguistically, and academically heterogeneous participants acquire knowledge—in this case, mathematical—through assisting one another in making sense of and solving challenging tasks (Gutiérrez, Baquedano-López, Alvarez, & Chiu, 1999). Blanton and Bremme (2006) argued that individual development requires certain kinds of social arrangements and multigenerational participation: "[T]here must be a functioning social level that includes both experienced and non-experienced members and a social setting that provides everyone with goals relevant to their joint participation" (pp. 22–23). These activity systems, even when they are in conflict, are reflective of the multiple points of views present in any social setting. In time, these diverse networks of participants, along with their repertoires and practices, might promote zones of development as they become tools for learning (Gutiérrez, Baquedano-López, & Tejeda, 1999; Morales, Díez-Palomar, Vomvoridi-Ivanović, & Khisty, 2007).

Moll, Amanti, Neff, and González (1992) developed the concept of *funds of knowledge* that places Latinas/os' cultural and social capital central to the learning process. This work stands out against U.S. schools' policies that reject teaching mathematics bilingually, or using Spanish to teach mathematics; or that there is even a need to consider students' home language and what that language means to what they know or the parental and community resources upon which these students draw. This perspective towards Spanish and those who speak Spanish has consequences for Latina/o students' mathematics achievement and creates the impression that Latino students and parents are unknowledgeable, thus creating a distance between school knowledge and their own knowledge simply because their home language is Spanish (Moll, 2001). Moll's (2001) investigation of funds of knowledge has been expanded by others (e.g., Civil & Andrade, 2002; Civil & Quintos, 2009; Díez-Palomar, Simic, & Varley, 2007; Willey, 2008) into the field of mathematics, with a focus on the development of mathematics learning contexts that build on Latina/o students' linguistic and cultural backgrounds. The study on which this chapter reports involved the investigation of the nature of learning mathematics among multigenerational participants in an after-school setting that sought to encourage networks to form and allow participants to draw on their home resources and school practices.

THE STUDY

The study draws on work carried out by the Center for the Mathematics Education of Latinas/os (CEMELA) that focuses on the research and practice of the teaching and learning of mathematics for Latinas/os in the United States through the integration of language, culture, and mathematics. This particular research was based on data gathered in an after-school project called "Los Rayos de CEMELA," adapted from the work of *The Fifth Dimension* (Cole, 2006) and *La Clase Mágica* (Vasquez, 2003). The after-school project was designed to give Latinas/os experiences engaging in nonremedial mathematical activities with an emphasis on problem solving and mathematics games, the intent of which were to enhance students' knowledge of probability and algebraic concepts. The primary purpose was to create a radically different environment that challenged traditional classroom norms.

Self-direction was the standard, and students had the freedom to choose their own mathematical activities. Students also were encouraged to work collaboratively with their peers and undergraduate facilitators to verbalize their thinking. One of the goals of the after-school project also was to promote mathematical biliteracy. With this objective in mind, it was important to advance the use of Spanish in interactions between adults and children. This objective was accomplished by engaging students in mathematical writing to a fictional online bilingual mathematics wizard called *El Maga*. The activities were written in both English and Spanish so that the students could practice reading the text in both languages.

Our research was conducted in a large, urban school district in a Midwestern city in the United States. According to information obtained from the school district's administration, 85.6% of the district's students were classified as coming from low-income families, and 13.7% were categorized as limited English proficient. To protect the identity of the school and the after-school program's participants, we refer to the research site as Rivera Elementary School. Rivera School's population consisted of approximately 425 students from pre-kindergarten through the sixth grade. The school is situated in a working-class neighborhood and the students' demographics are as follows: 99.4% self-reported as Latina/o, 98.3% were eligible for the government's free or reduced-price lunch program, and 68% of the students were categorized as English language learners (Chicago Public Schools, 2007).

During the 2005–2006 academic year, 13 third-grade Latina/o students, five undergraduate Latina/o facilitators, four graduate student researchers, and five Latina parents participated in the *Los Rayos de CEMELA* after-school project. All participants met twice a week for sessions lasting one and a half hours each for a ten-week period at the students' school. All sessions of the after-school project were captured by multiple video cameras. Descriptive and reflective field notes written by undergraduate and graduate student researchers documented participants' interactions as well as the facilitators' reflections of those interactions. Student work artifacts, as well as any electronic messages students exchanged with *El Maga*, the mathematics wizard, were collected.

The overarching goal of the research was to identify and describe patterns that emerged regarding how Latina/o children, undergraduate facilitators, and parents used language while engaged in mathematical activity, the resources the children and parents drew upon, and how social networks developed and enhanced students' mathematics learning. Specifically, we sought to understand and document the role played by multigenerational networks in students' mathematical development and identity as mathematics "knowers": What linguistic and cultural resources do students draw upon while engaged in mathematical activity as a consequence of interacting within multigenerational networks?

To answer our research questions, we focused our analysis on one episode in which children, parents, and undergraduate facilitators played a game called the *counters game*. Graduate researchers witnessed the activity. Data analysis was performed by individual researchers and through collective group analysis.[1] Qualitative methods (Lincoln & Guba, 1985) were used to examine how Latina/o students construct mathematical meanings through the mutually shaping influences of interactions among multiple and diverse networks in the after-school project.

METHOD: THE COUNTERS GAME

The study objective relative to the counters game activity was to encourage participation by our Latina/o children, undergraduate facilitators, and parents in a game of probability with the intent of engaging all participants to begin to think about ideas of chance and experimental/theoretical probability. The counters game activity provided a rich context within which to view multigenerational participation in mathematics. This rich mathematical activity engaged play among a wide range of ages. The activity afforded us a good example of multigenerational participation in mathematics in which linguistic, cultural, and mathematical resources were available and could be negotiated and distributed among participants. Students had the opportunity to play this game during two sessions—first with undergraduate facilitators and then in an expanded network that included some of the students' parents.

The counters game was an adaptation of a game from *Interactive Mathematics Program*. Its goal is to build on students' intuitive understandings of probability. To play the counters game, each players was given 11 counters

2	3	4	5	6	7	8	9	10	11	12

Figure 8.1 Sample of counters game.

and a self-made game board displaying all the possible sums of two dice. The board game resembles the layout shown in Figure 8.1.

Players can place as many counters as they choose on any of the sums represented in Figure 8.1. For example, a player may choose to place one counter on each of the possible sums or place all 11 counters on a single sum. After players have placed their counters on the game board, they take turns rolling two dice. Each time a player rolls the dice, the sum is calculated and any player who has a counter on the number corresponding to the sum removes one counter from his or her game board. For example, if a player rolls the dice and gets 4 and 5, any player with a counter on 9 removes a counter from her or his respective game board. The player who is first to clear all of the counters from his or her game board is the winner. In essence, players are encouraged to figure out strategies for placing their counters on their game boards to improve their likelihood of removing all of their counters first and winning the game.

To develop a good strategy for placing the counters on the game board, students must play many times. In time, they begin to see that the sums in the middle of the board (5 through 9) appear more frequently on the dice than those sums on the edges of the board. At any given throw, the sum with the highest probability of occurring is 7. The probability decreases as we move to greater or smaller sums.

Description of the Participants and the Context

During the first session, students in the after-school project played the counters game in small groups. Each group consisted of two to four students and one undergraduate facilitator. Some groups had a graduate student researcher participating as well. Approximately two weeks after the first session, the parents joined the students and undergraduate facilitators in playing the game for the first time all together. Merging the students and parents together was expected to foster further mathematical discussions in Spanish. We also assumed that parents would bring a more sophisticated level of Spanish to the discussions, thereby increasing everyone's repertoire in Spanish.

At this first session in which parents were introduced to the game, we first asked students to explain to the parents how to play the game. This explanation was intended to encourage the students to speak in Spanish. It also allowed us to establish the foundation for a home project on which students and their parents would work together. The home project required students, with the assistance of their parents, to create a mathematics board game and then explain, by recording a digital story with pictures, how the game was played.

The discussion we present in Findings focuses our analysis on the interactions of one student, Rodrigo, while he played the counters game on two different occasions and with two different groups. During the first session, Rodrigo played the counters game with a group consisting of one other student and an undergraduate facilitator. Three weeks later, Rodrigo played the counters game again with a group consisting of two other students, three mothers (including Rodrigo's mother, Olga), and a different undergraduate facilitator, Carlo. We specifically focused on how Rodrigo utilized linguistic (i.e., mathematics discourse) and cultural resources within the multigenerational learning communities in which he participated and how his mathematical understanding developed as a result of his participation. For practical purposes, we present our findings in chronological order, focusing first on Rodrigo's experiences playing the counters game, and then on Rodrigo's own math board game and digital story.

FINDINGS

The Counters Game Is Introduced

All undergraduate and graduate facilitators in *Los Rayos* who had worked with and/or observed Rodrigo considered him to be a very bright student in mathematics. He always seemed eager to engage in any type of mathematical activity and had expressed his inclination towards learning and doing mathematics in informal conversations with the second author of this chapter. The counters game activity showcased Rodrigo's enthusiasm for mathematics.

During the first session of playing the counters game, Rodrigo participated in a group with a student, Alfonso, and an undergraduate facilitator, Miguel. In this first session, Miguel spoke to Rodrigo in both Spanish and English. For the most part, however, Miguel used Spanish when addressing Alfonso and English when addressing Rodrigo. Alfonso spoke almost exclusively in Spanish and Rodrigo spoke predominantly in English and used Spanish only when he responded to Alfonso.

While playing the game, Miguel adopted the role of the expert and Rodrigo participated accordingly. Miguel made sure the students understood how the game was played and he also placed his own counters strategically so that he would win games more frequently. After they played a few rounds, Miguel decided to scaffold the students' understanding of the mathematics involved by having them observe the frequencies of the occurrence of the sums and by asking them to justify these frequencies. Miguel recommended that the students keep track of the sums each time the dice were rolled and prompted them to notice if any sums come up more or less often.

Rodrigo noticed that the sums 2 and 12 come up the least often. He explained that the sums 2 and 12 are the least likely to occur because there is only one combination of numbers that would result in each of these sums. When Miguel asked Rodrigo why he (Rodrigo) thought that other sums were more likely to occur, Rodrigo mentioned sum of 11 as an example and said that 11 could result from adding a 6 and a 5, or adding a 5 and a 6. He added that other sums, such as 9, 8, and 7 were also more likely to occur. Miguel prompted him to consider all these possibilities when deciding on how to place his counters.

We wish to highlight Miguel's role and how his line of questioning, scaffolding, and his suggestion for the boys to write down and keep track of their rolls helped Rodrigo begin to relate the likelihood of an event to the number of combinations that would lead to an event. Interacting with Miguel was a resource for Rodrigo's emergent mathematical thinking. There is evidence of Rodrigo having used this resource in Rodrigo's message to *El Maga* after the session: "We played with Miguel and Alfonso. I put my numbers in the numbers 5, 6, 7, 9, 9, 10, 10, 11, 11, 8, 8, 7. Because it is less possible to get 2 1 and 2 6. Miguel won all of the games."

As demonstrated by Rodrigo's message to *El Maga*, Rodrigo was able to describe in English how he placed his counters on his game board, and then justified why he placed them in such a way. By writing, "I put my numbers in the numbers 5, 6, 7, 9, 9, 10, 10, 11, 11, 8, 8, 7," Rodrigo suggested that he placed his counters, which he referred to as "numbers," on specific positions on the game board, which he also referred to as "numbers." He explained that he placed one counter on a position on his game board that corresponds to sum of 5, one counter on 6, one counter on 7, two counters on 9, two counters on 10, two counters on 11, two counters on 8, and one counter on 7. Rodrigo justified placing his counters in such a manner by explaining that "it is less possible to get 2 1 and 2 6," meaning that it is less possible to roll two dice and get two ones or two sixes, and therefore he did not place any counters on the game-board positions that corresponded to sums 2 and 12. Not only did Rodrigo realize that the game is not based on just "pure luck," but also he realized that there was a mathematical explanation for why some sums were less probable than others.

During previous after-school activities, Rodrigo spoke predominantly in English and demonstrated fluency in both his written and oral command of the language. This history led us initially to view him as English language dominant, but we quickly discovered that he was also fluent in Spanish. Our goal in conducting the after-school program was to create an environment that would help students to express themselves naturally and freely in Spanish and to help students gain a greater sense of confidence and agency, but even when Miguel and Alfonso spoke to Rodrigo in Spanish, he did not seem to engage in any significant way in Spanish. We experienced this same phenomenon with other students in the after-school project who preferred to only speak in English. To help these students overcome the dominance of English that had already influenced many of them by the third grade, we decided to expand the network. A few weeks later, we asked the parents to join the students in the after-school program setting and play the counters game together.

The Expanded Network

Of particular interest in establishing the after-school program was the creation of an environment that promoted communication in Spanish by students who had self-reported as Latina/o and were likely to be English language learners. We purposely wanted to include the parents of these students during the second session based on our belief that including the parents would naturally encourage the students to speak in Spanish, which we presumed was the language spoken in the home environment. We asked the students to explain to their parents the rules of the game and to demonstrate how to play the game.

When Rodrigo played the counters game during the second session, his group was more Spanish dominant than English dominant. His play group included two other students, Margarita and Rafael, Rodrigo's mother Olga, two other mothers, and an undergraduate facilitator, Carlo. All three mothers were Spanish language dominant, and their command of English was limited. When Rodrigo played the counters game with this group, he was more confident than he had been when he played with Alfonso and Miguel, an undergraduate facilitator. Rodrigo even adopted the role of referee, en-suring everyone—including the parents—played by the rules. This change in behavior was captured by a graduate student researcher's field notes:

> Margarita, Rafael, and Rodrigo played the counters game with Rodrigo's mom, Rafael's mom, and another mom. Rodrigo was very loud and laughing a lot; he kept saying that he hoped they wouldn't roll a 4; to me, it seemed that the way they were all talking and the arrangement of the table and the counters/chips, it looked that they were at a casino ☺ ... I don't think I've ever seen Rodrigo so animated or so talkative. The times I've seen him in the all-boys group, they all seem very quiet, structured, and not disruptive.

When the network was expanded to include the parents, Rodrigo's identity shifted, showing a greater sense of agency. Willey (2008) characterized *agency* as a participant's placement in the mathematical-meaning process. Participants who have a strong sense of agency chart their own path towards mathematical advancement. In this case, Rodrigo's sense of agency is evident by his shift in language from using exclusively English to using Spanish, and also by showing that he could play the counters game strategically. In Excerpt 8.1,[2] Rodrigo explained in Spanish to Carlo why the sum of 7 is more likely to occur.

Excerpt 8.1. Sums of 7

Carlo: "*¿Por qué tú crees que algunos salen más que otros?*"
["Why do you think that some come out more than others?"]

Rodrigo: "*No sale mucho, porque, porque no hay mucha probabilidad para hacer uno y uno con el dos, y también con el doce.*"
["They don't come out, because, because, there isn't much probability to make one with one for the two, and the same with twelve."]

Carlo: "*¿Y el siete porque sale tanto?*"
["And the seven, why does it come out so much?"]

Rodrigo: "*Porque hay más posibilidades para sacarlo...*"
["Because there is more probability of getting it."]

Carlo: "*¿Como qué?*"
["Like what?"]

Rodrigo: "*Como el cinco y el dos, cuatro y tres...*"
["Like five and two, four and three..."]

Carlo: "*Oh... Okay, me convenciste...*" (*rié*)
["Oh... okay, you convinced me."] (laughs)

In Excerpt 8.1, the evolution in Rodrigo's understanding of mathematics as it relates to the counters game was evident as he expressed for the first time the realization that some sums have higher probabilities of occurring and was also able to explain why 7 was the sum that was the most likely to occur. This understanding was based, in part, on his experience: he observed that some sums came up more frequently than others. In addition, Rodrigo's explanation in Spanish that "there is more probability of getting it (the seven)" because it can occur from rolling a "five and two" or a "four and three," showed his understanding that 7 was the sum with the greatest number of combinations. In other words, Rodrigo's thinking was not only based on an experiential model or playing the game (experimental probability), but also demonstrated that he was able to think about the game theoretically (theoretical probability).

After watching the video recording from the session in which the parents interacted with the children, we were struck by the fact that Rodrigo was so animated, talkative, and seemed so confident when playing the game. We were also surprised that he displayed such a fluent command of Spanish, including academic Spanish, and that he used Spanish during the entire session. What is significant in this shift of Rodrigo's language use and participation pattern was that it emerged naturally and even though his explanation was not particularly elaborate, it occurred, evolved, and was mediated by his interactions within the various networks in which he participated, rather than from instruction. As an agent in his own mathematical development, Rodrigo experienced a transformation in how he viewed himself from quiet and reserved to someone who was more confident in sharing his knowledge with others. In the next section, Rodrigo's mother shared with the group some of her knowledge.

Funds of Knowledge Are Realized: Rodrigo's Mom Shares Her Knowledge

During the second session of the counters game activity, Olga, Rodrigo's mother, suggested that they change the rules of the game so that no one could place any counters on 7. At this point, Rodrigo had already won twice and all participants were aware of the fact that 7 was the sum that was most likely to occur. Olga decided that the rules of the game must change. From Olga's point of view, this shared knowledge that 7 was most likely changed the entire activity and she felt the game would no longer be "fair." After negotiating how the rules should change, participants continued playing without placing any counters on 7. Later that day, Carlo documented in his field notes what had taken place; he also wondered about the implications of changing the rules of the game:

> Rodrigo's mom suggested when they were starting the third game that nobody put pieces on number 7 since it isn't fair and it comes out too often. I thought this was really interesting because it says something about group dynamic, there was an immediate agreement that this would indeed make the game more fair. Now the question is, does this limitation prevent one single person from taking advantage of number 7's frequency, or does it prevent a stalemate because too many people will have a tie at the end? Is it about making sure there is a defined winner, or is it about making sure it isn't too easy to become the winner?

Olga shared her knowledge with all of the participants. By changing the rule of the counters game, Olga mathematically changed the odds of winning and spurred the other participants to rethink their strategies for playing the game. This dynamic was an interesting one because it showed that Olga was not merely a passive player, but rather a participant who challenged others to think more deeply about the game. Initially, the students resisted the demand to change the rules of the game after they had already established a winning strategy. Olga, with the help of the other parents, convinced the students that this new approach was a good idea and consequently negotiated the new rules for playing the game. This challenge by Olga not only elevated her sense of agency, but also helped level the playing field for everyone else.

One of the reasons why we wanted the parents to play the counters game with the students was to help support parents in helping their children to create their own mathematics board games. We wanted to further encourage parents and their children to engage in creating a mathematics board game at home. Towards the end of the second session, we asked parents and students to brainstorm together about other possible mathematics board games they could create that were similar to the counters game and other spinner games they had played in the past.

Rodrigo's group started thinking about possible math board games they could create. At that point, Rodrigo's mother shared with others a mathematics game she said she had played at home as a young girl named "the game of the five numbers." Carlo described this game in his field-notes:

> Rodrigo's mom already seemed to be engaged in throwing out ideas based on games we already know in order to think of new ones. She suggested a game that they play a lot at home (but that's why I think Rodrigo's excellence in math is most definitely attributable to the influence at home and the comfort he feels as a math doer because of that influence) *se llama el juego de los cinco números* [it's called the game of the five numbers]. You generate five random numbers with a pair of dice or with some other method like a deck of cards or dominoes, then you try to find different arithmetic operations that will lead the first four numbers to equal the fifth. For example, you get 4, 10, 3, 2, and 8, so you need to use the first four numbers once each in any order to generate the answer 8. So you might try 4 + 10 = 14, then divide by 2 = 7, minus 3 = 4, nope, try again. Okay, so 4 – 3 = 1, 1 * 10 = 10, 10 – 2 = 8, and we have a solution. The idea is that through trial and error and using all four arithmetic operations, you all race to see who can get a solution first. I think we need to design an activity with this game, yes, it has the feel of drilling or even school, but it is also about "play," and increases comfort with math operations in an informal setting. . . .

Carlo, the undergraduate facilitator, attributed Rodrigo's excellence in mathematics to the mathematical practices he experienced at home. Carlo wrote that "Rodrigo's excellence in math is most definitely attributable to the influence at home and the comfort he feels as a math doer because of that influence." In addition, Carlo recognized the game Olga described as being a mathematical cultural resource from which the other students in the after-school project can benefit. Again, Olga positioned herself as a person who had knowledge, and her game of the five numbers demonstrated to others that their mathematics games could incorporate other areas of mathematics. This positioning was important for others—especially the children—to realize that parents are knowledgeable and can make valid and useful contributions to the meaning-making practice. In the next section, we describe Rodrigo's board game and how Olga played a major role in supporting him.

Rodrigo created his own math board game with his mother's help. His board game was an adaptation of various games he played in the past: the game of the five numbers, the spinner game, the counters game, and bingo. He named his game math bingo and created a digital story about his board game. Math bingo is played with two to four players. The materials needed for this game are a spinner, game boards, and counters. Each player creates a game board with a 5 × 5 square grid and assigns one number from 1 to 32 to each of the 25 grids on his or her game board. Each game board represents one of the four operations. A spinner with numbers from 1 to 32 is spun and the players write down the number on which the spinner lands. Any player whose game board includes the number on which the spinner landed places one counter on the position assigned for that number. The cycle of spinning and marking is repeated until a player has five counters in a row—vertically, horizontally, or diagonally. To win the game, a player must have five counters in a row and also be able to generate one of the five numbers on which the counters are placed using the rest of the four numbers and any of the four mathematical operations (i.e., addition, subtraction, multiplication, division).

Rodrigo played math bingo with his sisters at home and took pictures of them playing the game with him (see Figure 8.2). He included these pic-

Figure 8.2   Photograph of math bingo game taken by Rodrigo.

tures in his digital story, as well as an explanation of how the game is played. His explanation of the rules of math bingo is entirely in Spanish. Excerpt 8.2 is the transcript of Rodrigo's narration:

Excerpt 8.2. Rodrigo's math bingo experience

> Math bingo, starring Rodrigo. I am on the right and my sister, my...the one on the left is my sister and her name is Griselda, and the one on the bottom is my little sister and her name is Veronica.
>
> *Yo hice mi nuevo juego de Bingo usando matemáticas. Hice cuatro cartas y cada carta tiene diferentes operaciones. También hice una flecha, un...un tablero numérico con una flecha en el medio para girarla. Para ganar, tienes que hacer una línea vertical o horizontal o diagonal. Aquí, todos están tomando turnos girando la flecha y yo, y yo gané como dos veces. Estoy jugando con mi hermana que se llama Griselda y mi otra hermana que se llama Verónica. Cada quien está tomando turnos girando la flecha y apuntado el número que salga. Fin.*
>
> [I made my new bingo game using mathematics. I made four game pieces and each one has different operations. I also made an arrow, an...a numbered board with an arrow in the middle to spin it. To win, you have to make a vertical or horizontal or diagonal line. Here, everyone is taking turns spinning the arrow and I, and I won like two times. I am playing with my sister, whose name is Griselda, and with my other sister, whose name is Veronica. Everyone is taking turns spinning the arrow and writing down the number that comes up. The End.]

After introducing his sisters who played the game with him, Rodrigo described, in Spanish, how math bingo is played. Rodrigo used a spinner similar to one that he had used in the spinner game. He also used counters as well as game boards similar to the ones used in the counters game and bingo. In addition, he drew from the rules of bingo the process required to win: one needs to complete a row of numbers randomly generated. Finally, he incorporated from the game of the five numbers the rule requiring a player to generate one number using the other four numbers from his or her row. In essence, Rodrigo drew from games previously played at home and in *Los Rayos* to create his own math board game.

What is even more important than the initiative and creativity demonstrated by Rodrigo's board game and digital story was how he engaged at home with the resources he learned from his after-school project. This was not the typical interaction of a son sitting down with his mother checking over homework, but rather one of a true collaboration. Rodrigo narrated the description of his game in Spanish. This choice of language appears to be influenced by his mother's involvement and might have led Rodrigo to view his home resources, including his mother's insights, as valuable. These are the kind of interactions we hoped participants would achieve at home, where everyone's role and identities are transformed and where knowledge gets passed on to the whole family, including Rodrigo's siblings as he engaged them to play his game.

CONCLUSIONS

Designing an after-school program that gave Latinas/os experiences engaging in nonremedial mathematical activities where linguistic and cultural resources could be shared and distributed amongst multigenerational networks proved to be a challenging task. For many of the participants in the after-school project, the experience was a positive one that helped them explore mathematical ideas across various networks, and also helped students make connections with their parents' knowledge and experiences.

In Rodrigo's case, we observed him transform from a shy, soft-spoken boy into someone who was animated and enjoyed sharing his mathematical reasoning and being the expert. It was not until Rodrigo played the counters game the second time that he used Spanish as a resource to communicate his mathematical thinking. Rodrigo witnessed his mother play a game and offer alternate strategies. The objective we had hoped to achieve—the use of native Spanish language to enhance mathematical skills—was realized when Rodrigo's mother shared with the group a math game she used to play in the past. The connection between school mathematics and Rodrigo's mother's knowledge is critical for Rodrigo's mathematical development.

The importance of this connection between Rodrigo and his mother's game-playing experiences is evident in Rodrigo's digital story about the math board game he created with his mother's assistance. Rodrigo appropriated his mother's game as well as others to create a game of his own. Perhaps even more telling, Rodrigo narrated the description of his game in Spanish. His choice to use Spanish appears to be influenced by his mother's involvement during the last few weeks of the academic year, a preference that was very different from the one demonstrated earlier in the school year.

Research on Latinas/os in mathematics has emphasized the use of students' first language (e.g., Gutstein, Lipman, Hernández, & de los Reyes, 1997; Hernández, 1999; Khisty, 1995, 1997; Khisty & Viego, 1999; LoCicero, Fuson, & Allexsaht-Snider, 1999; Moschkovich, 1999a, 2000; Ron, 1999; Secada, 1991). Even though this body of research points to students' home language being a resource for learning mathematics, discussions of improving Latinas/os' performance in mathematics are still embedded in how to make mathematics taught in English comprehensible to students. Other publications focus on helping teachers effectively teach language minority students and bilingual students across content areas, including mathematics (e.g., Bresser, Melanese, & Sphar, 2009; Coggins, Kravin, Coates, &

Carroll, 2007; Colombo & Furbush, 2009; Kersaint, Thompson, & Petkova, 2009). These publications are directed towards helping teachers who do not share similar linguistic and cultural backgrounds with their students, and perhaps are monolingual themselves; they do not discuss ways in which teachers can build on students' home language and culture. Nothing in the public dialogue suggests teaching mathematics bilingually, or using Spanish to teach mathematics, or that there is even a need to consider students' home language and what that means for what they know or the parental and community resources on which they draw. This singular perspective has many consequences for Latina/o students' mathematics achievement. Among those consequences are perpetuated notions that Latina/o students are unknowledgeable, a fallacy that creates a distance between school knowledge and their own knowledge simply because their home language is Spanish (Moll, 2001).

In this chapter, we highlighted a study that demonstrated how multi-generational networks in an informal setting contributed to and mediated students' mathematical meaning-making practices, sense of agency, and participatory roles. This work illustrates the importance of these networks to creating and promoting zones of development as they become tools for learning (Gutiérrez, Baquedano-Lopez, & Tejeda, 1999). Some researchers have argued that beyond what teachers do in class, they need to involve students' families to support students to their fullest (Civil, 2000; Gutstein et al., 1997; LoCicero et al., 1999). The question of how we utilize multigenerational networks in traditional school settings that goes beyond "family math nights" remains unanswered. The goal is not merely to document that families have knowledge, but to determine how to transform school practices to capitalize on it.

ACKNOWLEDGEMENTS

The study presented here draws on work carried out by the Center for the Mathematics Education of Latinas/os (CEMELA). CEMELA is a Center for Learning and Teaching supported by the National Science Foundation, grant number ESI-0424983. The views expressed here are those of the authors and do not necessarily reflect the views of the funding agency.

NOTES

1. CEMELA-UIC research group: L. L. Khisty, H. Morales, Jr., C. Willey, G. Viego, E. Vomvoridi-Ivanović, C. López-Leiva., A. Radosavljevic, and B. Javier.

2. Utterances are spoken in Spanish are *italicized*, and the English translations are [bracketed].

REFERENCES

Blanton, W. & Bremme, D. (2006). The intellectual foundations of the fifth dimension. In M. Cole (Ed.), *The fifth dimension: An after-school program built on diversity* (pp. 15–33). New York: Russell Sage Foundation.

Bresser, R., Melanese, K., & Sphar, C. (2009). *Supporting English language learners in math class.* Sausalito, CA: Math Solutions.

Chicago Public Schools. (2007). *School district data.* Retrieved from the http://www.cps.edu/Schools/Pages/Schools.aspx

Civil, M. (2000, October). *Bridging in-school mathematics and out-of-school mathematics: A reflection.* Paper presented at the Diversity in Mathematics Education conference, Northwestern University, Evanston, IL.

Civil, M. & Andrade, R. (2002). Transitions between home and school mathematics: Rays of hope amidst the passing clouds. In G. de Abreu, A. J. Bishop, & N. C. Presmeg (Eds.), *Transitions between contexts of mathematical practices* (pp. 149–170). Dordrecht, The Netherlands: Kluwer Academic.

Civil, M. & Quintos, B. (2009). Latina mothers' perceptions about the teaching and learning of mathematics: Implications for parental participation. In B. Greer, S. Mukhopadhyay, S. Nelson-Barber, & A. B. Powell (Eds.), *Culturally responsive mathematics education* (pp. 321–343). New York: Routledge.

Coggins, D., Kravin, D., Coates, G. D., & Carroll, M. D. (2007). *English language learners in the mathematics classroom.* Thousand Oaks, CA: Corwin Press.

Cole, M. (Ed.). (2006). *The fifth dimension: An after-school program built on diversity.* New York: Russell Sage.

Colombo, M. & Furbush, D. (2009). *Teaching English language learners: Content and language in middle and secondary mainstream classrooms.* Thousand Oaks, CA: Sage.

Díez-Palomar, J., Simic, K., & Varley, M. (2007). "Mathematics is everywhere": Connecting mathematics to students' lives. *The Journal of Mathematics and Culture, 1*(2), 20–36. Retrieved from http://nasgem.rip.edu/pl/journal-mathematics-culture-s37

Gutiérrez, K. D., Baquedano-López, P., Alvarez, H. H., & Chiu, M. M. (1999). Building a culture of collaboration through hybrid language practices. *Theory Into Practice, 38*(2), 87–93. doi: 10.1080/00405849909543837

Gutiérrez, K. D., Baquedano-López, P., & Tejeda, C. (1999). Rethinking diversity: Hybridity and hybrid language practices in the third space. *Mind, Culture, & Activity: An International Journal, 6*(4), 286–303. doi: 10.1080/10749039909524733

Gutstein, E., Lipman, P., Hernández, P., & de los Reyes, R. (1997). Culturally relevant mathematics teaching in a Mexican American context. *Journal for Research in Mathematics Education, 28*(6), 709–737. doi: 10.2307/749639

Hernández, N. G. (1999). The mathematics-bilingual education connection: Two lessons. In L. Ortiz-Franco, N. G. Hernández, & Y. de la Cruz (Eds.), *Chang-

ing the faces of mathematics: Perspectives on Latinos (pp. 49–58). Reston, VA: National Council of Teachers of Mathematics.

Kersaint, G., Thompson, D. R., & Petkova, M. (2009). *Teaching mathematics to English language learners.* New York: Routledge.

KewalRamani, A., Gilbertson, L., Fox, M., & Provasnik, S. (2007). *Status and trends in the education of racial and ethnic minorities* (NCES 2007-039). National Center for Education Statistics, Institute of Education Sciences, U.S.

Khisty, L. L. (1995). Making inequality: Issues of language and meanings in mathematics teaching with Hispanic students. In W. G. Secada, E. Fennema, & L. B. Adajian (Eds.), *New directions for equity in mathematics education* (pp. 279–297). Cambridge, England: Cambridge University Press.

Khisty, L. L. (1997). Making mathematics accessible to Latino students: Rethinking instructional practice. In J. Trentacosta & M. J. Kenney (Eds.), *Multicultural and gender equity in the mathematics classroom: The gift of diversity* (pp. 92–101). Reston, VA: National Council of Teachers of Mathematics.

Khisty, L. L., & Chval, K. B. (2002). Pedagogic discourse and equity in mathematics: When teachers' talk matters. *Mathematics Education Research Journal, 14*(3), 154–168. Retrieved from http://www.merga.net.au/

Khisty, L. L. & Viego, G. (1999). Challenging conventional wisdom: A case study. In L. Ortiz-Franco, N. G. Hernández, & Y. de la Cruz (Eds.), *Changing the faces of mathematics: Perspectives on Latinos* (pp. 71–80). Reston, VA: National Council of Teachers of Mathematics.

Lincoln, Y. S. & Guba, E. G. (1985). *Naturalistic inquiry.* Newbury Park, CA: Sage.

LoCicero, A. M., Fuson, K. C., & Allexsaht-Snider, M. (1999). Mathematizing children's stories, helping children solve word problems, and supporting parental involvement. In L. Ortiz-Franco, N. G. Hernández, & Y. de la Cruz (Eds.), *Changing the faces of mathematics: Perspectives on Latinos* (pp. 59–70). Reston, VA: National Council of Teachers of Mathematics.

Moll, L. C. (2001). The diversity of schooling: A cultural-historical approach. In M. D. de la Luz Reyes & J. J. Halcón (Eds.), *The best of our children: Critical perspectives on literacy for Latino students* (pp. 13–28). New York: Teachers College Press.

Moll, L. C., Amanti, C., Neff, D., & González, N. (1992). Funds of knowledge for teaching: Using a qualitative approach to connect homes and classrooms. *Theory Into Practice, 31*(2), 132–141. doi: 10.1080/00405849209543534

Moll, L. C, & Ruiz, R. (2002). The schooling of Latino children. In M. M. Suárez-Orozco & M. Páez (Eds.), *Latinos: Remaking America* (pp. 362–374). Berkeley: University of California Press.

Morales Jr., H. (2004). *A naturalistic study of mathematical meaning-making by high school Latino students.* Unpublished doctoral dissertation, University of Illinois at Chicago.

Morales, H., Jr., Díez-Palomar, J., Vomvoridi-Ivanović, E., & Khisty, L. L. (2007, April). *Then after-school: Shifting paradigms for Latinas/os learning mathematics.* Paper presented at the American Educational Research Association, Chicago, IL.

Moschkovich, J. N. (1999a). Supporting the participation of English language learners in mathematical discussions. *For the Learning of Mathematics, 19*(1), 11–19. Retrieved from http://flm.edu.ualberta.ca/

Moschkovich, J. N. (1999b). Understanding the needs of Latino students in reform-oriented mathematics classrooms. In L. Ortiz-Franco, N. G. Hernández, & Y. de la Cruz (Eds.), *Changing the faces of mathematics: Perspectives on Latinos* (pp. 5–12). Reston, VA: National Council of Teachers of Mathematics.

Moschkovich, J. N. (2000). Learning mathematics in two languages: Moving from obstacles to resources. In W. G. Secada, (Ed.), *Changing the faces of mathematics: Perspectives on multiculturalism and gender equity* (pp. 85-93). Reston, VA: National Council of Teachers of Mathematics.

National Council of Teachers of Mathematics. (2000). *Principles and standards for school mathematics*. Reston, VA: Author.

Ron, P. (1999). Spanish-English language issues in the mathematics classroom. In L. Ortiz-Franco, N. G. Hernández, & Y. de la Cruz (Eds.), *Changing the faces of mathematics: Perspectives on Latinos* (pp. 23–33). Reston, VA: National Council of Teachers of Mathematics.

Secada, W. G. (1991). Degree of bilingualism and arithmetic problem solving in Hispanic first graders. *Elementary School Journal, 92*(2), 213–229. doi: 10.1086/461689

Stinson, D. W. (2004). Mathematics as "gate-keeper" (?): Three theoretical perspectives that aim toward empowering all children with a key to the gate. *The Mathematics Educator, 14*(1), 8–18. Retrieved from http://math.coe.uga.edu/tme/tmeonline.html

U.S. Department of Education (DOE). (2007). *Status and trends in the education of racial and ethnic minorities—Indicator 10: Reading and mathematics achievement* (NCES No. 2007-039). Retrieved on March 23, 2009 from http://nces.ed.gov/pubs2007/minoritytrends/ind_3_10.asp

Vasquez, O. A. (2003). *La clase mágica: Imagining optimal possibilities in a bilingual community of learners*. Mahwah, NJ: Erlbaum.

Vygotsky, L. S. & Cole, M. (Ed.). (1978). *Mind in society: The development of higher psychological processes*. Cambridge, MA: Harvard University Press.

Walqui, A. (2000). *Access and engagement : Program design and instructional approaches for immigrant students in secondary school*. McHenry, IL: Center for Applied Linguistics and Delta.

Willey, C. (2008). Immigrant Latina mothers' participation in a community mathematization project. *ALM International Journal, 3*(2a), 29–40. Retrieved from http://www.alm-online.net

CHAPTER 9

ALGEBRAIC AND GEOMETRIC REPRESENTATIONS OF PERIMETER WITH ALGEBRA BLOCKS

Professional Development for Teachers of Latino English Language Learners

Cynthia O. Anhalt
Department of Mathematics, The University of Arizona

Matthew Ondrus
Mathematics Department, Weber State University

INTRODUCTION

To empower students with mathematical thinking, teachers should be empowered first.
—Ma, 1999, p. 105

Algebra blocks are an effective tool for teaching prealgebraic and algebraic concepts (Leitze & Kitt, 2000). Typically, the blocks are used to provide con-

Latinos/as and Mathematics Education, pages 195–214
Copyright © 2011 by Information Age Publishing
All rights of reproduction in any form reserved.

crete representations of the distributive property, factoring, and polynomial expressions using the area of a rectangle as the organizing principle. They provide access to concepts by way of the physical manipulation of algebraic symbols, thus reducing the need for abstraction while maintaining complex, generalized understanding. In essence, these blocks encourage a geometric interpretation of symbol manipulation, thereby enriching students' connections between algebra and geometry. In addition, algebra blocks provide opportunities for students to engage in discourse that abstract symbols alone are unlikely to promote.

Algebra blocks provide a concrete representation of mathematical ideas; therefore, they can be used to teach in various mathematical strands, such as measurement, algebra, geometry, and number and operation. Using data taken from the 2000 National Assessment of Educational Progress, Lubiensky (2003) reported that the greatest gap between Caucasian and Latino students in the United States was found in the domain of measurement and suggested that "minority students of all SES levels need more opportunities to develop understanding in all strands of mathematics, but especially in the area of measurement" (p. 286). Because concepts in measurement are critical in the mathematics education of students and because measurement was the area of most marked disparity between Latino students and non-Latinos, we believed it was critical to address measurement concepts in a mathematics professional development course for middle-school teachers who work with Latino English language learners (ELLs).

Special attention to the improvement of instruction specifically geared for Latino ELLs is crucial for advancement in their mathematics learning. Moschkovich (2002) advocated a sociocultural perspective, which asserts that instruction for ELLs should focus on their mathematical competencies, rather than perceived deficiencies such as mispronunciation of words, accents, or code switching. The algebra blocks can be used as tools to aid students in expressing the mathematical ideas, and instruction can build on students' competencies and resources, thus creating more opportunities for students to participate in classroom discourse. Because mathematics is so often conveyed in symbols, oral and written communication about mathematical ideas is not always recognized as an important part of learning mathematics, yet it is crucial for the development and deepening of understanding the mathematical ideas. The National Council of Teachers of Mathematics ([NCTM], 2000) underscored the importance of communication of mathematical ideas among students to help them improve their mathematical discourse, and thus, deepening their understanding of mathematics.

Mathematical discourse, which involves conversations in which mathematical ideas are explored from multiple perspectives, helps the participants sharpen their thinking and make connections (NCTM, 2000). The

NCTM (2000) advocated for students to participate in mathematical discourse because

> such activity also helps students develop a language for expressing mathematical ideas and an appreciation of the need for precision in that language. Students who have opportunities, encouragement, and support for speaking, writing, reading, and listening in mathematics classes reap dual benefits: they communicate to learn mathematics, and they learn to communicate mathematically. (p. 60)

The activities described in this chapter were part of a professional development course for a cohort of middle-school mathematics teachers from the Center for the Mathematics Education of Latino/as (CEMELA), a U.S. National Science Foundation-funded project. The teachers in the semester-long course met in the evening once each week for three hours per meeting. A fundamental goal of the course was to broaden and deepen practicing teachers' knowledge of the mathematics they teach while helping them address the roles of language in the teaching and learning of mathematics. The 22 teachers in the course taught at schools with student populations of approximately 82% Latino, 7% Native American, 3% African American, 7% Anglo, and 1% Asian. Approximately 32% of the student populations were identified as ELLs, and the majority of the students came from middle to lower working-class families.

Because we were cognizant of the potential positive effects of teachers' increased content knowledge on their teaching, our goal for the class was to broaden teachers' mathematical knowledge. Sowder, Philipp, Armstrong, and Schappelle (1998) reported that teachers' improved content knowledge can have a positive effect on teaching and student learning and enables teachers to more easily answer student questions. Perhaps more interesting is the idea that improved content knowledge may cause teachers to rethink some of their classroom practices. Schifter (1998) suggested that teachers who are actively involved in learning new ideas are able to put what they learn into practice. Moreover, it can be useful for teachers to revisit the mathematics that they teach, as this seems to play an important role in helping teachers see connections between mathematical ideas (Brown, Smith, & Stein, 1996).

TEACHERS' KNOWLEDGE AND TEACHER
PROFESSIONAL DEVELOPMENT

The work of Ma (1999) compares U.S. teachers' and Chinese teachers' explorations of the relationship between area and perimeter of rectangles based on a student claim that as the perimeter of a rectangle increases, the area also increases. Ma found that U.S. teachers showed less enthusiasm for the topic than the Chinese teachers did, and that most of the Chinese teachers made mathematically legitimate explorations on their own, while most of the U.S. teachers did not. Additionally, the Chinese teachers demonstrated a better knowledge of elementary geometry and the formulas of area and perimeter. Ma claimed that in responding to the student's theory about the relationship between area and perimeter, the U.S. teachers behaved more like laypeople and engaged in limited explorations, while the Chinese teachers behaved more like mathematicians in their elaborate explorations and explanations. Ma suggested that the teachers who engage students in further discussions and explorations of mathematics are those who demonstrate a better understanding and are more comfortable in their own investigation of mathematics problems.

Shulman's (1987) conceptualization of teachers' knowledge is linked to the development of a knowledge base for teaching. He categorized teachers' knowledge into (1) content knowledge; (2) general pedagogical knowledge; (3) curriculum knowledge; (4) pedagogical content knowledge; (5) knowledge of learners and their characteristics; (6) knowledge of educational contexts; and (7) knowledge of educational ends, purposes, and values. Our focus in this professional development course was on several of these types of knowledge, with special attention paid to the teachers' mathematics content knowledge, pedagogical content knowledge, and knowledge of learners and their characteristics, specifically linguistic and cultural characteristics of Latino ELLs.

To address the teachers' mathematical knowledge, we asked them to investigate mathematical ideas in an exploratory setting. The algebra blocks, which we first used about halfway through the course, served the purpose of giving new meaning and learning experiences to the mathematics with which the teachers were already (to varying degrees) familiar. Additionally, the discussions that surrounded their learning of this content were interwoven with discussions about teaching it, and finally, the natural progression of the discussion led the teachers into the discussion of effective strategies for teaching ELLs. This discussion, in turn, pointed towards specific knowledge and characteristics of their students and the students' learning needs.

Shulman (1986) defined *pedagogical content knowledge* as the ability to represent ideas in ways that are understandable to students. Shulman and Quinlan (1996) further discussed pedagogical content knowledge as the transformation of the teachers' "own content knowledge into pedagogical representations that connect with the prior knowledge and disposition of the learner" (p. 409). It is domain-specific and includes a teacher's knowledge of students' interests and motivations to learn particular topics within a discipline and understandings about students' preconceptions that can interrupt or derail their learning (Shulman & Sykes, 1986). Shulman (1987) further elaborated on pedagogical content knowledge as the capacity "to transform the content knowledge he or she possesses into forms that are pedagogically powerful and yet adaptive to the variations in ability and background presented by the students" (p. 15). On the same notion, Shulman (1986) elaborated,

> What is also needed is knowledge of the most useful forms of representation of those ideas, the most powerful analogies, illustrations, examples, explanations, and demonstrations—in a word, the ways of representing and formulating the subject that make it comprehensible to others. . . . Pedagogical content knowledge also includes an understanding of what makes the learning of specific topics easy or difficult; the conceptions and preconceptions that students of different ages and backgrounds bring with them to the learning of those most frequently taught topics and lessons. (pp. 9–10)

In light of the many types of knowledge that are key to teaching and teacher professional development, the issue of context is of great importance. Webster-Wright (2009) characterized professional development as a context-dependent social activity. Two of the contexts playing an especially crucial role in professional development are the learning context (issues associated with the professional development experience) and also the professional context (the corresponding work environment). If, for example, mathematics teachers participate in professional development, the mathematics that is learned, the manner in which it is learned, and the other participating teachers are part of the learning context. The teachers' colleagues, their students, the students' parents, and even the required curriculum become part of the professional context. Webster-Wright argued that both contexts are important, and that viewing the professional and learning contexts as separate may suggest to participants in professional development a divide between theory and practice. When teachers, especially, view their learning through a lens that invites this dualism, they often interpret the learning experience as irrelevant. Consequently, it is imperative to view the mathematical and pedagogical issues of teaching mathematics in connection with context of teaching ELLs.

The knowledge that teachers possess and continue to develop regarding their students' learning characteristics is critical, especially because Latino ELL students are unique learners of mathematics due to the influence of language and culture (Khisty, 2002; Moschkovich, 2002). Because of these linguistic and cultural influences, the required specialized knowledge for teachers who are teaching mathematics to Latino ELL students is complex and often undermined. At the very least, the specialized knowledge essential for teaching Latino ELL students includes teachers' deep understanding and flexibility in mathematical knowledge with the ability to use multiple representations and relevant analogies that pertain to the students' background knowledge (Anhalt, Ondrus, & Horak, 2007).

The work of Ball, Lubienski, and Mewborn (2001) focused greatly on teachers' use of mathematical knowledge for teaching, and although their focus was not explicit for teaching ELLs, the findings are pertinent to teachers' use of mathematical knowledge for teaching ELL students. They claimed that a great challenge of teaching is to integrate many kinds of knowledge in the context of particular situations, including planned and unplanned situations. Teachers of ELL students are likely to be placed in these situations of unpredictability, especially because of the multiple meanings of mathematical terms and everyday language terms that may or may not coincide (Moschkovich, 2002). Ball and colleagues asserted that teachers need to be able to puzzle about the everyday common mathematics in an unanticipated idea or formulation proposed by a student, such as why $.7 \times 3$, $7 \times .3$, and $.7 \times .03$ are quite different problems, especially when represented through the use of base-10 blocks and area models of multiplication.

Kennedy (1998) supports the idea that "teachers need to be able to respond to questions and hypotheses that they might not have anticipated, provide students with guidance when they get in over their heads, clarify confusions, and ensure that misconceptions are not perpetuated" (p. 252). These situations may prove highly difficult for teachers who do not anticipate the misconceptions that ELL students may have about the mathematics content and the communication about the mathematical ideas. For teachers of ELLs to be able to clarify their students' misunderstandings, they must have the ability to explain, discuss, ask meaningful questions, allow for small group discussions in the students' academic language and using a variety of tools, such as concrete materials, and then be able to informally assess their understanding on a consistent and constant basis. This is no small task for teachers to undertake.

Ball and Bass (2000) asserted that to make mathematical knowledge usable, teachers must know content sufficiently and flexibly such that it can be used within a wide variety of contexts. For instance, Ma's (1999) investigation of teachers' knowledge found that not only must teachers know content deeply and conceptually and know the connections among ideas, but also they must know the representations for and the common student difficulties with particular ideas. We need to broaden the scope of these monumental ideas about teachers' knowledge to include the specialized knowledge for teaching ELL students, especially in light of our efforts to increase ELL student participation in mathematical discourse. An essential goal in working with the teachers was to help them transform the mathematics into forms that are pedagogically powerful for reaching all their students, especially Latino ELL students.

The mathematical content knowledge needed by teachers is substantial, and we cannot necessarily assume that K–8 teachers have expertise in both the teaching of the content matter and in the instructional practices that address learning of English as a second language. We therefore need examples of good teaching practices that are appropriate for working with ELL students. The use of algebra blocks has the potential for deepening and broadening teachers' mathematical perspectives about area and perimeter due to the nature of the unique concrete representation that the blocks can produce. By having opportunities to gain new perspectives on elementary mathematical knowledge through the use of algebra blocks, teachers may in turn strengthen their knowledge for teaching the mathematics, particularly in a setting with ELL students. Additionally, it is important to incorporate good practices from second language acquisition theory that advocate academic language scaffolding in the language of instruction. These practices include contextualizing the academic language through visuals and hands-on concrete models for increasing comprehensibility (Gibbons, 2002; Krashen, 1988).

LANGUAGE DEVELOPMENT AND MULTIPLE REPRESENTATIONS

Much of the literature on effective ways to teach mathematics to ELL students addresses the use of multiple representations for increasing comprehensible instruction (see, for example, Coggins, Kravin, Coates, & Carroll, 2007; Garrison & Mora, 1999). The use of multiple representations in teaching mathematics has the potential for increasing learning opportunities for students, particularly for ELLs. It is critical that teachers give students opportunities to verbally describe attributes of shapes constructed from the physical blocks, which we describe in the sections that follow. For example, if students are given blocks that represent the lengths a and b, they should be able to explain the meaning of $2a + b$. Given that the *Principles and Standards* (NCTM, 2000) recommended student explanations and justifications, it is imperative that teachers model such reasoning to help students, especially ELL students, develop mathematically and linguistically. Because algebra blocks are tangible mathematical objects, they allow for increased opportunities for mathematical ideas to be expressed comprehensibly in a classroom.

Language development can increase as students learn mathematical concepts in situations in which they are expected to explain and express their mathematical understandings through the use of multiple representations. Multiple representations (e.g., pictures or graphs drawn by students, physical objects that can be manipulated, and contexts and symbolism already familiar to the students) consequently become tools with which students can think and that students develop with time and experience (Davis & Maher, 1997). As the *Principles and Standards* report (NCTM, 2000) noted, "When students gain access to mathematical representations and the ideas they represent, they have a set of tools that significantly expands their capacity to think mathematically" (p. 67). Thus, representations can then be thought of as *thinking tools* to communicate mathematical ideas.

The concrete representations of area and perimeter using algebra blocks have the potential to bring meaning to the abstract notion of symbolic expressions. The algebra blocks offer tangible objects from which the mathematics can be extracted to make the mathematical ideas more transparent (Davis & Maher, 1997). They can provide a context for meaningful discussions about lengths that may ordinarily be expressed symbolically. Algebra blocks can represent, for example, a layout of a floor plan of a real-life building in which the measurements of perimeters are proportional and to scale. The inherent notion of variability in the algebra blocks is what makes them well suited to a variety of examples. Teachers can provide rich opportunities for ELL students to develop powerful mental representations that become part of their mathematical repertoire and thus contribute to their mathematical abilities (Lesh, Post, & Behr, 1987). When teachers and ELLs use tools (such as the algebra blocks) to facilitate comprehension of mathematics topics, we can potentially increase opportunities for students to express themselves mathematically.

Through the use of multiple representations, teachers of ELL students can provide linguistic and intellectual support for students to better understand the mathematical ideas of area and perimeter. We have expressed the need for teachers to provide students opportunities to develop their linguistic skills in mathematics via their reasoning and justification. We posit that this, in turn, will allow further development of mathematics and its academic language. Asking students to transform the ideas represented by the algebra blocks into symbolic, contextual, pictorial, and linguistic forms provides critical thinking opportunities for students. We encourage teachers and students to explore mathematical ideas through translations among the various representations and transformations within the representations to enhance their mathematical conversations.

In our professional development course, we asked teachers to think about the benefits of incorporating algebra blocks in the teaching of area and perimeter, especially in light of their ELL students. We now focus on the mathematical activities in which the teachers engaged on the topic of perimeter. We first briefly discuss the use of algebra blocks for area concepts, followed by a discussion of perimeter concepts with algebra blocks.

AREA CONCEPTS AND ALGEBRA BLOCKS

Several of the teachers enrolled in this course had heard of algebra blocks, but none had previously used them. Consequently, we chose to begin with activities related to area and its relationship to multiplication because algebra blocks are commonly used in this way. The blocks are based on the idea of representing multiplication in terms of area (sometimes referred to as the *area model* for multiplication). For example, the product 3×7 can be thought of as the area of a rectangle with height 3 and length 7. Algebra blocks add some abstraction to this representation of multiplication. For example, a set of algebra blocks typically contains pieces with the shapes and (implied) dimensions shown in Figure 9.1. It is important to note that the lengths, a and b, are incommensurable.

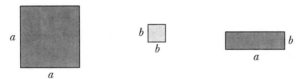

Figure 9.1   Dimensions of algebra blocks.

The rectangles shown in Figure 9.1 represent the quantities a^2, b^2, and ab, respectively. The teachers in our course used the tiles to construct models of various algebraic expressions. For example, they constructed the expression $a^2 + 2ab + b^2$ in several different ways, as demonstrated in Figure 9.2.

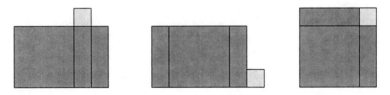

Figure 9.2   Teachers' models of $a^2 + 2ab + b^2$.

Similarly, the teachers wrote algebraic expressions corresponding to given arrangements of blocks. For instance, the areas in Figure 9.3 are both $a^2 + 3ab + 2b^2$.

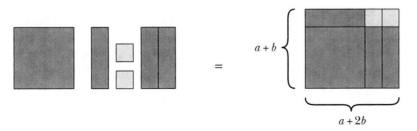

Figure 9.3   Two visual representations of $a^2 + 3ab + 2b^2$.

The area on the right, however, is arranged in the shape of a rectangle with dimensions $a + 2b$ and $a + b$, and its area is therefore $(a + 2b)(a + b)$. Thus the algebra blocks provide a visual representation for the equation $(a + 2b)(a + b) = a^2 + 3ab + 2b^2$, and more generally, they provide a geometric model for the distributive property and for factoring. Illustrating the distributive property and factoring of polynomials are typical topics for which algebra blocks were designed.

PERIMETER CONCEPTS AND ALGEBRA BLOCKS

The teachers in the course began an investigation of perimeter by finding the perimeters of several basic shapes built out of algebra blocks. For example, the shape on the left (in Figure 9.4) has a perimeter of $4a + 2b$, and the shape on the right has a perimeter of $2a + 6b$.

Figure 9.4   Basic shapes for investigating perimeter.

After the teachers investigated the perimeters of several shapes that were given to them, they created their own perimeter problems to pose to the class (see Figure 9.5). It became increasingly complex for the teachers to find the perimeters of the shapes they constructed, and the primary reason for the increase in difficulty is illustrated in the shape shown in Figure 9.5. Specifically, the indicated distance has a length that cannot be expressed as a sum of sides of length a or b.

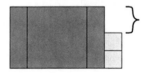

Figure 9.5   A challenging perimeter problem.

Rather, the labeled distance is obtained by subtracting two small distances from the large distance. Hence the missing length is $a - 2b$, and the total perimeter of the shape is $3a + 4b + 4b + (a - 2b) = 4a + 6b$.

After creating and studying several examples of this type, some of the teachers noticed a way to simplify their computations. If the *missing part* were inserted into the rectangle, as in Figure 9.6, the perimeter would not change. After this observation was investigated by a number of the other teachers, it became an accepted tool by which to solve problems. Thus, it was suddenly much easier for the teachers to compute that the perimeter of the given shape (in Figure 9.6) is $4a + 6b$.

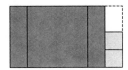

Figure 9.6   Filling in the missing corner.

Some of the teachers chose to think of the above idea in the terms, "Filling in a missing part of the rectangle doesn't change the perimeter." This seemed helpful until another teacher proposed the shape on the left side in Figure 9.7.

Figure 9.7   A counterexample to the teachers' conjecture.

The shape has a perimeter of $3a + 8b + (a - 2b) = 4a + 6b$, and the shape on the right side of Figure 9.7 (formed by filling in the missing part) has a perimeter of $4a + 4b$. This observation initially appeared to contradict the conjecture the teachers had made. After some discussion, however, the teachers decided to state the earlier conjecture more carefully. They decided that one can fill in the missing part of a rectangle, without changing the perimeter, as long as the missing part is a corner of the rectangle. From this discussion, it became necessary to examine why the modified conjecture is true. If we consider perimeter as "distance traveled around a shape," then the teachers' conjecture can be explained using the following reasoning.

If the top-right corner of a rectangle is missing (as in Figure 9.6), a bug walking clockwise along the edge of this shape must travel down and then right when it gets to the missing corner instead of right and then down. In either case, the bug must walk the same distance. (Algebraically, this is essentially due to the fact that $(a - 2b) + b = b + (a - 2b)$, and such an argument cannot be made for the missing piece in Figure 9.7.) Although the topic of study was a priori regarded as perimeter, this discussion led to discussion of the relationship between area and perimeter (addressed by Ma, 1999). The teachers realized that by removing a corner of a rectangle, they had changed the area without changing the perimeter.

As it turns out, there is a geometric shortcut for finding the perimeter of the shape (on the left) in Figure 9.7, and this method is illustrated in Figure 9.8.

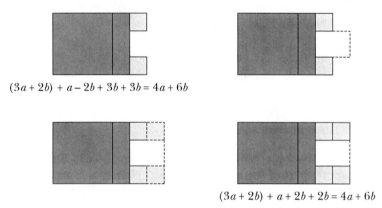

$(3a + 2b) + a - 2b + 3b + 3b = 4a + 6b$

$(3a + 2b) + a + 2b + 2b = 4a + 6b$

Figure 9.8 A geometric approach to finding the perimeter.

In planning for the lesson, we anticipated that teachers would discover this geometric method, but in fact, the teachers did not find it. One important goal was for the teachers to understand both algebraically and geometrically that area and perimeter may have very little to do with one another, and it was evident from the class discussion of these activities that this goal was met. Another critical goal was for teachers to learn to experiment mathematically and subsequently make and test mathematical conjectures. We believed that this goal was best achieved by encouraging the teachers to continue to search for a geometric method for finding the perimeter of a shape such as the one shown in Figure 9.8.

In recent years, there has been an interest in infusing early-grade curriculum with algebraic or prealgebraic thinking (see, for example, Greenes, 2003). The use of algebra blocks to study perimeter may provide a powerful way to teach algebraic thinking in earlier grades. For example, a teacher may arbitrarily designate that the lengths of the sides of the algebra blocks are, say, 2.1 (of some unit) and 7 (of the same unit), as shown in Figure 9.9. The essential point is that 7 is not an integer multiple of 2.1, and thus these lengths are consistent with the manner in which the blocks are designed.

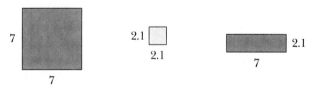

Figure 9.9 Algebra blocks with arbitrary concrete side-lengths.

With this designation, many questions and concepts similar to those mentioned here can be studied, but at a less abstract level. The usage of specific lengths instead of variables may help transition students towards algebraic thinking. For example, the task of finding the perimeter of the shape in Figure 9.10 is likely to involve the same algebraic thinking described for similar shapes. For instance, the marked distance in Figure 9.10 can be expressed as $7 - 2(2.1)$ instead of $a - 2b$ (as in Figure 9.5).

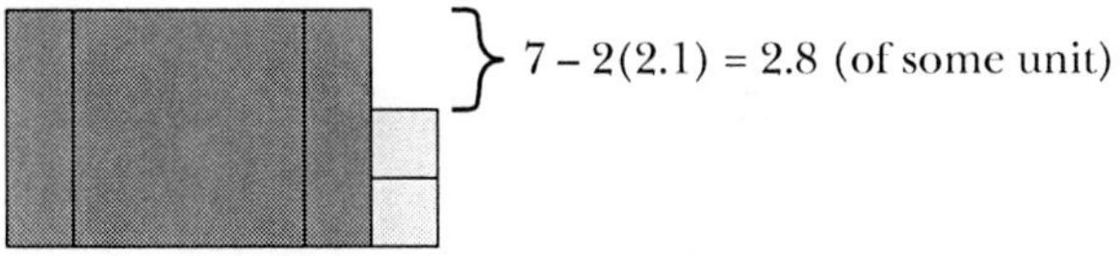

$$7 - 2(2.1) = 2.8 \text{ (of some unit)}$$

Figure 9.10   A concrete version of an earlier example.

The thinking is similar whether using variables or actual numbers, but the use of specific numbers removes a potential barrier in the transition from specific to general thinking. Thus we view this type of activity as a cognitive mechanism that facilitates the transition to abstract thinking.

TEACHERS' ANECDOTAL PERSPECTIVES

We believe that a professional development experience such as this one focusing on teachers' increased understanding of mathematics while attending to educational practices that support ELL students' learning of mathematics is critical. This experience is especially crucial in light of the growing number of ELL students in U.S. schools and the dangers posed by assuming that all middle-school mathematics teachers have extensive training in teaching mathematics to ELL students. Written feedback from the teachers and videotaped class sessions suggested that area and perimeter were the most beneficial topics from their professional development, specifically because of how the topics connected algebraic and geometric representations with algebra blocks.

One teacher confessed that she had had a boxful of the algebra tiles in her closet for a few years that were left from a previous teacher in that particular classroom, and that she did not know what they were or how they were used. She later shared that her level of motivation for teaching mathematics had been rejuvenated. Another teacher shared that he had never thought of algebra as anything beyond the symbolic notation of equations with numbers and variables. He mentioned that using area models and concrete objects to represent the mathematics helped him rethink students' perspectives on learning the mathematics via multiple representations. He realized the potential of multiple representations, especially when teaching mathematics concepts, the language of mathematics, and the English language to students whose primary language is not English. Other teachers had comments about the algebra blocks as a powerful tool to aid in the teaching and scaffolding of mathematical concepts, procedures, and formulas. In addition, the teachers expressed that the algebra blocks provided a setting for robust mathematical discussions because of the mathematics inherent in the blocks, and they regarded this as especially crucial for ELL students.

TEACHERS' QUESTIONNAIRE RESPONSES

We administered an anonymous open-ended questionnaire at the end of the course and asked the teachers to share their perceptions on the course experience. The questions are as follows:

1. What are your general impressions of having taken a professional development mathematics course with two instructors, one a mathematician and the other a mathematics educator?
2. What did you perceive as strengths of the course?
3. What did you perceive as weaknesses of the course?
4. What changes would you recommend to the instructors?

To more fully describe the teachers' perceptions of their experiences with the algebra blocks within the context of the professional development course, we have summarized their responses to the four questions. Despite the fact that the questions were asked about the course in general, many specific responses pertained to the experience with algebra blocks. After reading the responses to the questions, it became evident that the teachers strongly valued their explorations and corresponding discussions involving the algebra blocks.

General Impressions of Having Had Two Instructors

The responses to this question were overwhelmingly positive regarding the luxury of having two instructors. Many of the teachers appreciated the two different approaches and points of views in teaching the mathematics. One teacher eloquently stated, "I really enjoyed the balance of a well-versed and very knowledgeable doctor of mathematics who could explain intricacies and our doctor of mathematics education who could give us teaching suggestions. Your methods of teaching complemented each other." Another teacher commented, "It was good because you both had different styles of teaching and different points of view. This [difference] gave us 'permission' to voice our points of view that might be different yet." Another wrote, "I enjoyed the changes in personality and pace; the balance met the needs of different learners." Finally, one teacher explained, "Both teachers contributed to the learning and explaining to the class, and I learned from the multiple perspectives."

Perceived Strengths of the Course

Many of the responses referenced the use of algebra blocks as a highlight of the course: "I loved the algebra blocks, they were new to me"; "I really enjoyed working with the algebra blocks; I didn't think that algebra could be seen this way"; and "The algebra blocks helped me see math in a different way." Other relevant comments included, "I enjoyed the content and new methods for looking at algebraic concepts, especially the visuals and algebra blocks," and "I learned that I can implement a math lesson with manipulatives in my classroom." Many teachers expressed strong appreciation of the integrated nature of the course. For example, "I liked the balance between the 'pure math' and the educational strategies and issues that we discussed," and "I like the idea of this course that addressed the needs of middle school algebra and Latino students." One teacher commented that the hands-on investigations with the algebra blocks were beneficial because they helped her make the "aha" connections that will help her become a better teacher. Other general strengths of the course that were noted included using manipulatives, problem solving in groups, discussing articles on issues of teaching ELLs, interactions with fellow colleagues, variations in activities, and a relaxed atmosphere.

Perceived Weaknesses of the Course

There were several comments from the teachers suggesting that we may have misjudged the number of topics we could cover in the amount of time available (one semester). A teacher wrote that we could not cover as much material as we initially proposed because we chose to spend extra time on certain topics such as area and perimeter—which included the algebra blocks. Other comments that were unrelated to the use of algebra blocks referenced the reading of articles that were a required part of the course. Some of the responses suggested to us that the teachers felt overwhelmed with the new ways of looking at the mathematics and with the reading of related articles in addition to their full teaching load.

Recommendations for the Instructors

Ideas for us to consider in future teaching generally included suggestions such as, "[I'd like] more practice with the problems and algebra blocks during class because I've never taught with manipulatives, so that we can teach our students better." Other recommendations included a desire for more discussion on strategies of how to better teach ELLs that include the use of manipulatives and language, "more on how to reach Latinos like the article by Khisty on the case study" (Khisty, 2002). To paraphrase, a number of teachers simply wished to focus *more* on the issues that they found most relevant and most interesting. In many cases, these issues evidently (based on the corresponding response to the second question) related to our exploration with concrete algebra blocks, our discussions of the mathematics, and strategies for teaching mathematics to ELLs.

Further Thoughts on Representation and Variety

One reason for the appeal of the algebra blocks is that they offered another perspective on algebraic concepts. In other words, the algebra blocks are an alternative representation of algebraic ideas. The NCTM's (2000) publication of the *Principles and Standards for School Mathematics*, which incorporated *representation* as a process standard in the teaching and learning of mathematics, brought attention to the work of those emphasizing multiple representations as crucial for Latino ELLs in learning mathematics (for an example, see Garrison & Mora, 1999). More recent publications, such as Spitzer, White, and Flores (2009) and McGraw, Romero, and Krueger (2009), emphasize the multiple representations (concrete objects, graphs, table, and equations) of mathematical ideas for making these ideas more comprehensible and accessible to all students.

The influence of variety was not limited to the multiple mathematical representations in the context of this project. The backgrounds of the participating teachers varied substantially. Among the 22 participants, there were seven Latina women, five Latino men, five Anglo women, four Anglo men, and one Chinese woman. Their teaching experience ranged from one to 28 years, and their educational backgrounds ranged from a master's degree in education to a bachelor's degree in engineering.

Furthermore, the instructors for this course had substantially different backgrounds and perceptions of mathematics and of learning. The mathematician and the mathematics educator each brought different learning and teaching perspectives to the project. For example, the mathematics educator preferred to spend a large amount of time waiting, giving "think time" and work time in small groups, occasionally not allowing full coverage of the planned material, whereas the mathematician typically wanted to move through the planned material to stay on schedule, with the intent that the teachers would work through some of the mathematical details outside of class. When discussing mathematical material in class, the mathematician preferred to draw pictures and/or write equations, and the mathematics educator would frequently discuss the mathematics directly in terms of manipulatives (such as the algebra blocks). This preference may have accounted for the subsequent large group discussions that addressed both the benefits and the limitations of the manipulatives. The teachers saw how the concrete objects helped them to formulate and test conjectures, and they appreciated how the "visible" solutions encouraged participation in mathematical discourse, but they also recognized that some problems were best suited for more abstract analysis. Thus, while the apparent differences may a priori appear to be challenges, the classroom discussions and the participants' comments suggested that the opposite was true.

We sought to understand how this diversity of mathematical representations, participant backgrounds, and instructor perspectives could enrich a professional learning environment centered on mathematics teachers of Latino ELLs. A key mechanism in this process was the prevalence of mathematical discourse. This discourse allowed for the multiple perspectives to emerge, and (for example) it even led to a particularly meaningful demonstration of notions of conjecture, counterexample, and proof. The work of McGraw and colleagues (2009) and Maldonado, Turner, Domínguez, and Empson (2009) highlights the effectiveness of having students develop mathematical discourse by participating in mathematical discussions while making use of multiple representations to explain their thinking in mathematics. Although the inclusion of ELL students in hands-on activities and mathematical discussions may present challenges, these same challenges may be the ones that provide the richness in discussions embedded in the multiple representations that lead to access of more abstract mathematical ideas, which may not otherwise be accessible to ELLs.

The findings in this project corroborate with other successful projects with similar contexts. In a metasynthesis of qualitative research on effective teaching practices for ELLs, Téllez and Waxman (2006) found, in the studies they analyzed, that the use of multiple representations designed for understanding a target language is an effective instructional practice. This heavy reliance on multiple representations, such as the inclusion of visuals with language, allows for a multidimensional views of similar concepts. According to Tufte (1990), "visual displays of information encourage a diversity of individual viewer styles and rates of editing, personalizing, reasoning, and understanding" (p. 31). Tellez and Waxman noted that "Tufte's point is particularly germane to students' learning a second language, for whom rate of delivery, comprehensible input, and self-regulated attention are key factors in developing competence" (p. 263). The study of multiple representations, especially in the field of mathematics education for ELLs, deserves more attention from the research literature, especially because the use of multiple representations designed for teaching in the students' second language is, among others, a key practice likely to increase learning mathematics among ELLs.

CONCLUSIONS

The activities described in this chapter offer a concrete setting to study various additive algebraic properties while sacrificing little in terms of mathematical depth or generality. Not only is mathematical depth preserved, but the underlying mathematics is well suited to student-centered activities that involve significant mathematical analysis in the form of conjecture and generalization. This type of analysis has the additional benefit of highlighting connections between algebra and geometry.

Exploring mathematical concepts using algebra blocks and other representations is important for students' transition from arithmetic to algebraic thinking and for their development of mathematical language, which is especially critical for students who are learning English as a second language. The nature of conceptually understanding area and perimeter in abstract contexts can be cognitively demanding and yet necessary for *all* students to have equal access to mathematical skills and reasoning. The use of the linguistic representation plays a crucial role in understanding mathematics, especially for ELLs, thus explicit and deliberate linguistic and intellectual support for furthering language development during cognitively demanding tasks is vital.

ACKNOWLEDGMENT

This manuscript is based upon work supported in part by the National Science Foundation under Grant No. 0424983 to the Center for the Mathematics Education of Latinos/Latinas (CEMELA). Any opinions, findings, and conclusions or recommendations expressed in this material are those of the author(s) and do not necessarily reflect the views of the National Science Foundation. The authors wish to thank Virginia Horak, who reviewed the manuscript and offered support and feedback.

REFERENCES

Anhalt, C. O., Ondrus, M., & Horak, V. (2007). Issues of language: Teacher insights from mathematics lessons in Chinese. *Mathematics Teaching in the Middle School, 13*(1), 18–23. Retrieved from http://www.nctm.org

Ball, D. L. & Bass, H. (2000). Interweaving content and pedagogy in teaching and learning to teach: Knowing and using mathematics. In J. Boaler (Ed.), *Multiple perspectives on mathematics teaching and learning* (pp. 83–104). Westport, CT: Ablex.

Ball, D. L., Lubienski, S. T., & Mewborn, D. S. (2001). Research on teaching mathematics: The unsolved problem of teachers' mathematical knowledge. In V. Richardson (Ed.), *Handbook of research on teaching* (4th ed., pp. 433–456). Washington, DC: American Educational Research Association.

Brown, C. A., Smith, M. S., & Stein, M. K. (1996, April). *Linking teacher professional development to enhanced classroom instruction.* Paper presented at the meeting of the American Educational Research Association, New York, NY.

Coggins, D., Kravin, D., Coates, G. D., & Carroll, M. D. (2007). *English language learners in the mathematics classroom.* Thousand Oaks, CA: Corwin Press.

Davis, R. B. & Maher, C. A. (1997). How students think: The role of representations. In L. D. English (Ed.), *Mathematical reasoning: Analogies, metaphors, and images* (pp. 93–115). Mahwah, NJ: Erlbaum.

Garrison, L. & Mora, J. K. (1999). Adapting mathematics instruction for English-language learners: The language-concept connection. In L. Ortiz-Franco, N. G. Hernández, & Y. de la Cruz (Eds.), *Changing the faces of mathematics: Perspectives on Latinos* (pp. 35–47), Reston, VA: National Council of Teachers of Mathematics.

Gibbons, P. (2002). *Scaffolding language, scaffolding learning: Teaching second language learners in the mainstream classroom.* Portsmouth, NH: Heinemann.

Greenes, C. E. (2003). *Algebra for all ages.* Boston, MA: Houghton Mifflin. Retrieved from http://www.eduplace.com/state/pdf/author/greenes.pdf

Kennedy, M. M. (1998). Education reform and subject matter knowledge. *Journal of Research in Teaching Science, 35*(3), 249–263. doi: 10.1002/(SICI)1098-2736(199803)35:3<249::AID-TEA2>3.3.CO;2-T

Khisty, L. L. (2002) Mathematics learning and the Latino student: Suggestions from research for classroom practice. *Teaching Children Mathematics, 9*(1), 32–35. Retrieved from http://www.nctm.org/

Krashen, S. D. (1988). *Second language acquisition and second language learning.* Upper Saddle River, NJ: Prentice Hall.

Leitze, A. R. & Kitt, N. A. (2000) Algebra for all: Using homemade algebra tiles to develop algebra and prealgebra concepts. *Mathematics Teacher, 93*(6), 462–665. Retrieved from http://www.nctm.org/

Lesh, R., Post, T., & Behr, M. J. (1987). Representations and translations among representations in mathematics learning and problem solving. In C. Janvier (Ed.), *Problems of representation in the teaching and learning of mathematics* (pp. 33–40). Hillsdale, NJ: Erlbaum.

Lubiensky, S. L. (2003). Is our teaching measuring up? Race-, SES-, and gender-related gaps in measurement achievement. In D. H. Clements & G. Bright

(Eds.), *Learning and teaching measurement, 65th yearbook* (pp. 282–292). Reston, VA: National Council of Teachers of Mathematics.

Ma, L. (1999). *Knowing and teaching elementary mathematics: Teachers' understanding of fundamental mathematics in China and the United States.* Mahwah, NJ: Erlbaum.

Maldonado, L. A., Turner, E., Domínguez, H., & Empson, S. (2009). English-language learners learning from, and contributing to, mathematical discussions. In C. E. Malloy, D. Y. White, & J. S. Sitzer (Eds.), *Mathematics for every student: Responding to diversity, grades pre-K–5* (pp. 7–22). Reston, VA: National Council of Teachers of Mathematics.

McGraw, R., Romero, D., & Krueger, R. (2009). Facilitating whole-class discussions in diverse classrooms: Strategies for engaging all students. In C. E. Malloy, D. Y. White, & J. S. Sitzer (Eds.), *Mathematics for every student: Responding to diversity, grades 9-12* (pp. 17–28). Reston, VA: National Council of Teachers of Mathematics.

Moschkovich, J. N. (2002). A situated and sociocultural perspective on bilingual mathematics learners. *Mathematical Thinking and Learning, 4*(2/3), 189–212. doi: 10.1207/S15327833MTL04023_5

National Council of Teachers of Mathematics (NCTM). (2000). *Principles and standards for school mathematics.* Reston, VA: Author.

Schifter, D. (1998). Learning mathematics for teaching: From a teachers' seminar to the classroom. *Journal of Mathematics Teacher Education, 1*(1), 55–87. doi: 10.1023/A:1009911200478

Shulman, L. S. (1986). Those who understand: Knowledge growth in teaching. *Educational Researcher, 15*(2), 4–14. doi: 10.3102/0013189X015002004

Shulman, L. S. (1987). Knowledge and teaching: Foundations of the new reform. *Harvard Educational Review, 57*(1), 1–22. Retrieved from http://www.hepg. org/her/

Shulman, L. S. & Quinlan, K. M. (1996). The comparative psychology of school subjects. In D. C. Berliner & R. C. Calfee (Eds.), *Handbook of educational psychology* (pp. 399–422). New York, NY: Simon & Schuster Macmillan.

Shulman, L. S. & Sykes, G. (1986). *A national board for teaching? In search of a bold standard: A report for the task force on teaching as a profession.* New York: Carnegie Corporation.

Sowder, J. T., Philipp, R. A., Armstrong, B. E., & Schappelle, B. P. (1998). *Middle-grade teachers' mathematical knowledge and its relationship to instruction: A research monograph.* Albany: State University of New York Press.

Spitzer, J. S., White, D. Y., & Flores, A. (2009). Help one, help all. *Mathematics for every student: responding to diversity, grades 9-12* (pp. 39–48). Reston, VA: National Council of Teachers of Mathematics.

Téllez, K. & Waxman, H. C. (2006). A meta-synthesis of qualitative research on effective teaching practices for English language learners. In J. M. Norris & L. Ortega (Eds.), *Synthesizing research on language learning and teaching* (pp. 245–277). Amsterdam, The Netherlands: John Benjamins.

Tufte, E. R. (1990). *Envisioning information.* Cheshire, CT: Graphics Press.

Webster-Wright, A. (2009). Reframing professional development through understanding authentic professional learning. *Review of Educational Research, 79*(2), 702–739. doi: 10.3102/0034654308330970

CHAPTER 10

SITUATING MATHEMATICS PROFESSIONAL DEVELOPMENT

A Bilingual Teacher and Researchers' Collaboration

Sandra I. Musanti, Ph.D.
Universidad Nacional de San Martin, Argentina

Mary E. Marshall
Albuquerque Public Schools

Karla Ceballos
La Mesa Elementary, Albuquerque Public Schools

Sylvia Celedón-Pattichis
Department of Language, Literacy, and Sociocultural Studies
The University of New Mexico

INTRODUCTION

All of us who engage in professional development activities work to introduce new approaches to teachers that will elevate their practice and improve their students' learning. Researchers who explore teaching practices through pro-

Latinos/as and Mathematics Education, pages 215–232
Copyright © 2011 by Information Age Publishing
215

fessional development strive to discover that special combination of support and information that teachers need to take an idea and make it their own. It is reasonable to assume the teachers with whom we work hope that the time and effort they put into learning will be worthwhile.

Even when professional development is successful and all the hopes and expectations of the researchers and teachers come together, rarely do the participants have an opportunity to reflect on the experience and collectively learn. In this chapter, we report on a three-year project that became an important professional development experience for the three university researchers and the one kindergarten teacher involved. During this time, we constructed a collaborative partnership, learned from each other, grew professionally, developed warm and supportive relationships, and together, we believe, enhanced children's mathematical learning.

Equity drove our work and research to improve mathematics teaching and learning in a bilingual kindergarten classroom, where the majority of students were from Mexican immigrant families. We developed our collaboration agenda around mathematics word problem solving using Cognitively Guided Instruction (CGI) (Carpenter, Fennema, Franke, Levi, & Empson, 1999). Students were encouraged to develop communication, reasoning, and justification skills as they engaged with important mathematical concepts. Our goal was to demonstrate that these students could successfully solve complex word problems if the problems were based in familiar linguistic and cultural contexts (Turner, Celedón-Pattichis, & Marshall, 2008). Key to this development was a teaching approach that connected with students' cultural knowledge, assessed students' thinking about the problems, and built on students' own emerging strategies to move students forward.

In the following sections, we outline the theoretical framework that guided our work and the previous research on which we built our study. Because few studies have explored the mathematical professional development of bilingual teachers, especially for those who are teaching content areas in Spanish, our literature review integrates different areas of bilingual teaching (Flores, 2001; Varghese, 2004). In addition, we explain the grounding of our work in a sociocultural understanding of collaboration to generate a mutually beneficial partnership (John-Steiner, 2000; Wenger, 1998) and a definition of situated professional development in mathematics that recognizes the uniqueness of each situation and the multiple factors that affect classroom and school dynamics (Cobb, McClain, Lamberg, & Dean, 2003). Specific to the bilingual population in this study, we discuss equity in mathematics education and particularly the language challenges Latina/o students face to be successful mathematics learners (Secada, 1995). We end the chapter with a detailed description of the context and characteristics of our collaboration, as well as how it influenced the kindergarten teacher and her students.

THEORETICAL ROOTS TO A SITUATED APPROACH TO PROFESSIONAL DEVELOPMENT

Bilingual Teacher Education Research

In the political context of the early 21st century, bilingual education, the education of bilingual teachers, and their role in the education of Latina/o students is under close scrutiny. With increasing Latino, Spanish-speaking populations across every region of the United States and persistently low mathematics achievement rates of these same students (The Education Trust, 2008), school districts with bilingual programs should offer customized professional development opportunities that address teachers' needs and those of their students. Specifically, bilingual mathematics education has received little attention in what counts as effective professional development (Musanti, Celedón-Pattichis, & Marshall, 2009).

Teacher education and professional development that specifically prepare teachers of the Latino, Spanish-speaking population are needed (Téllez, 2004/2005). Research has shown that teachers' positive personal experiences in relation to language and culture affect their beliefs regarding the benefits of bilingual education (Flores, 2001; Varghese, 2004). Professional development designed for bilingual teachers should grow from a careful consideration of the local teaching context, teachers' beliefs and unique teaching styles, and the learning needs of their specific group of students. Varghese (2004) explained that contrary to the view of bilingual education as a profession unified under similar conceptions, bilingual teachers tend to hold dissimilar beliefs regarding how to approach their practice. It is important to recognize "such differences rather than assuming an unified *a priori* (italics in original) understanding of bilingual teaching, so as to assist bilingual teachers in exploring different configurations of their roles and ultimately attempt to create more quality bilingual programmes" (Varghese, 2004, p. 223).

Considering the politically charged nature of bilingual education and the lack of research in professional development for bilingual mathematics teachers, we argue that bilingual teacher development must be reconceptualized as a situated practice aimed at generating collaborative partnerships that promote localized and contextualized learning. Consequently, we need to reconsider the potential of professional development initiatives that recover teachers' experiences as learners and teachers (Musanti, 2005), and validate bilingual teachers' agency in terms of enacting curriculum and language policies (Varghese, 2004).

Sociocultural Understanding of Collaboration and Professional Development

In our long-term professional development project, we came to realize the importance of complementarity in collaborative efforts (John-Steiner, 2000) among the researchers and teacher. As researchers, we approached our work with Karla, a bilingual kindergarten teacher and the third author of this chapter, from a sociocultural understanding of collaboration and coconstruction of knowledge among those engaged in a shared enterprise (Musanti, 2005). Our approach to situated professional development began with the acknowledgment that successful learning collaboration draws on the unique strengths each learner brings to the partnership and requires a joint purpose or vision (John-Steiner, 2000). We knew that Karla's unique strengths and beliefs were built on her life experiences, especially as a learner, and they influenced her approach to teaching and her understanding about her students' learning needs (Musanti, 2005). We knew our own strengths and beliefs came from our life experiences as well. Our theoretical stance became clearer as the project unfolded, and we constructed a common agenda for professional development. As a true collaboration, we came to realize our interdependence and that our collaborative teaching was increasingly guided by a wider perspective, one informed equally by our own research-based insights and Karla's expanding sense of her own efficacy as a mathematics educator.

From a sociocultural perspective, building learning communities encourages teachers and professional development facilitators to participate in their own development and thus transform their understanding of student and teacher learning, ultimately altering teaching practice, which in turn may transform their identities (Wenger, 1998). We built on the idea of engagement and participation, relying on Rogoff's (2003) conceptualization of development and cognition. As Rogoff explained, "a person develops through *participation in* an activity, *changing* to be involved in the situation at hand in ways that contribute both to the ongoing event and to the person's preparation for involvement in other similar events" (p. 254).

Central to our work with teachers was our engagement and participation with their mathematics teaching, grounded in the importance for teachers to have organized opportunities in which to learn and form practice (Whitcomb, Borko, & Liston, 2009). This approach to professional development focuses on understanding children's learning and situating teacher development in relation to their practice (Franke, Carpenter, Levi, & Fennema, 2001; Kazemi & Franke, 2004). Contemporary conceptualizations of professional development emphasize teachers learning in collaboration with others, reflecting on their practices, and collegially designing teaching approaches that respond to students' needs. Unfortunately, these conceptualizations do not explain how those who conduct the professional development are also learners, and how they can benefit from collaboration, reflection, and collegial design as well. Without this realization, opportunities for continuous improvement in the facilitator's role in professional development are often missed.

A situated approach to professional development (i.e., one that suits teacher's needs, generates reciprocal learning between teacher and researchers, and affords opportunities to have an impact on student learning) requires a deep understanding of teachers' instructional realities and their underlying assumptions about teaching and learning (Cobb, McClain et al., 2003). Because of this importance, we contend it is necessary to reconceptualize professional development as a collaborative enterprise that engages researchers and teachers in a mutual learning and teaching relationship that requires an ongoing reflective approach on the impact of practice (Guskey, 2002; John-Steiner, 2000; Whitcomb et al., 2009). "The crucial point is that it is not the professional development *per se*, but the experience of successful implementation that changes teachers' attitudes and beliefs. They believe it works because they have seen it work, and that experience shapes their attitudes and beliefs" (Guskey, 2002, p. 383).

This premise was true for the researchers in this study as well. In the process of situating mathematics professional development into a Spanish-taught kindergarten classroom, we collectively learned about Latina/o students' mathematical learning, how to teach problem solving, and how to better support bilingual teachers to teach mathematics in Spanish.

Equity-Driven Professional Development

Equitable mathematics learning environments recognize that all students have a greater opportunity for success when teachers view the specific language and cultural backgrounds of their students as strengths and use these to support student learning (Secada, 1995). It was equity that drove our professional development and we were aware that the statistics showing unacceptably low mathematics achievement for Spanish-speaking Latina/o children do not reflect their true potential (The Education Trust, 2008).

Lack of access to challenging curricula for Latina/o students and teachers with inadequate training and weak backgrounds in mathematics are listed among the factors contributing to testing disparities between Latino and Caucasian students (The Education Trust, 2008). To promote Latina/o students' academic success, it is critical that mathematics instruction move increasingly towards a language-rich and contextually based problem-solving approach outlined in the National Council of Teachers of Mathematics (2000) standards. To facilitate mathematical communication, support for English language learner Latina/o students in their native and second language is critical (Celedón-Pattichis, 2008; Cummins, 2001; Khisty, 1995; Moschkovich, 2007).

METHOD

We use a narrative approach to describe the professional development project and our work with the students. As Clandinin and Connelly (2000) suggested, narrative research strategies place an emphasis on documenting ongoing reflections and shared stories, which served to highlight the dynamics of our developing partnership and how we learned from each other. The data presented in this chapter are part of a qualitative longitudinal study.

Data Collection

Here we focus on data collected from our work with a kindergarten teacher and third author of this chapter (Karla), during a period of two years, between January 2007 and December 2008. During this period, we conducted four interviews with Karla, one at the end of each semester, to explore her ideas on mathematics teaching to Latina/o students, her understandings of CGI, how she integrated it into her curriculum, and how she perceived the impact it had on students. The final interview took the form of an open conversation. As a result of our prolonged involvement and our relationship, we believed the most appropriate approach for this final interview was a conversation without a preset script to elicit the topics that each of us, teacher and researchers, believed important.

Another source of data was the debriefing sessions we held with Karla during fall 2007 and spring 2008. These sessions involved open-ended conversations about the events of the CGI lesson of the day. It is important to note that during many of the lessons the researchers and teacher each took a small group of students to continue solving CGI problems after a whole-group introduction. Because of this experience, our conversations were based on common successes and challenges. Even though our intent was to hold debriefing sessions weekly after each CGI session, Karla's classroom schedule was busy and time availability was scarce, so we were only able to debrief formally 11 times during fall 2007 and spring 2008. Debriefing became shorter and more informal during fall 2008 because time availability was scarcer due to changes in the school's daily agenda. We managed to briefly speak after each session.

We also used video data collected between fall 2007 and spring 2008 on eight CGI classroom sessions. We developed content logs of each videotape over the course of the project. At the conclusion of the project, we selected the episodes that best illustrated the impact of our collaborative work on how to integrate problem solving into the kindergarten classroom.

A final source of data came from the informal conversations with Karla as we prepared to present our work with her and other teachers at a language teaching conference. Karla took a leadership role in this presentation, during which she explained her experiences and perceptions of teaching mathematics problem solving. We relied on some of her statements during this presentation because they summarized relevant insights achieved during our work together. Additionally, our prolonged involvement with Karla, her kindergarten class, and our close collaboration allows us to provide a description of our partnership that integrates data from researchers' memos, debriefing sessions, e-mails exchanged, and notes from researchers' planning meetings.

The main goal of this chapter is to present a detailed description of our professional development experience and reflect on the impact of working together for two years. Therefore, our analysis consisted mainly of reading and rereading the data to identify stories and reflections. Our purpose is to illustrate the main characteristics of our collective work that shaped and situated the professional development experience, especially in how practice can inform and shape theory.

A CONTEXT FOR COLLABORATION AND PROFESSIONAL DEVELOPMENT

In 2006, the Center for the Mathematics Education of Latinas/os (CEME-LA) researchers had initiated professional development work with bilingual teachers from a local school district's elementary school. This Title I school is located in the southwestern United States, and 85% of its student population is of Mexican descent, mostly immigrant families. All students receive free breakfast and lunches. The school implements a bilingual program involving instruction in both native language and English as second language (ESL) designed to meet the linguistic and academic needs of students, adjusting the percentage of instruction in each language accordingly. At the time of our collaboration, kindergarten instruction in content areas was done almost exclusively in Spanish, given that 100% of the students spoke Spanish as a first language. Typically, afternoon segments of instruction were dedicated to ESL and mostly focused on introducing students to basic academic vocabulary.

Regarding mathematics instruction, the school had adopted Everyday Mathematics as its mathematics reform curriculum. The curriculum emphasized the mathematical processes of problem solving, communication, reasoning, connections, and representation. Our professional development proposal provided teachers ways to supplement this curriculum by introducing contextualized problem solving and focusing on understanding students' mathematical thinking through their communication.

The CEMELA research team offered professional development opportunities for teachers who would be willing to learn about mathematical reasoning, problem solving, and language and culture issues in the mathematics learning of Latina/o students. During summer 2005 and 2006, primary-grade bilingual teachers at the school were invited to participate in two-week institutes dedicated to learning about the integration of language, culture, and mathematics, a graduate course that was offered for credit and was taught in 2005 by Sylvia, the fourth author, and CGI (Carpenter et al., 1999). Initially, a partnership with a kindergarten teacher at the school who had participated in our first CGI summer institute opened the door for a longitudinal research project that focuses on following a small group of bilingual students from kindergarten through third grade (for research findings see Turner et al., 2008).

Our involvement with teachers at the school site expanded during the fall 2006. We initiated a systematic project with three teachers at the school, providing weekly visits to their classrooms. In-class support involved frequent researchers' visits to the teachers' classrooms to observe mathematics lessons, participate or model CGI problem-solving lessons, discuss different ways to implement problem-solving activities, provide resources to supplement mathematics curriculum, and offer time for debriefing conversations to discuss classroom events related to mathematics instruction. Additionally, between September and November 2006, the first and second authors (Sandra and Mary) had attended five kindergarten collaboration meetings to work with teachers on the CGI approach. During these meetings, we shared videotapes from the kindergarten study and discussed CGI main assumptions.

Our work with Karla, who participated in the second and final summer institute during summer 2006, started with every other week visits to the classroom by the first author, Sandra, in January 2007. In September 2007, the second author, Mary, joined Sandra, and the visits increased to a weekly frequency. In January 2008, the fourth author, Sylvia, joined in our weekly visits to Karla's classroom.

The partnership we created grew from the recognition that we were all essentially novices in using CGI. The first author, Sandra, a native Spanish speaker from Argentina, had done her doctorate work in collaboration and bilingual teacher professional development. She had participated in the second summer institute on CGI but had no experience implementing it in the classroom. The second author, Mary, a doctoral candidate, had a background in mathematics and experience in elementary mathematics teaching in the United States, but was a Spanish language learner. She also had some experience in CGI from a previous year's research in the first kindergarten classroom, as did Sylvia. The third author, Karla was the kindergarten teacher with three years of teaching experience at the time. She was a native of Mexico and shared the culture and language of her students. She admitted that her background in mathematics was not strong. The fourth author, Sylvia, was the faculty advisor with a strong mathematics background and theoretical experience in elementary mathematics teaching methods, but no elementary classroom teaching experience.

The collaborative professional development approach described in this chapter focused on mathematics problem solving using CGI (Carpenter et al., 1999) in a Spanish-language kindergarten classroom. This work grew from extending conclusions of a previous kindergarten study (Turner et al., 2008), which demonstrated the power of integrating problem solving in two bilingual kindergarten classrooms and an ESL kindergarten classroom with Latina/o students. The evidence in the previous study showed that a CGI approach to problem solving that focused on students solving mathematical stories created from their own cultural experiences had a positive impact on students' capacity to communicate their mathematical thinking, develop problem-solving and basic number skills, and connect home and school contexts.

Situating Ourselves in a Spanish-Speaking Bilingual Classroom

The professional development approach is based on the idea of situated mathematics professional development that responds to the cultural and linguistic needs of the student population and recognizes the uniqueness of each situation and the multiple factors that affect classroom and school dynamics (Cobb & McClain, 2006). In our research, we extended this notion to situate our efforts based on the needs of the teacher as well, and recognized that each classroom has a unique dynamic relationship among students and between them and their teacher (Musanti et al., 2009). Each year, curriculum implementation issues, administrative agendas, the issues surrounding the lives of the students, and teacher reactions to these issues play a role in the classroom. With all these factors in mind, situating our professional development also meant redefining our role with the teacher and recognizing that it was unrealistic to arrive as "the experts" in the middle of these classroom dynamics. We knew that our best chance of success depended on developing a partnership with the teacher and developing the problem-solving approaches that worked for her and her students. We recognized that essential elements of this process were mutuality, trust, and shared purpose, which required prolonged involvement and reciprocal learning to unfold (John-Steiner, 2000; Musanti, 2005). This effort incorporated components of a design experiment framework (Cobb, Confrey et al., 2003); that is, our collaborative goal was to ultimately develop theory about how to support teacher and students' mathematics teaching and learning in a Spanish-speaking classroom.

Sandra initiated the partnership in 2007 at the invitation of Karla, who had been inspired by the success of the other kindergarten classroom teacher who had implemented CGI the previous year—her mentor, Ms. Arenas (see Turner et al., 2008). Karla's decision to enter into this collaboration with CE-MELA showed professional initiative, dedication to her students, and personal courage. Her own experience with mathematics learning in Mexico and the United States had been painful and her confidence was low. She admitted during the summer 2006 institute that she knew very little about mathematics beyond basic operations, but was determined to grow professionally in this area and give her students the best education possible.

Aware of her inexperience with CGI and mathematics learning in general, Sandra did not enter into this partnership with high levels of confidence. Instead, Sandra focused on learning from Karla's class and on becoming a thinking partner for Karla, someone with whom she could discuss ideas and plan the next step. Both approached the work as novices. After each session, they would get together when possible to talk about their impressions of students' problem-solving strategies and how to support students to verbalize their thinking. Karla's thoughts, shared in May 2007 during one of those brief conversations with Sandra, capture the essence of our initial learning:

> CGI is more about having them think, and about having them explain, and having them orally give their thoughts and see what they were doing, by themselves and with the teacher, so I could really see: Well, he's thinking this and he's doing this, and this is why.

In September 2007, we started the school year with some changes. The CEMELA research team at the time, Sandra and Mary, had decided to expand and intensify the work with the teachers who had asked us to continue the collaboration. Mary joined the partnership with Sandra and Karla, bringing a stronger mathematics background, but only slightly more confidence in CGI implementation and no experience in teaching at the kindergarten level, especially in Spanish. For this academic year, we proposed to the teachers who were engaged in implementing CGI, including Karla, to participate in monthly professional development workshops that we tailored to teachers' and students' needs and gave teachers an opportunity to discuss their CGI experiences with each other. Because we did not want to be positioned as experts, we approached this work from a collegial stance, focusing on learning from each other and reflecting on students' work. During fall 2007 and spring 2008, we held six workshops with six primary-grade teachers who were implementing CGI in their classrooms. In addition, we sought approval from Karla to increase the frequency of our visits to her classroom to a weekly basis so we could work more closely with her and her students. She also agreed to be videotaped during some of her lessons.

Initially, to deepen our involvement in the classroom, Sandra and Mary offered to work with students, mostly in small-group format, when Karla considered it appropriate. Typically, we discussed and planned each session during the debriefing conversation the previous week, and either Sandra or Mary e-mailed to Karla the outlined plan. Sometimes, this plan was modified by Karla based on her assessment of students' needs. We offer a quote from an e-mail sent from Mary to Karla with the ideas for the session in October 2007. It illustrates the way we constructed our collegial work with a shared vision of improving the quality of the mathematics teaching and learning experience while contemplating the needs of students and the emphasis the teacher wanted to bring to the session. In this case, the focus was on students telling their own mathematics stories:

> You have a challenging group, but we think you are making real progress with them! We [Karla, Mary and Sandra] decided that this week we would take small groups in the same way you work with the whole group. We will each go to a corner of the classroom, have them sit in front of us, an then come forward one at a time to tell their own number story. We will keep the blocks and only the student telling the story will work blocks. Hopefully, we can get them to focus more.

During the next session, Karla started with the whole group sitting on the carpet. She posed a math story for the students: "*Compré 6 panes y mi esposo se comió 3. ¿Cuántos quedaron?*" ["I bought six rolls and my husband ate three. How many were left?"] Her focus at this time was on students retelling the story and recalling the information embedded in the story. What happened next (see Excerpt 10.1) illustrates how challenging it was, initially, for most students in this group to retell the stories and to verbalize their thinking. The interaction has been translated from Spanish and reconstructed from field notes.

Excerpt 10.1. Whole-group math stories

>   **Karla:** "Who can repeat the story? Fabian?" (Fabian stands up and comes to the front.)
>   **Fabian:** (doesn't say anything)

> **Karla:** "What happens in the story? What was the story about?"
> **Fabian:** (He remains silent looking at the teacher.)
> **Karla:** (to the group) "How many rolls did I buy?"
> **Students:** "Six." (few students answer)
> **Karla:** "And how many did my husband eat?"
> **Students:** "Three." (few students respond, Fabian remains silent)

Karla called a second student to help Fabian solve the problem with manipulatives. During the process of solving the problems, students were asked similar questions ("How many did I buy? How many did he eat?") to help them recall the facts. Students solved the problem by modeling, first showing six cubes and then taking three away and counting the remaining cubes.

At this point in the year, students needed a lot of support to stay focused during the process of solving the problem. Most of these students had no previous schooling, some of them were still working on one-to-one correspondence, and some had difficulties expressing themselves verbally. Therefore, we had decided that this whole-class activity would be followed by small-group work. Each of us facilitated a group, focusing on giving students opportunities to tell mathematics stories or retell stories made up by peers before working on the solution. Our involvement in the class became a powerful experience that confronted researchers with the challenges of teaching kindergarten students, afforded a unique opportunity for complementing each other's roles, and strengthened the bidirectionality of the learning process.

This type of activity afforded Karla the opportunity to work closely with students who needed more individualized attention, and for Mary and Sandra, it was a chance to get involved in the classroom's dynamics while getting to know students better, work on eliciting their math thinking, and implement CGI with kindergartners. For all of us, it was a chance to build our partnership by sharing roles that typically are out of bounds when research and professional development are involved. This opportunity for researchers to cross over to the teaching side was a central element in the process of situating professional development in the context of localized practice. By embedding ourselves in the teaching process, we added a new dimension to the professional development approach, that of a more truthful co-construction of knowledge and collegial learning.

In what follows, we share our reflections of the impact of situated mathematics professional development on Karla's level of confidence in herself as a mathematics learner and teacher, and the centrality of confidence for equity in bilingual teachers and Latina/o students' learning.

Gaining Confidence in Teaching and Learning Mathematics

During our first interview with Karla in May 2007, she explained:

> Before CGI, I had more questions. I had more questions about how I was teaching mathematics, but after CGI, I think I'm understanding mathematics better myself, because I never was a good student in math. . . . I always had to take algebra. I took algebra three times. I don't know how they let me take it three times, but I had to take it. Because I wasn't good at math. I was always afraid of it and I never thought I was going to understand as well. But now I feel more confident and more able to teach it, I mean, not as a mathematician, but at a level that I feel confident, and just good.

A central and unexpected realization from our research was the importance of building confidence for the teacher, the students, and the researchers in this project. We initiated this collaboration, not from an expert stance, but with the genuine understanding that we all had something to learn from students and from each other. Often, this awareness runs parallel to how confident we feel as we approach a new task. Karla was aware that her previous experiences as a mathematics learner had left her with a feeling of inadequacy that generated discomfort and lowered her confidence as a teacher of mathematics. As she explained it, understanding mathematics, becoming aware of the achieved understanding, and being confident in this new knowledge were very important elements of her change and professional development efficacy.

We contend that change in knowledge and practice happens when educators see that change in teaching can have an effect on students' learning and not the other way around (Guskey, 2002). In May 2008, Karla explained to us that after implementing CGI for two years, she was feeling more comfortable because "I see that my students and I have evolved, and that now, like them, I've also started seeing different ways to solve a problem and have more confidence" (translated from Spanish). Confidence as a learning outcome, as a teaching goal, and as a personal achievement has been underrated. Confidence is a crucial component of bilingual teachers' sense of agency to enact curriculum that attends to students' needs (Varghese, 2004). Therefore, both teachers and students can benefit from putting confidence at the center of a professional development agenda.

Being confident entails understanding our practice, the theory behind it, and a reflective attitude towards our role and beliefs. Confidence also recognizes the value in others' contributions. As Karla's words from an interview we conducted with her in May 2008 illustrate, valuing and respecting the knowledge that others (students or teachers) bring to our endeavor is essential for genuine understanding:

They come with a lot of knowledge, not without it. They know a lot, but they don't know how to show it. Only if we value it and we tell them, "But you knew it, you learned it at home. Well done." But they think they don't know anything. And that's not the case. On the contrary, many of these kids know how to go shopping at the flea market, they know how to deal with money, how much things cost. Maybe they don't know the quantities, but they know to make tamales, and sell them, and who has more or who has less. But they believe that is not education. (translated from Spanish)

Becoming a confident teacher in terms of understanding students' needs means higher teacher expectations of students' mathematical learning, a central component of educational equity (Turner et al., 2008). As Karla explained to us in an interview in May 2008,

I think that my main achievement is that they feel more confident. Because I see how much more confident they are, and how secure they feel either in mathematics or anything else. I enjoy that because at the beginning they would lower their heads. Their self-esteem was very low. Not now. (translated from Spanish)

Over time, Karla's students became more confident in their capabilities, were able to provide math stories to be solved by peers, take risks solving problems in different ways even when they reached an incorrect answer, or explain their thinking to the class as they solved a problem. The students' intense engagement in the CGI problem-solving lessons and their excitement about the researchers' visits to their classroom were proof of their developing confidence as mathematics problem solvers. We believe this is the result of an intense teacher's work to validate their voice and thinking, for instance acknowledging all answers as potentially valid and/or correct. Karla expressed this sentiment succinctly during our presentation at La Cosecha conference in November 2008:

I ask different kids and if I have three that have different answers, I make all three come up and explain to the whole class. And then the class decides, who do you think is right? And then some of them know and some of them don't and then we work out all of those three problems and then they know.

We observed over time how Karla constructed a sense of agency and confidence in herself and her students' capabilities to learn mathematics. She created a safe classroom environment in which students felt that they could freely think and talk without fear of being wrong. By the end of the school year, in April 2008, Karla posed a comparison problem for students: "Juan had 10 cookies and Anthony had 5. How many more cookies does Anthony need to have like Juan?" Comparison problems tend to be challenging for kindergarten students because they need to compare two static quantities, reflecting a relationship rather than an action that can be modeled (Carpenter et al., 1999). Ivan's attempts to explain his thinking after solving the comparison problem is an example of the effect of Karla's confidence in her students' mathematics learning.

> **Ivan:** "*Le faltan a Anthony cinco.*"
> ["Anthony needs five."]
> **Karla:** "*¿Cómo supo? A ver, enséñeme.*"
> ["How did you know? Let's see, show me."]
> **Ivan:** "*Usted cuando dijo que Anthony tenía 10 galletas, yo puse así con mis deditos, y luego (muestra 10 dedos extendidos), y luego cuando dijo 5, saqué así [saca una mano] y luego supe que eran 5.*" (*mirando la mano restante*)
> ["When you said that Anthony had ten cookies, I put my little fingers like this (showing 10 extended fingers) and then when you said five, I took one out (taking a hand away) and then I knew that it was five." (looking at the remaining hand)]

Rather than simply acknowledging the right answer, as she might have done earlier before our professional development, Karla recognized the value in Ivan's explanation and was confidently able to let Ivan take over in the role of modeling his strategy. Here, teacher confidence was intertwined with a deeper understanding of the impact that validating student thinking and problem solving strategies have in students' mathematics performance.

CONCLUSIONS

Our research and professional development agenda focused on building relationships and locating actions in the classroom context (Whitcomb et al., 2009). We experienced the importance of working with a teacher's needs and her understanding of students' mathematical learning without imposing our vision. When researchers and teachers come together for long-term collaborative projects that draw on the strengths of all participants to reach a common goal, each participant gains new skills and insights, having grown from the experience and developed in ways he or she did not think possible before. This is one of the benefits of a genuine collaboration (John-Steiner, 2000). It sets participants on a trajectory that allows them to reshape their identity as they move from novice to expert. One of the most rewarding results of our collaboration was the discovery that Karla's talents as a dynamic teacher, and her ability to respond instantly and build on her students' thinking, are being realized in her increasing role in professional presentations. Her commitment to learning from her students inspired us as researchers. Karla's courage to share her story also inspired us to share ours. When researchers and teachers come together to generate a learning community that pursues to construct knowledge both ways, everyone grows. This vignette from a conference illustrates this point:

> **Audience:** "I just noticed that a lot of my kids have a very negative attitude, because I teach algebra. . . . It's really hard to turn them around once they're in algebra and they shut down."
>
> **Karla:** "So that's why we're trying to show in this workshop, to let you see that it works and if we start them in kinder[garten] and we keep going up to sixth, seventh grade, that would really give the students a lot of confidence and they wouldn't be afraid to come up [to the front], and not talk. [By doing this] we'll change their attitudes in math."

We agree with the growing consensus that professional development "should help teachers learn how to elicit and interpret students' ideas, examine student work, and use what they learn about students' ideas and work to inform their instructional decisions and actions" (Whitcomb et al., 2009, p. 209). In addition, we contend that researchers and teacher educators involved in professional development initiatives should see themselves as catalysts for confidence. Researchers and teacher educators engaged in collaborative endeavors with teachers need to consider and inquire about the short- and long-term impact of confidence. The importance of creating environments and relationships based on mutual trust requires that teachers and students' needs become the focus of the joint work over any research agenda previously established.

We believe that this long-term professional development project worked because we accomplished what we set out to do. Our objective was to make a difference in a teacher's practice and her students' learning. A key aspect was our research basis in a powerful problem-solving framework, CGI, that helps students bridge their experiential knowledge with classroom learning (Carpenter et al., 1999) and an iterative approach that revisited biases and strengthened actions to respond to the unique dynamics of the classroom community.

ACKNOWLEDGMENT

This manuscript is based upon work supported in part by the National Science Foundation under Grant No. 0424983 to the Center for the Mathematics Education of Latinos/Latinas (CEMELA). Any opinions, findings, and conclusions or recommendations expressed in this material are those of the author(s) and do not necessarily reflect the views of the National Science Foundation.

REFERENCES

Carpenter, T. P., Fennema, E., Franke, M. L., Levi, L., & Empson, S. B. (1999). *Children's mathematics: Cognitively guided instruction.* Portsmouth, NH: Heinemann.

Celedón-Pattichis, S. (2008). "What does that mean?": Drawing on Latino and Latina students' language and culture to make mathematical meaning. In M. W. Ellis (Ed.), *Mathematics for every student: Responding to diversity, grades 6–8* (pp. 59–73). Reston, VA: National Council of Teachers of Mathematics.

Clandinin, D. J. & Connelly, F. M. (2000). *Narrative inquiry: Experience and story in qualitative research.* San Francisco, CA: Jossey-Bass.

Cobb, P., Confrey, J., diSessa, A., Lehrer, R., & Schauble, L. (2003). Design experiments in educational research. *Educational Researcher, 32*(1), 9–13. doi: 10.3102/0013189X032001009

Cobb, P. & McClain, K. (2006). The collective mediation of a high-stakes accountability program: Communities and networks of practice. *Mind, Culture, and Activity, 13*(2), 80–100. doi: 10.1207/s15327884mca1302_2

Cobb, P., McClain, K., Lamberg, T. D., & Dean, C. (2003). Situating teachers' instructional practices in the institutional setting of the school and school district. *Educational Researcher, 32*(6), 13–24. doi: 10.3102/0013189X032006013

Cummins, J. (2001). Empowering minority students: A framework for intervention. *Harvard Educational Review, 71*(4), 656–675. Retrieved from http://www.hepg.org/her/

The Education Trust. (2008). *Latino achievement in America.* Retrieved from http://www.edtrust.org

Flores, B. B. (2001). Bilingual education teachers' beliefs and their relation to self-reported practices. *Bilingual Research Journal, 25*(3), 251–275. Retrieved from http://www.nabe.org/journals.html

Franke, M. L., Carpenter, T. P., Levi, L., & Fennema, E. (2001). Capturing teachers' generative change: A follow-up study of professional development in mathematics. *American Educational Research Journal, 38*(3), 653–689. doi: 10.3102/00028312038003653

Guskey, T. R. (2002). Professional development and teacher change. *Teachers and Teaching: Theory and Practice, 8*(3), 381–391. doi: 10.1080/135406002100000512

John-Steiner, V. (2000). *Creative collaboration.* Oxford, UK: Oxford University Press.

Kazemi, E. & Franke, M. L. (2004). Teacher learning in mathematics: Using student work to promote collective inquiry. *Journal of Mathematics Teacher Education, 7*(3), 203–235. doi: 10.1023/B:JMTE.0000033084.26326.19

Khisty, L. L. (1995). Making inequality: Issues of language and meanings in mathematics teaching with Hispanic students. In W. G. Secada, E. Fennema, & L. B.

Adajian (Eds.), *New directions for equity in mathematics education* (pp. 279–297). Cambridge, England: Cambridge University Press.

Moschkovich, J. N. (2007). Bilingual mathematics learners: How views of language, bilingual learners, and mathematical communication impact instruction. In N. S. Nassir & P. Cobb (Eds.), *Diversity, equity, and access to mathematical ideas* (pp. 121–144). New York: Teachers College Press.

Musanti, S. I. (2005). *Collaboration and inservice teachers' professional development: A qualitative study on knowledge, identity and practice.* Doctoral dissertation, The University of New Mexico. Retrieved from ProQuest Dissertations and Theses database. (AAT 3201647)

Musanti, S. I., Celedón-Pattichis, S., & Marshall, M. E. (2009). Reflections on language and mathematics problem solving: A case study of a bilingual first-grade teacher. *Bilingual Research Journal, 32*(1), 25–41. doi: 10.1080/15235880902965763

National Council of Teachers of Mathematics. (2000). *Principles and standards for school mathematics.* Reston, VA: Author.

Rogoff, B. (2003). *The cultural nature of human development.* Oxford, England: Oxford University Press.

Secada, W. G. (1995). Social and critical dimensions for equity in mathematics education. In W. G. Secada, E. Fennema, & L. B. Adajian (Eds.), *New directions for equity in mathematics education* (pp. 146–164). Cambridge, England: Cambridge University Press.

Téllez, K. (2004/2005). Preparing teachers for Latino children and youth: Policies and practices. *The High School Journal, 88*(2), 43–54. doi: 10.1353/hsj.2004.0026

Turner, E. E., Celedón-Pattichis, S., & Marshall, M. E. (2008). Cultural and linguistic resources to promote problem solving and mathematical discourse among Latino/a kindergarten students. In R. Kitchen & E. Silver (Eds.), *Promoting high participation and success in mathematics by Hispanic students: Examining opportunities and probing promising practices* [A Research Monograph of TODOS: Mathematics for ALL], *1*, 19–42. Washington, DC: National Education Association Press. Available from http://www.todos-math.org

Varghese, M. (2004). Professional development for bilingual teachers in the United States: A site for articulating and contesting professional roles. *International Journal of Bilingual Education and Bilingualism, 7*(2/3), 222–237. doi: 10.1080/13670050408667810

Wenger, E. (1998). *Communities of practice: Learning, meaning, and identity.* Cambridge, UK: Cambridge University Press.

Whitcomb, J., Borko, H., & Liston, D. (2009). Growing talent: Promising professional development models and practices. *Journal of Teacher Education, 60*(3), 207–212. doi: 10.1177/0022487109337280

CHAPTER 11

MATHEMATICS TEACHING WITH A VISION OF SOCIAL JUSTICE

Using the Lens of Communities of Practice

Beatriz Quintos
*Department of Curriculum & Instruction,
University of Maryland*

Marta Civil
Department of Mathematics, The University of Arizona

with **Olga Torres**
CEMELA, The University of Arizona

INTRODUCTION

In this chapter, we analyze a mathematics teaching practice guided by a vision of social justice at the heart of a Latino community. This study builds on contemporary understandings about mathematics learning from a criti-

Latinos/as and Mathematics Education, pages 233–258

cal and situated perspective that includes the historical and sociocultural milieu as constituting the academic opportunities of Latino students and the workspace of teachers.

Educational institutions often ground mathematics teaching on the assumptions that learning is an individual endeavor best learned if the curriculum is decontextualized and that learning is always the result of direct instruction (Wenger, 1998). In the sociopolitical context of the early 21st century, many mathematics educators are challenging this perspective, suggesting that the underlying mandated initiatives found in the contemporary policy climate ignore the purposes and needs of disenfranchised communities. An education that positions students as objects to change rather than agents of change reproduces unequal power structures.

The theory of legitimate peripheral participation contests the narrowing of mathematics education to a universal body of knowledge. The use of the lens of communities of practice (Lave & Wenger, 1991; Wenger, 1998) highlights that critical aspects of learning within classrooms are commonly overlooked. Aspects such as community norms, power relations, the mathematical identities of teachers and students are opportunities that have the potential of disrupting the student-as-object position.

The study presented in this chapter represents a counter-narrative of mathematics instruction by exploring the work of an experienced elementary teacher working in a Latino, mostly Mexican-descent community. Olga's goals were to develop a collaborative community in which her students negotiated mathematical meanings to read and write their world, as well as develop identities as critical Latina/o citizens through mathematics. As we learned, Olga's educational goals went well beyond the narrow curricular aims defined in contemporary accountability climate. She encouraged children to challenge the racist views and biases surrounding them, and this critical mathematics practice, in all its complexity, was key to achieving her goals as their mathematics teacher. As a member of her students' community, she saw her work as both a moral and professional obligation.

In this chapter, we focus on the analysis of Olga's teaching practice within the classroom, informed by her reflections, as well as the views of students and some parents. It is essential to frame this analysis with a historical review of the academic experiences of these Latino students. Our analysis demands a comprehensive perspective to include the prevalent inequities within and beyond mathematics education (Apple, 1992; Gutstein, 2003; Stinson, 2004). This same perspective moved Olga to focus her efforts on developing students' identities as critical citizens.

As a note of caution, in this chapter and the study it presents, our purpose is not to evaluate Olga's practice. Olga, like any teacher, had challenges, made mistakes, and faced contradictions and dilemmas. Our goal is to describe the mathematics learning in a community through a lens that brings to the forefront aspects of learning that otherwise are ignored. To achieve this goal, we chose to describe those experiences and reflections that evinced a connection to her stated goals of social justice. We hope this focus is not misinterpreted as a presentation of an ideal classroom rather than a real one.

THEORETICAL FRAMEWORK

Educational researchers have described the "encapsulation" of school learning as a historical challenge of formal education (Brown, Collins, & Duguid, 1989; Engestrom, 1991). The school curricula, especially mathematics education, too often promote the memorization of inert facts and procedures, which then get lost within the walls of the classrooms, rarely gaining any meaning in the lives of students. Two standard approaches to instruction routinely result in learning devoid of meaning: "transmission of knowledge from others [and] acquisition or discovery of knowledge by oneself" (Rogoff, 1994, p. 209). These approaches focus on the learner as an individual who is disconnected from others for his or her development. In contrast to perspectives that focus on the individual are the sociohistorical frameworks that consider the political, social, and historical milieu of the experiences as well as the situated and distributed nature of learning (Hutchins, 1993; Lave & Wenger, 1991). These perspectives situate learning in the social interactions of an individual with particular communities. These views also consider the agency of the individual in interaction with his or her sociocultural context.

This study uses the concept of communities of practice and, more broadly, the framework of situated cognition to underscore issues of access, relation among members of a community, artifacts, and the participation in activities of the whole individual in interaction with the world. We use the dynamic and intersecting dimensions of practice, community, meanings, and identities to analyze a teaching practice crafted by a teacher with a vision of social justice. We contend this lens uncovers dimensions of mathematics learning otherwise overlooked that can bring to light the everyday inequities in mathematics education that disenfranchise Latino students. The following sections offer brief descriptions of these four dimensions of learning.

Practice

The first dimension, *practice*, includes a view of learning as the social pursuit of an enterprise considered from a sociohistorical perspective. Learning as a result of participating in a practice involves "shared historical and social resources, frameworks, and perspectives that can sustain mutual engagement in action" (Wenger, 1998, p. 5). Activity theory underscores the significance of the different levels of history as an integral component of activity as well as the central role of the goals of the activity (Engestrom, 1991). In this case, the practice of mathematics education within the classroom includes the history of those involved within this practice, as well as the unequal power relations mediated through factors such as race, social class, and gender, which result in historical differential access to social and cultural capital. This history and sociocultural milieu influence the experiences of the teacher and students who, at the same time, reconstruct the practice of schooling and become part of the history and tradition of those who follow. In the analysis of the data, as part of this dimension, we identify the goals of the teacher as structuring components for this classroom community.

Community

The second dimension, *community*, underscores the view of learning as belonging. In this view, one's learning is influenced and constituted by the changing community to which one belongs. The concept of community highlights the relevance of its members to define the learning experiences. In this project, we define the community of practice as the classroom participants: the teacher and the students. This community, then, was a space in which the students and the teacher negotiated their understandings of society and themselves and established relationships with others. Inevitably, other communities and individuals influenced each individual outside of the school; however, these influences were not the focus of this chapter.

Identity

Identity, the third dimension of learning, suggests that one's knowledge, beliefs, and history are not merely parallel or peripheral to learning, but rather an essential component of the learning process. Through participation in a community, individual members transform their identities. *Learning*, then, is defined as this process in which an individual's identities are constantly modified. As Lave and Wenger (1991) explained, "Learning implies becoming a different person with respect to the possibilities enabled by these systems of relations" (p. 53). This definition of identity means that it is not an entity that enters a community with the individual, but it is co-constituted by the individual and the community; in other words, identity is situated and distributed (Roth, Tobin, Elmesky, Carambo, McKnight, & Beers, 2004; Wenger, 1998). Efforts to improve the education of Latino and other disenfranchised populations underscore the critical role of opening spaces for students' cultural identities to become part of school learning (Cobb & Hodge, 2002; Cummins, 1996; Delpit, 1995; Gutiérrez & Rogoff, 2003; Khisty, 1997; Ladson-Billings, 1994; Ladson-Billings & Tate, 1995; Martin, 2000; Nasir, 2002; Roth et al., 2004; Sfard & Prusak, 2005; Turner, 2003).

Valenzuela (1999) endorsed an additive education that considers students' cultural identities as an asset to their education. In the area of mathematics, Martin (2000) focused on students' mathematical identity and considered it to be pivotal in their learning. Finally, those educators and researchers who advocated for democratic schools also used this argument, promoting a process they believed ought to begin within the same structures of schools (Dewey, 1916). Students need to develop a democratic character that becomes part of their experiences in this process of learning.

Meanings

Wenger (1998) defined the *meanings* as the fourth dimension of learning: "the process by which we experience the world and our engagement in it as meaningful" (p. 53). The term *negotiation* makes evident the distributed nature of meanings; in other words, meanings are settled among members of particular communities. These meanings are also situated in practices, social relations, activities, and the environment; the context, then, is part of the structure and content of the meanings (Brown et al., 1989). Wells (1999) suggested that school learning is primarily a semiotic process "to expand one's action potential as well as one's potential for meaning through language" (p. 48).

For this semiotic process to enable the participation of a learner, meanings need to be interconnected. When these meanings hide their connections to the community and identities of individuals, they become bits and pieces of information stored only with the use of artificial strategies (rote memorization) and without significance. Traditional models of teaching treat students as objects, assuming that they do not have any responsibility in the negotiation of the meanings that they learn. This passive view of the learners is a misconception. Humans negotiate meanings, participate in practices, become part of communities, have identities of participation.

The situated perspective contrasts with commonplace views about mathematics teaching and learning. The failure of school to expand its definition of learning is most troubling for students whose communities' funds of knowledge and perspectives are systematically ignored in school (González, Andrade, Civil, & Moll, 2001; Moll & González, 2004; Moll & Greenberg, 1990). This exclusion is one of the factors that blocks students from marginalized communities, including Latinos, from having access to a culturally relevant mathematics education (Civil & Quintos, 2009; Ladson-Billings, 1995; Quintos & Civil, 2008).

Dimensional Intersections

An education that considers the intersection of four dimensions can scaffold students to learn to think critically and to ask questions, to be life-long learners and curious individuals, to care about others and their world, and to realize they are valuable citizens and need to make informed decisions (Nieto, 1999). Particularly relevant for this study, students need to learn to read and write their world through mathematics (Gutstein, 2006). This phrase, based on Freire's early work, argues that students learn to use mathematics to understand their context and learn that these mathematical discourses can be key in the transformation of themselves, the environment, and their communities.

For instance, multicultural educators focus on an education for a more democratic and socially just society. These educators critically revise the successes and failures of the school system, especially in relation to those communities that have historically been disenfranchised. Multicultural education, in Nieto's (1999) view, calls for an education that is embedded in the sociopolitical context, is basic and antiracist, includes all schooling areas, and is committed to social justice. This definition considers the content and the process of learning as inseparable. At the same time, it calls for teachers to learn about the individual students, their background, and social contexts, while it considers the sociopolitical context that influence their learning experiences. The individual learner and his or her context are indissoluble. Gutstein (2003), a critical mathematics education scholar, called for a mathematics that serves the purposes of the learners and their communities, a tool to think and make meaning of daily life situations, a vehicle to explore the world and its relationships, and a way to critically participate for a more socially just society.

Critical mathematics (Gutstein, 2003) and culturally relevant pedagogy (Khisty, 1997; Ladson-Billings, 1995) advocate for a situated notion of mathematics, as well as a need for political awareness. Based on Freire's ideas, Gutstein (2003) described the need for students to develop socio-political consciousness, a sense of agency, and positive cultural identities. These dispositions are evident when students are able to read and write the world using mathematics and to develop mathematical power. Gutstein, who works with Latino communities, highlighted as a critical goal of learning that students realize that they themselves are part of the solution to injustice. Ladson-Billings (1995) described parallel characteristics to those of Gutstein (2003) when she proposed a culturally relevant pedagogy. In her work, she portrayed exemplary teachers of African American students. She advocated for a pedagogical model that includes student performance, but also strengthens students' cultural identity and helps them develop a critical view of inequities.

For Latina/o students, Khisty (1997) added that culturally relevant teaching must include bilingual education and theories of English as a second language. Bilingualism is seen not only as a resource but also as an integral part of students' identities. These pedagogical frameworks concur that mathematics education needs to go into classrooms without losing its power to bridge learning between classrooms and the outside world in transformative ways. Despite concurrence, actual examples of critical mathematics education are rare (Frankenstein, 1983, 1990, 1997a, 1997b), especially at the elementary-school level in Latino bilingual communities. Therefore, the overarching purpose of this chapter is to share an in-depth exploration of Olga's practice, as viewed through the analysis of the researcher-authors, Beatriz and Marta. Although somewhat unorthodox as a methodology, our collaborative approach to research and writing underscores our own theoretical commitments to community and shared understandings.

METHOD

Setting and Participants: The Classroom Community

This study took place in a fifth-grade classroom at an urban elementary school in which 90% of the students were of Latino background and almost 70% of the students received free or reduced-cost lunch. All the students in the classroom spoke English and Spanish, although several were more inclined to use one language exclusively. Instruction in this classroom was bilingual; however, many of the children were previously in English-only classrooms.

The teacher in the study, Olga, has been nationally and locally recognized for her teaching practice: She was the 1995 recipient of the Presidential Award of Excellence in Mathematics Teaching at the Elementary Level. She remains a bilingual teacher-researcher who is articulate about her beliefs and values about teaching and learning, mathematics, and curriculum. She is also an expert teacher with in-depth knowledge of second-language learning, child development, and mathematics teaching and learning.

Olga had taught for over 35 years at the time of the study. She had been an adjunct professor teaching mathematics education courses at the college level, an educational consultant in mathematics working with districts around the United States, and a teacher leader in her school district and in the Center for the Mathematics Education of Latinos/as. Furthermore, this study is the second research conducted in her classroom, in addition to Olga's own research.

The participants in the study were 19 fifth graders, the parents of five of these students, and the classroom teacher. We selected five of the 19 students, all Mexican immigrants or Mexican Americans, to develop in-depth case studies. These students were selected in consultation with the teacher to include diversity in gender, mathematical proficiency, as well as their language fluency in English and in Spanish, as determined by the teacher.

Data Collection and Analysis

This year-long qualitative study explored the practice of a teacher and the mathematics learning of a fifth-grade classroom in a Latino community. The use of multiple case studies (Dyson & Genishi, 2005) bridges local particulars of this classroom to the abstract social phenomenon of communities of practice. We used an ethnographic approach for data collection, which took place in three sites: the classroom, students' households, and three after-school programs. The data consisted of field notes and transcripts from classroom observations, a collection of selected artifacts from the case study students, and transcripts from semistructured interviews with the teacher, parents, and children. In this chapter, we focus on the analysis from Olga's teaching practice as well as her reflections. These reflections were collected throughout the school year, before or after the observations, and some in semistructured interviews.

The analysis of the video transcripts, field notes of classroom observations, and interview transcripts was based on grounded theory (Charmaz, 1983), a process that explores emergent themes. This inductive analysis explored a comprehensive and dynamic picture of the students, the teacher, and parents (Moschkovich & Brenner, 2000). The different sources were used to triangulate themes and build thick descriptions. Ongoing reflections were the basis of a continual and cyclical analysis of the collected data. After this first cycle of analysis, we used the dimensions of learning from Wenger (1998) to organize and highlight the major themes of our analysis.

We discuss the dimension of practice as goal-oriented. In this case, the goals of the classroom teacher steered the trajectories of this community of practice in negotiation with the goals of students, other communities, and individuals. We explore two interrelated goals of the teacher to create a space to nurture: a community of mathematical learners and critical mathematics citizens. Both of these identities represent different foci of the vision Olga carefully crafted for this community of practice. These goals are not ones she described as such; they are an analytical effort to identify her expectations in relation to students' mathematics learning. We separated these goals only for presentation purposes. In practice, however, they are indivisible and overlap.

MATHEMATICS LEARNING WITH A VISION FOR SOCIAL JUSTICE

Identity

The mathematical identities proposed in this classroom were strongly influenced by Olga's identities. She was keenly aware of her influence on children's dispositions towards mathematics. The foremost goal of Olga's teaching focused on the identity of her students as valuable human beings. During one of our interviews with her, Olga said, "My expectation is that they (students) realize that they are important human beings and anything that I do is to make sure that they are seen in that light."

Olga's belief motivated her efforts to explore students' knowledge to create circumstances that uncover and expand students' possibilities of participation and the transformation of their identities. This approach countered a deficit view of students that determines what students do not know; instead, it supports and values students' unique ways of participation. This belief was explicitly stated in Olga's description of her practice, which she shared in an interview:

> It's not my job to judge them but to discover them, so my goal in my teaching is to create teaching circumstances that allow me to discover more and more about the kids and what they bring to me and how I can use those experiences as the core of my curriculum.

Consequently, Olga promoted specific dispositions towards mathematics learning to develop students' identities for empowerment. The development of students' self-confidence was one of the stated goals in Olga's pedagogy. Throughout the year, she highlighted the importance of children's willingness to take risks, be confident, accept confusion, and celebrate mistakes. Olga explicitly explained to children that to learn, they sometimes have to go through some confusion and work their way out of it. She talked with her students about how right answers often hide confusion, and therefore she celebrated mistakes as a sign of learning. We captured these frequently repeated words in our field notes:

> **Olga:** *"Aquí celebramos las equivocaciones."*
> ["Here we celebrate mistakes."]

"We can't learn if we don't make mistakes."

"How a child perceives himself or herself in a learning situation matters, because if the environment doesn't allow a child to make mistakes or get confused then they are not going to take the risks, because it is too uncomfortable. So if the culture allows kids to be learners, and when I say learners, it means the right to make mistakes, the right to get confused."

To illustrate some students' process of transformation in their identities as learners, we share two significant events. The first occurred during a test; the second during a mathematics investigation. Early in the school year, Olga's students were getting ready to start a test when Gloria stated she was scared. This short exchange, captured in our field notes, is presented in Excerpt 11.1.

Excerpt 11.1. Admitting fear

 Olga: "Boys and girls, this is just a pretest."
Gloria: "I'm scared."
 Olga: "Why are you scared?"
Gloria: "Because I'm afraid of getting it wrong."
 Peter: "I'm afraid of being a loser."

In the interaction presented in Excerpt 11.1, dominant ideologies appear to have been imposed on students who have had multiple experiences with being "wrong" in school. Olga explicitly and deftly addressed this attitude by reinforcing the importance of language and of mistakes as celebrations of learning. At the end of the year, a conversation among Gloria, Yessenia, and another student gave evidence of a shift in their participation. Gloria and Yessenia volunteered to explain their reasoning on a chart board for the whole class. The whole class had been asked to confirm or refute the following mathematical sentence: $1/16 + 1/8 + 1/4 + 1/2 = 1$. Yessenia and Gloria argued that this equation was true and described their thinking on the chart board.

After some discussion in their groups and an exploration with paper strips, they learned their answer was "wrong." Gloria and Yessenia wrote their process again for the class when someone teased them for writing the "wrong" answer. The answer from Yessenia and Gloria, captured in a video transcript, is presented in Excerpt 11.2:

Excerpt 11.2. Mistakes are part of learning

Yessenia: "So? Mistakes are part of learning."
 Gloria: "Yeah, we made a mistake, so we tried something new."

In addition to the explicit discourse in which the community celebrates mistakes, Olga believed that encouraging children to be in control of their decisions when they participated in mathematical practices built this confidence. This control entailed being able to make sense of mathematics. This promotion of sense making contrasts with most mathematics education classrooms in which children are given an algorithm to follow or definitions to memorize. By contrast, Olga asked the students to explore and share their own ideas. One strategy Olga used was inspired by a children's literature book, *Ish* (Reynolds, 2004). Pedro and Gloria's ideas became "Pedro-ish" and "Gloria-ish." Olga used this expression to validate children's own approach to solving problems in mathematics. For example, as part of a larger investigation, students had to use the commutative and distributive properties of multiplication to write equivalent expressions.

Monica shared that a difficult equation for her was $9 \times 8 = 72$. Olga used the area of rectangles to help students make sense of the distributive property and broke the area in four rectangles of 9 by 2 (see Figure 11.1).

Adriana suggested adding $18 + 18$ starting with the tens $(10 + 10)$, then the ones $(8 + 8)$ and then adding the partial sums $(20 + 16 = 36)$, thus $9 \times 4 = 36$. Finally, she doubled this number to find out 9×8, as sequenced in Excerpt 11.3:

Excerpt 11.3. *Using distributive property to determine area*

$18 + 18 = (10 + 10) + (8 + 8) =$
$20 + 16 = 36$
$9 \times 4 = 36$
$9 \times 8 = 72$

From this point on, Olga referred to this strategy as Adriana's strategy, giving her ownership of this process. As captured in our field notes, she told students, "Solve the problems, but do them in an Adriana-ish, Pedro-ish, Gloria-ish way, in whatever way makes sense to you." This discourse was a way to encourage children to develop their own voice in mathematics in a collaborative environment. Students' confidence is supported when they make decisions on how to solve problems and take control of the mathematics tools to represent their thinking.

Finally, another aspect of student identities that Olga underscored is that they are citizens of the world. The particular characteristics of this citizen-

9×2	9×2	9×2	9×2

Figure 11.1 Example of commutative and distributive properties of multiplication.

ship gain meaning based on students' identities and their specific historical and sociopolitical context. The history of the western United States is filled with examples of discrimination and racism against Latino students, as well as instances of activism and resistance. Most of Olga's students were Latino and came from working-class families; she believed they particularly needed to leverage for their rights against stereotypes, discrimination, or prejudice. In a personal conversation with us, she expressed her desire, saying, "I want these kids to have any choice in the future they want, I want that key that unlocks opportunities."

At the same time, Olga made an effort to counter the prejudices against Latino students so they did not internalize a cultural view of inferiority, but instead, were critical and valued their cultural identities. The concept of social justice was a guiding principle in her teaching. In her definition, these concepts are based on the human and civil rights of individuals. In a personal conversation with us, Olga explained that, to her, the word "social" emphasized the idea of learning happening in the company of others; "justice" referred to voice and diversity as assets:

> For me, social justice in the classroom begins with human and civil rights. The "social" meaning being in the company of others and 'justice' is individuals having a voice and that diversity of ideas, experiences, and culture are assets to be capitalized on. This social justice then transcends into decisions that eventually affect society.

These definitions underscored Olga's concept of education; it is not meant to stay within the walls of the classroom. She framed students' participation in her classroom as connected to their life as critical citizens. For example, she countered the hegemonic views of Spanish as an obstacle in these children's education. She defended her classroom as a bilingual space. In opposition to the state law that curtailed the use of any other language for educational purposes, Spanish and English were both used to enhance learning. Children had the right to choose the language in which they were going to work at any time. Furthermore, Olga highlighted the benefits of developing a bilingual communicative competency. She discussed the connection of Spanish and Latin to support their sense making of mathematics terminology. For example, when she was teaching a geometry investigation, she explained that the word rectangle in Spanish connects to the mathematical definition of a polygon with right angles, "*rectángulos y ángulos rectos*" ["rectangles and right angles"]. The use of Spanish as a resource confronted the status quo in the particular location of the study.

Community

Students engage in the practice of learning mathematics not only by attending school or being in the same classroom, but also by having access to those engagements that are relevant to the community. From Olga's perspective, collaboration in the community was both a goal and a means for learning in all the academic areas, especially in mathematics. Olga's commitment to facilitate and support a collaborative community relied on her deep belief in the social nature of learning as well as her view of the community as a way to learn how to collaborate. To be a member of this community meant to learn from others through dialogue and collaboration in given investigations. Olga promoted opportunities of collaboration to increase the human capital available in the community.

Her goal was to create situations in which students benefited from each other's experiences and expertise and generated new knowledge that would not exist if students worked individually. In this manner, the community became a structuring resource that facilitated students' access to full participation. This expanded learning was a result of discussing their understanding, sharing connections, justifying their perspectives, defining concepts, and problem solving, among other discourse interactions—all of which required or at least were enriched by interaction. Furthermore, even when some activities were performed in apparent isolation (e.g., writing), they were profoundly social. For example, this notion of the distributed nature of learning was evident in one interaction between Marcela, Rebeca, and Hernan, who were investigating the relations and factors of the numbers 1, 11, 21, 6, 16, and 26. Their interaction, captured in field notes and represented in Excerpt 11.4, shows some of the ways children learned or participated in this community:

Excerpt 11.4. Shared learning

Marcela and Rebeca begin to work promptly while Hernan takes a bit longer to start. Rebeca started to solve the problems without much difficulty. Marcela started more slowly, following Rebeca. She would write some numbers like 1, but she would rely on Rebeca to finish or to check her work. After a while, Rebeca started talking with Hernan, and Marcela was able to continue without stopping. Rebeca explained to Hernan how to find the factors. Hernan relied on Rebeca to do his work as he started later. Rebeca went back to her own work. Later on, there was one time where Marcela and Rebeca disagreed and each explained their answer and tried to convince the other.

In this case, Hernan asked Rebeca for support to get started, so he got a second explanation after Olga's account, and then continued to work independently. Marcela also learned by observing Rebeca, working independently, and by discussing a specific disagreement with her teammate.

Finally, although Rebeca started the project with more independence, her learning was supported by having to explain her thinking to Hernan and discussing her thinking with Marcela.

The norms of collaboration had to be established early on because the students did not view one another as a legitimate source for learning. Often, at the beginning of the school year, the students used only their own materials and knowledge to participate in academic activities. For example, on the first day of classes, students had to brainstorm predictions about what they would learn during the coming year. Olga invited them to explore their environment and discuss their ideas with their peers. She said, "Find a partner, walk and look around the room. You have to look and discuss. What do you think you are going to learn this year? *¿Qué voy a aprender este año?*" ["What am I going to learn this year?"] Children used books, objects, and signs, but they only talked to each other occasionally. At a certain point, Olga explicitly encouraged them to value and recognize each other as a resource.

Another example of these collaborative relations is Diego's letter to Olga. When Olga was absent, each student had to write about the actions of a randomly assigned student. In his letter, Diego described Monica's actions helping others and the norm of "setting an example" for other students:

> *Estimada Señora, la persona que yo observé durante que usted estaba ausente fue Mónica. Le voy a decir tres decisiones que hizo Mónica. La primera decisión que hizo fue que cooperó en la mesa, eso le ayudó a la clase a cooperar con su grupo. La segunda decisión que hizo Mónica fue que se juntó con su compañero y eso le ayudó a la clase para que ellos se juntaran con su compañero. Finalmente, ella respetó al maestro y esto ayudó a la clase para que todos respetaran al maestro. Sinceramente, Diego*

> [Dear Mrs., the person I observed while you were absent was Monica. I am going to tell you three decisions that Monica made. The first decision she made was to cooperate at the table, that helped the class to cooperate with their group. Monica's second decision was that she got together with her buddy and that helped the class to get together with their buddy. Lastly, she was respectful with the teacher and that helped the class to respect the teacher. Sincerely, Diego]

This social view of learning is a process Olga reinforced and developed throughout the year. Olga structured the mathematics experiences based on collaboration (Boaler & Staples, 2008; Esmonde, 2009a, 2009b). Children were expected to share their thoughts and understandings regardless of their different experiences with mathematics in school. For example, in an investigation of probability, each small group had the task to collect the data of 20 coin tosses. After each small group finished, Olga collected the data for the whole class and got the results for a sample of 100. Each student was responsible for recording his or her personal and group outcomes. In this way, the activities were based on the assumption that each student contributed their work to the group and together generated a new product.

Collaboration would not be possible if the concept of "relationships" was not situated at the center of this community of learners. Olga believed the most important aspect for learning is the quality of the relationships of students with each other and the teacher. Therefore, she explicitly talked about the nature of relationships she expected in this community. At the center of students' tables, she had an excerpt by Jim Cummins (1996) printed for children. Olga discussed this excerpt with students in the first days of school, revisited these ideas throughout the year, which served as a reminder from the teacher to the students (and teacher) to be cognizant of the decisions they were making each day (Figure 11.2). The print was a constant reminder that human relationships were at the heart of learning. More importantly, each interaction and discussion built on the dynamic nature of the culture of the classroom.

Olga's deep belief in the community as the center of learning was eloquently expressed to the students on the eighth day of classes:

> It's not what you know, is what you know about others by the way you feel, if you have a voice in the class. When we share ideas, do we respect and listen? Because when someone stands up and says something, she or he is taking a risk and we have to respect that risk. It's not about academics, it's about how you relate to each other and how I relate to you.

The type of experiences and relationships that were provided within this community of practice had profound implications for students' engage-

Negotiating Identities: Education for Empowerment in a Diverse Society
by Jim Cummins (p 1 and 15-16)

"... human relationships are at the heart of schooling." The interactions that take place between students and teachers and among students are more central to student success than any method for teaching literacy, or science or math. When powerful relationships are established between teachers and students, these relationships frequently can transcend the economic and social disadvantages that afflict communities and schools alike in inner city and rural areas.

Students whose schooling experiences reflect collaborative relations of power develop the ability, confidence and motivation to succeed academically. They participate competently in instruction as a result of having developed a secure sense of identity and the knowledge that their voices will be heard and respected within the classroom. They feel a sense of ownership for the learning that goes on in the classroom and a sense that they belong in the classroom learning environment. . . .**Empowerment derives from the process of negotiating identities in the classroom. Identities are not static or fixed but rather are constantly being shaped through experiences and interactions.**

Negociando Identidades: Educación Para dar Facultad a una Sociedad Diversa
Jim Cummins (p 1 y 15-16)

"... las relaciones humanas son el corazón del sistema educativo. Las interacciones que se llevan a cabo entre estudiantes y maestros y entre los mismos estudiantes contribuyen más al éxito del estudiante que qualquier método sobre la enseñanza de literatura, o ciencia, o matemática. Cuando se establecen relaciones poderosas entre maestros y estudiantes, estas relaciones frequentemente trascienden las desventajas económicas y sociales que afligen comunidades y escuelas, lo mismo en áreas céntricas que en áreas rurales.

Las experiencias escolares que reflejan poderosas relaciones colaborativas, desarrollan en los estudiantes habilidad, confianza, y motivación para lograr éxito académico. Estos estudiantes son capaces de participar completamente en su propia educación como resultado de haber desarrollado un sentido seguro de identidad y el conocimiento que sus voces tendrán oído y respeto en el salón de clase. Ellos se sienten dueños del aprendizaje que se lleva acabo en el salón de clase y sienten que pertenecen al ambiente educativo del salón de clase. . . .Esta facultad deriba del proceso de negociar identidades en el salón de clase. **Las identidades no son estáticas ni fijas, sino al contrario, constantemente se están forjando por medio de las experiencias e interacciones.**

Figure 11.2 Olga's handout: Excerpt of the work of Jim Cummins (1996).

ment and their mathematics identities. The children were engaged in the activities, cared about the outcomes in the experiments, collaborated with each other, and often reported that they enjoyed the investigations. At the end of the probability investigation, one boy said "Time went fast! Ms. You know what they say? When you are having a lot of fun, time goes fast but when you are boring, when you're bored, time goes slow."

MEANINGS

Olga recognized that elementary-aged students often have been participants in doing mathematics by the method of drill and practice. However, such participation is bereft of student meaning. For true meaning to emerge from mathematics instruction, it must be informed by students' life experiences. This use of students' history means that occasionally, they import habits (Dewey, 1916) from their previous experiences that clash with the practice of this community. Not only do children bring their views of school mathematics from their previous experiences, but also the views and beliefs of their parents, caretakers, or family members, and other individuals in their lives. These entrenched habits sometimes imply that they use mathematical tools without questioning their purpose or without the need to take responsibility of their meaning.

For example, when Olga asked the students to discuss at their tables the difference between the multiples of 20, the class responded, "It's going by 2s and you add a zero." This notion of "adding a zero" is common in the teaching of algorithms that isolates the process from the meaning of the number system. Olga told students,

> My argument is that people are throwing out numbers and you've got to be able to explain. Nothing in math just adds zeros. *Todo tiene su valor y su razón* [Everything has its value and its reason]. This is not counting by 2s and adding a zero. What does 20 mean?

As recorded in our field notes, from this moment, the children focused on numbers using place value in this lesson. However, these habits persisted in many students.

It was Olga's belief that the learning of mathematics involves developing significant reasoning and communicative competencies. During a series of activities exploring factors, Olga expected children to discuss problems in their groups. She asked them, "What is the function of a factor? What can a factor do? What is the meaning of a factor?" Olga told the students, "*No es bastante que sepan etiquetar que es un factor, tienen que saber para que sirve, que hace, poderlo explicar.*" ["It is not enough that you know how to label what is a factor, you need to know what it is for, what it does, be able to explain it."]

Olga asked children to explain and listen to each other share their definitions and ways of thinking with the whole class, and she or other peers built on their explanations. For example, children discussed the concept of factors. Their definitions were part of the multiple inquiries that involved these concepts throughout the year. As captured in our field notes, Valeria read a definition she had in a card in English and in Spanish for the class: "*El factor es un número entero que divide a otro número entero en grupos iguales*" ["A factor is a whole number that divides another whole number in equal groups."] Olga emphasized the idea of children's need to make sense of mathematics. She believed children need to have concrete experiences and create connections with the abstract symbols of mathematics. For instance, she created opportunities for students to visualize or use a model to understand the relationships represented in the number system. Olga explained that if children missed these opportunities, they began to rely on rules created by others rather than using their experiences to make sense of the symbolic systems. These rules, then, are based on others' understandings and children lose control, instead of making sense of the mathematics.

The connections that Olga established were not only within mathematics, but also extended to other content areas. To elaborate this point, I describe Olga's introduction to the investigation, "Ways to Count," which illustrates the interconnections between mathematics and other areas of study in this community—interconnections that are not only context to the mathematics, but also that become part of the mathematical meanings.

The students had been working on a science exploration of owl pellets. Students dissected this indigestible material regurgitated by an owl and searched for bones, such as teeth, skulls, or claws. The class then discussed their conclusions, based on the types and number of bones they found in each of the regurgitated pellets. Olga explained the sense of the term conclusions which was captured in our field notes: "You are trying to make sense of what you are seeing; they are based on what you know." In one of the pellets, children found seven jaws, so the group of children concluded there were four rodents, because jaws come in pairs. Olga wrote 7/2 and Adriana spontaneously described it as an improper fraction. Our field notes captured a few salient exchanges. Yessenia said, "It is 4, 7 divided by 2 is 4 rodents and 1 jaw missing." This conversation ended with their theories about the gender and age of the rodents. The children deduced it was a family (a male, a female and two babies), while Olga theorized there were two female mice and some babies. She concluded:

> Do you see how experiences help us draw conclusions? *Ustedes sacaron la conclusión de que había una hembra y un macho. Yo les digo, que pensé que eran dos hembras. Mi pensamiento fue que quizá la lechuza se comió las dos hembras y los bebés que tienen los ojos cerrados.*

[You drew the conclusion that there was one female and one male. I am saying, I thought there were two females. My thought was that maybe the owl ate the two females and the babies who have their eyes closed]. We both used our experiences.

This discussion connects to the second key characteristic of this community: the regular sharing of stories from Olga and the students. Olga regularly brought students' life experiences into their school learning with the goal of enhancing their participation outside of the classroom. Through the stories shared, Olga connected the curriculum to the world, in particular, to the life of students and their identities, as well as to herself. All students are legitimized when they are appreciated and valued equitably. Olga explicitly raised their awareness of the interactions between school mathematics and mathematics in the everyday world. Throughout the year, children also established these connections between school mathematics and mathematics in everyday experiences. For example, our field notes captured an exchange between Yessenia and Olga. Yessenia shared, "Miss, at soccer practice the captain made small groups, we were working with math." Olga smiled and replied, "We are always dealing with math." Yessenia connected the activity of making groups from a specific number of players at her soccer practice.

Olga provided opportunities for students to understand, interpret, and think critically about their world. She modeled this attitude towards mathematics by narrating stories from her personal life and their geographical context—from their neighborhood to the world—in which she highlighted the use of the different areas of mathematics. For example, she introduced the investigation in probability with examples of its use. In her stories, she described weather predictions, medical diagnosis based on blood samples, electoral predictions published in the newspaper, and the last basketball game statistics from the local team. Excerpt 11.4, taken from her video-taped narration of the last basketball game she watched on television, is an example of Olga's narratives in which she used mathematics to interpret the world.

Excerpt 11.5. Olga's narrative highlighting mathematics in the world

> Olga: "Now, when I was watching the game on Sunday, probability was really important because ... [our team] could win if they could make two points. There was a two point difference! So they are playing basketball, and this really good player has the ball. Our player can't help it, he's got to foul that player because he's got to stop the clock. So they foul the guy, that guy had an 85.7% chance of making the free throw. How close it that?"

Students: "Really close." (in chorus)

Olga: "*Ay!* An 85.7% and he had six shots out of the seven (Olga writes 6/7) during the whole game he had made those shots on free throws. Do you think it is likely that he is going to make that basket?"

Students: "Yeah!"

(Olga continued narrative of game)

Olga: "So probability, oh and basketball, Ah! All the time! So it's (mathematics) in everything we do."

Olga was able to model how the outcome of the game was dependent on the mathematical reasoning of the coaches in utilizing data and probability. This narrative prompted children to share stories in which they used mathematics for interpreting their world. For example, Yessenia asked light-heartedly, "What's the probability that we are going to play basketball, Ms.?" Another example is how Andres connected the concept of probability to a science experiment. The previous day, Andres had investigated the law of motion by rapidly removing a piece of paper that was between the top of a cup and some coins and allowing the coins to drop into the cup. He said he had a high probability to get the coins in the cup. Students spontaneously shared these stories in which they recognized the use of probability. These examples showed how the classroom community embraced the idea that mathematics is a way to learn about the world.

A third salient aspect of this community of practice was how the teacher supported students' agency in their own learning (Freire, 1998) by using a pedagogy that continuously built on the background knowledge of students. At the beginning of the investigation of probability, Olga reminded students that they needed to establish connections with their previous experiences and expertise. Olga told the students, "Whenever you investigate in mathematics you always have to think about what you know." In this context, their previous knowledge included their experiences outside and within this community, their communicative competency, and their cultural background.

The teacher treated students as individuals with a wealth of experiences relevant for their learning of mathematics. The teacher tapped into students' funds of knowledge in the introduction to these activities, as she framed probability as something occurring in students' everyday life experiences. In the first activity, the coin toss, children were asked to use probability as a tool to make sense of their experiences in the classroom. In another activity, the children were invited to think of themselves as citizens of the world and connect their actions to the environment by calculating the probability of an animal going extinct.

One day, Olga read to the class from the book *If the World Were a Village* (Smith, 2002). The author of this book invites the readers to consider the world as if it was the size of a village and includes topics such as world population, religions, nationalities, food distribution, schooling and literacy, money and possessions, and electricity, among other topics. During the read-aloud, Olga highlighted some aspects for the children to consider as citizens of the world. She read, "Sixty percent of the world population is hungry and of those, 26% are severely undernourished, and 24% of the population always has enough food." A girl said, "That's mean."

Then, Olga stopped reading and posed the question to the students, "Why does this happen? That's what's important." Olga continued reading about the languages most spoken in the world. Some of the languages listed were Chinese, Hindi, English, and Spanish. After Olga read these data, she said to the students, "If you speak Spanish, you are at a great advantage because it is one of the four most spoken languages in the world." Olga connected the data presented in this book to the students' own experiences and countered a demeaning view of Spanish. She used this information to highlight the value of students' linguistic knowledge.

These connections underscore the instrumental use of mathematics, but also as a tool to be critical in their participation as citizens in this world. Her explorations launched from real-life contexts, emphasizing the relevance and their familiarity with these concepts. Olga began one math lesson highlighting different practices that included the use of decimals, fractions, and percents in the real world. A transcribed videotape of one of Olga's lessons is offered here:

> When you are learning mathematics, you are learning mathematics so you can understand the world that surrounds you. Now Kellogg's is really working hard, it is trying to convince the public that they are trying to do the best they can to serve good food. . . . Then, the news came out saying that a lot of cereals have a lot of sugar. So, Kellogg's is trying to win the public back and they say that the Frosted Flakes, on that box, is 1/3 less sugar. What do you say?

These problems were presented in the context in which children negotiated meanings, as well as understood their role as individuals and as a community. The task invited students to be part of a community that does not passively receive messages, but that questions their meaning and implications. Olga negotiated the meanings necessary with students to promote a collaborative community as well as the interconnections with students' out-of-school life.

CONCLUSIONS

Those interested in manipulating learning—accelerating it, making it happen, or assessing it—need to pay careful attention to their assumptions about learning (Wenger, 1998). This fact is also evident when one considers its historical "encapsulation" (Engestrom, 1991, p. 243) within schools and the imbalance of opportunities of quality education for Latino students and other marginalized students in the United States. The framework of communities of practice is not tied to any particular educational practice. Nonetheless, it offers an analytical framework of existent practices and, on this basis, some suggestions come to the fore.

These suggestions ought to include the voice of community members as well as those previous efforts in mathematics education for a more inclusive and transformative education, such as a culturally relevant pedagogy, multicultural education, and democratic education (Dewey, 1916; Ladson-Billings, 1995; Ladson-Billings & Tate, 1995; Nieto, 1999). In particular, there have been research studies in the area of mathematics education of Latino students that included their particular cultural and linguistic resources. Some leading work is being done by mathematics education researchers in the Center for the Mathematics Education of Latinos/as (Celedón-Pattichis, 2003; Civil, 2007; González et al., 2001; Khisty, 1997; Khisty & Chval, 2002; Kitchen, 2004; Moschkovich, 2002, 2007; Turner, 2003), as well as by other researchers (Allexsaht-Snider, 2006; Combs, Evans, Fletcher, Parra, & Jiménez, 2005; Escalante & Dirmann, 1990; Gutstein, 2003, 2006; Secada, 1991; Sleeter, 1997).

The analysis of the learning practices in this fifth-grade classroom speaks to the structuring role of the goals of the teacher. A goal-oriented analysis emerges from the evident connection between this teacher's vision and the participation of the different members of this community of practice. The goals of the teacher influence her participation and that of students—in other words, their learning and hers.

Cummins, a well-known scholar in second-language learning and literacy development, has written comprehensively about the goal of the empowerment of Latino and other minoritized students (Cummins, 1996, 2001, 2003). In his book, *Negotiating Identities: Education for Empowerment in a Diverse Society*, Cummins explains:

> Culturally diverse students are disempowered educationally in very much the same way that their communities have been disempowered historically in their interactions with societal institutions. The logical implication is that these students will succeed academically to the extent that the patterns of interaction in school reverse those that prevail in the society at large. (Cummins, 1996, p. iii)

Cummins (1996) connected the historical and ontogenic history of Latino students to ground his vision to reverse the patterns of oppression that disenfranchise students. He suggested that collaborative relations have a transformative power that allows Latino students to be motivated, confident, and able to succeed academically. Our study supports Cummins's suggestion: Teachers need to take thoughtful consideration of students' identities and the nature of the classroom community. Teacher education and professional development efforts need to support teachers in taking control over their teaching in the midst of the many contradictions that emerge from the sociopolitical milieu. Teachers need time and critical communities that support them in being reflective and leveraging for the rights of students. The experiences described in this study suggest that making explicit the connections between the meanings and the identity of Latino students supports them in developing a sense of ownership in the negotiation of mathematical meanings.

Olga's teaching considered students' learning in a broader sense than the transformation of meanings, which is generally the focus in many classrooms. Reform mathematics, for instance, suggests experiences that support students' conceptual understanding of mathematics. Instead, Olga used these conceptual understandings as the means to her main goals that focused on students' agency and critical disposition. A vision of social justice grounded on the human being and the community is a key means of learning. It reminds us that multicultural education is not only about content, but also about the relationships established within the learning space. The community in Olga's classroom was a structuring resource that was part of students' learning. Part of the learning in her classroom involved students becoming participants in a collaborative community that respected and valued diversity.

This form of teaching required Olga's participation in several professional development communities that helped her to reflect on, question, and improve her practice. Throughout her career, Olga has been a member of several professional communities that allowed her to become an expert teacher. She has continued to revise her practice and address her areas of weakness as learning opportunities. She struggled with the time limits of an academic year and the dilemmas of a sociopolitical milieu that reified mathematics as inert knowledge. Children had to be ready for standardized tests in which they were not allowed to use each other as a resource and mistakes were not "celebrations from which students could learn." These were difficult challenges that Olga and countless other teachers have faced. However, having a vision that kept students and their families at the center moved her teaching forward.

The implications from this case study highlight the nature of one example of mathematics teaching and learning. The teaching of this classroom was a counter-narrative to dominant models of teaching and learning. The purpose of this chapter was to present a case study; we did not intend to operationalize a model of instruction. Even though we presented an example of mathematics pedagogy, transformative learning cannot be transferred as a recipe for other classrooms (Darder, 1997). This discussion is an invitation to examine the learning experiences of students and to understand the vision and practice of one teacher committed to social justice.

ACKNOWLEDGMENT

This research was supported in part by the National Science Foundation under Grant No. 0424983 to the Center for the Mathematics Education of Latinos/as (CEMELA). Any opinions, findings, and conclusions or recommendations expressed here are those of the authors and do not necessarily reflect the views of the National Science Foundation.

REFERENCES

Allexsaht-Snider, M. (2006). Editorial: Urban parents' perspectives on children's mathematics learning and issues of equity in mathematics education. *Mathematical Thinking and Learning, 8*(3), 187–195. doi: 10.1207/s15327833mtl0803_1

Apple, M. W. (1992). Do the standards go far enough? Power, policy, and practice in mathematics education. *Journal for Research in Mathematics Education, 23*(5), 412–431. doi: 10.2307/749562

Boaler, J. & Staples, M. (2008). Creating mathematical futures through an equitable teaching approach: The case of Railside School. *Teachers College Record, 110*(3), 608–645. Retrieved from http://www.tcrecord.org/

Brown, J. S., Collins, A., & Duguid, P. (1989). Situated cognition and the culture of learning. *Educational Researcher, 18*(1), 32–42. doi: 10.3102/0013189X018001032

Celedón-Pattichis, S. (2003). Constructing meaning: Think-aloud protocols of ELLs on English and Spanish word problems. *Educators for Urban Minorities, 2*(2), 74–90. Retrieved from http://www.liu.edu/

Charmaz, K. (1983). The grounded theory method: An explication and interpretation. In R. M. Emerson (Ed.), *Contemporary field research: A collection of readings* (pp. 109–126). Boston, MA: Little, Brown.

Civil, M. (2007). Building on community knowledge: An avenue to equity in mathematics education. In N. S. Nasir & P. Cobb (Eds.), *Improving access to mathematics: Diversity and equity in the classroom* (pp. 105–117). New York: Teachers College Press.

Civil, M. & Quintos, B. (2009). Latina mothers' perceptions about the teaching and learning of mathematics: Implications for parental participation. In S. M. B. Greer, S. Mukhopadhyay, A. B. Powell , & S. Nelson-Barber (Ed.), *Culturally responsive mathematics education* (pp. 321–343). New York: Routledge.

Cobb, P. & Hodge, L. L. (2002). A relational perspective on issues of cultural diversity and equity as they play out in the mathematics classroom. *Mathematical Thinking and Learning, 4*(2/3), 249–284. doi: 10.1207/S15327833MTL04023_7

Combs, M. C., Evans, C., Fletcher, T., Parra, E., & Jiménez, A. (2005). Bilingualism for the children: Implementing a dual-language program in an English-only state. *Educational Policy, 19*(5), 701–728. doi: 10.1177/0895904805278063

Cummins, J. (1996). *Negotiating identities: Education for empowerment in a diverse society.* Ontario, CA: California Association for Bilingual Education.

Cummins, J. (2001). *Negotiating identities: Education for empowerment in a diverse society* (2nd ed.). Ontario, CA: California Association for Bilingual Education.

Cummins, J. (2003). *Every student learns: Scott Foresman social studies.* Glenview, IL: Scott Foresman.

Darder, A. (1997). Creating the conditions for cultural democracy in the classroom. In A. Darder, R. D. Torres, & H. Gutiérrez (Eds.), *Latinos and education: A critical reader* (pp. 331–350). New York: Routledge.

Delpit, L. D. (1995). *Other people's children: cultural conflict in the classroom.* New York: New Press.

Dewey, J. (1916). *Democracy and education: An introduction to the philosophy of education.* New York: Macmillan.

Dyson, A. H. & Genishi, C. (2005). *On the case. Approaches to language and literacy research.* New York: Teachers College Press.

Engestrom, Y. (1991). Non scolae sed vitae discimus: Toward overcoming the encapsulation of school learning. *Learning and Instruction, 1*(3), 243–259. doi: 10.1016/0959-4752(91)90006-T

Escalante, J., & Dirmann, J. (1990). The Jaime Escalante math program. *The Journal of Negro Education, 59*(3), 407–423. doi: 10.2307/2295573

Esmonde, I. (2009a). Ideas and identities: Supporting equity in cooperative mathematics learning. *Review of Educational Research, 79*(2), 1008–1043. doi: 10.3102/0034654309332562

Esmonde, I. (2009b). Mathematics learning in groups: Analyzing equity in two cooperative activity structures. *Journal of the Learning Sciences, 18*(2), 247–284. doi: 10.1080/10508400902797958

Frankenstein, M. (1983). Critical mathematics education: An application of Paulo Freire's epistemology. *Journal of Education, 165*(4), 315–340.

Frankenstein, M. (1990). Incorporating race, gender, and class issues into a critical mathematical literacy curriculum. *Journal of Negro Education, 59*(3), 336–347. doi: 10.2307/2295568

Frankenstein, M. (1997a). Breaking down the dichotomy between learning and teaching mathematics. In P. Freire, J. Fraser, D. Macedo, & T. McKinnon (Eds.), *Mentoring the mentor: A critical dialogue with Paulo Freire* (pp. 59–88). New York: Peter Lang.

Frankenstein, M. (1997b). In addition to the mathematics: Including equity issues in the curriculum. In J. Trentacosta & M. J. Kenney (Eds.), *Multicultural and gender equity in the mathematics classroom: The gift of diversity* (pp. 10–22). Reston, VA: National Council of Teachers of Mathematics.

Freire, P. (1998). Pedagogy of the oppressed. In P. Friere, A. M. Araújo Friere, & D. P. Macedo (Eds.), *The Paulo Freire reader* (pp. 45–79). New York: Continuum.

González, N., Andrade, R., Civil, M., & Moll, L. C. (2001). Bridging funds of distributed knowledge: Creating zones of practices in mathematics. *Journal of Education for Student Placed at Risk, 6*(1/2), 115–132. doi: 10.1207/S15327671ES PR0601-2_7

Gutiérrez, K. & Rogoff, B. (2003). Cultural ways of learning: Individual traits or repertoires of practice. *Educational Researcher, 32*(5), 19–25. doi: 10.3102/0013189X032005019

Gutstein, E. (2003). Teaching and learning mathematics for social justice in an urban, Latino school. *Journal for Research in Mathematics Education, 34*(1), 37–73. doi: 10.2307/30034699

Gutstein, E. (2006). *Reading and writing the world with mathematics: Toward a pedagogy for social justice.* New York: Routledge.

Hutchins, E. (1993). Learning to navigate. In S. Chaiklin, & J. Lave (Eds.), *Understanding practice: Perspectives on activity and context* (pp. 35–63). Cambridge, UK: Cambridge University Press.

Khisty, L. L. (1997). Making mathematics accessible to Latino students. In J. Trentacosta & M. J. Kenney (Eds.), *Multicultural and gender equity in the mathematics classroom: The gift of diversity* (National Council of Teachers of Mathematics 1997 Yearbook, pp. 92–101). Reston, VA: National Council of Teachers of Mathematics.

Khisty, L. L. & Chval, K. B. (2002). Pedagogic discourse and equity in mathematics: When teachers' talk matters. *Mathematics Education Research Journal, 14*(3), 154–168. Retrieved from http://www.merga.net.au/

Kitchen, R. S. (2004). Challenges associated with developing discursive classrooms in high-poverty, rural schools. *Mathematics Teacher, 97*(1), 28–31. Retrieved from http://www.nctm.org/publications/mt.aspx/

Ladson-Billings, G. (1994). *The dreamkeepers: Successful teachers of African American children.* San Francisco, CA: Jossey-Bass.

Ladson-Billings, G. (1995). Toward a theory of culturally relevant pedagogy. *American Educational Research Journal, 32*(3), 465–491. doi: 10.3102/00028312032003465

Ladson-Billings, G. & Tate, W. (1995). Toward a critical race theory of education. *Teachers College Record, 97*(1), 47–68. Retrieved from http://www.tcrecord.org/

Lave, J. & Wenger, E. (1991). *Situated learning: Legitimate peripheral participation.* Cambridge, England: Cambridge University Press.

Martin, D. B. (2000). *Mathematics success and failure among African-American youth: The roles of sociohistorical context, community forces, school influence, and individual agency.* Mahwah, NJ: Erlbaum.

Moll, L. C. & González, N. (2004). Engaging life: A funds-of-knowledge approach to multicultural education. In J. A. Banks & C. A. M. Banks (Eds.), *Handbook of research on multicultural education* (2nd ed., pp. 699–715). San Francisco, CA: Jossey-Bass.

Moll, L. C. & Greenberg, J. B. (1990). Creating zones of possibilities: Combining social contexts for instruction. In L. C. Moll (Ed.), *Vygotsky and education: Instructional implications and applications of sociohistorical psychology* (pp. 319–348). Cambridge, England: Cambridge University Press.

Moschkovich, J. N. (2002). A situated and sociocultural perspective on bilingual mathematics learners. *Mathematical Thinking and Learning, 4*(2/3), 189–212. doi: 10.1207/S15327833MTL04023_5

Moschkovich, J. N. (2007). Examining mathematical discourse practices. *For the Learning of Mathematics, 27*(1), 24–30. Retrieved from http://www.flm.educ.ualberta.ca/

Moschkovich, J. N. & Brenner, M. E. (2000). Integrating a naturalistic paradigm into research on mathematics and science cognition and learning. In A. E. Kelly & R. A. Lesh (Eds.), *Handbook of research design in mathematics and science education* (pp. 457–486). Mahwah, NJ: Erlbaum.

Nasir, N. S. (2002). Identity, goals, and learning: Mathematics in cultural practice. *Mathematical Thinking and Learning, 4*(2/3), 213–247. doi: 10.1207/S15327833MTL04023_6

Nieto, S. (1999). *The light in their eyes: Creating multicultural learning communities.* New York: Teachers College Press.

Quintos, B. & Civil, M. (2008). Parental engagement in a classroom community of practice: Boundary practices as part of a culturally relevant pedagogy. *Adults Learning Mathematics: An International Journal, 3*(2a), 59–71. Retrieved from http://www.alm-online.net

Reynolds, P. H. (2004). *Ish.* Cambridge, MA: Candlewick Press.

Rogoff, B. (1994). Developing understanding of the idea of communities of learners. *Mind, Culture, and Activity, 1*(4), 209–229. doi: 10.1080/10749039409524673

Roth, W.-M., Tobin, K., Elmesky, R., Carambo, C., McKnight, Y.-M., & Beers, J. (2004). Re/making identities in the praxis of urban schooling: A cultural historical perspective. *Mind, Culture, and Activity, 11*(1), 48–69. doi: 10.1207/s15327884mca1101_4

Secada, W. G. (1991). Degree of bilingualism and arithmetic problem solving in Hispanic first graders. *The Elementary School Journal, 92*(2), 213–231. doi: 10.1086/461689

Sfard, A. & Prusak, A. (2005). Telling identities: In search of an analytic tool for investigating learning as a culturally shaped activity. *Educational Researcher, 34*(4), 14–22. doi: 10.3102/0013189X034004014

Sleeter, C. E. (1997). Mathematics, multicultural education, and professional development. *Journal for Research in Mathematics Education, 28*(6), 680–696. doi: 10.2307/749637

Smith, D. J. (2002). *If the world were a village: A book about the world's people..* Toronto: Kids Can Press.

Stinson, D. W. (2004). Mathematics as "gate-keeper" (?): Three theoretical perspectives that aim toward empowering all children with a key to the gate. *The Mathematics Educator, 14*(1), 8–18. Retrieved from http://math.coe.uga.edu/tme/tmeonline.html

Turner, E. E. (2003). *Critical mathematical agency: Urban middle school students engage in mathematics to investigate, critique, and act upon their world.* Doctoral dissertation. Retrieved from https://repositories1.lib.utexas.edu/

Valenzuela, A. (1999). *Subtractive schooling: U.S.-Mexican youth and the politics of caring.* Albany: State University of New York Press.

Wells, C. G. (1999). *Dialogic inquiry: Towards a sociocultural practice and theory of education.* Cambridge, UK: Cambridge University Press.

Wenger, E. (1998). *Communities of practice: Learning, meaning, and identity.* Cambridge, UK: Cambridge University Press.

CHAPTER 12

ENGLISH LANGUAGE LEARNERS' CONCEPTUAL UNDERSTANDING OF FRACTIONS

An Interactive Interview Approach as a Means to Learn with Understanding

Libni Berenice Castellón
Laura G. Burr
Richard S. Kitchen, Ph.D.
The University of New Mexico

INTRODUCTION

The number of English language learners (ELLs) enrolled in schools in the United States increased 57% from 1995 to 2006 (National Clearinghouse for English Language Acquisition and Language Instruction Educational Programs, 2007). The rapidly growing population of ELLs is the fastest growing demographic subgroup in the United States. In response to the increase of ELLs in schools, accommodations must be made in instruction

Latinos/as and Mathematics Education, pages 259–282
Copyright © 2011 by Information Age Publishing
All rights of reproduction in any form reserved.

and assessment to support their diverse learning needs (Abedi & Gándara, 2006). This need may not be readily apparent to teachers of mathematics, many of whom view mathematics as a universal language (Lager, 2006). However, Abedi and Lord (2001) found that both students' mathematical knowledge and proficiency in English were strong predictors of students' achievement in mathematics.

In addition to recognizing the strong association between language and mathematics, researchers have documented how ELL students' prior knowledge and culture should be integrated into instruction and assessment tasks (Abedi & Gándara, 2006; Abedi & Lord, 2001; Lockwood & Secada, 1999). ELLs benefit from the use of their home language, from teachers and peers revoicing their explanations, and from the translation and explanation of key words and sentences (Abedi & Gándara, 2006; Borjian, 2008; Lockwood & Secada, 1999). They also learn best if given regular opportunities to reflect on their own thinking and to assess their own errors. Instruction of ELLs should support students by using techniques such as gestures, concrete representations including drawings, and the use of their first language to communicate mathematical thinking (Moschkovich, 2007).

For many students, including ELLs, understanding fractions and their different interpretations and meanings is very challenging (Brown & Quinn, 2006; Chan, Leu, & Chen; 2007; Charalambos & Pitta-Pantazi, 2007). Fractions are usually studied in middle school because of the complexity of the concepts, but when the curriculum was examined, the concepts of fractions appeared at elementary, secondary, and university levels (Lamon, 2007). Results from the National Assessment Educational Progress test reveals that high school students "recurrently demonstrate a lack of proficiency with fraction understanding" (Brown & Quinn, 2006, p. 28). Research concerning students' understanding of fractions has attributed their difficulties to the multiple interpretations of fractions (e.g., part–whole, ratio, operator, quotient, and measure), their lack of knowledge of these interpretations, and their role in the learning of fractions with understanding (Brown & Quinn, 2006; Chan et al., 2007; Charalambos & Pitta-Pantazi, 2007; Clarke, Roche, & Mitchell, 2007; Lamon, 2007; Saxe, Taylor, McIntosh, & Gearhart, 2005; Watson, Campbell, & Collis, 1993). Enhanced knowledge of the different interpretations of fractions facilitates teachers' capacities to analyze students' thinking related to fractions and to design instruction and assessment that will support the learning of fractions (Charalambos & Pitta-Pantazi, 2007; Clarke et al., 2007; Lamon, 2005). Lamon (2007) argued that building fraction, ratio, and proportional knowledge is a lengthy and complex process.

The purpose of this chapter is to document the results of a study conducted by the authors to examine the value of a formative assessment format to gather in-depth information about ELLs' knowledge of the fraction subconstructs. We describe a research study conducted during spring of 2008 that focused on ELLs' conceptual understanding of the fraction subconstructs that was uncovered with the use of an interactive interview research protocol. The research study sought to answer the question, How does the use of the interactive interview research protocol as a type of formative assessment contribute to ELLs' conceptual understanding of fractions? To answer this question, we considered three issues: (1) ELLs' knowledge and misunderstandings related to fractions, (2) the nature of the information gathered about ELLs' understanding of fractions through the use of the interactive interview research protocol, and (3) the power of the interactive interview research protocol as a tool to foster ELLs' mathematical understanding.

We chose to use the interactive interview protocol with ELLs because they historically have been described from a deficit viewpoint that highlights their lack of mastery of academic language. However, the use of the interactive interview protocol fostered a safe environment in which students' levels of fluency with mathematical terminology would not be the criteria used when determining their understanding of mathematical concepts; students could communicate by writing on a white board, drawing pictures to represent ideas, and pointing to items, possibly without naming them. This approach allowed students to explain their thinking using methods that also represent competent mathematical communication (Moschkovich, 2007).

Rolón (2003) recommended assessing understanding by asking questions and focusing on students' understanding, not their language skills. We learned that through focusing on students' understanding and not on their deficiencies, we could gain valuable insights about what students, particularly ELLs, can achieve mathematically. In this study, we also discovered that the use of the research protocol provided detailed information about ELL students' understanding of fractions that could be used to inform instruction.

Elsewhere, we described how the learning environment engendered by the research protocol motivated student responses that were often well developed and innovative (see Kitchen, Burr, & Castellón, 2010). Research participants frequently developed creative problem-solving strategies, communicated their ideas, and justified their solutions by reflecting on their own thinking. Moreover, we found the use of the research protocol cultivated a culturally affirming and empowering learning environment for the participating ELL students. We learned of the potential of the interactive interview research protocol to support the development of trusting and affirming relationships, which ultimately led to mathematically inspiring Latino/a youth. Through the fruition of these positive relations, the research protocol provided a means to position these students as competent problem solvers (Empson, 2003; Forman, 2003; Kitchen et al., 2010; Turner, Celedón-Pattichis, & Marshall, 2008) and to support bilingual learners using the resources that they bring to the learning process (Moschkovich, 1999). The result was a revelation of sorts of what is possible if formative assessment practices are coupled with attention to the cultures and social identities of Latino/a youth.

In this chapter, we focus primarily on cognition and the effectiveness of the interactive interview research protocol to assess ELL students' understanding of the five fraction subconstructs (part–whole, ratio, operator, quotient, and measure). Before describing the study and our findings in more detail, an overview of a theoretical model describing fractional understanding and the different interpretations of fractions is provided. We then summarize the research findings of assessments of ELLs and their understanding of fractional concepts. We proceed by offering the theoretical framework used to interpret the mathematical thinking of the students and the context within which this thinking took place. After delineating the methodology used in this investigation, we summarize and analyze the research findings. We conclude with a final discussion of the study and possible implications and contributions of this study to the research literature.

UNDERSTANDING FRACTIONS: A THEORETICAL MODEL

The overview presented in this chapter follows an epistemological stance, which framed the study of rational numbers according to construct and subconstructs as a means to classify them and to better understand how they are interpreted (Moss & Case, 1999). We assumed this stance because of the importance we placed on the development of students' abilities to think about and make sense of different interpretations of fractions, and to understand how those interpretations influence the ways they solve mathematical tasks (Lamon, 2005). Another reason for following an epistemological stance is that many of the difficulties in learning and teaching fractions appear to be due to the multiple interpretations of fractions and their representations (Clarke et al., 2007; Chan et al., 2007). Those difficulties persist in the upper grade levels.

Kieren (1980) described five ideas that represented subcategories or subconstructs of rational numbers—part–whole, ratio, operator, quotient, and measure—as emerging from a pool of constructs. Kieren emphasized the need for differentiating and connecting those subconstructs (Brown & Quinn, 2006; Chan et al., 2007; Charalambos & Pitta-Pantazi, 2007; Clarke et al, 2007; Lamon, 2007; Saxe et al., 2005; Watson et al., 1993). The subconstructs were expanded upon by Behr, Lesh, Post, and Silver (1983) as part of their work on the Rational Number Project. Behr and colleagues proposed a theoretical model relating the five fraction subconstructs to the basic operations of fractions, fraction equivalence, and problem solving.

Charalambos and Pitta-Pantazi (2007) presented a theoretical model of the five subconstructs of fractions. The model presents the part–whole subconstruct as the basis for learning the other interpretations of fractions and suggests the use of this subconstruct as a starting point to teach the other subconstructs. Based on this model, the ratio subconstruct influences the understanding of equivalent fractions. The operator and measure subconstructs influence the understanding of the multiplication and addition of fractions, respectively.

Mastering the five fraction subconstructs influences how students perform in problem solving situations (Behr et al., 1983; Lamon, 2007). The fraction subconstructs have been used as the basis for studying children's understanding, planning instruction, and designing assessment tasks (Brown & Quinn, 2006; Charalambos & Pitta-Pantazi, 2007; Clarke et al., 2007; Chan et al., 2007; Lamon, 2007; Saxe et al., 2005; Watson et al., 1993). By targeting the subconstructs separately, researchers and teachers can measure students' understanding and draw conclusions concerning each of them. In the following section, each subconstruct is described in detail.

Definitions of the Fraction Subconstructs

The *part–whole* subconstruct is the most common interpretation of fractions (Clarke et al., 2007) and is defined as the partition of a quantity or objects into parts of equal size (Charalambos & Pitta-Pantazi, 2007; Clarke et al., 2007). Lamon (2007) found that through developing a strong understanding of the part–whole construct, children will be able to understand equivalent fractions, and the operations of addition and subtraction of fractions.

The *ratio* subconstruct of fractions is defined as the comparison between two quantities or two sets and may not be emphasized enough in the school curriculum (Charalambos & Pitta-Pantazi, 2007; Clarke et al., 2007). Lamon (2005) took the stance that there is no reason to delay the study of ratios until middle school because children use ratios in sharing and comparing situations.

The interpretation of the *operator* subconstruct includes "shrinking and enlarging, contracting and expanding, enlarging and reducing or multiplying and dividing" (Lamon, 2005, p. 151). The operator subconstruct is also described as a function, or a set of operations performed to derive a result (Behr et al., 1983; Lamon, 2005). A pervasive misconception among many students is that multiplication always results in a larger number and division always results in a smaller number. This misunderstanding can be attributed to a lack of experience using fractions as operators (Clarke et al., 2007).

The *quotient* subconstruct, also called division, can be seen as the numerical value of a/b. The foundation for building an understanding of this subconstruct is generally developed in the early years through fair-sharing activities (Lamon, 2007). Because the result of a/b refers to the numerical value and not to the parts, there is no restriction about the fraction size; the numerator can be smaller, equal to, or bigger than the denominator.

The *measure* subconstruct describes the unit and subintervals, equivalence, and the density of the rational numbers (Lamon, 2007). This subconstruct has been associated with using number lines showing that the number of equal parts in a unit can vary depending on the number of partitions (Charalambos & Pitta-Pantazi, 2007; Clarke et al., 2007). Students can develop strong notions of the operations of addition and subtraction by mastering the measure subconstruct (Lamon, 2007).

The five fraction subconstructs provide the means to study student strategies and common mistakes. Because students' interpretations of fractions are based upon the subconstruct under consideration, there is a need for different assessment formats to understand how students think about fractions. The next section gives an overview of assessment in general, followed by a section on the assessment of students' understanding of fraction.

Assessment and Students' Understanding of Fractions

For almost two decades, researchers and policy makers have been advocating for revisions in assessment practices to bring about changes in instruction based on how children learn (e.g., Kulm, 1994; O'Day & Smith, 1993). No longer is it enough to determine if the student simply gets the correct answer; attention has shifted to assessment being used to inform teachers of students' knowledge of, ability to use, and disposition toward mathematics (National Counil of Teachers of Mathematics, 1995). Gearhart and Saxe (2004) noted that assessment is necessary to reveal students' thinking. Designing assessment tasks is complex because the items should capture the mathematics that students know, foster learning, and provide valid inferences about students' understanding. At the classroom level, teachers can effectively implement formative assessments, "assessment that focuses on teacher's responses to student learning data they encounter on a daily basis" (Wilson & Kenney, 2003, p. 55) to shed light on student understanding and subsequently inform instruction.

Wilson and Kenney (2003) reported that formative assessment has positively influenced student learning and supports the development of equitable classrooms. It also gives more accurate information about student understanding that will help to inform instruction (Wilson & Kenney, 2003). Examples of formative assessments include observations, portfolios, projects, classroom questioning and discourse, and clinical interviews (Shepard, 2000; Wilson & Kenney, 2003). When implementing formative assessment, teachers are gathering evidence and making conjectures about students' learning. This information will allow them to provide feedback and target instruction. Decisions are based on data and not on assumptions concerning what students can or cannot do. When teachers use formative assessment, they are taking into account students' prior knowledge and the language and cultural resources that they bring as important components in assessment and instruction (Wilson & Kenney, 2003).

Researchers have proposed different ways to evaluate proficiency in fraction understanding and fraction computations (Chan et al., 2007; Clarke at al., 2007; Cramer, Post, & delMas, 2002; Niemi, 1996). Niemi (1996) employed written assessments to evaluate students' conceptual knowledge of fractions. He drew on mathematical representations, problem solving, explanation measures, and multifaceted assessment strategies as indices of understanding of fractions. To score student responses, he designed a scoring rubric with five dimensions: (1) general quality of content knowledge, (2) concepts and principles, (3) knowledge of facts and procedures, (4) misconceptions, and (5) integration of knowledge.

Since Niemi's (1996) work, researchers have used one-on-one interviews to assess student understanding of fractions in relation to the five subconstructs (Clarke et al., 2007; Cramer et al., 2002). The use of interviews gave students opportunities to explain their ideas using resources other than paper and pencil, and allowed the interviewer to address questions. For large-scale assessments, one-on-one interviews may be impractical, but for smaller groups, one-on-one interviews permit a better understanding of students' thinking (Chan et al., 2007).

Cramer and colleagues (2002) designed and analyzed interviews to evaluate the understanding of fractions of two groups of students: a control group and a treatment group. They used ordering and estimation tasks, and the interviews were done by participating teachers. The ordering questions showed how students made sense of the relative size of fractions, and the estimation tasks gave information about students' use of fraction size to estimate solutions to addition and subtraction tasks. They analyzed the data according to conceptual or procedural knowledge, students' explanations, manipulatives used, and students' reasoning. They found the treatment group, which had received instruction focusing more on conceptual experiences, developed a conceptual foundation to solve more procedural tasks despite the limited time devoted to those kinds of tasks during the intervention.

Taking a different approach than Cramer and colleagues (2002), others have trained interviewers and assessed student knowledge on a large number of fraction subconstructs. For example, Clarke and colleagues (2007) collected data for a large group of sixth-grade students ($n = 323$) to assess fraction understanding using one-on-one, task-based interviews. They evaluated the five fraction subconstructs and found that students benefited from greater exposure to these subconstructs. Furthermore, they recommended that teachers use tasks based on the subconstructs to gather evidence about student understanding and common misconceptions; more importantly, they encouraged teachers to inform their instruction and possibly modify their curriculum.

THEORETICAL FRAMEWORK

The theoretical framework on which our data analysis is based draws upon the area of social constructivism. The emergent social-constructivist paradigm borrows from cognitive, constructivist, and sociocultural theories (Shepard, 2000). Within the cognitive psychology paradigm, scholars seek to understand an individual's learning in terms of internal cognitive structures and processes (Cobb, 2007). Within this paradigm, frameworks have been developed to locate students' thinking within specific mathematical domains such as multiplicative reasoning (e.g., Confrey & Smith, 1995). The learning of mathematics is viewed as an active process of mental construction and sense making for a constructivist. A potential pitfall of cognitive and constructivist frameworks is that they may not take into account cultural and social issues such as the cultural practices of the communities in which the learner lives; another possibility is that issues of equity and access are not necessarily considered.

In the sociocultural perspective, learning is developed through socially supported interactions. We will borrow a central idea from Vygotsky's work (1925/1999), that learning and child development are brought about from the beginning through communication. "Instruction and development do not meet for the first time at school age; rather, they are in fact connected with each other from the very first day of a child's life" (Vygotsky, as cited in Lerman, 2001, p. 5). From this perspective, cognition is inherently social, and learning is viewed as an element of a system of cultural practices (Cobb, 2007). Vygotsky advocated that we not only look at mental activity, but also at situated practices and that the process must be studied, not just the outcome of activities (Forman, 2003). Thus, sociocultural theory provides a means to explain the complex relationship between social context and learning.

METHOD

This study was designed to examine the effectiveness of the interactive interview research protocol that we describe next to assess students' understanding of the five fraction subconstructs. The study sought answers to the following research question and subquestions:

1. How does the use of the interactive interview research protocol as a type of formative assessment contribute to ELL students' conceptual understanding of fractions?
2. What are ELL students' knowledge and misunderstandings related to fractions?
3. What is the nature of the information gathered about ELL students' understanding of fractions through the use of the interactive interview research protocol?
4. How can the interactive interview research protocol be used as a tool to foster ELL students' mathematical understanding?

Data Collection

In spring of 2008, videotape data were collected on four students as they estimated, calculated, and explained their solutions to tasks involving fractions, decimals, percents, and proportional reasoning, first on a preassessment administered prior to instruction in a reform mathematics curriculum, then on a postassessment administered after two to four weeks of instruction. The four ELL (Spanish as first language and English as a second language) students were in a sixth-grade class taught by the third author. A four-stage interactive interview protocol was designed and used twice with the students, first throughout the preassessment and second during postassessments. The interviews were conducted by the first and second authors; the first author is Spanish dominant (Interviewer B), and the other is English dominant (Interviewer A). They had developed close relationships with the students. During the fall of 2007, they taught a few classes and assisted twice a week to help the students during their mathematics class.

The interactive interview protocol is synthesized in Figure 12.1. The design of the interactive interview protocol built upon and was an extension of an interview protocol used by the third author in a previous study (see Kitchen & Wilson, 2004; Kulm, Wilson, & Kitchen, 2005). The four stages of the interactive interview protocol shown in Figure 12.1 took place over two sessions; Session 1 was composed of two stages of the interactive interview, estimation, and writing; and Session 2 occurred a few days later and included an interview and a simulated phone interview.

In Stage 1, the estimation stage, the student was presented with mathematics tasks in English and given the option of having them read in Spanish. The student was asked to estimate the solutions to the tasks. The student could not use any tools (e.g., ruler, paper and pencil, calculator, and

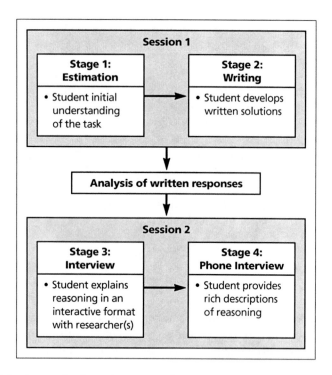

Figure 12.1 Interactive interview protocol.

so on) during this stage and was not permitted to write down ideas while estimating—this technique removed the temptation students often have to immediately calculate the answer. The purpose of this stage was to ensure that the student understood the task as indicated by the reasonableness of their estimation.

In Stage 2, the writing stage, the student worked independently to develop written solutions to all the tasks for which the student had developed estimates in Stage 1. Between the two sessions, the researchers analyzed the student's answers to determine what questions might clarify the student's work and reveal the student's thinking during subsequent stages. In Stage 3, the interview stage, the student was asked by Interviewer A to explain the reasoning used to solve each task. During this stage, a copy of the student's work was provided so the student could review the work completed and recall how the work was done. The student used a dry-erase board, as needed, to demonstrate his or her mathematical thinking. Also, during this process, Interviewer A asked clarifying questions, revoiced the student's explanations, and/or referenced aspects of the student's work.

Finally, in Stage 4, the phone interview stage, the student was asked to explain his or her mathematical thinking for each task by Interviewer B in a simulated telephone interview. Interviewer B sat with her back to the student and could not view any of the student's written work during this stage because the goal was to motivate the student to provide rich descriptions of the mathematical reasoning used in solving the task. Similar to Stage 3, Interviewer B could ask clarifying questions, revoice explanations, and/or reference explanations given by the student throughout this stage.

Students were videotaped during stages 1, 3, and 4 to capture student work, gestures, and interactions with the interviewers. The videotapes were used to analyze students' strategies to solve tasks, to identify common strategies and mistakes, and to examine students' thinking through the various stages of the process. Gestures observed on the videos were part of students' explanations and served as evidence of how the students understood the task and made sense of it (e.g., moving hands to demonstrate how values change from positive to negative on a number line).

Data Analysis

The data subsets were analyzed using interpretive methods (Erickson, 1986; Maxwell, 2005). This method of analysis coupled with the integrated theoretical framework used enabled an analysis of student understanding of mathematical concepts in the context of a highly relational learning environment engendered by the two interviewers. The data were analyzed for three of the fraction subconstructs: part–whole, measure, and ratio. When we examined students' thinking, we explored how students used traditional mathematical algorithms, developed representations such as graphs, interpreted number lines, applied reasoning, formed mathematical connections, and produced generalizations. We also analyzed the nature of students' interactions with the interviewers, their responses to the instructional scaffolding provided, and their willingness to persevere in their attempts to problem solve.

FINDINGS

In this study, we found that the interactive interview protocol provided the means to reveal the in-depth understanding of students' mathematical knowledge, reasoning, and procedural abilities used to determine solutions to tasks. The interactive interview research protocol provided students with the opportunity to ask questions, try a variety of approaches, and test and revise mathematical hypotheses in their attempts to arrive at solutions to the given tasks. The conditions inherent to the research protocol such as the extensive time provided students for problem solving, language support, instructional scaffolding, and adult collaboration provided the means for students to explore fraction concepts deeply. Students could request explanations or ask clarifying questions in English or Spanish, and could explain their ideas in either language. They had the time needed to think and talk about their task solution. They could use different strategies; the knowledge of algorithms was not a prerequisite to solving tasks. During the process, it was not unusual for students to develop and connect mathematical ideas as they solved problems.

The interviewers played an important role during the process. Having two interviewers, one a native English speaker and the other a native Spanish speaker, created a linguistically and culturally supportive learning environment. The interviewers formulated questions that led students to find their mistakes and to try new strategies to solve tasks. The interviewers acknowledged students' mathematical ideas and helped the students to refine those ideas when needed. We found that the dynamic interactions that took place between the students and interviewers were crucial to motivate students' thinking and often led to the students demonstrating innovative approaches. At times, the interviewers acted as teachers, using questioning as a tool to cause disequilibrium to help students find mistakes and think about new strategies to solve the tasks. We used the interactive interview research protocol because we wanted to foster students' thinking so that we could be better informed about their knowledge of fractions. A notion that guided this work was our belief that greater insight could be elicited about student understanding through the use of a formative assessment model in which social interaction helps students elaborate upon their conceptual understanding.

In the next section, vignettes are presented in which students revealed their understanding of three of the fraction subconstructs—part–whole, measure, and quotient. We focused on how students made sense of the different tasks and applied the fraction subconstructs to solve them. Although we conducted interviews using a pre- and posttest, we do not compare their work in this paper. We begin with a vignette of a student solving a fraction problem involving the part–whole subconstruct.

Part–Whole Subconstruct

Lamon (2005) found that the part–whole subconstruct influenced how students made sense of equivalent fractions and how they performed the operations of addition and subtraction on fractions. Two of the tasks in the pre- and postassessments required students to obtain equivalent fractions to add or subtract them. The task discussed here is a word problem that asked students to subtract mixed numbers. Specifically, students were presented with the following task: Andres drove his bike $39\frac{1}{6}$ meters and Ned drove his bike $28\frac{5}{9}$ meters. How many more meters did Andres drive than Ned?

Students approached this task involving mixed numbers in different ways, converting the mixed number into an improper fraction or subtracting the whole and fractional parts separately. A description of the process used by Zenia to solve this task during the postassessment as she progressed through the four stages of the interactive interview protocol exemplified how one student made sense of this task.

Zenia began by reading aloud the task: "Andres drove his bike $39\frac{1}{6}$ meters and Ned drove his bike $28\frac{5}{9}$ meters. How many more meters did Andres drive than Ned?" During the estimation stage, she gave a reasonable approximation; the answer was going to be a little bit less than 11, because 39 minus 28 is 11 but she still needed to account for the fractional portions of the numbers. When Zenia actually worked on the problem, she used a different strategy—she applied the algorithm and converted the mixed numbers into improper fractions. In this case, she got 11 as an answer due to an error in multiplication.

During the interview, Zenia solved this task converting the mixed numbers into improper fractions and then found a common denominator to get equivalent fractions. After this conversion, Zenia ended up computing

$$\frac{2115}{54} - \frac{1542}{54} = \frac{573}{54}.$$

She converted the resulting improper fraction into a mixed number to get her final answer, $10\frac{6}{10}$, by dividing 573 by 54, as shown in Figure 12.2. Note that Zenia's reliance on the division algorithm resulted in her obtaining an approximation with the decimal solution instead of deriving the more precise solution of $10\frac{33}{54}$ or $10\frac{11}{18}$.

We discovered numerous aspects of Zenia's thinking in this example. First, Zenia did not use the least common multiple to derive equivalent fractions, a strategy that would have made it easier to perform the calculations. She did, however, recognize the need and understood the procedure

```
        1 0.6
54) 5 7 3.0
    5 4
    ─────
    3 3
      0
    ─────
    3 3 0
    3 2 4
    ─────
        6
```

Figure 12.2 Zenia's computation.

to get equivalent fractions to subtract. Zenia explained that she multiplied the existing denominators to get 54 ($6 \times 9 = 54$), but then the interviewer provided scaffolding for Zenia, as presented in Excerpt 12.1.

Excerpt 12.1. Lowest common denominator

Interviewer: "I have another question for you on this same problem. You used 54 for your common denominator. Is there a smaller number that you could have used?"

Zenia: "36." (after a brief exchange with Zenia)

Interviewer: "Okay, could you have used an even smaller number?"

Zenia: "18?"

Interviewer: "And why 18?"

Zenia: "9 goes into 18 two times and 6 goes into 18 three times."

Interviewer: "Is there one number that is better than another to use or does it matter?"

Zenia: "It doesn't matter."

During the phone interview, the interviewer asked her if she could solve the problem in a different way to avoid having to deal with such large numbers. During her explanation, Zenia demonstrated the ability to manipulate fractions, decomposing and combining them in different ways while always conserving their equivalence. She ultimately solved the task by subtracting the whole numbers and the fractional portions of the mixed numbers separately, and then combined the results. Zenia explained her solution this way:

> I subtracted 39 minus 28 and it gave me 11, and now I am going to multiply 1/6 times 3 over 3 and it's gonna give me 3/18. Then I am going to multiply 5/9 times 2 over 2 and it gives me 10/18. And, so then I need to subtract 3/18 minus 10/18 and it gives me negative 7/18. Then I need to subtract negative 7/18 minus 11. Maybe if I just subtract 11 minus 7/18 equals... 10 and... 11/18ths.

Throughout this process, Zenia manipulated the fractions and the whole numbers, showing a deep understanding of fraction size and equivalence of fractions. When the interviewer asked her how she went from $11\frac{-7}{18}$ to $10\frac{11}{18}$, she answered that she took 1 from the 11 and left the 10 as the whole number, then she represented the one as $\frac{18}{18}$ and subtracted $\frac{7}{18}$ from that, getting the fractional part of the final answer.

In this vignette, Zenia's thinking was uncovered and advanced through the use of extensive questioning. As the student and teacher interacted, knowledge was socially constructed, each giving rise to comments and explanations that furthered the understanding of the mathematical concepts for the student and reciprocally furthering the knowledge of the interviewer concerning the student's reasoning. The interactive interview research protocol provided a means to both probe student learning and to prompt the students to think in new directions.

Veronica, another student in the study, solved a different task during the postassessment involving the subtraction of mixed numbers. The problem statement was as follows: Veronica has $5\frac{1}{4}$ pounds of grapes. She gave $2\frac{2}{3}$ pounds to Marisol. How many pounds of grapes does Veronica have left? On the written work, Veronica solved the problem by subtracting the whole numbers and then the fractions. She converted 1/4 into 3/12 and 2/3 into 8/12. During the interview, she explained that 5 minus 2 will be 3, but since 3/12 is less than 8/12, she needed to reduce the whole number by 1, resulting in 2 as the whole number part of the resulting fraction. She then added the fractions and got 11/12. Her answer was $2\frac{11}{12}$.

The interviewer questioned Veronica's answer, asking, "How did you get 11/12? How did you decide what operation to use?" When Veronica explained the reasons, she realized that the answer was wrong and decided to subtract the fractions, determining $3\frac{-5}{12}$ to be the solution. The interviewer questioned her thinking, as presented in Excerpt 12.2.

Excerpt 12.2. Subtracting mixed numbers

Veronica: "It would equal like 2 something."

Interviewer: "Okay, I'm not sure I understand, what is this?"

Veronica: "Negative 5/12 but if I multiply 5 times 3 [the whole number resulting when she subtracted 5 – 2] it would be 48 over 12."

Interviewer: "I'm not following that."

Veronica: "12 times 3 over 12, the answer over 12 and you can subtract it from that [–5/12]."

Interviewer: "Oh, you could. You could do that. Yeah, but 3 times 12, think again..."

Veronica: "Is 36."

Interviewer: "You wanna show us how you do that. So you're replacing the 3 with..."

Veronica: "5 over 12 and then you would do the same for 36."

Interviewer: "Okay, yeah."

Veronica: "And you get 31."

Interviewer: "Okay, you have 31, very good."

Veronica: "31 over 12. And then it's going to equal $2\frac{11}{12}$."

Interviewer: "Okay, 2, because, how'd you get 2?"

Veronica: "How many times 12 goes into 31."

Interviewer: "Good, that's 2, and what's 2 times 12?"

Veronica: "24."

Interviewer: "Good, and then how many more do you need to get to 31?"

Veronica: "7, yeah, 7." (Writes $2\frac{7}{12}$ on the white board)
Interviewer: "So you like that answer better?"
Veronica: "Yeah."

Veronica had derived two different mixed number answers, $2\frac{11}{12}$ and $3\frac{-5}{12}$. She knew that fractions could be represented in different ways, but still denote the same value as equivalent fractions. The interviewer asked her to represent $3\frac{-5}{12}$ with only positive values and Veronica wrote it as $2\frac{11}{12}$. The interviewer then solicited further explanation on how she determined her solution. Veronica assumed that the mixed numbers were equivalent, but after working on an equivalent representation for $3\frac{-5}{12}$, she recognized that $2\frac{11}{12}$ was not an equivalent representation. Understanding that fractions can be written in different ways and still represent the same value helped Veronica to become aware of the error in her thinking.

The examples of Zenia and Veronica's exchanges illustrate some of the ways knowledge is socially constructed in the interview process. The interviewer interacted with students to extend their understanding of fractions and, at the same time, helped students identify mistakes in their use of mathematical terms or in their mathematical thinking. The interviewer also learned about the solidity or fragility of students' understanding.

Quotient Subconstruct

The quotient interpretation of fraction is defined as the numerical value of the fraction—the fraction represents the division of the numerator by the denominator. One of the problems on both the pre- and postassessment required comparing the size of a decimal to a mixed number. The common strategy was to convert the mixed number into a decimal to compare the numbers. Students showed creative strategies to convert the fractions into decimals and demonstrated a clear understanding of fraction size (e.g., how changes in the denominator affected the size of the fraction).

One of the problems involved a comparison between 4.86 and $4\frac{3}{8}$. Andres solved this problem by initially noting that only .86 and $\frac{3}{8}$ needed to be compared because the whole numbers in each number are equivalent. When he converted $\frac{3}{8}$ into a decimal, Andres developed a strategy and established a relationship between the fraction size and the corresponding decimal representation. In Andres' strategy, he recognized that $\frac{3}{8}$ is close to $\frac{3}{10}$. In the following exchange, Andres explained how he got a decimal representation for $\frac{3}{8}$. He demonstrated a clear understanding of fraction size and the relationship between the numerator and denominator and the actual numerical value that the fraction represents, as highlighted in Excerpt 12.3.

Excerpt 12.3. Relationship between numerator and denominator

Andres: "I changed 3/8 into 3/10 and basically in a decimal it was .30. And I changed it into 3/9, and it gave me [point] 33."

Interviewer: "How did you get the 33?"

Andres: "The smaller the number on the bottom, the bigger the decimal gets. The bigger it gets in a decimal."

Interviewer: "How do you know that would be .33?"

Andres: "... Now, instead of making 3/9, I make it into 3/8. So, as a decimal it is going to be higher, .36."

Interviewer: "I don't understand how you got the 36 and 33. How do you know that would be 33 and not 34, or ..."

Andres: "Because I'm adding by 3s. The number on top, I'm adding by 3s, because the number on top will be ... yes. I'm just adding by 3s."

Interviewer: "That's because the number on top is 3."

Andres: "Yeah."

Even though Andres made mistakes estimating how changes in the denominator affected changes in the numerical value (i.e., 3/8 ≠ .36), he was able to explain that the value of the fraction increases as the denominator decreases when the numerator is constant. He found a close approximation of the actual value, but further activities need to be developed to lead him to find the mistake in his reasoning.

Andres socially constructed a solution to this problem as he interacted with the interviewer. He understood the fraction size to be greater when the number of pieces (denominator) is smaller. Andres did not know how to determine the exact decimal value of the fraction. He developed a very creative way to solve the problem, partially because, as Andres stated in an informal conversation, he did not like to memorize and use algorithms. He preferred to derive a task solution. Teachers and researchers can share strategies like those derived by Andres with other students to help them make sense of task solutions.

Measure Subconstruct

Assessing the subconstruct of measure provides evidence about student understanding of the density of the rational numbers and also the idea that the number of equal parts in a unit depends upon the number of partitions. Clear ideas of equivalent fractions are needed to efficiently solve measurement tasks. One task in the pre- and postassessments required students to subtract fractions with the aid of a number line. On the preassessment, the task was to compute 1/4 – 1/2. To discourage students from changing fractions into decimals, the numbers on the postassessment were fractions with nonterminating decimal representations (2/3 and 1/6). This change elicited the application of more complex strategies to derive a solution such as applying distance concepts and dividing the number line into thirds and sixths.

During the postassessment, Andres initially struggled to find a way to find $1/6 - 2/3$ and made common mistakes when estimating the answer (e.g., subtracting numerators and denominators). The interviewer asked questions to help him identify his errors and ultimately derive the correct answer. To compute $1/6 - 2/3$, Andres divided the units into thirds and sixths and labeled them on the number line. He then explained that the distance between 1/6 and 2/3 is the same distance that he needed to move to the left starting at 1/6. He found that 2/3 is equivalent to 4/6. He noted that the distance from 1/6 to 4/6 is 3/6 and explained that this is the equivalent to the distance from zero to 3/6 and consequently is equivalent to the distance from zero to –3/6. To illustrate the strategy, he explained that if the distance between the two numbers is 5", then he needed to move 5" to the left because he was subtracting to find the answer. During the phone interview stage, Andres was able to explain clearly how he solved the problem and synthesized all the procedures with the following explanation. He had already divided the number line into sixths and noted 2/3 = 4/6 (see Excerpt 12.4).

Excerpt 12.4. Distance between numbers

> I tried to subtract that [$1/6 - 2/3$] and well I thought that if I had zero through 4/6 and if I subtracted that, the answer would just be –4/6. Since I have 1/6 through 4/6, I'm going to try to subtract that. And the space that I have between zero and 1/6 is going to be the same space that I have from 3 over 6 to 4 over 6. Okay? So then I'm going to like move the number line. So now I'm just going to make it from zero to 3/6, 'cause now it's going to be the same distance.

Though Andres successfully derived $1/4 - 1/2$ in the preassessment by using decimals and coin relationships to represent the fractions (1/4 is the same as one quarter of a dollar and 1/2 is equal to two quarters), it did not necessarily follow that he could find $1/6 - 2/3$. Using the interactive interview research protocol, we gathered information about Andres's ability to work with fractions as measure and his capacity to transfer strategies that can be used with whole numbers to work with fractions. It is important to note that the process Andres followed to derive the answer in the postassessment was quite involved and that the interviewer was intimately involved in supporting Andres to draw on his existing ideas and to construct new ones.

CONCLUSIONS

Similar to Abedi and Lord (2001), we found that participating students' written responses gave a very limited snapshot of their mathematical reasoning and communication. Students just wrote down their solutions, giving little or no explanation of their thought process. However, through the different stages of the interactive interview research protocol, students demonstrated their mathematical understanding in diverse ways. They solved problems using different strategies, using an algorithm in some cases or inventing procedures in others, as demonstrated in Zenia's and Andres's vignettes (excerpts 12.1 and 12.3–12.4, respectively). Sometimes, students chose to privilege the use of algorithms and often did not trust their own thinking (e.g., Veronica). Other times, they realized that their reasoning led to the correct answer and was a more direct way to arrive at a solution than applying a complex algorithm, as Zenia did when she subtracted the mixed numbers first using improper fractions and then applying her reasoning and subtracting wholes and fractions separately. The students became more aware of their thinking and what they did or did not understand well. During the interactive interview process, they were often able to find their own mistakes and explain their strategies, as illustrated in Veronica's vignette (see Excerpt 12.2).

Using a socioconstructivist perspective (Shepard, 2000), we were able to gather accurate information about the students' understanding of fractions and their mathematical gaps. The fraction subconstructs provided a framework to make sense of participating students' thinking vis-à-vis their differing interpretations of fractions. The interactive interview research protocol proved to be quite effective as a formative assessment format to uncover the four participating students' reasoning. Throughout, we had opportunities to teach ideas related to fractions as we engaged in socially constructed interactions with students—exploring students' understanding, encouraging student communication, and providing scaffolding when students struggled to connect ideas.

The findings reported in this research study also showed that the participants, all of whom were ELLs at the time the study was undertaken, were quite capable of solving complex mathematical tasks and communicating their mathematical ideas in detail by using means that go beyond their mastery of English or academic language. As students and interviewers interacted, new knowledge was constructed and acquired by students, and a greater understanding of students' ideas about fractions was determined. Sometimes, the ELLs did not use academic language to communicate their ideas, but used both mathematical terms, common words, and gestures to describe their ideas. Had the students' knowledge been judged based only on their use of academic language, the results would not have been accurate. For example, Andres use the term "minus numbers" when he referred to negative numbers, and both Marisol and Andres asked the interviewers for the English equivalent of a Spanish term during their explanations.

It was important to acknowledge the ELL students' prior knowledge and their strategies because this recognition led to students being more willing to try different approaches without fear of being judged negatively by the interviewers. We found it was important that the interviewers had established positive relationships with the students prior to the use of the research protocol because this familiarity promoted the participants' greater comfort with sharing their mathematical thinking and even taking risks while problem solving. Through the fruition of these positive relations, the research protocol provided a means to position these students as competent problem solvers (Empson, 2003; Kitchen et al., 2010; Turner et al., 2008) and to support bilingual learners using the resources that they bring to the learning process (Moschkovich, 2002). Because of the interactive interview protocol's usefulness, we argue that this alternative assessment format has great potential for use in classrooms that serve majority Latino/a populations.

Based on the ideas discussed in this chapter, we encourage teachers to include the theoretical model of fraction subconstructs in their teaching with the use of one-on-one, task-based interviews to evaluate student conceptual understanding of fractions. We also recommend that teachers use assessment results to inform instruction. Teachers are likely to find that their students' understanding of these concepts influences their learning and achievement as they operate on fractions, derive equivalent fractions, and solve problems with fractions.

Our research contributes to a body of knowledge on effective formative assessment formats. One of the limitations we found in this study was the time needed to implement the research protocol. Researchers should explore how instruction of the different fraction subconstructs supports ELL students to develop a better understanding of fractions. Other research questions worth investigating include the following: How can teachers modify their fraction instruction to help ELL students? What adaptations in assessment can be made to better understand ELLs' understanding of fractions?

We believe that the interactive interview research protocol has great potential as a formative assessment tool to provide teachers with in-depth information that they generally cannot gather about their students' mathematical knowledge. Through the use of the research protocol, we were able to collect much more information about students' thinking than could be derived from simply examining students' written responses to mathematical prompts. Finally, the interactive interview research protocol can be used to inform instruction in general, and to improve the mathematical learning of ELLs in particular.

ACKNOWLEDGMENT

This research was supported by the National Science Foundation, under Grant No. ESI-0424983, awarded to the Center for the Mathematics Education of Latino/as (CEMELA). The views expressed here are those of the authors and do not necessarily reflect the views of the funding agency.

REFERENCES

Abedi, J., & Gándara, P. (2006). Performance on English language learners as a subgroup in large-scale assessment: Interaction of research and policy. *Educational Measurement: Issues and Practices, 25*(4), 36–46. doi: 10.1111/j.1745-3992.2006.00077.x

Abedi, J., & Lord, C. (2001). The language factor in mathematics tests. *Applied Measurement in Education, 14*(3), 219–234. doi: 10.1207/S15324818AME1403_2

Behr, M., Lesh, R., Post, T., & Silver E. (1983). Rational number concepts. In R. A. Lesh & M. Landau (Eds.), *Acquisition of mathematics concepts and processes* (pp. 91–125). New York, NY: Academic Press.

Borjian, A. (2008). A new approach in meeting the needs of Latinos in American schools: Students' views on attending a redesigned small high school. *The International Journal of Learning, 15*(2), 277–285. Retrieved from http://ijl.cgpublisher.com

Brown, G. & Quinn, R. J. (2006). Algebra students' difficulty with fractions: An error analysis. Australian Mathematics Teacher, 62(4), 28–40. Retrieved from http://www.aamt.edu.au/Webshop/Entire-catalogue-Australian-Mathematics-Teacher

Chan, W.-H., Leu, Y.-C., & Chen, C.-M. (2007). Exploring group-wise conceptual deficiencies of fractions for fifth and sixth graders in Taiwan. *Journal of Experimental Education, 76*(1), 26–57. doi: 10.3200/JEXE.76.1.26-58

Charalambos, C. Y. & Pitta-Pantazi, D. (2007). Drawing on a theoretical model to study students' understandings of fractions. *Educational Studies in Mathematics, 64*(3), 293–316. doi: 10.1007/s10649-006-9036-2

Clarke, D. M., Roche, A., & Mitchell, A. (2007). Year six fraction understanding: A part of the whole story. In. J. Watson & K. Beswick (Eds.), *Proceedings of the 30th Annual Conference of the Mathematics Education Group of Australasia, Tasmania* (pp. 207–216). Retrieved from http://www.merga.net.au/documents/RP152007.pdf

Cobb, P. (2007). Putting philosophy to work: Coping with multiple theoretical perspectives. In F. K. Lester, Jr. (Ed.), *Second handbook of research on mathematics teaching and learning* (2nd ed., pp. 3–38). Charlotte, NC: Information Age.

Confrey, J. & Smith, E. (1995). Splitting, covariation, and their role in the development of exponential functions. *Journal for Research in Mathematics Education, 26*(1), 66–86. doi: 10.2307/749228

Cramer, K. A., Post, T. R., & delMas, R. C. (2002). Initial fraction learning by fourth- and fifth- grade students: A comparison of the effects of using commercial curricula with the effects of using the Rational Number Project curriculum. *Journal for Research in Mathematics Education, 33*(2), 111–144. doi: 10.2307/749646

Empson, S. B. (2003). Low-performing students and teaching fractions for understanding: An interactional analysis. *Journal for Research in Mathematics Education, 34*(4), 305–343. doi: 10.2307/30034786

Erickson, F. (1986). Qualitative methods in research on teaching. In M. C. Wittrock (Ed.), *Handbook of research on teaching* (3rd ed., pp. 119–161). New York: Macmillan.

Forman, E. A. (2003). A sociocultural approach to mathematics reform: Speaking, inscribing, and doing mathematics within communities of practice. In J. Kilpatrick, W. G. Martin, & D. Schifter (Eds.), *A research companion to principles and standards for school mathematics* (pp. 333–352). Reston, VA: National Council of Teachers of Mathematics.

Gearhart, M. & Saxe, G. B. (2004). When teachers know what students know: Integrating mathematics assessment. *Theory Into Practice 43*(4), 304–313. doi: 10.1207/s15430421tip4304_9

Kieren, T. E. (1980). The rational number construct—Its elements and mechanisms. In T. E. Kieren (Ed.), *Recent research on number learning* (pp. 125–149). Columbus, OH: ERIC/SMEAC.

Kitchen, R. S., Burr, L. G., & Castellón, L. B. (2010). Cultivating a culturally affirming and empowering learning environment for Latino/a youth through formative assessment. In R. S. Kitchen, & E. Silver (Eds.), *Assessing English language learners in mathematics* [A Research Monograph of TODOS: Mathematics for All] (pp. 59–82). Washington, DC: National Education Association.

Kitchen, R. S. & Wilson, L. D. (2004). Lessons learned from students about assessment and instruction. *Teaching Children Mathematics, 10*(8), 394–399. Retrieved from http://www.nctm.org

Kulm, G. (1994). *Mathematics assessment: What works in the classroom.* San Francisco, CA: Jossey-Bass.

Kulm, G., Wilson, L. D., & Kitchen, R. S. (2005). Alignment of content and effectiveness of mathematics assessment items. *Educational Assessment Journal, 10*(4), 333–356. doi: 10.1207/s15326977ea1004_2

Lager, C. A. (2006). Types of mathematics-language reading interactions that unnecessarily hinder algebra learning. *Reading Psychology, 27*(2/3), 165–204. doi: 10.1080/02702710600642475

Lamon, S. J. (2005). *Teaching fractions and ratios for understanding* (2nd ed.). Mahwah, NJ: Erlbaum.

Lamon, S. J. (2007). Rational numbers and proportional reasoning: Toward a theoretical framework for research. In F. K. Lester (Ed.). *Second handbook of research on mathematics teaching and learning* (pp. 629–667). Reston, VA: The National Council of Teachers of Mathematics.

Lerman, S. (2001). A cultural/discursive psychology for mathematics teaching and learning. In W. Atweh, H. Forgasz, & B. Nebres (Eds.), *Sociocultural research on mathematics education: An international perspective* (pp. 3–17). Mahwah, NJ: Erlbaum.

Lockwood, A. T. & Secada, W. G. (1999). *Transforming education for Hispanic youth: Exemplary practices, programs, and schools* [NCBE Resource Collection Series No. 12]. Washington, DC: National Clearinghouse for Bilingual Education.

Maxwell, J. A. (2005). *Qualitative research design: An interactive approach* (2nd ed.). Thousand Oaks, CA: Sage.

Moschkovich, J. N. (1999). Supporting the participation of English language learners in mathematical discussions. *For the Learning of Mathematics, 19*(1), 11–19. Retrieved from http://flm.educ/ualberta.ca/

Moschkovich, J. N. (2002). A situated and sociocultural perspective on bilingual mathematics learners. *Mathematical Thinking and Learning, 4*(2/3), 189–212. doi: 10.1207/S15327833MTL04023_5

Moschkovich, J. N. (2007). Bilingual mathematics learners: How views of language, bilingual learners, and mathematical communication affect instruction. In N. S. Nasir & P. Cobb (Eds.), *Improving access to mathematics* (pp. 89–104). New York: Teachers College Press.

Moss, J. & Case, R. (1999). Developing children's understanding of the rational numbers: A new model and an experimental curriculum. *Journal for Research in Mathematics Education, 30*(2), 122–147. doi: 10.2307/749607

National Clearinghouse for English Language Acquisition and Language Instruction Educational Programs (NCELA). (2007). *The growing numbers of limited English proficient students, 1995/96–2005/06.* Washington, DC: U.S. Department of Education. Retrieved from http://www.ncela.gwu.edu/files/uploads/4/GrowingLEP_0506.pdf

National Council of Teachers of Mathematics. (1995). *Assessment standards for school mathematics.* Reston, VA: Author.

Niemi, D. (1996). Assessing conceptual understanding in mathematics: Representations, problem solutions, justifications, and explanations. *Journal of Educational Research, 89*(6), 351–363. doi: 10.1080/00220671.1996.9941339

O'Day, J. A. & Smith, M. S. (1993). Systemic school reform and educational opportunity. In S. H. Fuhrman (Ed.), *Designing coherent educational policy: Improving the system* (pp. 250–311). San Francisco, CA: Jossey-Bass.

Rolón, C. A. (2003). Educating Latino students. *Educational Leadership, 60*(4), 40–43. Retrieved from http://www.ascd.org/publications/educational-leadership

Saxe, G. B., Taylor, E. V., McIntosh, C., & Gearhart, M. (2005). Representing fractions with standard notation: A developmental analysis. *Journal for Research in Mathematics Education, 36*(2), 137–157. Retrieved from http://www.nctm.org/

Shepard, L. (2000). *The role of classroom assessment in teaching and learning CSE* (CSE Technical Report 517). Los Angeles: University of California, Los Angeles, Center for the Study of Evaluation, Standards, and Student Testing.

Turner, E. E., Celedón-Pattichis, S., & Marshall, M. (2008). Cultural and linguistic resources to promote problem solving and mathematical discourse among Latino/a kindergarten students. *TODOS Research Monograph, 1,* 19–40.

Vygotsky, L. S. (1999). Consciousness as a problem in the psychology of behavior (Original work published in 1925). In N. Veresov (Ed. & Trans.), *Europaische studien zur ideen- und wissenschaftsgeschichte, Bd. 8* [*Undiscovered Vygotsky: Etudes on the pre-history of cultural-historical psychology*]. Pieterlen, Switzerland: Peter Lang. Retrieved from http://www.marxists.org/archive/vygotsky/

Watson, J. M., Campbell, K. J., & Collis, K. F. (1993). Multimodal functioning in understanding fractions. *Journal of Mathematical Behavior, 12*, 45–62. Retrieved from http://www.elsevier.com/

Wilson, L. D., & Kenney, P. A. (2003) Classroom and large-scale assessment. In J. Kilpatrick, W. G. Martin, & D. Schifter (Eds.), *A research companion to principles and standards for school mathematics* (pp. 53–67). Reston, VA: National Council of Teachers of Mathematics.

CHAPTER 13

LANGUAGE ISSUES IN MATHEMATICS AND THE ASSESSMENT OF ENGLISH LANGUAGE LEARNERS

Guillermo Solano-Flores, Ph.D.
University of Colorado at Boulder

INTRODUCTION

In the 21st century, as at no other time in history, educators need to be more knowledgeable of the basic principles underlying assessment and the practice and policy of testing. In the United States, students are being tested more frequently now than ever before. Important decisions affecting their lives and their schools are made based on test scores. Legislation mandates frequent testing of students for purposes of accountability, and requirements of adequate yearly progress are being used with the intent to assess the success of schools (see Abedi, 2004; Durán, 2010; Linn, Baker, & Betebenner, 2002).

Unfortunately, this increased role of testing in education has no corresponding more critical attitude towards our testing practices and the premises underlying them. We have become heavy consumers of tests without

Latinos/as and Mathematics Education, pages 283–314
Copyright © 2011 by Information Age Publishing
All rights of reproduction in any form reserved.

asking what we should be doing differently with them now than has been done in the past. Indeed, policy and decision makers and the general public appear to view tests as more precise instruments than they really are.

In times of accountability and standards-based education, the danger of overuse and misuse of tests is clear (Shepard, 1992; Shepard, Hannaway, & Baker, 2009). The consequences of not thinking critically about these issues are especially relevant to the testing of English language learners (ELLs)—students who are developing English as a second language while they are still developing their first language in a society in which English is the predominant language. Although it has long been recognized that cultural differences and limited proficiency in the language in which tests are administered affect the performance of students in tests, testing practices for these students have not changed significantly. There are strong reasons to believe that some current testing practices intended to address linguistic diversity are flawed because they lack appropriate theoretical foundation, underestimate the complexity of language, or are poorly implemented (Solano-Flores, 2008, 2009).

This chapter discusses language issues that are relevant to valid and fair mathematics assessment for ELLs in the context of large-scale assessment. The achievement gap between this group of students and non-ELL students is a source of serious concern. In the National Assessment of Educational Progress (NAEP) mathematics assessment of 2009, only 12% and 5% of ELLs in grades 4 and 8, respectively, performed at or above the level of proficient. In contrast, 42% and 35% of non-ELL students in grades 4 and 8, respectively, performed at or above the proficient level (National Center for Education Statistics, 2010).

To be regarded as valid, measures of mathematics academic achievement should not be due to attributes other than the knowledge and skills measured by tests (Messick, 1989). Because language is the means through which tests are administered, proficiency in the language of testing can be an important source of test invalidity and the reason for unfair score differences between those who are and those who are not proficient in the language of testing (see American Educational Research Association, American Psychological Association, and National Council on Measurement in Education, 1999).

Language issues are discussed along with main principles from the field of psychometrics—which, for the purposes of this chapter, can be defined as the discipline concerned with the measurement of behavior, knowledge, and skills in humans and social systems. The chapter shows how proper consideration of the complex relationship of language and mathematics at all stages of the assessment process is critical to attaining sound assessment practices for ELLs. The chapter also points at the limitations of current testing practice and discusses how this practice can be improved.

Available to readers are a number of publications intended to introduce educators in the field of assessment (e.g., Green, 1981; Gronlund & Waugh, 2009; Nitko & Brookhart, 2007; Popham, 2007; Reynolds, Livingston, & Wilson, 2006), and in the field of ELL assessment (e.g., Gottlieb, 2006; O'Malley & Valdez-Pierce, 1996). Also available are important publications for researchers and policy makers that discuss technical issues in the assessment of diverse populations and students with limited proficiency in English (e.g., Abedi, 2006; Camilli & Shepard, 1994; Wolf, Herman, Bachman, Bailey, & Griffin, 2008; Zieky, 2006). Unlike that body of literature, this chapter addresses language issues in ELL mathematics assessment according to a conceptual framework created with the specific purpose of examining the relationship between language and mathematics in educational research (Solano-Flores, 2010).

This chapter is guided by the notion that effective approaches to ELL testing require more serious consideration of the specific linguistic features and challenges that are inherent to disciplinary knowledge. Each discipline has its own register—its own set of meanings and words and structures expressing those meanings (Halliday, 1978)—and each discipline poses a unique set of linguistic challenges to any student learning that discipline (Halliday, 1993; Schlepegrell, 2010; Wellington & Osborne, 2001). This set of challenges is more complex for ELL students, who are developing a second language at the same time that they are learning the language of the discipline (Trumbull & Koelsch, 2011; Trumbull & Solano-Flores, 2011).

The chapter is divided in four sections. The first section, "The Complex Relationship of Language and Mathematics," discusses how history, linguistic variation, and cultural diversity shape the many ways in which mathematical ideas are represented and understood. As a result of this complex relationship, individuals with different cultural and linguistic backgrounds face different sets of challenges in learning mathematics and demonstrating mathematical knowledge in tests, whether they are tested in their first language (L1) or in their second language (L2). This section examines how approaches intended to address these challenges are guided by different views (conceptions) of language—as a system, process, structure, and factor (Solano-Flores, 2010).

The second section, "Measurement Error in Mathematics Assessment and the Need for a View of Language as a System," discusses measurement error and sampling as critical notions in examining the testing of ELLs. Given the complexity of language, the multiple linguistic features of mathematics test items, and the linguistic heterogeneity of ELL populations, effective approaches to ELL testing should be based on properly addressing the relationship between language variation and score variation. The chapter discusses evidence of research that addresses this relationship with a probabilistic approach. In this probabilistic approach, views of language as a factor and as a system are used in combination, and language is treated as a source of measurement error.

The third section, "Mathematics Assessment Development and the Need for a View of Language as a Process," discusses the process of assessment development in large-scale assessment and examines the limitations of current practice in the testing of ELLs that result from not properly incorporating a view of language as a process. Normative documents such as standards, assessment frameworks, and item specifications play a critical role in the ways in which content is sampled to develop tests. Not taking into consideration the interaction of language, culture, and cognition, and the absence of a deep treatment of the development of mathematical academic language in those normative documents hampers the ability to properly identify and address critical language issues. The chapter also discusses the consequences of not including ELLs in the pilot stages of the process of assessment development—when the wording of test items is refined to ensure that students understand them as test developers intend. It also discusses the limitations of testing accommodations for ELLs, many of which lack a solid theoretical foundation.

The fourth section, "Conclusions," provides a summary of the chapter and ends with a simple deduction: Given the complex relationship between language and mathematics, valid, fair mathematics assessment for ELLs will not take place without a deep transformation of assessment practices.

For the purposes of this chapter, the terms *assessment* and *test* are used interchangeably when they refer to an instrument; *assessment* and *testing* are used interchangeably when they refer to an activity or system; and *task* and *item* are used as synonyms.

THE COMPLEX RELATIONSHIP OF LANGUAGE AND MATHEMATICS

An Example: Fractions and Ordinal Numbers

In his book, *A History of* π, Beckmann (1971) speculated about the early stages of development of the notions of fraction and infinity and discussed the fact that, in many languages, fractions and ordinal numbers tend to be named with the same words—as in *fifth*, which refers to both the result of dividing a whole in five parts and the order of an event taking place after four events of the same kind have taken place. Beckmann also discussed the fact that this commonality usually does not exist for the fractional and ordinal expressions of 2 or 3. In English, these expressions are different for 2 (*half* and *second*), but the same for 3 or more (*third, fourth, fifth*, etc.). In Spanish, these expressions are different for 2 (*medio* and *segundo*) and also different for 3 (*tercio* and *tercero*), but the same for 4 or more (*cuarto, quinto, sexto,* etc.).

These two facts appear to reflect the realization that the fraction of a whole is closely related to the number of times an action, such as cutting or distributing that whole in equal parts, needs to be repeated. They also reflect the realization, after three or four cuts, that the number of cuts may have no limit. The conventions for naming both fractions and ordinal numbers (e.g., hundred*th*, in English; cent*ésimo,* in Spanish) meet the need to describe that an *n*th is the result of dividing a whole *n* number of times (by 1, 2, 3, etc.) or that an *n*th is the size of a piece after the *n*th cut.[1]

This story illustrates two facts that should not escape consideration in discussing issues of language in mathematics education and assessment. One is that language is a cultural phenomenon that encodes experience accumulated through history (Nettle & Romaine, 2002). Due to their likely common origin, we have inherited the use of the same word to refer to such different (though related) concepts as fraction and ordinal number. Thus, in learning mathematics, we have had to negotiate meaning across contexts and cope with the fact that a word such as *fifth* does not always have the same meaning. Moreover, we have had to learn multiple forms of representation (e.g., 5th, 1/5, 0.20) that serve different purposes in mathematical reasoning.

The second fact is that different languages do not encode experience following the same rules (Greenfield, 1997), as shown by the fact that *third* as a fraction and *third* as sequential order are described by the same word in English, but not in Spanish. Due to these differences, those who learn mathematics in a second language or in two languages have to negotiate meaning not only across contexts, but also across languages.

Some potential challenges that the use of notation conventions for representing basic mathematical ideas may pose to learners when mathematics is learned in a second language are presented in Table 13.1. Indicated in the table are some forms of representation of (*one*) *fifth* as a fraction and

TABLE 13.1 Conventions Used in English (United States) and in Spanish (Latin American countries) to represent (*one*) *fifth* as a Fraction and as an Ordinal Number

Language	Fraction			Ordinal number	
	Quotient	Decimal	Graphic		
	1/5	0.20	0,20	▱▱▱▱▱	5th	5°
English	yes [a]	yes [b]	no [c]	yes [d]	yes [e]	no [f]
Spanish	yes [g]	yes [h]	yes [i]	no [j]	no [k]	yes [l]

Note: A yes or a no in the corresponding cell indicates respectively that a given form of representation is common or uncommon in each language. Letters in parenthesis are used to refer to specific cells.

as an ordinal number in English and in Spanish. As a fraction, *one fifth* can be represented as a quotient (1/5), in decimal form (0.20 and 0,20), or graphically (as a bar with light and shaded segments). As an ordinal number, (*one*) *fifth* can be represented as 5th and 5°.

Comparing specific cells in the table allows us to appreciate whether and how specific notation conventions may be challenging for ELL students.

1. In the simplest case, the representation of a fraction as a quotient (cells a and g) poses no challenge because it is the same across languages.

2. The representation of a fraction in decimals with a point or a comma varies across Spanish-speaking cultures (cells h and i). As a consequence, 0.20 is familiar to some students (see cells b and h), not for others (see cells b and i).

3. The graphic representation of a fraction as a bar with shaded segments, which is popular in mathematics curricula and frequently used in assessment systems in the United States (e.g., NAEP) or in international test comparisons (e.g., Trends in Mathematics and Science Study—TIMMS), is not common in some Spanish-speaking cultures (cells d and j). As clear and concrete as this form of representation may look, it may take some time and practice for students before they become familiar with it and use it properly.

4. The representation of *fifth* as an ordinal number (5th) is different in the United State and in Latin American countries. Students from Spanish-speaking countries learning mathematics in English in the United States need to learn a new convention for representing ordinal numbers (cells e and k), which is different from the superscript of the letter *o* (°) frequently used in Latin American countries. Because in Spanish, there are gender forms of adjectives, this superscript needs to be the letter *a* (5ª) if the noun modified by the ordinal is feminine.

5. The use of the superscript *o* in Spanish (5°) brings another complication—it can be mistaken as the symbol of degrees. Whereas this symbol is different from the superscript *o*, the difference between 5° and 5° may be extremely difficult to appreciate for many (even highly educated individuals living in Latin American countries), especially when the medium is written, not printed text.[2] In the past, the superscripts for denoting ordinals in *o* and *a* were accompanied by a dashed line below them (e.g., 5° and 5ª), but those conventions tend to disappear in modern printed materials.

There is another important difference in the ways in which fractions and ordinal numbers are named in English and in Spanish. Whereas in

English, fraction numbers are, in general, denoted by simply modifying the ending of the name for the ordinal number (*twenty* becomes *twentieth; thirty* becomes *thirtieth; forty* becomes *fortieth*), in Spanish ordinal numbers are denoted in a more complex way by both expressing the ordinal number according to its form in Latin and modifying the ending of the word. The ordinal forms of *veinte* (*twenty*), *treinta* (*thirty*), and *cuarenta* (*forty*) are, respectively, *vigésimo, trigésimo,* and *cuadragésimo;* the ordinal form of *cuarenta y cinco* (*forty-five*) is *cuadragésimo quinto.*

Due to this difference between languages, learning the rules for naming fractions and ordinal numbers appears to be more challenging when learning mathematical academic language in Spanish than in English. These rules are influenced by sociolinguistic factors that have to do with social status and stratification. A popular, simple convention for naming ordinal numbers exists in informal Spanish. It consists of simply adding the ending, *avo* (or *ava*) to the cardinal form.[3] For example, the ordinal form of *cuarenta y cinco* is *cuarenta y cincoavo,* instead of *cuadragésimo quinto,* which is more complicated. However, in spite of its efficiency, this system is not always regarded as correct in mathematics curricula or is not used in formal writing contexts in many Spanish-speaking cultures.[4]

This intricate set of influences that shape how effectively mathematical ideas are expressed in ELL students' L1 and L2 is an important part of the challenges they face when they acquire and demonstrate mathematical knowledge.[5] In the context of classroom assessment, unless educators are well aware of both the differences in notation conventions and the specific cultural backgrounds of their students, they are more likely to interpret the use of comma in *0,20* as an indicator of low achievement, not cultural differences.

In the context of large-scale testing, the situation is even more detrimental to ELLs, mainly because raters have no information on the students' histories or learning contexts that could help them interpret the responses they score. In some cases, testing ELLs in their native language is an option, but it is not necessarily an effective solution when the students tested have different histories of schooling in L1 and in L2. Even if testing ELLs in their native language is possible, there are multiple dilemmas that need to be resolved. For example, in a test administered in Spanish, which of the two systems for naming ordinal numbers described in "An Example: Fractions and Ordinal Numbers" should be used—formal (academic) or informal?

Language Views

In addition to illustrating the complex relationship of language and mathematics, the topics of fractions and ordinal numbers come in handy to explain the notion of language views. Language views can be defined as ways of thinking of language as a phenomenon. These views are not necessarily explicit; they may be implicit in the sets of methods and practices researchers, educators, and assessment systems regard as sound, acceptable, and sufficient to properly address language (Solano-Flores, 2010).

Definitions and illustrations of four basic types of language views—as a system, process, structure, and factor—are presented in Table 13.2. These categories are not clear cut; rather, they describe patterns in which research and practice address the relationship of language and mathematics. None of these views is better than the others because language is, at the same time, a system, a process, a structure, and a factor. Thus, I contend that more effective approaches to addressing the relationship of language and mathematics in the assessment for ELLs can be developed by using multiple views of language in combination.

As indicated in Table 13.2, views of language as a system and as a process are common in research and practice in mathematics instruction, and views of language as a structure and as a factor are common in research and practice in mathematics assessment. These views are reflected, respectively, in the approaches used to characterize populations (e.g., by classifying ELLs into a small number of categories of English proficiency) and to examine the linguistic complexity of text in tests (e.g., by examining the structural complexity of sentences in test items and examining its value as a predictor of student performance; Shaftel, Belton-Kocher, Glasnapp, & Poggio, 2006). Although these approaches are necessary in assessment, they are more effective if they are used in combination with views of language as a system and as a process. For example, a view of language as a system makes us appreciate the tremendous linguistic variation that exists within broad linguistic groups of ELLs (e.g., native speakers of Spanish) and the tremendous variation in ELL language proficiency across the four language modes (listening, speaking, reading, and writing) in both L1 and L2. Also, a view of language as a process makes us see that language is not only in tests but also in the individuals who take tests.

MEASUREMENT ERROR IN MATHEMATICS ASSESSMENT AND THE NEED FOR A VIEW OF LANGUAGE AS A SYSTEM

Sampling and Measurement Error

Critical to understanding assessment is the notion of *sampling*, the action of taking a portion of a whole with the intent to make inferences about that whole based on characteristics observed in the sample. We use samples in any situation in which we need to draw conclusions about something that is not possible to examine in its entirety. An example of sampling is

TABLE 13.2 Views of Language in Research on Language and Mathematics

Concept	As a system	As a process	As a structure	As a factor
Treatment of language	As a resource in learning	As a means for knowledge construction	As a source of complexity in mathematics problems	As an extraneous variable
Examples of issues addressed	Dynamic nature of languages and dialects	Process of acquiring academic language	Morpho-syntactic properties of text	Existence of different broad linguistic groups
Use of the terms, *language* and *linguistic*	*Language*, as in *English language or language dialect (Standard English or African American Vernacular English)*	*Language*, as in *the language development or the construction of mathematical academic language*	*Linguistic*, as in *the linguistic features of items*	*Linguistic*, as in *broad linguistic group (native Spanish speakers)*
Examples of investigations	Language variation and its effect in language use in multilingual mathematics classrooms	The influence of language on cognition and the construction of meaning	The influence of text complexity and semantic structure on student performance in mathematics problems	Test score variation within linguistic groups
Issues relevant to the teaching and assessment of fractions and ordinal numbers	• English and Spanish dialect diversity among ELL Spanish speaking population • Diversity of registers in the naming of ordinal numbers in Spanish	• Negotiating meaning across contexts and languages when ELLs learn fractions • Challenges faced by ELLs in the learning of notation conventions for ordinal numbers	• Types of notation conventions for fraction numbers • Complexity of rules for naming ordinal numbers	• Test score differences on fraction numbers between ELLs and non-ELLs • Dependability of test scores on fraction numbers when ELLs are tested in English and in Spanish

Note: Adapted from Solano-Flores, G. (2010). Function and form in research on language and mathematics education. In J. N. Moschkovich (Ed.), *Language and mathematics in education: Multiple perspectives and directions for research* (pp. 113–149). Charlotte, NC: Information Age.

tasting the soup when it is boiling with the purpose of deciding whether it has reached the desired flavor—tasting all the soup would be impractical and pointless. Another example is asking students a few questions on the content being taught during a lesson to gauge their understanding—asking them too many questions during the lesson would be too time-consuming.

The term *population* is used to refer to the universe of cases from which a sample is drawn. Although it is used frequently to refer to the students being tested, population may refer to other things. For example, we can talk about a population of raters from which some are selected to score the responses of students to constructed response tasks. Also, we can talk about a population of items from which a sample is drawn to be included in a test.

To be able to lead to accurate conclusions about the characteristics of a population, a sample must be representative of that population; the makeup of the sample should reflect the makeup of the population about which generalizations are to be made. When a sample is not representative of the population it is drawn from, it is said to be a biased sample. Bias is a form of systematic error that leads to erroneous conclusions about the population studied (see Camilli, 2006, for a discussion of the relation between test fairness and bias).

A sample may be biased due to imprecise criteria for selecting the cases to be included in it or to poor implementation of those criteria. For example, a student can be included in a sample of Latino ELL students based on the fact that he or she has a Spanish last name. Whereas being Latino and having a Spanish last name are associated with limited English proficiency, one thing does not necessarily imply the other. Even when this blatant form of error is not made, ELL populations are often misspecified due to inaccurate and insufficient measures of English proficiency (Solano-Flores, 2009).

Sampling is not only about students. Sampling issues are also relevant to determining the different types of tasks that should be included in the same test. A wide variety of tasks can be used in assessment. Each is sensitive to different types of knowledge and skills. For example, whereas multiple-choice items tend to be suitable for assessing factual knowledge, essay and hands-on tasks may be more appropriate, respectively, for assessing critical thinking and problem-solving skills (e.g., Shavelson, Baxter, & Gao, 1993; Shavelson, Ruiz-Primo, & Wiley, 1999). There is evidence that not all types of tasks are exchangeable. If students are given different types of tasks that assess knowledge on the same content area, their performance will be unstable across tasks. A student who performs well on a multiple-choice test may not perform well on an open-ended test, or vice versa, even if the two tests are intended to assess knowledge on the same content area. Thus, ideally, to make appropriate generalizations about individual students' knowledge of a domain, assessment systems should use different types of tasks in combination (see Baker, Linn, Herman, & Koretz, 2002).

A part of the reason for this limited exchangeability is that different types of tasks tend to pose different sets of linguistic and reading demands on the test taker (Bernardo, 2002; Thurber, Shinn, & Smolkowski, 2002). For example, traditional multiple-choice items tend to consist of one or two sentences with syntactical structures that are uncommon in everyday life (nonschool) language and tend to ask questions without providing much context to the student (see Solano-Flores, 2006). In contrast, constructed-response word problems provide more context in dense text and the continuity of ideas from one sentence is scant (Noonan, 1990).[6] This trade-off between different types of tasks (Lee, 1999) is another reason to support the notion that better generalizations about ELL students' academic achievement can be made based on test scores if those students are assessed with different types of tasks in combination.

Measurement Error in the Testing of ELLs

Measurement error can be defined as the extent to which test scores are due to factors other than the construct a test is intended to measure. Ideally, we would like to be certain that a substantial amount of the score variation observed among students on a given test is due to the construct measured (i.e., the knowledge and skills being measured), not other sources such as the linguistic features of the items included in a test, or inconsistency between raters in their scoring (see Kane, 2006; Messick, 1989, 1995). When the amount of measurement error is considerable, test scores lead to improper generalizations about the students' knowledge on the construct being measured.

Generalizability (G) theory (Brennan, 1992; Cronbach, Gleser, Nanda, & Rajaratnam, 1972; Shavelson & Webb, 1991, 2009) is a theory of measurement error. According to the theory, there are two types of score variation: student—the object of study—and facets (factors)—sources of systematic measurement introduced by observations such as item, rater, and occasion. The theory allows identification of the magnitude of score variation due to student, the facets, and the interaction of student and the facets.

The series of investigations that my colleagues and I (Solano-Flores & Li, 2006, 2008, 2009a, 2009b; Prosser & Solano-Flores, submitted) have conducted using G theory in assessment of mathematics achievement for ELLs constitutes an example of research that combines the view of language as both a factor and a system. In these studies, ELLs are given the same set of items in English and in Spanish. The intent is not to assess them in bilingual formats, but to examine how their scores vary across languages.[7,8]

Shown in Table 13.3 are the results from a G study from one of our investigations (Solano-Flores & Li, 2009b). The first column lists the sources of score variation: student (the object of study), three facets (item, rater, and language), and the interactions of different combinations of the four sources of score variation. The *e* in the last term (sirl,*e*) indicates random error due to sources that cannot be accounted for and that is confounded with error due to the interaction of student, item, rater, and language. Percentages of score variation due to each source are indicated in the table.

As indicated in Table 13.3, the most important source of measurement error was the interaction of student, item, and language (45% of the total score variation). This means that the performance of ELL students was inconsistent across languages and across items. In addition to knowledge of the content measured by the items, each student tends to perform well or poorly in English or in Spanish, depending on the item. In other words, each ELL student has a unique set of strengths and weaknesses in English and a unique set of strengths and weaknesses in Spanish. At the same time, each item poses a unique set of linguistic demands in English and a unique set of linguistic demands in Spanish. The results are consistent with an im-

TABLE 13.3 Estimated Variance Components and Percentage of Score Variation for Items Administered in English and in Spanish: Random $s \times i \times r \times l$ Model

Source of score variation	Sample size	Estimated variance component	Rounded % of score variation
student (s)	30	0.0236	17
i (item)	10	0.0113	8
r (rater)	4	0	0
l (language)	2	0	0
si		0.0334	24
sr		0	0
sl		0	0
ir		0	0
il		0.0005	0
rl		0.0000	0
sir		0.0010	1
sil		0.0646	45
srl		0	0
irl		0.0001	0
sirl, e		0.0075	5
Total variance		0.1420	

Note: Adapted from "Language variation and score variation in the testing of English language learners, native Spanish speakers," by G. Solano-Flores & M. Li, (2009), *Educational Assessment, 14*(3), 180–194. Copyright 2009 by Taylor & Francis.

portant notion in the field of sociolinguistics—that bilingual individuals vary considerably in their proficiency in each of their two languages across contexts (Fishman, 1965).

From the estimated variance components obtained in G studies, it is possible to model the minimum numbers of observations (numbers of items and the number of raters, in this case) needed to obtain dependable scores if students are tested in English or in Spanish. The results favor testing in English for some schools and testing in Spanish for other schools. When we have tested students in their first language but across dialects (e.g., standard Spanish and the local Spanish dialect used in their communities), we have found similar patterns of score variation. For some schools, more dependable test scores can be obtained by testing ELLs in the local dialect rather than in the standard dialect of Spanish; for other schools, the results are similar across dialects.

These results are consistent with the notion that there is a tremendous linguistic variation among ELL populations and that every ELL has a unique pattern of language dominance (Bachman, 1990, Bialystok, 2001; Grosjean, 1985; MacSwan, 2000). The implication of these findings is that language variation needs to be taken into account if effective testing models for ELLs are to be developed. When it is appropriate to test ELLs in L1 or in L2 should be determined based on G studies like the one described performed at the local (e.g., school, school district) level (Solano-Flores & Trumbull, 2008).

An approach based on examining language as a source of measurement error can be described as probabilistic because it is sensitive to language variation (a view of language as a system) and recognizes that many events related to language cannot be known with precision or are beyond control (Solano-Flores, 2008). For example, even ELL students from the same broad linguistic group (e.g., native Spanish speakers) have multiple cultural origins, multiple patterns of language proficiency in L1 and in L2, and multiple schooling histories in both L1 and L2. As a result of this heterogeneity, the actions intended to minimize limited proficiency in English as a source of measurement error cannot be expected to work for all ELLs. This approach contrasts with current approaches in ELL testing, which assume homogeneity of broad linguistic groups and use short categories of English proficiency to characterize ELL students.

As represented in the discussion of fractions and ordinal numbers, even notation conventions in mathematics vary tremendously across cultures within the same broad linguistic group. An item with certain linguistic features (e.g., certain forms of notation) may be effective in minimizing measurement error due to language proficiency for some, but not all ELL students. This variation can be addressed by increasing the size of the sample of items included in tests. Notice that this approach is not based on using mainstream, native English-speaking students as a reference group—which is typical in approaches that examine test bias (e.g., Allalouf, Hambleton, & Sireci, 1999; Camilli & Shepard, 1994; Ercikan, 2002). Most of the approaches used in research and practice in the testing of ELLs are based on comparing the performance of these students with the performance of mainstream students. In contrast, this approach is based on estimating measurement error, not score differences across populations. It is consistent with the notion that validity should be assessed separately for students with different language backgrounds (see Baker et al., 2002).

MATHEMATICS ASSESSMENT DEVELOPMENT AND THE NEED FOR A VIEW OF LANGUAGE AS A PROCESS

The Process of Assessment Development

From the perspective of sampling, tests can be examined as samples of a knowledge domain. An illustration of these tests, examined as samples of a knowledge domain, is presented in Figure 13.1. A *knowledge domain* can be thought of as the universe of all possible pieces of information, problems, and situations (and their combinations) of a content area (Bormuth, 1970)

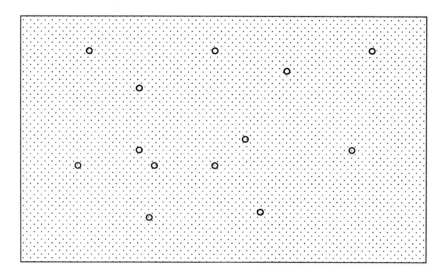

Figure 13.1 A representation of a test based on the notion of sample. Dots represent the pieces of information and the problems and situations that comprise the knowledge domain. Circles represent specific combinations of pieces of information, problems, and situations sampled from that knowledge domain that are to be included in a test.

such as fourth-grade mathematics. These pieces of information, problems, and situations are indicated as dots in Figure 13.1.

A knowledge domain like this one involving ELLs is vast, if not infinite. For example, think about all the forms in which subtraction problems can be expressed or all the possible situations that may involve subtraction problems. Because of this vastness, we cannot expect to be able to examine the performance of students by exposing them to all these pieces of information, problems, and situations. Rather, we have to content ourselves with using a limited set of tasks intended to represent them. That is why *generating (writing) items* for a test sometimes is referred to as *drawing a sample of items from a knowledge domain.*

How well a set of tasks represents a given knowledge domain determines, to a large extent, the quality of a test, hence the importance of ensuring that the tasks included in a test have been selected through a logical, systematic process. For example, in the case of subtraction, should the problems included in the test pose real-world situations with rich contextual information? Should the test be restricted to subtraction problems involving integers, or should it also include fractional numbers? Should *subtraction* be understood as including cases in which the first term is smaller than the second term? Should negative numbers be included? Should problems that involve other mathematical operations be included?

Knowledge domain specification is the term used to refer to the actions taken and the rules used to determine what counts as belonging to a given knowledge domain and to identify categories of pieces of information, problems, and situations of that domain (see Hively, Patterson, & Page, 1968). In current testing practice, a knowledge domain is specified based on a conceptual framework of knowledge. This conceptual framework identifies the cognitive processes a test is intended to target (Pellegrino, Chudowsky, & Glaser, 2001). To develop a test on subtraction, we need to formalize our beliefs about the processes that take place when students solve different kinds of subtraction problems. For example, subtraction may involve, among many other processes, constructing certain problem-solving strategies to new problems, retrieving from memory certain information, and applying certain computation routines.

A conceptual framework can be developed based on four types of knowledge, like those proposed by Li, Ruiz-Primo, and Shavelson (2006): *Declarative knowledge* (*knowing that*), which includes factual knowledge (e.g., the fact that $4 - 2 = 2$); *procedural knowledge* (*knowing how*), which includes routines and sequences of decisions and activities (e.g., a subtraction algorithm); *schematic knowledge* (*knowing why*), which includes understanding and explaining facts and processes (e.g., viewing a subtraction as reverse addition); and *strategic knowledge* (e.g., *knowing when, where, and how to apply knowledge*), which includes developing domain-specific problem-solving

TABLE 13.4 Representation of a Knowledge Domain Based on the Intersection of Types of Knowledge and Content Area

	Content Area				
Type of knowledge	Number properties and operations	Measurement	Geometry	Data analysis and probability	Algebra
Declarative					
Procedural					
Schematic					
Strategic					

strategies or efficiently integrating the other types of knowledge (e.g., correctly framing a given problem as a subtraction problem).

Presented in Table 13.4 is an example of representation of a knowledge domain. This arrangement of rows and columns shows the intersection of different kinds of knowledge and the different kinds of content areas within the knowledge domain, usually defined by content standards and other normative documents. In this example, five content areas times four types of knowledge gives a total of 20 cells.

Multiple factors determine how many and what types of tasks are to be generated for each cell. One is that certain tasks are more suitable than others for assessing certain types of knowledge. Another is that some tasks are more costly than others to develop, administer, and score, which poses a limit, for example, to the number of constructed-response tasks that can be included in a test. Theory, logical reasoning, and practical limitations shape the content and configuration of a test. A great deal of the work done by psychometricians consists of figuring out an optimal combination of tasks that strikes a balance between score quality and cost- and time-effectiveness.

In large-scale assessment, the job of specifying a given knowledge domain is supported and regulated by two kinds of documents: a *content standards* document (e.g., National Council of Teachers of Mathematics, 2000)—which establishes what students should know and be able to do at each grade and for the corresponding content area—and an *assessment framework*—a document that provides a description of the knowledge domain (a vision of the test that is to assess that knowledge domain) and the areas of knowledge that the test is to emphasize (see National Assessment Governing Board, 2009a).

In the context of large-scale assessment, it is important to distinguish between individual-score tests and group-score tests. The latter are designed to assess the achievement of groups of people, for example at the national or international level (Mazzeo, Lazer, & Zieky, 2006). In group-score assessments, the number of tasks needed to properly sample large knowledge domains is, by far, larger than the number of tasks included in the test booklet each student is given. It is not uncommon that several hundred items are developed for an assessment for a given content area in a given year, whereas the booklets given to students cannot have more than about 40 items. Because it would not be practical or recommendable to give more items to students, the assessment has to be administered to students in different *blocks* of items. In this arrangement, there may be, say, 16 different blocks, each with a different combination of items, although some items are common across blocks. In this arrangement, the content sampled is much larger than the content covered by each individual block. Thus, this kind of test allows for generalizing about the population's (not individual students') knowledge of the domain.

The development of tasks for large-scale assessment programs like NAEP, PISA, TIMSS, and state assessments is supported by *item specifications*, documents that lay out "the basic design of the assessment by describing the mathematics content that should be tested and the types of assessment questions that should be included. It also describes how the various design factors should be balanced across the assessment" (National Assessment Governing Board, 2009b, p. 1). Among these item characteristics are style, length (e.g., number of sentences), use of contextual information, and the use of charts and other sources of information.[9]

Item specifications documents ensure standardization in the process of task development by making it possible that all items generated by different item writers for a given combination of type of knowledge and content area have similar characteristics and comparable complexities. This standardization is important because many item writers can be involved in the process of assessment development; the characteristics of the items should not be determined by idiosyncratic factors such as the item writers' personal styles. Also, item specifications documents allow the development of considerable numbers of items in a relatively short time. Efficiency in test development is not a trivial matter if we consider that behind the 300 items or so needed for a given content area in a given year in the case of group-score assessments, there are many other items that need to be discarded somewhere along the process of test development because they have poor psychometric qualities.

In the current context of standards reform, the importance of assessment frameworks and item specifications documents cannot be overstated. They are primary sources for contractors (test developers) to determine the numbers and kinds of items to develop for each content area and each type of knowledge, and the complexity and structural properties of the items. Because an important criterion for judging content validity in large-scale assessments is the degree of their alignment with standards (see Hamilton & Koretz, 2002; Sloane & Kelly, 2003), poor assessment frameworks and item specifications documents may result in low-quality tests (e.g., tests that do not represent properly the corresponding knowledge domain), which nonetheless are deemed valid.

Assessment Development and the Testing of ELLs

Several limitations of current assessment development practices can be identified concerning their effectiveness in addressing language issues and the needs of ELLs. Those limitations can be attributed to their failure to properly address the nature of language as a process. Four aspects deserve discussion: the interaction of language, culture, and cognition; the ways in which language is addressed in normative documents; the inclusion of ELLs in the process of assessment development; and the use of testing accommodations in the assessment of ELLs.

Interaction of Language, Culture, and Cognition

Most of the research on cognition that supports educational practice has been done with mainstream populations. The limits to the generalizations of findings from that research to individuals from different languages and cultures are uncertain (Pellegrino et al., 2001). According to current knowledge from the fields of cultural anthropology and language development, culture and language play an important role in the ways in which individuals make sense of experience and construct knowledge (e.g., Bialystok, 2002; Vygotsky, 1978; Wertsch, 1985).

Not properly recognizing that culture and language may influence the way in which students interpret items and respond to them may bias the process of assessment development in favor of mainstream students. In fact, we have evidence that indicates that fourth-grade students draw considerably on their personal experiences outside the classroom to make sense of mathematics items and that students from different cultural groups tend to relate the content of the items to different sets of contexts of their personal lives (Solano-Flores & Li, 2009a; Solano-Flores & Trumbull, 2008). It is possible that the contextual information included in many mathematics test items may over-represent the situations and contexts with which mainstream students are familiar—situations and contexts that may not be equally meaningful to students from different linguistic and cultural backgrounds.

Normative Documents

One way or another, standards documents discuss the role of language in the learning of disciplinary knowledge and recognize the importance of providing appropriate support to ELLs. However, these documents do not provide information about the linguistic demands involved in learning content, which could be used by test developers to better address language issues in mathematics. To a large extent, these linguistic demands concern the development of academic language—the set of terms, expressions, and discursive and argumentation forms used in a discipline, and which are frequently used in textbooks and tests. Consider the question, *How much time does it take for Joan's mom to drive from her house to the market if she drives at a steady speed of 35 MPH and the market is 6 miles away?*

The sentence is complex, not only because it is long, but also because it combines the interrogative and conditional modes. Some would argue that this sentence is unnecessarily complex and that it could be reworded as, for example, *Joan's mom drives from home to the market at 35 PMH. The market is 6 miles away. How much time does it take Joan's mom to get to the market?*

At the same time, others would argue that the first version of the item reflects more accurately the ways in which problems are phrased in mathematics. However, regardless of the debate, it is difficult to know from content standards documents at what grades it is reasonable to expect students to understand complex discursive forms like this one. In the same venue, rarely do item specifications documents provide detailed information on the discursive forms that should be used or avoided in mathematics items. This limitation is especially serious in mathematics assessment, as problem solving is greatly influenced by language skills (Barwell, 2009; Durán, 1985).

Future versions of mathematics standards, assessment frameworks, and item specifications documents should be more deeply informed by research that examines the process of development of mathematical academic language among ELLs and by conceptual frameworks of academic language that address the complex, multidimensional nature of academic language (e.g., Butler, Lord, Stevens, Borrego, & Bailey, 2004; Scarcella, 2003).

Inclusion of ELLs in the Process of Assessment Development

Typically, a task needs to go through a series of revisions and needs to be piloted with students before it is ready for inclusion in an assessment (Solano-Flores & Shavelson, 1997). This iterative process, represented in Figure 13.2, comprises four stages: (1) preparing a draft of the task, and, in the case of constructed-response tasks, its accompanying response format, scoring system, and administration procedure; (2) having colleagues, teachers, and content specialists review the task to ensure content accuracy and appropriateness to the corresponding age or grade; (3) trying out the task with a group of pilot students to see if they can understand its wording and what they are being asked to do; and (4) making appropriate modifications based on the information collected. In each iteration, appropriate modifications are made to ensure that students interpret the items as in-

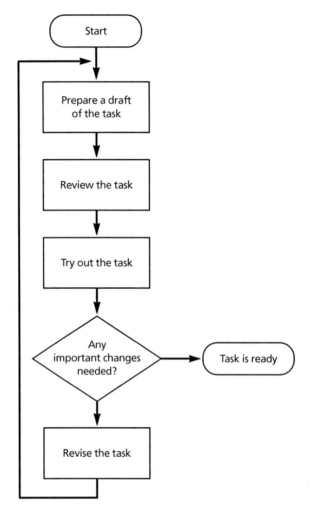

Figure 13.2 Iterative process of test development. Adapted from Source: Solano-Flores, Trumbull, & Nelson-Barber (2002).

tended. This sequence of steps may need to be repeated several times until no or few further substantial improvements are needed.

To identify what modifications need to be made on the assessments, test developers examine the pilot students' responses to determine whether they understand the items as they are intended and to make sure that the items have an adequate level of difficulty. As part of the process of development, test developers may also conduct cognitive interviews—which include verbal protocols in which students verbalize their thinking while they respond to items or after they respond to them and a series of questions students are asked about the ways in which they interpret the items and respond to them (see Baxter, Elder, & Glaser, 1996; DeBarger, Ayala, Minstrell, Kraus, & Stanford, 2009; Ericsson & Simon, 1993; Hamilton, Nussbaum, & Snow, 1997; Ruiz-Primo, Shavelson, Li, & Schultz, 2001). Cognitive interviews may reveal, among other things, whether students have difficulty understanding the items due to linguistic features that are not related to the constructs targeted.

Whereas legislation mandates the inclusion of ELLs in large-scale assessment, no norm in current testing practices prescribes their inclusion in the process of assessment development—when draft versions of the items are tried out with pilot students (!). This situation is particularly disturbing because a great number of the modifications made on items have to do with the ways in which they are worded. As a result, the long process of assessment development ends up serving the linguistic needs of mainstream students and excluding ELLs—the students in more serious need of linguistic support.

Well known in bilingual education is the notion that, while it takes a short time for ELLs to develop a basic English proficiency that allows them to communicate in this language through informal conversations, it takes several years to develop the academic language in English that allows them to fully benefit from instruction in English and to be fairly tested in this language (Cummins, 1981; Hakuta, Butler, & Witt, 2000). (Indeed, to a large extent, ELLs' development of their basic communication skills in English rapidly has contributed to the misconception that ELLs benefit more from English-only immersion programs than bilingual programs and that ELLs can be validly and fairly tested in English after one or two years of schooling in English.) Because most of the revisions test items undergo have to do with non-academic language (e.g., the phrasing of contextual information included in test items with the intent to make them meaningful to students), there is no reason why ELLs should not participate as pilot students in the process of assessment development. Indeed, as part of an investigation that examines how cognitive interviews can be used with ELLs, we (Prosser & Solano-Flores, 2010) have observed that many students classified as ELLs can interact with the interviewer in English when they participate in cognitive interviews.

Testing Accommodations

Unfortunately, the inclusion of ELLs in large-scale state and national assessment programs appears to be based on the false premise that somehow testing accommodations will ensure fair and valid testing for these students. This overreliance on testing accommodations appears to reflect the assumption that language issues can be effectively addressed at the end, not throughout the entire process of assessment development. Testing accommodations are modifications made in the ways in which tests are administered to ELLs with the intent to remove the effects of limited proficiency in the language of testing as an extraneous factor that may influence their performance in tests, but without altering the construct measured or unfairly favoring them over students who do not receive accommodations.

The spectrum of testing accommodations is wide (see, for example, Abedi, Hofstetter, & Lord, 2004; Sireci, Li, & Scarpati, 2003). Accommodations include giving students more time for completing the test, sitting them in areas where they are less likely to be distracted, reading aloud for them (in either L1 or L2) test items that normally are administered in a paper and pencil format, and simplifying the language in which items are phrased. Those accommodations that operate directly on the language features of items appear to be the most effective to reduce the score gap between ELL and non-ELL students (Abedi, 2002; Abedi & Hejri, 2004; Abedi & Lord, 2001). Among these accommodations, the linguistic simplification of the text of items has been proven to be the most effective (Abedi, Lord, Hofstetter, & Baker, 2000) in reducing that gap without affecting the comparability between ELL and non-ELL student scores (Rivera & Stansfield, 2004).

As simple and compelling as testing accommodations may appear as a strategy for eliminating language proficiency as an extraneous factor in testing, the effectiveness of most of them has proven to be limited. Evidence from recent investigations demonstrates that assigning ELLs to accommodations based on the information on their English proficiency that is available to schools is as effective in reducing the score gap between these students and native English speakers as randomly assigning them to those accommodations (Kopriva, Emick, Hipolito-Delgado, & Cameron, 2007). Poor theoretical defensibility of some accommodations, lack of fidelity in their implementation, and the limited and inaccurate information on the students' language proficiency can account for these limitations.

More research and conceptual developments need to take place before the use of testing accommodations can be legitimately assumed to minimize measurement error due to limited proficiency in the language of testing for ELLs. Certain approaches based on collecting detailed information on the students' proficiency in English in different language modes (listening, speaking, reading, and writing) and on constructing complex algorithms for determining the optimal set of accommodations needed by each student (Kopriva & Koran, 2008) hold promise for future improved practice. However, cost-effectiveness and the accessibility of full and accurate data on the proficiency of each ELL are challenges that will need to be addressed before these important advances can be used on a large scale. For now, the use of testing accommodations should be thought, at best, as a necessary but hardly sufficient approach for addressing limited proficiency in the language of testing.

CONCLUSIONS

In this chapter, I have discussed main issues in the assessment of mathematics for ELLs. First, I examined how the complex relationship of language and mathematics is shaped by cultural factors and how each ELL student faces a unique set of challenges in learning mathematics. Given this complexity, to validly test ELL students, language needs to be addressed from multiple perspectives. Although views of language as a system and as a process are more prevalent in the field of teaching and learning in mathematics, views of language as a structure and as a factor are more prevalent in the field of mathematics assessment.

I have submitted the notion that, to ensure valid, fair mathematics assessment for ELLs, views of language as a structure and as a factor need to be used in combination with views of language as a system and as a process. I have discussed measurement error as critical to examining testing practices for ELLs and shared findings from current research concerned with the development of testing models that are sensitive to language variation and the tremendous cultural and linguistic heterogeneity of ELL populations. This research uses views of language as a factor and as a system in combination. It views language as a source of measurement error and recognizes the fact that, to a large extent, variation in performance across languages results from linguistic variation within ELL populations.

In this research, ELL students are given the same set of items in both L1 and L2 with the purpose of examining how their performance varies across languages and items (not to obtain scores based on averaging across languages). These findings indicate that each ELL student has a unique set of strengths and weaknesses in L1 and in L2, and each item poses a unique set of linguistic challenges in L1 and in L2. Similar findings also indicate a considerable amount of measurement error due to dialect (e.g., standard and local dialect) and speak to the fact that ELLs are tremendously sensitive to language variation in testing. Appropriate sampling that addresses the diversity of linguistic features of mathematics test items is critical to ensuring valid, fair testing for ELLs.

Also, I have discussed the process of assessment development in large-scale assessment and the limitations of current practice in the testing of ELLs from a view of language as a process. Normative documents such as standards, assessment frameworks, and item specifications play a critical role in the ways in which content is sampled to develop tests. I have examined the limitations of current practice in relation to four aspects relevant to the testing of ELLs—the interaction of language, culture, and cognition; the ways in which language is addressed in normative documents; the inclusion of ELLs in the process of assessment development; and the use of testing accommodations in the assessment of ELLs. I conclude that, in order to improve assessment practices concerning ELLs, language needs to be taken into consideration at all stages of the process of assessment development. More specifically, the development of cognitive models on test taking should incorporate how language and culture shape cognition; standards and assessment frameworks should address mathematical academic language in more detail; ELLs can and should participate in the pilot stages of assessment development; and, to be effective, testing accommodations for ELLs should be more firmly grounded on theory from the language sciences.

Presented in Figure 13.3 is an attempt to summarize my discussion on the ways in which language views influence assessment practices in the context

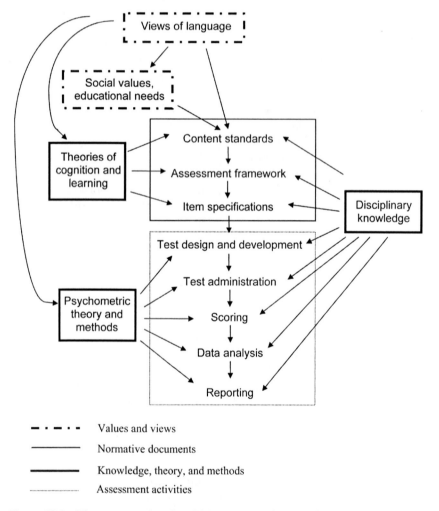

Figure 13.3 The process of testing: Main actors and their relationships.

of large-scale assessment. Normative documents (content standards, assessment frameworks, and item specifications)—based on which assessments are developed—reflect current disciplinary, mathematical knowledge and theories of cognition and learning. The main activities in the process of assessment (test design and development, test administration, scoring, data analysis, and reporting) are performed according to prescriptions made by normative documents, according to psychometric theory and methods, and according to disciplinary, mathematical knowledge. Social values and educational needs influence the content of normative documents. Explicit or implicit views of language influence how normative documents and methods from the field of psychometrics—key components in the assessment process—address language.

Although there are important documents that point at ways in which assessment systems should be improved to better serve ELL students (e.g., Baker et al., 2002; Wolf, Herman, & Dietel, 2010), improved testing for these students requires a change in mentality and a deep transformation of all the components in the process of testing. If we are serious about fairly and validly testing ELLs in mathematics, we need to enrich our understanding of the complex relationship between language and mathematics and make a serious effort to address the multifaceted nature of language.

NOTES

1. Of course, this varies depending on the way in which the cuts are made.
2. The potential for confusion is greater if, in addition to $5°$ and $5°$, we take 5^0 (5 with a zero exponent) into consideration. Whether or not this is an issue may depend on school grade.
3. In this system, the rule of adding the ending *avo* (or *ava*) is applicable to most numbers equal to or greater than 12 (*doceavo, treceavo, catorceavo, quinceavo...*).
4. To complicate matters, adding the ending *avo* (or *ava*) is more acceptable when the rule is used to name some fractions. However, this varies across Latin American countries.
5. Of course which of these challenges each ELL faces depends on individual personal and schooling histories.
6. An important issue, not discussed here, is that, in some cases, word problems may be wrongly assumed to assess complex problem-solving skills, when in fact they are simple translations of computation problems (see Schoenfeld, 2004).
7. These studies have been conducted also with ELL students who are native speakers of Haitian-Creole. The findings are the same.
8. The design used ensures that students do not take the same items in two languages on the same occasion. Appropriate actions have been taken to control for the effects of fatigue and practice.

9. The reader is invited to conduct a web search of international, national, and state assessment frameworks and item specifications documents. A tremendous variation in quality should become apparent from comparing these documents.

REFERENCES

Abedi, J. (2002). Standardized achievement tests and English language learners: Psychometric issues. *Educational Assessment, 8*(3), 231–257. doi: 10.1207/S15326977EA0803_02

Abedi, J. (2004). The No Child Left Behind Act and English language learners: Assessment and accountability issues. *Educational Researcher, 33*(1), 1–14. doi: 10.3102/0013189X033001004

Abedi, J. (2006). Language issues in item development. In S. M. Downing & T. M. Haladyna (Eds.), *Handbook of test development* (pp. 377–398). Mahwah, NJ: Erlbaum.

Abedi, J. & Hejri, F. (2004). Accommodations for students with limited English proficiency in the National Assessment of Educational Progress. *Applied Measurement in Education, 17*(4), 371-392. doi: 10.1207/s15324818ame1704_3

Abedi, J., Hofstetter, C. H., & Lord, C. (2004). Assessment accommodations for English language learners: Implications for policy-based empirical research. *Review of Educational Research, 74*(1), 1–28. doi: 10.3102/00346543074001001

Abedi, J. & Lord, C. (2001). The language factor in mathematics tests. *Applied Measurement in Education, 14*(3), 219–234. doi: 10.1207/S15324818AME1403_2

Abedi, J., Lord, C., Hofstetter, C. H., & Baker, E. (2000). Impact of accommodation strategies on English language learners' test performance. *Educational Measurement: Issues and Practice, 19*(3), 16–26. doi: 10.1111/j.1745-3992.2000.tb00034.x

Allalouf, A., Hambleton, R. K., & Sireci, S. G. (1999). Identifying the causes of DIF in translated verbal items. *Journal of Educational Measurement, 36*(3), 185–198. doi: 10.1111/j.1745-3984.1999.tb00553.x

American Educational Research Association, American Psychological Association, and National Council on Measurement in Education. (1999). *Standards for educational and psychological testing* (2nd ed.). Washington, DC: American Educational Research Association.

Bachman, L. F. (1990). *Fundamental considerations in language testing.* Oxford, England: Oxford University Press.

Baker, E. L., Linn, R. L., Herman, J. L. & Koretz, D. (2002, Winter). *Standards for educational accountability systems* (CRESST Policy Brief 5). Los Angeles: University of California, National Center for Research on Evaluation, Standards, and Student Testing.

Barwell, R. (2009). Mathematical word problems and bilingual learners in England. In R. Barwell (Ed.), *Multilingualism in mathematics classrooms: Global perspectives* (pp. 63–77). Bristol, UK: Multilingual Matters.

Baxter, G. P., Elder, A. D., & Glaser, R. (1996). Knowledge-based cognition and performance assessment in the science classroom. *Educational Psychologist, 31*(2), 133–140. doi: 10.1207/s15326985ep3102_5

Beckmann, P. (1971). *A history of π (pi).* New York: St. Martin's Press.

Bernardo, A. B. I. (2002). Language and mathematical problem solving among bilinguals. *Journal of Psychology, 136*(3), 283–297. doi: 10.1080/00223980209604156

Bialystok, E. (2001). *Bilingualism in development.* Cambridge, UK: Cambridge University Press.

Bialystok, E. (2002). Cognitive processes of L2 users. In V. J. Cook (Ed.), *Portraits of the L2 user* (pp. 145–165). Clevedon, UK: Multilingual Matters.

Bormuth, J. R. (1970). *On the theory of achievement test items.* Chicago: University of Chicago Press.

Brennan, R. L. (1992). *Elements of generalizability theory.* Iowa City, IA: The American College Testing Program.

Butler, F. A., Lord, C., Stevens, R., Borrego, M., & Bailey, A. L. (2004). *An approach to operationalizing academic language for language test Development purposes: Evidence from fifth-grade science and math* (CSE Technical Report No. 626). Los Angeles: University of California, Los Angeles, National Center for Research on Evaluation, Standards, and Student Testing.

Camilli, G. (2006). Test fairness. In R. L. Brennan (Ed.), *Educational measurement* (4th ed., pp. 221–256). Westport, CT: Praeger.

Camilli, G. & Shepard, L. A. (1994). *Methods for identifying biased test items.* Thousands Oaks, CA: Sage.

Cronbach, L. J., Gleser, G. C., Nanda, H., & Rajaratnam, N. (1972). *The dependability of behavioral measurements.* New York: Wiley.

Cummins, J. (1981). The role of primary language development in promoting educational success for language minority students. In *Schooling and language minority students: A theoretical framework* (pp. 3–49). Sacramento, CA: Office of Bilingual Bicultural Education, Department of Education.

DeBarger, A. H., Ayala, C., Minstrell, J. A., Kraus, P., & Stanford, T. (2009). Facet-based *progressions of student understanding in chemistry* (Chemistry Facets Technical Report 1). Menlo Park, CA: SRI International.

Durán, R. P. (1985). Influences of language skills on bilinguals' problem solving. In J. W. Segal, S. F. Chipman, & R. Glaser (Eds.), *Thinking and learning skills: Relating instruction to research* (Vol. 2, pp. 187–207). Hillsdale, NJ: Erlbaum.

Durán, R. P. (2010). Ensuring valid educational assessments for ELL students: Scores, score interpretation, and assessment uses. In M. del R. Basterra, E. Trumbull, & G. Solano-Flores (Eds.), *Cultural validity in assessment: Addressing linguistic and cultural diversity* (pp. 115–142). New York: Routledge.

Ercikan, K. (2002). Disentangling sources of differential item functioning in multilanguage assessments. *International Journal of Testing, 2*(3/4), 199–215. doi: 10.1207/S15327574IJT023&4_2

Ericsson, K. A. & Simon, H. A. (1993). *Protocol analysis: Verbal reports as data.* Cambridge, MA: Massachusetts Institute of Technology Press.

Fishman, J. A. (1965). Who speaks what language to whom and when? *La Linguistique, 1*(2), 67–88. Retrieved from http://www.puf.com/wiki/La_Linguistique

Gottlieb, M. (2006). *Assessing English language learners: Bridges from language proficiency to academic achievement.* Thousands Oaks, CA: Corwin Press.

Green, B. F. (1981). A primer of testing. *American Psychologist, 36*(10), 1001–1011. doi: 10.1037/0003-066X.36.10.1001

Greenfield, P.M. (1997). You can't take it with you: Why ability assessments don't cross cultures. *American Psychologist, 52*(10) 1115–1124. doi: 10.1037/0003-066X.52.10.1115

Gronlund, N. E., & Waugh, C. K. (2009). *Assessment of student achievment* (9th Edition). Columbus, OH: Pearson.

Grosjean, F. (1985). The bilingual as a competent but specific speaker-hearer. *Journal of Multilingual and Multicultural Development, 6*(6), 467–477. doi: 10.1080/01434632.1985.9994221

Hakuta, K., Butler, Y. G., & Witt, D. (2000). *How long does it take English learners to attain proficiency?* (Policy Report 2000-1). Berkeley: The University of California Linguistic Minority Research Institute.

Halliday, M. A. K. (1978). *Language as social semiotic: The social interpretation of language and meaning.* London: Edward Arnold.

Halliday, M. A. K. (1993). Some grammatical problems in scientific English. In M. A. K. Halliday & J. R. Martin (Eds.), *Writing science: Literacy and discursive power* (pp. 69–85). Pittsburgh, PA: University of Pittsburgh Press.

Hamilton, L. S. & Koretz, D. M. (2002). Tests and their use in test-based accountability. In L. S. Hamilton, B. M. Stecher, & S. P. Klein (Eds.), *Making sense of test-based accountability in education* (pp. 13–49). Santa Monica, CA: RAND.

Hamilton, L. S., Nussbaum, E. M., & Snow, R. E. (1997). Interview procedures for validating science assessments. *Applied Measurement in Education, 10*(2), 181–200. doi: 10.1207/s15324818ame1002_5

Hively, W., Patterson, H. L., & Page, S. H. (1968). A "universe-defined" system of arithmetic achievement tests. *Journal of Educational Measurement, 5*(4), 275–290. doi: 10.1111/j.1745-3984.1968.tb00639.x

Kane, M. T. (2006). Validation. In R. L. Brennan (Ed.), *Educational measurement* (4th ed., pp. 17–64). Westport, CT: American Council on Education and Praeger Publishers.

Kopriva, R. J., & Koran, J. (2008). Proper assignment of accommodations to individual students. In R. J. Kopriva (Ed.), *Improving testing for English language learners* (pp. 217–254). New York: Routledge.

Kopriva, R. J., Emick, J. E., Hipolito-Delgado, C. P., & Cameron, C. A. (2007). Do proper accommodation assignments make a difference? Examining the impact of improved decision making on scores for English language learners. *Educational Measurement: Issues & Practice, 26*(3), 11–20. doi: 10.1111/j.1745-3992.2007.00097.x

Lee, O. (1999). Equity implications based on the conceptions of science achievement in major reform documents. *Review of Educational Research, 69*(1), 83–115. doi: 10.3102/00346543069001083

Li, M., Ruiz-Primo, M. A., & Shavelson, R. J. (2006). Towards a science achievement framework: The case of TIMSS 1999. In S. J. Howie & T. Plomp (Eds.), *Contexts of learning mathematics and science: Lessons learned from TIMSS* (pp. 291–311). Florence, KY: Routledge.

Linn, R. L., Baker, E. L., & Betebenner, D. W. (2002). Accountability systems: Implications of requirements of the No Child Left Behind Act of 2001. *Educational Researcher, 31*(6), 3–16. doi: 10.3102/0013189X031006003

MacSwan, J. (2000). The threshold hypothesis, semilingualism, and other contributions to a deficit view of linguistic minorities. *Hispanic Journal of Behavioral Sciences, 22*(1), 3–45. doi: 10.1177/0739986300221001

Mazzeo, J., Lazer, S., & Zieky, M. J. (2006). Monitoring educational progress with group-score assessments. In R. L. Brennan (Ed.), *Educational measurement* (4th ed., pp. 681–699). Westport, CT: American Council on Education and Praeger Publishers.

Messick, S. (1989). Validity. In R. L. Linn (Ed.), *Educational measurement* (3rd ed., pp. 13–103). Washington, DC: American Council on Education & National Council on Measurement in Education.

Messick, S. (1995). Validity of psychological assessments: Validation of inferences from person's responses and performances as scientific inquiry into score meaning. *American Psychologist, 50*(9), 741–749. doi: 10.1037/0003-066X.50.9.741

Moschkovich, J. N. (2010). Language(s) and learning mathematics: Resources, challenges, and issues for research. In J. N. Moschkovich (Ed.), *Language and mathematics education: Multiple perspectives and directions for research* (pp. 1–28). Charlotte, NC: Information Age.

National Assessment Governing Board. (2009a). *Assessment and item specifications for the NAEP 2009 mathematics assessment.* Washington, DC: Author. Retrieved from http://www.nagb.org/publications/frameworks.htm

National Assessment Governing Board. (2009b). *Mathematics framework for the 2009 National Assessment of Educational Progress.* Washington, DC: Author. Retrieved from http://www.nagb.org/publications/frameworks/math-framework09.pdf

National Center for Education Statistics. (2010). *The nation's report card: Mathematics.* Washington, DC: U.S. Department of Education. Retrieved from http://nces.ed.gov/nationsreportcard/mathematics/

National Council of Teachers of Mathematics. (2000). *Principles and standards for school mathematics.* Reston, VA: Author.

Nettle, D. & Romaine, S. (2002). *Vanishing voices: The extinction of the world's languages.* New York: Oxford University Press

Nitko, A. J. & Brookhart, S. M. (2007). *Educational assessment of students* (5th ed.). Upper Saddle River, NJ: Pearson Education.

Noonan, J. (1990). Readability problems presented by mathematics text. Early Child Development & Care, 54(1), 57–81. doi: 10.1080/0300443900540104

O'Malley, M. & Valdez-Pierce, L. (1996). *Authentic assessment for English language learners.* New York: Addison-Wesley.

Pellegrino, J. W., Chudowsky, N., & Glaser, R. (2001). *Knowing what students know: The science and design of educational assessment.* Washington, DC: National Academies Press.

Popham, W. J. (2007). *Classroom assessment: What teachers need to know* (5th ed.). Boston: Allyn & Bacon.

Prosser, R., & Solano-Flores, G. (submitted). *Rater language background as a source of measurement error in the testing of English language learners.* Manuscript submitted for publication.

Prosser, R. R. & Solano-Flores, G. (2010, April). *Including English language learners in the process of test development: a study on instrument linguistic adaptation for cognitive validity.* Paper presented at the Annual Conference of the National Council of Measurement in Education, Denver, CO.

Reynolds, C. R., Livingston, R. B., & Wilson, V. (2006). *Measurement and evaluation in education.* Boston: Pearson Education.

Rivera, C. & Stansfield, C. W. (2004). The effect of linguistic simplification of science test items on score comparability. *Educational Assessment, 9*(3/4), 79–105. doi: 10.1207/s15326977ea0903&4_1

Ruiz-Primo, M. A., Shavelson, R. J., Li, M., & Schultz, S. E. (2001). On the validity of cognitive interpretations of scores from alternative concept-mapping techniques. *Educational Assessment, 7*(2), 99–141. doi: 10.1207/S15326977EA0702_2

Scarcella, R. C. (2003). *Academic English: A conceptual framework* (Report 2003-1). Santa Barbara: University of California Linguistic Minority Research Institute.

Schleppegrell, M. (2010). Language in mathematics teaching and learning: A research review. In J. N. Moschkovich (Ed.), *Language and mathematics in education: Multiple perspectives and directions for research* (pp. 73-112). Charlotte, NC: Information Age.

Schoenfeld, A. H. (2004). The math wars. *Educational Policy, 18*(1), 253–286. doi: 10.1177/0895904803260042

Shaftel, J., Belton-Kocher, E., Glasnapp, D., & Poggio, G. (2006). The impact of language characteristics in mathematics test items on the performance of English language learners and students with disabilities. *Educational Assessment, 11*(2), 105–126. doi: 10.1207/s15326977ea1102_2

Shavelson, R. J., Baxter, G. P., & Gao, X. (1993). Sampling variability of performance assessments. *Journal of Educational Measurement, 30*(3), 215–232. doi: 10.1111/j.1745-3984.1993.tb00424.x

Shavelson, R. J., Ruiz-Primo, M. A., & Wiley, E. W. (1999). Notes on sources sampling variability in science performance assessments. *Journal of Educational Measurement, 36*(1), 61–71. doi: 10.1111/j.1745-3984.1999.tb00546.x

Shavelson, R. J. & Webb, N. M. (1991). *Generalizability theory: A primer.* Newbury Park, CA: Sage.

Shavelson, R. J. & Webb, N. M. (2009). Generalizability theory and its contributions to the discussion of the generalizability of research findings. In K. Ercikan & W. M. Roth (Eds.), *Generalizing from educational research* (pp. 13–32). New York: Routledge.

Shepard, L. A. (1992). Uses and abuses of testing. In M. C. Alkin (Ed.), *Encyclopedia of educational research* (6th ed., pp. 1477–1485). New York: Macmillan.

Shepard, L., Hannaway, J., & Baker, E. (2009). *Standards, assessments, and accountability.* Washington, DC: National Academy of Education. Retrieved from http://www.naeducation.org/Standards_Assessments_Accountability_White_Paper.pdf

Sireci, S. G., Li, S., & Scarpati, S. (2003). *The effects of test accommodation on test performance: A review of the literature* (Research Report 485). Amherst, MA: Center for Educational Assessment.

Sloane, F. C. & Kelly, A. E. (2003). Issues in high stakes testing programs. *Theory Into Practice, 42*(1), 12–17. doi: 10.1207/s15430421tip4201_3

Solano-Flores, G. (2006). Language, dialect, and register: Sociolinguistics and the estimation of measurement error in the testing of English-language learners. *Teachers College Record, 108*(11), 2354–2379. doi: 10.1111/j.1467-9620.2006.00785.x

Solano-Flores, G. (2008). Who is given tests in what language by whom, when, and where? The need for probabilistic views of language in the testing of English language learners. *Educational Researcher, 37*(4), 189–199. doi: 10.3102/0013189X08319569

Solano-Flores, G. (2009). The testing of English language learners as a stochastic process: Population misspecification, measurement error, and overgeneralization. In K. Ercikan & W. M. Roth (Eds.), *Generalizing from Educational Research* (pp. 33–45) New York: Routledge.

Solano-Flores, G. (2010). Function and form in research on language and mathematics education. In J. N. Moschkovich (Ed.), *Language and mathematics in education: Multiple perspectives and directions for research* (pp. 113–149). Charlotte, NC: Information Age.

Solano-Flores, G. & Li, M. (2006). The use of generalizability (G) theory in the testing of linguistic minorities. *Educational Measurement: Issues and Practice 25*(1), 13–22. doi: 10.1111/j.1745-3992.2006.00048.x

Solano-Flores, G. & Li, M. (2008). Examining the dependability of academic achievement measures for English language learners. *Assessment for Effective Intervention, 33*(3), 135–144. doi: 10.1177/1534508407313238

Solano-Flores, G. & Li, M. (2009a). Generalizability of cognitive interview-based measures across cultural groups. *Educational Measurement: Issues and Practice, 28*(2), 9–18. doi: 10.1111/j.1745-3992.2009.00143.x

Solano-Flores, G. & Li, M. (2009b). Language variation and score variation in the testing of English language learners, native Spanish speakers. *Educational Assessment, 14*(3), 180–194. 10.1080/10627190903422880

Solano-Flores, G. & Shavelson, R. J. (1997). Development of performance assessments in science: Conceptual, practical, and logistical issues. *Educational Measurement: Issues and Practice, 16*(3), 16–24. doi: 10.1111/j.1745-3992.1997.tb00596.x

Solano-Flores, G. & Trumbull, E. (2008). In what language should English language learners be tested?. In R. J. Kopriva. (Ed.), *Improving testing for English language learners* (pp. 169–200). New York: Routledge.

Thurber, R. S., Shinn, M. R., & Smolkowski, K. (2002). What is measured in mathematics tests? Construct validity of curriculum-based mathematics measures. *School Psychology Review, 31*(4), 498–513. Retrieved from http://www.nasponline.org/publications/spr/

Trumbull, E. & Koelsch, N. (2011). Language arts: Designing and using a reading assessment for learners transitioning to English-only instruction. In M. R. Basterra, E. Trumbull, & G. Solano-Flores (Eds.), *Cultural validity in assessment: Addressing linguistic and cultural diversity* (pp. 195–217). New York, NY: Routledge.

Trumbull, E. & Solano-Flores, G. (2011). Addressing the language demands of mathematics assessments: Using a language framework and field research findings. In M. R. Basterra, E. Trumbull, & G. Solano-Flores (Eds.), *Cultural validity in assessment: Addressing linguistic and cultural diversity* (pp. 218–253) New York, NY: Routledge.

Vygotsky, L. S. (1978). *Mind in society: The development of higher psychological processes.* Cambridge, MA: Harvard University Press.

Wellington, J. & Osborne, J. (2001). *Language and literacy in science education.* Buckingham, UK: Open University Press.

Wertsch, J. V. (1985). *Vygotsky and the social formation of mind.* Cambridge, MA: Harvard University Press.

Wolf, M. K., Herman, J. L., Bachman, L. F., Bailey, A. L., & Griffin, N. (2008). *Recommendations for assessing English language learners: English language proficiency measures and accommodation uses—Recommendations report* (CRESST Report 737). Los Angeles: University of California, National Center for Research on Evaluation, Standards, and Student Testing.

Wolf, M. K., Herman, J. L., & Dietel, R. (2010, Spring). *Improving the validity of English language learner assessment systems* (CRESST Policy Brief No. 10 - Executive Summary). Los Angeles: University of California, National Center for Research on Evaluation, Standards, and Student Testing.

Zieky, M. J. (2006). Fairness review in assessment. In S. M. Downing & T. M. Haladyna (Eds.), *Handbook of test development* (pp. 359–376). Mahwah, NJ: Erlbaum.

CHAPTER 14

TEACHER QUALITY, ACADEMIC TRACKING AND THE MATHEMATICS PERFORMANCE OF LATINO ENGLISH LEARNERS

Eduardo Mosqueda
University of California, Santa Cruz

INTRODUCTION

The mathematics performance of Latino students on standardized assessments has been described as pervasively, disproportionately, and persistently low relative to similar outcomes for white students (Valencia, 2002). Results from the National Assessment of Education Progress and other standardized tests of mathematics performance show that the scores of Latino English language learners (ELLs) are considerably lower compared to the scores of their native English-speaking peers (Abedi, 2004; Abedi & Lord, 2000; Mosqueda, 2010; Secada, 1992; Tate, 1997). The underperformance of Latino ELLs relative to their English-speaking peers suggests that low levels or emergent levels English proficiency plays an important role in explaining their underachievement in mathematics.

Latinos/as and Mathematics Education, pages 315–339
Copyright © 2011 by Information Age Publishing
All rights of reproduction in any form reserved.

The academic success of Latino ELLs, however, depends of many factors, not only learning English. In this chapter, I argue that language is not the cause of the performance disparities in mathematics of Latinos, particularly Latino ELLs; instead, I examine the potential of language to be a critical part of a solution towards redressing these enduring inequitable outcomes. A step in this direction requires us to consider the institutional complexities or *instructional contexts* that differentially influence the educational opportunities of Latino ELLs as a consequence of their English proficiency. By instructional context, I refer primarily to two relationships: the students' English proficiency and the relationship with their mathematics teacher, and the students' level of access to the mathematics content and their language proficiency. Specifically, I focus on the interrelatedness of the English proficiency of ELLs, the rigor of the mathematics content to which students are exposed, and their teachers' professional qualifications in both the content itself and their specific training in providing linguistic support for ELLs.

I hypothesized that these central features of the instructional context have the potential to help make mathematics content conceptually and linguistically accessible for Latino ELLs and therefore help facilitate the development of their mathematics language register. To test this hypothesis, I analyzed how instructional contextual features, both *within* classrooms and *between* schools, influence mathematics performance of Latino ELLs and whether having access to a mathematics teacher with specialized training to provide linguistic support for ELLs can reduce the effect of low English proficiency on performance in mathematics.

BACKGROUND

Latino ELLs who have not developed the requisite English skills to understand a teacher's explanations or the textbook, for example, are unlikely to meet their potential in mathematical understanding. One common response is to ensure that mathematics teachers working with Latino ELLs are specially prepared to make the content both conceptually and linguistically accessible. Another less common approach is to provide native language support in the teaching of mathematics. This strategy suggests that Latino ELLs who are taught mathematics in their native language will gain the necessary conceptual understanding while also learning English, thus making the transition to mathematics instruction in English much smoother and resulting in fewer gaps in their understanding.

Whereas a bilingual approach to mathematics instruction is a viable strategy supported by research (Celedón-Pattichis, 2004; Cuevas, 1984; Dentler & Hafner, 1997; Garrison & Mora, 1999; Khisty, 1995; Lucas, Henze, & Donato, 1990; Ron, 1999), finding a sufficient number of teachers with the specialized training to provide native language support is a formidable policy challenge because the vast majority of the teaching force in U.S. schools is white, middle class, and predominantly monolingual English-speaking (Gandara & Maxwell-Jolly, 2006). Moreover, recent trends have shown that as the number of school-aged ELLs has rapidly increased at the national level, the provision of native language instruction and support has dramatically declined. During the decade between 1990 and 2000, the ELL population increased by approximately 105%, while the general school population grew by just 12% (Kindler, 2002). During almost the same time period (between 1992 and 2002), the percentage of all ELLs who received services in *English only* increased substantially, from 34% to 48%, while the percentage of those who received support services with significant native language use decreased by more than half, from 37% to 17%, across all content areas (Zehler, Fleischman, Hopstock, Stephenson, Pendzick, & Sapru, 2003). Furthermore, the percentage of ELLs who received no primary language services at all increased from 4% to 12% (Zehler et al., 2003).

The dearth in native language support during instruction juxtaposed against the alarmingly low performance of Latino ELLs raises important questions that force us to look beyond the English proficiency levels of ELLs and to examine the influence of the preparation of teachers to meet both their academic and linguistic needs. Therefore, the mathematics performance on standardized tests of native and nonnative English-speaking Latinos, and of ELLs in particular, is analyzed because instructional context features such as access to rigorous (or college preparatory) mathematics content and access to adequately prepared mathematics teachers are not only linked to ELL underachievement, but also continue to raise significant barriers to their academic success at the secondary school level.

A focus on the mathematics outcomes of all Latino students is important, given the research findings that have shown high school students who complete advanced mathematics courses (e.g., algebra 2, trigonometry, precalculus, or calculus) were more likely to graduate from high school and were twice as likely to attend college, compared to students who completed only low-level mathematics courses (Adelman, 1999, 2006). By examining the relationship between the English proficiency, academic tracking, access to teachers with an adequate preparation to teach math to ELLs, and the mathematics performance on standardized tests among native and nonnative English-speaking Latino 10th-grade students, the present study offers a more complete explanation for the underperformance of Latino ELLs.

Access to Adequately Trained Teachers

Because exposure to low-quality teaching has a detrimental impact on academic achievement, many researchers have argued that improving teacher quality is what matters most in the improvement of educational quality and equity (Darling-Hammond, Berry, & Thoreson, 2001; Darling-Hammond & Youngs, 2002; Gándara & Maxwell-Jolly, 2006; Gándara & Rumberger, 2003; Téllez & Waxman, 2006). Although research suggests that students learn more from qualified teachers, a teacher with low qualifications can severely hamper assessment performance "by more than a one grade-level equivalent" (Hanushek, 1992, p. 107). In fact, educators can expect little to no growth in the performance of students between their previous school year to the end of the next grade if their teacher lacks the appropriate qualifications. The Educational Trust (1998) has argued that low-income Latino students, who have less to begin with, are systematically given less in school. Education researchers have shown that it is not at all uncommon for low-income Latinos to be taught by under-qualified teachers who lack the appropriate preparation and certification, background content knowledge, and the experience to meet the learning needs of their students (Flores, 2007; Gándara & Rumberger, 2003; Maxwell-Jolly, Gándara, & Driscoll, 2005).

Latino students, particularly Latino ELLs, are disproportionately exposed to poor-quality teachers (August & Hakuta, 1997; Gándara & Rumberger, 2003; Ruiz-de-Velazco & Fix, 2000; Tellez & Waxman, 2006). Latino ELLs experience an even greater disadvantage because, in addition to the poor learning opportunities, their language needs are often not met. For instance, in an analysis of 26 high schools in California with large concentrations of first- and second-generation immigrants, Minicucci and Olsen (1993) found that Latino ELLs are linguistically *isolated* from mainstream students and grouped in sheltered classes with the least trained teachers, only limited access to appropriate materials, and little primary-language support or instruction.

Large-scale studies conducted since the late 20th century found that Latino students lack access to teachers who are trained to provide native language support, and that the little training teachers do have is often inadequate. Although 40% of all teachers nationwide have at least one ELL in their classroom, researchers found that each teacher received little to no preparation to work with these students. For instance, teachers who taught at least three ELLs in their classroom reported receiving an average of five hours of training in the last five years (Gándara & Maxwell-Jolly, 2006). In mathematics classrooms that serve ELLs, one must also consider whether the teacher has a background in mathematics, given the research findings that show how ELLs are often taught mathematics by teachers who are out of their field and therefore do not have a background in a mathematics-related field (Gándara & Rumberger, 2003; Miniccuci & Olsen, 1992; Valdés, 1998).

Native Language Support and the Development of a Mathematics Language Register

Research has shown that English proficiency is a critical component of learning mathematics for Latino ELLs (August & Hakuta, 1997). The provision of native language support for Latino ELLs during mathematics instruction has been shown to facilitate their comprehension of content. Nonnative English speakers with low levels of proficiency, however, face the added difficulty of becoming proficient in English while they also develop proficiency in the academic language of the mathematics classroom. *Academic language* is the language used in schools to learn, speak, and write about academic subjects such as mathematics (Valdés, Bunch, Snow, & Lee, 2005). Therefore, simply becoming proficient in English may not be sufficient for students to become successful in rigorous mathematics courses.

English proficiency plays a critical role in learning rigorous secondary school mathematics because both the academic language of instruction and the content are highly abstract and complex (August & Hakuta, 1997; Cuevas, 1984; Flores, 1997; Khisty, 1995). Each students' level of English proficiency must be considered to ensure that ELLs are able to comprehend the complex mathematical concepts that the teacher is presenting (Garrison & Mora, 1999). Considerable research has shown that mathematics is itself a language that is more complex than everyday English (Cuevas, 1984; Garrison & Mora, 1999; Gutierrez, 2002; Khisty, 1995, 1997). The language of mathematics has been described as a "register" of words, expressions, and meanings that differ from those of everyday language (Cuevas, 1984; Mestre, 1988; Secada, 1992, 1996). For example, the language of mathematics has specialized meanings for words and phrases such as "horizontal," "vertical," "subtract," "difference," "equivalence," and "inverse," to name a few, that differ from the everyday conversational and academic meanings that ELLs were learning in their English-language arts courses (Ron, 1999).

Research also suggests that as all Latino students, and ELLs in particular, develop their mathematics language register, they are better able to both understand the lesson and to express their ideas with greater specificity in their dominant language. For instance, in their work with Latino immigrant ELLs during a reading lesson in English language arts, Moll and Díaz (1987) found that students were better able to understand and comprehend much more about the content that was being taught (in English) than they could verbally articulate in English. The use of Latino ELLs' native language, Spanish in this case, was critical because it allowed them to describe what they had understood during the lesson with greater detail and precision.

Similar results have been obtained with Latino ELLs in a secondary school algebra class (Garrison & Mora, 1999). In this latter research, following a lesson on determining the area of a triangle that was drawn on graph paper, students were asked to work in groups and then explain the process in English. Janet, a recently arrived Latina immigrant with a low level of English proficiency, was asked to explain how to find the area of the triangle. Garrison and Mora (1999) noted that Janet's initial response in English to a question about how she and her group had calculated the area was "because we count the squares" (p. 43). Her response in English was limited and provided little information about her understanding of the concept of the area of triangles (Garrison & Mora, 1999). However, the teacher then asked her to provide an explanation in Spanish, and Janet provided the following response (translated to English by the authors):

> We think the area is 18 squares. We counted the whole squares and got 12. There were some incomplete squares left over, some were big, others were smaller. We joined the big ones with the small ones and got 6. We added 12 + 6, and our result was 18 squares. (Garrison & Mora, 1999, p. 44)

It is clear that Janet's response in Spanish provided greater insight into her grasp of the concept of area than her terse response in English. This excerpt suggests that Janet's native language was an important medium for communicating her mathematical thinking.

Similarly, a few other important studies have demonstrated higher levels of success in secondary school mathematics courses that provide native language support for Latino ELLs (Celedón-Pattichis, 2004; Dentler & Hafner, 1997; Gutiérrez, 2002, 2007; Lucas et al., 1990; Moschkovich, 1999a, 1999b, 2007). In a large-scale study of districts in the Southwest that served large numbers of immigrant children, Dentler and Hafner (1997) found that districts that were successful in educating Latino ELLs were more likely to have a well-established language program that used "the student's primary language to build comprehension" (p. 67). Yet, programs that provide native language support in mathematics content courses and foster the success of Latino ELLs are rare (Gándara, 1995; Minicucci & Olsen, 1992; Olsen, 1995, 1997). Taken together, these studies underscore the missed opportunity to capitalize on students' native language to facilitate deeper learning of complex mathematics content. However, English proficiency is not the only important factor that has an impact on mathematics achievement.

English Proficiency and Access to Rigorous Content

English proficiency is important, but it is just one of many factors contributing to low academic achievement for nonnative English speakers. Institutional factors such as tracking also play an important role in structuring the academic success and failure of Latinos in general, and Latino ELLs in particular (Conchas, 2001, 2006; Gándara, 1995, 1997; Lucas et al., 1990; Mehan, Villanueva, Hubbard, & Lintz, 1996; Oakes, 1985; Olsen 1995). Tracking practices are questionable, particularly because placement decisions are often made without an accurate assessment of students' mathematics background in their native language, given the limitation of tests in the English medium to assess the mathematics content knowledge of ELLs (Abedi, 2004; Abedi & Lord, 2000; Durán, 2008; Martiniello, 2008; Solano-Flores, 2008).

Research has shown that Latinos are denied access to rigorous courses at disproportionate rates compared to white and Asian students (Oakes, 1985). Specifically, studies on Latino ELLs suggest that English proficiency significantly factors into educators' decision about Latino ELLs' mathematics track placement (Gándara, 1999; Harklau, 1994a, 1994b; Lucas, 1997; Walqui, 2000). In their research on schools in the Southwest with large numbers of Latinos, for instance, Donato, Menchaca, and Valencia (1991) found that track assignments were strongly influenced by students' level of English-language proficiency, and resulted in remedial or vocational track placements. Furthermore, the placement of all ELLs, including Latino ELLs, in low-track classes was often justified by the misguided assumption that those classes are not as difficult linguistically, compared to higher level courses (Harklau, 1994b; Katz, 1999).

Latino ELLs are particularly vulnerable to low-track placement in mathematics courses. Secada and Carey (1990), for example, contended that a lack of understanding of the role of language in the mathematics instruction of Latino ELLs has led to placement of these students in courses in which they receive no linguistic support and, as a result, are denied access to high-level mathematical skills and reasoning. Such practices can have important implications on achievement because it can be argued that the absence of native-language support in mathematics classrooms, coupled with the denial of access to rigorous mathematics content, may limit the potential for further development of academic language or the mathematics language register of Latino ELLs and, in turn, contribute to their lower mathematics performance. A growing body of research has analyzed the practice of placing ELLs in low-track classes and has consistently found that low-track placements have a negative impact on students' achievement in mathematics (Callahan, 2005; Katz, 1999; Mosqueda, 2010; Wang & Goldschmidt, 1999).

Literature on tracking has also shown that once students are sorted into tracks, they become locked in to those arrangements (Heubert & Hauser, 1999). Thus, Latinos placed in remedial mathematics classes that produce lower and slower rates of learning (Oakes, Gamoran, & Page, 1992) have a lower probability of receiving better track assignments in the future (Heubert & Hauser, 1999). The long-term effects of permanent placement in low-track classes have been linked to lower academic achievement and higher dropout rates for Latino ELLs (Romo & Falbo, 1996; Rumberger & Larson, 1998). However, acquiring a higher level of English fluency is rarely a guarantee for promotion into high-track classes (Olsen, 1997). In fact, in her study of Mexican-origin high school students in low-track classes, Valenzuela (1999) found that after students became proficient in English, they were only promoted horizontally in the tracking system. That is, students with high levels of English proficiency were removed from the low-track English as a second language classes and reassigned to the English-only low-level track.

This review of the literature illustrates the manifold causes of Latino ELL underperformance in mathematics. Although all the studies reviewed addressed important factors that help to explain the persistent achievement disparities between Latinos and whites, none have systematically combined academic tracking, teacher preparation, and English proficiency into a single study. Using this combination of variables, this study adds to our knowledge of the sources of Latino ELL underperformance in mathematics by addressing the following two research questions:

1. Does the relationship between academic tracking and the math teachers' content knowledge and teaching preparation influence the mathematics performance on standardized tests of Latino native and nonnative English-speaking secondary school students?
2. Does having access to a mathematics teacher with training in teaching ELLs improve the performance of Latino ELLs relative to their English-proficient and their native English-speaking peers?

Before discussing the methods and analyses, I want to first point out that this study used a cross-sectional design model testing the association of variables, and thus no causal statements can be made about the direction of these relationships.

METHOD

The data were drawn from the first wave of the Educational Longitudinal Study of 2002 (ELS: 2002), a large, nationally representative data set provided by the National Center for Education Statistics. The base year of the ELS: 2002 represented the first stage of a longitudinal study that will ultimately provide policy-relevant trend data about critical transitions experienced by a national probability sample of students as they proceed through high school and into college or their careers (Ingels, Pratt, Rogers, Siegel,

& Stutts, 2004). The first wave, from which the subsample for this chapter was drawn, was composed of students in the 10th grade in 2002 and included 15,362 students from a random sample of 752 public, Catholic, and other private schools. The data set contained assessments of students in reading and mathematics performance, in addition to measures of important student, family, teacher, classroom, and school characteristics. It also contained information on students' immigrant status, language proficiency, and track placement. It was especially suited for this study because Latinos were oversampled.

The analysis is based on the subsample of 2,234 first-generation Latino immigrants and U.S.-born second-generation and third-generation Latinos present in the ELS: 2002 data set. Statistical power analyses (Light, Singer, & Willett, 1990) suggested that this sample size provides power (.90) sufficient to detect small effects at the typical levels of statistical significance.

Variables in the Models

Question Predictors

The primary question predictors for each student (i.e., i in school j) include three measures of the mathematics teacher preparation. A list of these predictors, along with descriptive data for each variable, is presented in Table 14.1. The first predictor, certified ($MTHCERT_{ij}$) is a dummy variable used to distinguish between teachers who are certified to teach and those who do not have a teacher certification (1 = is certified to teach, 0 = is not certified to teach). Second, mathematics major ($MTHMAJOR_{ij}$) is a dummy variable used to distinguish between weather or not the teacher has an undergraduate degree in mathematics (1 = undergraduate mathematics major, 0 = does not have an undergraduate degree in mathematics). Third, also tested is whether the mathematics teacher participated in training (EL_TRAIN_{ij}) to support ELLs in their classrooms. In the ELS: 2002 survey, mathematics teachers were specifically asked if they had at least eight hours of specialized LEP training in the last 3 years.

To distinguish between native and nonnative English speakers in the analysis and to account for differences in the level of English proficiency of each student, the variables that follow are also included in this analysis. Nonnative ($NONNATIV_{ij}$) is a dummy variable used to distinguish between Latino native and nonnative English speakers (1 = non-native English speaker, 0 = native English speaking Latino). About 50.5% of the Latino students in this sample reported being nonnative English speakers. To differentiate among the level of English proficiency of nonnative English speakers, the cross-product $NONNATIV_{ij}*ENGPROF_{ij}$ is used. $NONNATIV_{ij}$ is a dummy variable used to distinguish between Latino native and nonnative English

TABLE 14.1 Descriptive Statistics for All Variables

Variable	Description	*n*	Mean	SD	Min	Max
Student background						
SES	ELS:2002 Standardized SES Composite	2222	8.12	2.50	1	13
FEMALE	Sex (0 = male and 1 = female)	2222	0.50	0.50	0	1
NONNATIVE	Nonnative English speaker (0 = native English speaker)	2222	0.51	0.50	0	1
Immigration status						
FIRSTGEN	First-generation immigrant	2222	0.15	0.42	0	1
SECGEN	Second-generation immigrant	2222	0.25	0.43	0	1
THIRDGEN	Third-generation immigrant	2222	0.60	0.48	0	1
English proficiency						
ENGPROF	Level of English proficiency	2222	6.90	1.22	3	8
Track level placement						
GENTRACK	General track placement	2222	0.53	0.50	0	1
Teacher preparation						
MTHMAJOR	Math teacher has math degree	2222	0.51	0.50	0	1
MTHCERT	Math teacher is certified	2222	0.76	0.43	0	1
EL_TRAIN	Math teacher received at least 8 hrs training in EL strategies in the last 3 years.	2222	0.22	0.45	0	1
School context measures						
PCT_LEP	Percent of 10th-graders who are LEP students in the high school	524	0.78	0.81	0	4
PCTLUNCH	Percent of 10th-grade students who qualify for free lunch	524	3.42	1.96	1	7
PUBLIC	School control (1 = public high and 0 = Catholic or other private)	524	92.35	17.31	0	1

speakers (1 = non-native English speaker, 0 = native English speaking Latino) above. $ENGPROF_{ij}$ is a composite that ranges from 3 to 8 (low to high), based on each student's self-reported level of English proficiency.[1] This weighted composite score is constituted from students' responses to four ordinal dimensions of self-reported English proficiency that include how well students understand spoken English, speak English, read English, and write English.

For each of these dimensions of English proficiency, students provided one of following ordinal responses: very well, well, not well, or not at all. The inclusion of this interaction in a hypothesized regression model allows for the comparison between nonnative English speakers with varying levels of English proficiency and their native English-speaking peers. Finally, the variable GENTRACK$_{ij}$ is a dichotomous predictor that indicates whether a student was placed in the general/vocational academic track or in the college preparatory track (1 = general/vocational track, 0 = college preparatory track). Approximately 52.6% of the students reported general track placement, and the remaining 47.4% reported being placed in the academic track.

Outcome variable

Math achievement (MTH_ACH$_{ij}$) represents an item response theory (IRT) scaled mathematics achievement score (Ingels et al., 2004) variable for each student i in school j. The ELS: 2002 assessment itself contained items in arithmetic, algebra, geometry, data/probability, and advanced topics (Ingels et al., 2004). These scores are standardized to a mean of 50 and a standard deviation of 10 in the full ELS: 2002 sample (Ingels et al., 2004). The test score for the subsample of Latinos is 45.7 and an SD of 9.6 points on the ELS: 2002 assessment. IRT scores were used because they simplify the interpretation of the impact of predictors on the outcome. A one-point difference associated with the outcome variable equals one item correct on the ELS: 2002 assessment.

Control Predictors

The analysis includes a series of control predictors to account for individual background and school context variation that may have an impact on the outcomes, and to assess the potential impact of selectivity bias. These controls include individual-level gender, SES, parental education, and each immigrant student's prior level of education in his or her native country. At Level 2, included are a set controls for selected aggregate measures of the school context, such as the percentage of students who are placed in the general track, the percentage of all EL students, and the percentage of poor students within each school—the number of students within each school that qualify for free or reduced-price lunch is used as a proxy for poverty. For a description of the definitions and coding of each variable in this analysis, see Table 14.2.

Missing Data and Sample Weights

Multiple imputation was used to replace missing data in the ELS: 2002 survey (Rubin, 1987). The procedure (PROC MI) in the SAS statistical software package was used to replace missing values with randomly generated values from the sample distributions of the variables in the analysis. Using multiple imputation, five data sets were generated, each with different ran-

TABLE 14.2   Data and Coding for All Variables

Variable	Definition	Notes/coding
Student background		
SES	Standardized composite measure that includes family income, parent education, and occupational status	Ranges from −1.98 to 1.79
FEMALE	Student's gender	1 = female, 0 = male
NONNATIV	Indicates whether student is a nonnative English speaker or a native English speaker	1 = nonnative, 0 = native speaker
Immigration status		
FIRSTGEN	Indicates whether both the student and parent are foreign-born	1 = yes, 0 = no
SECGEN	Indicates whether the student is U.S.-born while at least one parent is foreign-born	1 = yes, 0 = no
THIRDGEN	Indicates whether both the student and parents are U.S.-born	1 = yes, 0 = no
Teacher preparation		
MTHMAJOR	Indicates whether each student's mathematics teacher has a bachelor's degree in mathematics or a math-related field.	1 = yes, 0 = no
MTHCERT	Indicates whether each student's mathematics teacher is certified to teach	1 = yes, 0 = no
School context measures		
PCTLUNCH	Proxy for school SES and measured by the percentage of 10th-grade students who are eligible for free or reduced-cost lunch in the school	1 = 0–5% 2 = 6–10% 3 = 11–20% 4 = 21–30% 5 = 21–30% 6 = 51–75% 7 = 76–100%
PCT_LEP	Percentage of 10th-grade LEP students enrolled in the school	0 = none 1 = 1–10% 2 = 11–25% 3 = 25–50% 4 = 51% or more
PUBLIC	Indicates whether the school is public, or Catholic or other type of private	1 = public 0 = Catholic or private
English proficiency		
ENGPROF	Weighted composite of the self-reported level of English proficiency of each respondent, based on their ability to understand, speak, read, and write English	Ranges from 3 to 8.
Track-level placement		
GENTRACK	Indicates the academic track placement of each respondent—the general/vocational or college preparatory track	1 = general/ vocational, 0 = college track

domly imputed individual-level values. The regression models were then fitted separately in each of the imputed data sets, and the results were averaged and corrected for the inclusion of the random variation in each of the imputed datasets. The ELS: 2002 student-level panel weights and school-level weights were applied to the analysis according to the guidelines provided for the hierarchical linear model software (Raudenbush & Bryk, 2002).

Data Analysis

Using hierarchical linear models, three fitted multilevel models were evaluated in which the mathematics achievement of Latino students was modeled as a function of the control and question predictors. Multilevel modeling is well suited for this analysis because it can account for the clustering of students within schools. The first fitted model (M1) is the null or unconditional model that contains no predictors and estimates the average mathematics achievement for the subsample of Latino 10th graders in the ELS: 2002 data set. The second fitted model (M2) is the baseline control model and includes all of the individual-level and school-level control predictors. The third model (M3) adds the key question predictors and presents the main effect of having access to a mathematics teacher who was certified to teach, a teacher who majored in mathematics as an undergraduate, and a mathematics teacher with training to support ELLs.

FINDINGS

The results shown in Table 14.3 help to answer the three research questions. In particular, the results represent the effect of having access to an adequately prepared teacher (certified to teach, with an undergraduate mathematics major, and with training in support of ELLs) on native or nonnative English-speaking students (NONNATIV), the self-reported level of English proficiency (ENG_PROF) of nonnative English speakers, along with their academic track placement on the mathematics performance on the ELS: 2002 assessment.

First, the parameter estimates indicate that students with a mathematics teacher who has a degree in mathematics scored higher than students with teachers without a degree in mathematics. The parameter estimates also show that Latino native-English speakers, on average, scored higher than most nonnative English speakers, and students in the college preparatory track scored higher than Latinos in the general track.

The results from Model 3 in Table 14.3 show that of the three teacher preparation measures, only having a mathematics teacher with a degree

TABLE 14.3   Final Estimated Hierarchical Linear Models

Fixed effects	Model 1 coeff. (SE)	Model 2 coeff. (SE)	Model 3 coeff. (SE)
Intercept	45.46***	47.49***	45.87***
	(0.46)	(0.65)	(0.88)
Student characteristics			
Socioeconomic status		2.75***	2.68***
		(0.69)	(0.71)
Female (male is omitted)		–0.70	–0.71
		(0.43)	(0.54)
Immigration status			
First generation		–0.53	–0.09
		(0.95)	(0.69)
Second generation (third generation omitted)		1.69*	1.60*
		(0.89)	(0.81)
English proficiency			
Nonnative English speaker (native English speaker omitted)		–10.32***	–9.93***
		(2.72)	(1.88)
Level of English proficiency (nonnative)		1.21***	1.16***
		(0.27)	(0.40)
Track-level placement			
General/vocational track		–2.50***	–2.42***
		(.47)	(.64)
School context features			
10th-grade % free lunch		–0.98***	–0.95**
		(0.25)	(0.26)
10th-grade % LEP		–1.11*	–1.08
		(0.51)	(0.49)
Public school (Catholic & other private omitted)		0.60	–0.85**
		(1.02)	(1.71)
Teacher preparation			
Math major			1.85*
			(0.71)
Standard certification			0.99
			(0.54)
EL training			–0.18
			(0.67)
Random effects			
Within schools[a] ($\tau00$)	18.30	11.37	11.00
Between schools[b] ($\sigma2$)	66.20	61.11	60.36
Chi-square	1165.74***	1003.01***	777.06***

[a] Indicates the amount of residual variance within schools.
[b] Variance component indicating whether there are differences between schools.
* $p < .05$; ** $p < .01$; *** $p < .001$.

in that subject was related ($p < .05$) to improved mathematics scores on the ELS: 2002 assessment. Latino native and nonnative English speakers with a teacher who had a degree in mathematics scored nearly two points higher that their peers whose mathematics teacher was teaching out-of-field ($\beta = 1.85$, $p < .05$). This difference in test scores is not negligible because it totals nearly 20% of a standard deviation. The effect on Latino student performance of having a teacher with a standard certification compared to those with a temporary or an emergency credential was not statistically significant ($\beta = 0.99$, $p > .05$). The results also indicate that the mathematics achievement of nonnative English speakers who had access to a mathematics teacher with at least eight hours of specialized LEP training in the last three years is not impacted ($\beta = -0.18$, $p > .05$) when controlling for students' background characteristics, their mathematics teacher's preparation, and selected school context measures.

The results also show that the mathematics achievement of Latino nonnative English speakers with low levels of English proficiency is lower than the test scores of their nonnative English-speaking peers with higher levels of English proficiency.[2] Thus, there is a positive relationship between mathematics achievement and English proficiency ($\beta = 1.16$, $p < .01$). More specifically, a one-unit positive difference in the level of English proficiency of nonnative English speakers is associated with a 1.21 positive difference in their mathematics score on the ELS: 2002 standardized test, all other predictors being equal. This difference in performance is slightly greater than 10% of a standard deviation for every unit difference in English proficiency. Additionally, the results from Model 3 also show that placement in the general track has a negative effect on mathematics achievement. On average, general track placement is associated with a 2.4-point lower difference (or 24% of a standard deviation) in mathematics test scores for both Latino native and nonnative English speakers, compared to their peers in the college preparatory track.

These relationships are illustrated graphically on the fitted plot in Figure 14.1 for students with a teacher who has a degree in a mathematics-related field, and with all other control predictors set to their mean in the Latino subsample. It is important to note that because there is no measured variation in the English proficiency of *native* English speakers, as shown in Figure 14.1, the horizontal line represents their mean mathematics achievement. Thus the horizontal fitted (dashed) line serves only as a reference for comparison with the mathematics achievement of nonnative English speakers at their reported level of English proficiency.

In Figure 14.1, the main effect of academic tracking is shown to be similar for nonnative English speakers at each level of English proficiency. It is critical to also note that nonnative English speakers at the lowest level of English proficiency (ENG_PROF = 3) are not represented in the col-

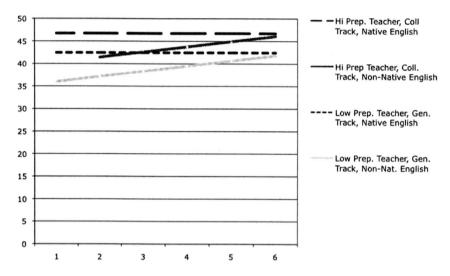

Figure 14.1 Main effect plot of mathematics performance of Latino 10th-grade native and nonnative English speakers by the mathematics teacher's preparation, English proficiency, and academic track placement.

lege preparatory track. Instead, the lowest level of English proficiency of students in the college preparatory track is 4 (ENG_PROF = 4). Also represented in Figure 14.1 is another important relationship between native and nonnative English speakers in the college and general track. Nonnative English speakers at the *highest* level of English proficiency (ENG_PROF = 8) performed at levels that are nearly equal to the students with the highest test scores in this study—Latino native English speakers.

The findings suggest that the relationship between English proficiency and mathematics test performance are negatively influenced simultaneously by low track placement and by the teacher's preparation, and, in turn, illustrate a disturbing pattern. Within each academic track, the scores of nonnative English speakers at the lowest level of English proficiency are over five points lower (or .5 of a standard deviation) below the scores of native English speakers. More alarming still is the difference in test scores between native English speakers and nonnative English speakers at the highest level of English proficiency (ENG_PROF = 8) in the college preparatory track and Latino ELLs in the general track. As illustrated in Figure 14.1, the difference in the predicted test scores among these groups across academic tracks is ten points on the ELS: 2002 assessment, the equivalent of one standard deviation, on average.

The individual and school-level control variables were also related to the mathematics performance of Latino students in ways that were consistent with existing research in this area. At the individual level, having a higher

SES was strongly related to the mathematics performance of Latino native and nonnative English speakers. A one-unit standard deviation difference in SES was associated with a positive difference of 2.75 points on the ELS: 2002 assessment, a difference of about .28 of a standard deviation. The results also show a small and statistically nonsignificant difference between male and female students, suggesting that there are no differences in performance among these groups. Finally, another interesting finding suggests that second-generation Latino students (the U.S.-born children of foreign-born parents) scored higher than both first-generation immigrants and third-generation immigrants. At the school level, both the proportion of ELLs and the proportion of students who qualified for free and reduced-price lunch were negatively related to mathematics performance. These findings suggest that the higher the percentage of ELLs in the school and the higher the percentage of students who qualified for free lunch, the lower the predicted test scores of Latino students in those schools.

CONCLUSIONS

This study highlights the complex nature of the relationship between the English proficiency of Latino ELLs and their mathematics performance. The analysis focuses on the relationship between multiple features of the instructional context on the mathematics achievement of Latino native and nonnative English speakers, including the mathematics teacher's preparation, English proficiency, and access to rigorous content (academic tracking) while controlling for important individual characteristics and aspects of the school context. Particular attention was placed on the lowest achieving students, Latino ELLs, to further examine whether having access to a teacher with specialized language support training can help facilitate learning and improve their performance, particularly in rigorous mathematics classrooms.

The findings reveal that the relationship between access to a qualified teacher, academic tracking, and the level of English proficiency of nonnative English-speaking Latino students is indeed an important predictor of their performance on standardized mathematics tests. The analysis also shows that the mathematics test scores of Latino ELLs are unacceptably low and considerably lower than the test scores of both nonnative English-proficient students and native English speakers. For example, at the lowest level of English proficiency (ENGPROF = 3), Latino ELLs scored nearly seven points—equaling over .66 of a standard deviation—below both Latino English-proficient (ENGPROF = 8) and Latino native speakers. A test score difference of this proportion is both substantial and alarming.

Due to the large disparity between Latino ELLs and their native English-speaking and English-proficient peers, these findings suggest that there is an urgent need to address the English proficiency needs of Latino ELLs as they simultaneously learn rigorous mathematics content and English. The role of the teacher in mitigating the negative effects of English proficiency on mathematics scores is indeed important. In this study, having access to an adequately trained teacher was associated with higher achievement on some important measures. Latino students with access to a teacher with a degree in mathematics scored nearly two points higher on the ELS: 2002 assessment compared to students who had a mathematics teacher with a bachelor's degree in another field. This difference in test scores is not negligible because it totals nearly .30 of a standard deviation. This is an important finding with critical policy implications, given the research that has shown that Latino ELLs are often taught by teachers who do not have a background in mathematics (Gándara & Rumberger, 2003; Minicucci & Olsen, 1992).

On the other hand, having access to teachers with a standard certification was not associated with a statistically significant difference in the test scores compared to students whose teacher had an emergency or a temporary credential or not credential at all. This distinction does not mean that a standard credential is not an important aspect of the preparation of teachers. It may be the case in this analysis that there is not sufficient variation in this particular teacher preparation measure to influence differences in student achievement. This finding is not so surprising when one considers that teachers with an emergency or a temporary credential are typically enrolled in programs in which they have met some of their requirements but may still be working toward the completion of their standard credential through a university or a school district internship program. Future research should investigate whether there are differences when teachers without a credential are disaggregated from those with temporary/emergency credential and from those with full standard teaching credentials.

Also analyzed was whether the presence of a mathematics teacher with specialized LEP training was associated with higher Latino ELL mathematics test scores. The analysis reveals that the presence of teachers with specialized LEP training did not have an impact on the assessment outcomes of Latino ELLs (see Model 3 in Table 14.3). This finding, however, is not conclusive. The measure of the linguistic training of teachers was very crude. The survey asked whether teachers had at least eight hours of specialized training over the last three years in working with ELLs. For those teachers reporting having had such training, some may have attended a single day (eight-hour) workshop for training on teaching ELLs over the last three-year period. Alternatively, it could mean that a teacher earned a graduate degree in second language instruction. Given the wide range of this measure, more work is needed to create a more reliable measure of specialized linguistic training for future data collection.

Consistent with the literature cited in this study, the findings also showed that tracking has a negative effect on the mathematics achievement of both Latino native and nonnative English speakers that is the equivalent of about .24 of a standard deviation. This statistic suggests exposure to rigorous mathematics content plays an important role in mediating the mathematics test scores of all Latinos. Not surprisingly, Latino native and nonnative English speakers with varying levels of English proficiency who are placed in the general academic track do have lower mathematics achievement scores than their respective peers in the college preparatory track. For all Latino students, the effect of low-track placement was linked to a lower test score of two points (or .25 of a standard deviation) on average, compared to students in the college preparatory track. This difference in test scores is also sizeable.

These findings also suggest that the placement of nonnative English speakers in the general track disadvantages them once they acquire English proficiency if nonnative English speakers remain in low-level mathematics courses that teach unchallenging basic mathematics skills. The English proficiency level of Latino ELLs will invariably improve over time, but if they are placed in remedial mathematics instruction, they will not gain benefit from their English proficiency, nor will they reach their full potential in mathematics. This study challenges the common practice of making English proficiency a prerequisite for enrollment in rigorous mathematics courses. Given the complexity of the mathematics language, deficit theories that limit ELLs' opportunities to take challenging courses based on their level of English proficiency will continue to have long-term negative consequences on their learning and test performance because this practice delays ELLs' entry into rigorous courses until they reach an "academic" level of English proficiency.

These results support the placement of ELLs in rigorous courses and suggest that exposure to more rigorous content may facilitate the development of their mathematics language register. Given that academic proficiency may take anywhere up to seven years to develop (Gándara, 1997), by the time ELLs develop a level of English proficiency deemed "appropriate" to be able to handle the linguistic complexity of secondary school mathematics content, it may be too late for them to meet the mathematics requirements for graduation and college entrance. Furthermore, deficit-oriented practices that lead to the placement of ELLs in low-level mathematics courses solely based on their English proficiency are unjustifiably using English proficiency as a measure of an ELL's capacity in mathematics.

Finally, it is important to note that the cumulative disadvantage of both a low-track placement and the lack of access to a teacher with a background in mathematics has a large impact on the test scores of Latino students. Having access to a teacher with a background in mathematics is associated with a nearly two-point difference (or .20 of a standard deviation) on the ELS: 2002 scores, while low track placement is associated with a 2.4 lower difference in test scores (the equivalent of .24 of a standard deviation). Taken together, Latino students in a low track who do have access to a teacher with a background in mathematics score more than four points, or .40 of a standard deviation, lower on the ELS: 2002 mathematics assessment.

The results of this study suggest that the English proficiency of ELLs should be used to assess the types of linguistic support these students will need in rigorous mathematics courses, instead of using English proficiency to deny these learning opportunities to ELLs. In other words, Latino ELLs should be offered mathematics instruction that simultaneously promotes learning rigorous, college-track mathematics content and proficiency in English, as well as the academic language of the mathematics classroom. These findings underscore the need for more research that examines the provision of native-language support for Latino ELLs until they become proficient enough in English to understand rigorous content without their English proficiency inhibiting the opportunity to learn and understand mathematics content at high levels. In particular, more research is needed to influence policies and practices that promote simultaneous exposure to rigorous content and language development support for the purpose of fostering the development of the mathematics language register. Because the role of the teacher's background preparation is central, training teachers to provide English language development in mathematics courses for ELLs seems to be a critical feature of the instructional context that is necessary to help promote the mathematics achievement of Latino ELLs.

NOTES

1. Widely cited large-scale sociological studies of immigrants using similar types of data sets have used these same self-reported English proficiency measures and find that they are relatively reliable measures of language skills (Portes & Rumbaut, 2001)
2. In the previous section, I described predictor ENG_PROF as a cross product of non-native status and English proficiency (NONNATIV*ENGPROF).

REFERENCES

Abedi, J. (2004). The No Child Left Behind Act and English language learners: Assessment and accountability issues. *American Educational Research Association, 33*(1), 4–14. doi: 10.3102/0013189X033001004

Abedi, J. & Lord, C. (2000). The language factor in mathematics. *Applied Measurement in Education, 14*(3), 219–234. doi: 10.1207/S15324818AME1403_2

Adelman, C. (1999). *Answers in the tool box: Academic intensity, attendance patterns, and bachelor's degree attainment* [Monograph]. Washington, DC: U.S. Department of Education. Retrieved from http://www2.ed.gov/pubs/Toolbox/

Adelman, C. (2006). *The toolbox revisited: Paths to degree completion from high school through college.* Washington, DC: U.S. Department of Education. Retrieved from http://www2.ed.gov/rschstat/research/pubs/toolboxrevisit/toolbox.pdf

August, D. & Hakuta, K. (Eds.). (1997). *Improving schooling for language-minority children: A research agenda.* Washington, DC: National Research Council, Institute of Medicine, National Academy Press.

Callahan, R. M. (2005). Tracking and high school English learners: Limiting opportunity to learn. *American Educational Research Journal, 42*(2), 305–328. doi: 10.3102/00028312042002305

Celedón-Pattichis, S. (2004). Research findings involving English-language learners and implications for mathematics teachers. In M. F. Chappell & T. Pateracki (Eds.), *Empowering the beginning teacher of mathematics in middle school* (pp. 47–48). Reston, VA: National Council of Teachers of Mathematics.

Conchas, G. Q. (2001, Fall). Structuring failure and success: Understanding the variability in Latino school engagement. *Harvard Educational Review, 71,* 475–504. Retrieved from http://www.hepg.org/her/

Conchas, G. Q. (2006). *The color of success: Race and high-achieving urban youth.* New York: Teachers College Press.

Cuevas, G. J. (1984). Mathematics learning in English as a second language. *Journal for Research in Mathematics Education, 15*(2), 134–144. doi: 10.2307/748889

Darling-Hammond, L., Berry, B., & Thoreson, A. (2001). Does teacher certification matter? Evaluating the evidence. *Educational Evaluation and Policy Analysis, 23*(1), 57–77. doi: 10.3102/01623737023001057

Darling-Hammond, L. & Youngs, P. (2002). Defining "highly qualified teachers": What does "scientifically-based research" actually tell us? *Educational Researcher, 31*(9), 13–25. doi: 10.3102/0013189X031009013

Dentler, R. A. & Hafner, A. L. (1997). *Hosting newcomers: Structuring educational opportunities for immigrant children.* New York: Teachers College Press.

Donato, R., Menchaca, M., & Valencia, R. R. (1991). Segregation, desegregation, and the integration of Chicano students: Problems and prospects. In R. R. Valencia (Ed.), *Chicano school failure and success: Research and policy agendas for the 1990s* (pp. 27–63). New York: Falmer Press.

Durán, R. P. (2008). Assessing English-language learners' achievement. *Review of Research in Education, 32*(1), 292–327. doi: 10.3102/0091732X07309372

The Educational Trust. (1998). Good teaching matters: How well qualified teachers can close the achievement gap. *Thinking K–16, 3*(2), 1–14. Retrieved from http://www.edtrust.org/sites/edtrust.org/files/publications/files/k16_summer98.pdf

Flores, A. (1997). *Si se puede,* "It can be done": Quality mathematics in more than one language. In J. Trentacosta & M. J. Kenney (Eds.), *Multicultural and gender equity in the mathematics classroom: The gift of diversity* (pp. 81–91). Reston, VA: National Council of Teachers of Mathematics.

Flores, A. (2007). Examining disparities in mathematics education: Achievement gap or opportunity gap? *The High School Journal, 91*(1), 29–42. doi: 10.1353/hsj.2007.0022

Gándara, P. C. (1995). *Over the ivy walls: The educational mobility of low-income Chicanos.* Albany: State University of New York Press.

Gándara, P. C. (1997). *Review of research on the instruction of limited English proficient students: A report to the California legislature.* Davis, CA: University of California Linguistic Minority Research Institute.

Gándara, P. C. (1999). Staying in the race: The challenge for Chicanos in higher education. In J. F. Moreno (Ed.), *The elusive quest for equality: 150 years of Chicano/Chicana education* (pp. 169–196). Cambridge, MA: Harvard Educational Press.

Gándara, P. C. & Maxwell-Jolly, J. (2006). Critical issues in developing a teacher corps for English learners. In K. Téllez & H. C. Waxman (Eds.). *Preparing quality educators for English language learners: Research, policies, and practices* (pp. 99–120). Mahwah, NJ: Erlbaum.

Gándara, P. C. & Rumberger, R. W. (2003). *The inequitable treatment of English learners in California's public schools.* Santa Barbara, CA: University of California Linguistic Minority Research Institute.

Garrison, L. & Mora, J. K. (1999). Adapting mathematics instruction for English language learners: The language concept. In L. Ortiz-Franco, N. G. Hernandez, & Y. de la Cruz (Eds.), *Changing the faces of mathematics: Perspectives on Latinos* (pp. 35–48). Reston, VA: National Council of Teachers of Mathematics.

Gutiérrez, R. (2002). Beyond essentialism: The complexity of language in teaching mathematics to Latina/o students. *American Educational Research Journal, 39*(4), 1047–1088. doi: 10.3102/000283120390041047

Gutiérrez, R. (2007). (Re)defining equity: The importance of a critical perspective. In N. S. Nasir & P. Cobb (Eds.), *Improving access to mathematics: Diversity and equity in the classroom* (pp. 37–50). New York: Teachers College Press.

Hanushek, E. A. (1992). The trade-off between child quantity and quality. *Journal of Poltical Economy, 100*(1), 84–117. doi: 10.1086/261808

Harklau, L. (1994a). "Jumping tracks": How language-minority students negotiate evaluations of ability. *Anthropology & Education Quarterly, 25*(3), 347–363. doi: 10.1525/aeq.1994.25.3.04x0149s

Harklau, L. (1994b). Tracking and linguistic minority students: Consequences of ability grouping for second language learners. *Linguistics and Education, 6*(3), 217–244. doi: 10.1016/0898-5898(94)90012-4

Heubert, J. P. & Hauser, R. M. (1999). *High stakes: Testing for tracking, promotion, and graduation.* Washington, DC: National Research Council, National Academies Press.

Ingels, S. J., Pratt, D. J., Rogers, J. E., Siegel, P. H., & Stutts, E. S. (2004). *Education Longitudinal Study of 2002: Base year data file user's manual* (NCES 2004-405). Washington, DC: U.S. Department of Education, National Center for Education Statistics.

Katz, S. R. (1999). Teaching in tensions: Latino immigrant youth, their teachers, and the structures of schooling. *Teachers College Record, 100*(4), 809–840. doi: 10.1111/0161-4681.00017

Khisty, L. L. (1995). Making inequality: Issues of language and meanings in mathematics teaching with Hispanic students. In W. G. Secada, E. Fennema, & L. B. Adajian (Eds.), *New directions for equity in mathematics education* (pp. 279–297). New York: Cambridge University Press.

Khisty, L. L. (1997). Making mathematics accessible to Latino students: Rethinking instructional practice. In J. Trentacosta and M. J. Kenney (Eds.), *Multicultural and gender equity in the mathematics classroom: The gift of diversity* (pp. 92–101). Reston, VA: National Council of Teachers of Mathematics.

Kindler, A. L. (2002). *Survey of the states' limited English proficient students and available educational programs and services: 2000–2001 summary report.* Washington, DC: U.S. Department of Education, Office of English Language Acquisition, Language Enhancement and Academic Achievement for Limited English Proficient Students.

Light, R. J., Singer, J. D., & Willett, J. B. (1990). *By design: Planning research in higher education.* Cambridge, MA: Harvard University Press.

Lucas, T. (1997). *Into, through, and beyond secondary school: Critical transitions for immigrant youth.* Washington, DC: Center for Applied Linguistics.

Lucas, T., Henze, R., & Donato, R. (1990, Fall). Promoting the success of Latino language-minority students: An exploratory study of six high schools. *Harvard Educational Review, 60,* 315–340. Retrieved from http://www.hepg.org/her/

Martiniello, M. (2008, Summer). Language and the performance of English-language learners in math word problems. *Harvard Educational Review, 78,* 333–368. Retrieved from http://www.hepg.org/her/

Maxwell-Jolly, J., Gándara, P. G., & Driscoll, L. (2005). *Promoting academic literacy among secondary English language learners.* Davis: University of California, Davis School of Education, Linguistic Minority Research Institute Education Policy Center.

Mehan, H., Villanueva, I., Hubbard, L., & Lintz, A. (1996). *Constructing school success: The consequences of un-tracking low-achieving students.* Cambridge, UK: Cambridge University Press.

Mestre, J. P. (1988). The role of language comprehension in mathematics and problem solving. In R. R. Cocking & J. P. Mestre (Eds.), *Linguistic and cultural influences on learning mathematics* (pp. 201–225). Hillsdale, NJ: Erlbaum.

Minicucci, C. & Olsen, L. (1992). *Programs for secondary limited English proficient students: A California study* [Occasional Papers in Bilingual Education No. 5]. Washington, DC: National Clearinghouse for Bilingual Education.

Moll, L. C. & Díaz, S. (1987). Change as the goal of educational research. *Anthropology & Education Quarterly, 18*(4), 300–311. doi: 10.1525/aeq.1987.18.4.04x0021u

Moschkovich, J. N. (1999a). Supporting the participation of English language learners in mathematical discussions. *For the Learning of Mathematics, 19*(1), 11–19. Retrieved from http://flm.educ.ualberta.ca/

Moschkovich, J. N. (1999b). Understanding the needs of Latino students in reform-oriented mathematics classrooms. In L. Ortiz-Franco, N. G. Hernandez, & Y. de la Cruz (Eds.), *Changing the faces of mathematics: Perspectives on Latinos* (pp. 5–12). Reston, VA: National Council of Teachers of Mathematics.

Moschkovich, J. N. (2007). Bilingual mathematics learners: How views of language, bilingual learners, and mathematical communication affect instruction. In N.

S. Nasir & P. Cobb (Eds.), *Improving access to mathematics: Diversity and equity in the classroom* (pp. 89-104). New York: Teachers College Press.

Mosqueda, E. (2010). Compounding inequalities: English proficiency and tracking and their relation to mathematics performance among Latina/o secondary school youth. *Journal of Urban Mathematics Education, 3*(1), 57–81. Retrieved from http://education.gsu.edu/JUME

Oakes, J. (1985). *Keeping track: How schools structure inequality.* New Haven, CT: Yale University Press.

Oakes, J., Gamoran, A., & Page, R. N. (1992). Curriculum differentiation: Opportunities, outcomes, and meanings. In P. W. Jackson (Ed.), *Handbook of research on curriculum: A project of the American Education Research Association* (pp. 570–608). New York: Macmillan.

Olsen, L. (1995). School restructuring and the needs of immigrant students. In R. G. Rumbaut & W. A. Cornelius (Eds.), *California's immigrant children: Theory, research, and implications for educational policy* (pp. 209–232). San Diego: University of California, San Diego, Center for U.S.-Mexican Studies.

Olsen, L. (1997). *Made in America: Immigrant students in our public schools.* New York: New Press.

Portes, A. & Rumbaut, R. G. (2001). *Legacies: The story of the immigrant second generation.* Berkeley, CA: University Press and Russell Sage Foundation.

Raudenbush, S. W. & Bryk, A. S. (2002). *Hierarchical linear models: Applications and data analysis methods* (2nd ed.). Newbury Park, CA: Sage.

Romo, H. D. & Falbo, T. (1996). *Latino high school graduation: Defying the odds.* Austin: University of Texas Press.

Ron, P. (1999). Spanish-English language issues in the mathematics classroom. In L. Ortiz-Franco, N. G. Hernandez, & Y. de la Cruz (Eds.), *Changing the faces of mathematics: Perspectives on Latinos* (pp. 23–33). Reston, VA: National Council of Teachers of Mathematics.

Rubin, D. B. (1987). *Multiple imputation for nonresponse in surveys.* New York: Wiley.

Ruiz-de-Velasco, J. & Fix, M. E. (with Clewell, B. C.). (2000). *Overlooked and underserved: Immigrant students in U.S. secondary schools.* Washington, DC: Urban Institute.

Rumberger, R. W. & Larson, K. A. (1998). Toward explaining differences in educational achievement among Mexican American language-minority students. *Sociology of Education, 71*(1), 68–92. doi: 10.2307/2673222

Secada, W. G. (1992). Race, ethnicity, social class, language, and achievement in mathematics. In D. A. Grouws (Ed.), *Handbook of research on mathematics teaching and learning* (pp. 623–660). New York, NY: Macmillan.

Secada, W. G. (1996). Urban students acquiring English and learning mathematics in the context of reform. *Urban Education, 30*(4), 422–448. doi: 10.1177/0042085996030004004

Secada, W. G. & Carey, D. A. (1990). *Teaching mathematics with understanding to limited English proficient students.* New York: ERIC Clearinghouse on Urban Education, Institute on Urban and Minority Education.

Solano-Flores, G. (2008). Language, dialect, and register: Sociolinguistics and the estimation of measurement error in the testing of English language learners. *Teachers College Record, 108*(11), 2354–2379. doi: 10.1111/j.1467-9620.2006.00785.x

Tate, W. F. (1997). Race-ethnicity, SES, gender, and language proficiency trends in mathematics achievement: An update. *Journal for Research in Mathematics Education, 28*(6), 652–679. doi: 10.2307/749636

Téllez, K., & Waxman, H. C. (2006). *Preparing quality educators for English language learners: Research, policies, and practices.* Mahwah, NJ: Erlbaum.

Valdés, G. (1998). The world outside and inside schools: Language and immigrant children. *Educational Researcher, 27*(6), 4–18. doi: 10.3102/0013189X027006004

Valdés, G., Bunch, G., Snow, C., & Lee, C. (with Matos, L.). (2005). Enhancing the development of students' language(s). In L. Darling-Hammond & J. Bransford (Eds.), *Preparing teachers for a changing world: What teachers should learn and be able to do* (pp. 126–168). San Francisco, CA: Jossey-Bass.

Valencia, R. R. (Ed.). (2002). *Chicano school failure and success: Past, present, and future* (2nd ed.). New York: Routledge/Falmer.

Valenzuela, A. (1999). *Subtractive schooling: U.S.-Mexican youth and the politics of caring.* Albany: State University of New York Press.

Walqui, A. (2000). *Access and engagement: Program design and instructional approaches for immigrant students in secondary school.* McHenry, IL: Center for Applied Linguistics and Delta.

Wang, J., & Goldschmidt, P. (1999). Opportunity to learn, language proficiency, and immigrant status effects on mathematics achievement. *Journal of Educational Research, 93*(2), 101–111. doi: 10.1080/00220679909597634

Zehler, A. M., Fleischman, H. L., Hopstock, P. J., Stephenson, T. G. Pendzick, M. L., & Sapru, S. (2003). *Descriptive study of services to LEP students and LEP students with disabilities* (No. 4 Special Topic Report: Findings on Special Education LEP Students). Arlington, VA: Development Associates.

ABOUT THE CONTRIBUTORS

Beatriz Quintos-Alonso

Beatriz Quintos is a Lecturer in the Curriculum and Instruction Department at the University of Maryland, College Park. Her research interests include parental engagement that draws from the knowledge and perspectives of Latina/o communities and socio-cultural and critical perspectives to explore student learning at the elementary level. She earned her PhD from University of Arizona and was a fellow in the Center for the Mathematics of Latinos. Her previous research has appeared in journals such as *Adults Learning Mathematics: International Journal* and *Multicultural Education.*

Cynthia O. Anhalt

Cynthia Oropesa Anhalt is Instructional Faculty and the Director of the Secondary Mathematics Education Program in the Department of Mathematics at The University of Arizona. Her research interests include mathematics teacher education, teaching and learning of mathematics, equity issues in mathematics education, and in particular, Latino/a students learning of mathematics. She earned her PhD from the University of Arizona in 2004 in Mathematics Teaching and Teacher Education. Her publications have appeared in journals such as the *Journal of Latinos and Education, TODOS Mathematics for All Research Monograph II,* and NCTM's *Mathematics Teaching in the Middle School* and *Teaching Children Mathematics.*

Eduardo Mosqueda

Eduardo Mosqueda is an Assistant Professor of Education at UC Santa Cruz. His primary research uses the Education Longitudinal Study of 2002 (collected by the National Center of Education Statistics) and analyzes the relationship between the English proficiency of non-native English speakers,

Latinos/as and Mathematics Education, pages 341–348
Copyright © 2011 by Information Age Publishing
341

their access to rigorous courses, and their performance on standardized mathematics assessments. His most recent research examines the impact of science content integrated with language and literacy development strategies on the beliefs and practices of pre-service teachers of Latino English learners. He completed his doctoral studies at the Harvard Graduate School of Education and was awarded a Spencer Dissertation Fellowship. He has taught both middle and high school mathematics.

Erin Turner

Erin Turner is an Assistant Professor in the Teaching, Learning and Sociocultural Studies Department at the University of Arizona. Her research interests include equity, diversity, and social justice in mathematics education, preparing elementary teachers to teach mathematics to diverse groups of children, English learners and mathematics teaching and learning, and issues related to the mathematics education of Latino/as. Prior to her work at the university, she was a bilingual elementary teacher in Phoenix, Arizona. She earned her PhD from the University of Texas at Austin, where she studied mathematics and science education. Her previous research has appeared in journals such as *Educational Studies in Mathematics, Mathematical Thinking and Learning,* the *Journal of Mathematical Behavior,* and the *Journal of Latinos and Education.*

Eugenia Vomvoridi-Ivanović

Eugenia Vomvoridi-Ivanović is an Assistant Professor in the Department of Secondary Education at the University of South Florida. She earned her PhD in Curriculum and Instruction with an emphasis in Mathematics Education from the University of Illinois at Chicago in 2009. Her interests in research and teaching include: the mathematics education of language minority students, mathematics teacher preparation for diverse student populations, teacher development in informal mathematics learning contexts, teaching mathematics for social justice, and culturally responsive mathematics teacher education.

Guillermo Solano-Flores

Guillermo Solano-Flores is an Associate Professor of Bilingual Education and English as a Second Language at the School of Education of the University of Colorado, Boulder. He specializes in educational measurement. His work focuses on the development of alternative, multidisciplinary approaches that address linguistic and cultural diversity in testing. Current research projects investigate the measurement of mathematics academic language load in tests and the design and use of illustrations as a form of testing accommodations for English language learners with an approach that uses cognitive science, semiotics, and sociolinguistics in combination.

Heather Cavell

Heather Cavell recently graduated with her PhD from the University of Arizona where she studied language and culture in education with a focus in mathematics education. Her research interests include teacher education and professional development, issues in the mathematics education of Latinos/as, the education of English Language Learners, and educational policy. Prior to graduate work, she taught secondary school (mathematics) in Vail, AZ. Her work with undergraduate teacher training in mathematics education with a graduate colleague has appeared in *Teaching Children Mathematics.*

Hector Morales

Hector Morales, Jr. is a Visiting Assistant Professor at DePaul University. His research interests include mathematics teaching and learning in urban contexts with racially, culturally, and linguistically diverse student populations. Prior to his work at the university, he taught secondary school mathematics in Chicago, IL. He earned his PhD from the University of Illinois at Chicago in Curriculum Studies: Mathematics Education Concentration.

Higinio Dominguez

Higinio Dominguez is an Assistant Professor in Curriculum and Instruction at Texas State University. He earned his PhD from the University of Texas at Austin. He is currently conducting classroom-based investigations that focus on bilingual students' thinking—including the resources that support this thinking—as the foundation to inform teachers' practices with bilingual students in mathematics. His research has been published in various journals, including *Bilingual Research Journal, Educational Studies in Mathematics,* and the *Journal for Research in Mathematics Education.*

Javier Diez-Palomar

Javier Díez-Palomar, PhD, is associate professor (lecturer) at the Universitat Autonoma de Barcelona, in the Department of Mathematics Education and Sciences. He has been working with dialogic learning, family training, mathematics education, and multicultural approaches. He is also part of CEMELA, where he was involved as Fulbright Visitor Scholar for two years, in Tucson, Arizona. Some of his last works have been published in the *Adult Learning Mathematics: International Journal, Journal of Mathematics and Culture,* and *Enseñanza de las Ciencias.*

Jesus Acosta-Iriqui

Jesus Acosta-Iriqui received his undergraduate degree in Public Accounting (CPA) from Universidad del Noroeste in Sonora, Mexico in 1995. His master's degree is in bilingual/multicultural education from The University of Arizona in 2006. He is currently a doctoral student there, where he studies the interplay of language, culture, and the teaching and learning of mathematics. As a CEMELA doctoral fellow, his research has been focused on language and culture, and the teaching and learning of mathematics around Mexican parents, teachers working with ELLs, and ELLs from Mexican background.

Judit Moschkovich

Judit Moschkovich is Professor of Mathematics Education in the Education Department at the University of California at Santa Cruz. Her research uses sociocultural approaches to examine mathematical thinking and learning in three areas: algebraic thinking, mathematical discourse practices, and bilingual mathematics learners, especially Latino/a students. Dr. Moschkovich was the co-editor, with M. Brenner, of JRME monograph Number 11, E*veryday and Academic Mathematics: Implications for the Classroom* (2002) and editor of *Language and Mathematics Education: Multiple Perspectives and Directions for Research* (2010). Her work has been published in journals such as *The Journal for the Learning Sciences, Educational Studies in Mathematics*, and *For the Learning of Mathematics*. She was the Principal Investigator of an NSF project (1998–2003) titled "Mathematical discourse in bilingual settings: Learning mathematics in two languages" and a Co-PI for the Center for the Mathematics Education of Latinos/as (CEMELA). She served on the Editorial Panel for the *Journal for Research in Mathematics Education*, the Review Board for *The Journal for the Learning Sciences*, as the Chair for the SIG (Special Interest Group) Research in Mathematics Education in AERA (American Educational Research Association), and is a member of the International Program Committee of the International Council for Mathematics Instruction (ICMI) Study #21: Mathematics education and language diversity.

Karla Ceballos

Karla Ceballos is a bilingual kindergarten teacher at La Mesa Elementary in Albuquerque, New Mexico. She earned her Bachelor of Arts degree in elementary and bilingual education as well as a Masters in Education from the University of New Mexico.

Kip Téllez

Kip Téllez is an Associate Professor and current Chair in Education Department at the University of California at Santa Cruz. His research interests include teacher education, second language teaching, and issues in the education of Latino/as. Prior to his work at the university, he taught elementary and secondary school (mathematics) in La Puente, CA. He earned his PhD from the Claremont Graduate University where he studied educational linguistics. His previous research has appeared in journals such as *Bilingual Research Journal, Journal of Teacher Education,* and *Teaching and Teacher Education.*

Laura Burr

Laura G. Burr is enrolled in the Mathematics Education PhD program at the University of New Mexico in Albuquerque, NM. Her research focus is on student–teacher interactions in a reform mathematics classroom with Latino/a students. Earlier in her career, she taught mathematics, was an elementary school principal, then was the Director of Curriculum. She has spent her career in various public school settings with predominantly Latino/a students.

Lena Licon Khisty

Lena Licón Khisty is Professor Emerita in Curriculum and Instruction at the University of Illinois at Chicago. Her research focuses on improving the schooling of Latinos, classroom and discourse processes, and equity and the sociopolitical contexts of schooling. She has combined her research interests with teacher preparation and development emphasizing the integration of bilingual instruction and mathematics teaching and learning. She has had several funded projects, including a multi-year whole-school improvement project based on teacher action research and integrating mathematics, science, and dual language. Her research on equity in mathematics appears in national and international journals and books, primarily in the area of mathematics education.

Libni Berenice Castellón

Libni B. Castellon is a Professor in Mathematics Department at the Universidad Pedagógica Nacional Francisco Morazán at Honduras, C.A. Her professional interests include teacher education, teacher development, Student learning and standard based assessment. She worked as research assistant at the University of New Mexico. She developed research on Latino students and mathematics education at the Center for the Mathematics Education of Latinos (CEMELA). She earned her Master's degree from the University of New Mexico where she studied Secondary Education with an emphasis on Mathematics.

Marta Civil

Marta Civil is a Professor in the Department of Mathematics at the University of Arizona. Her research interests encompass teacher education, cultural, social, and language aspects in the teaching and learning of mathematics, equity, and parental engagement in mathematics, primarily in working-class, Latino/a communities. She has directed several initiatives aimed at engaging children ages 8–13 in hands-on mathematics and science explorations in informal and after-school settings as well as programs focused on involving parents in mathematics education. She is the Principal Investigator for NSF-funded CEMELA (Center for the Mathematics Education of Latinos/as), a Center for Learning and Teaching. She has presented her work at national and international conferences and has multiple publications in her main areas of research.

Mary Marshall

Mary Marshall is a 7th grade mathematics teacher at John Adams Middle School in Albuquerque, New Mexico. She received her Ph.D. in August 2009 in Language, Literacy and Sociocultural Studies from the University of New Mexico. In her dissertation research, she explored primary grade bilingual students' mathematical thinking during individual problem solving.

Matthew Ondrus

Matthew Ondrus is an assistant professor in the Mathematics Department at Weber State University. His scholarly interests include Lie algebra representation theory as well as the preparation and professional growth of mathematics teachers. He earned his PhD in mathematics at the University of Wisconsin–Madison, and he spent three years as a post doc at the University of Arizona, where he was a was a fellow at The Center for the Mathematics Education of Latinos/as.

Maura Varley

Maura Varley Gutiérrez is an adjunct assistant professor in the Teaching and Teacher Education Program at the University of Arizona. Her research interests include the intersection of race and gender in mathematics education and critical mathematics education at the elementary and preservice teacher levels. She previously taught upper elementary grades in Washington, DC and was a Peace Corps Volunteer in Belize.

Nancy O'Rode

Nancy O'Rode is an Associate Professor of Elementary Education in the Michael D. Eisner College of Education at California State University Northridge. In addition to teaching mathematics methods courses for the teacher preparation program, Dr. O'Rode conducts research on algebraic thinking, teacher leadership and mathematics teacher preparation. She earned a Ph.D. in Education from the University of California Santa Barbara. Her classroom experience, spanning grades 4–11, began as a Peace Corps volunteer in the Fiji Islands and continued in Spain, Kenya and California. Dr. O'Rode recently published several articles in NCTM's Empowering the Mentor series for pre-service, beginning, and experienced mathematics teachers.

Olga Torres

Olga Torres has been an educator in multiage, multilingual, multicultural classrooms for more than 30 years. She has been a project math specialist and co-director of the Title I/ExxonMobil Mathematics/Science Project for the Tucson Unified School District in Arizona. Olga has taught grades K through 5 and has been an adjunct professor for the University of Arizona teaching a math methods course for pre-service teachers. Olga was also the 1995 recipient of the Presidential Award of Excellence in Mathematics for the state of Arizona. Olga received her Master's degree in Bilingual/Multicultural Education and her work outside the classroom includes work with teachers on equity issues and teaching mathematics for understanding. Olga worked as a teacher leader for CEMELA working with teachers and students. Currently, she is an independent mathematics educational consultant and works part-time with Math Solutions Professional Development.

Richard Kitchen

Richard Kitchen is a Professor of Leadership in Mathematics Education at the University of New Mexico. He was a co-Principal Investigator of the Center for the Mathematics Education of Latinos/as (CEMELA) at UNM. His research interests include equity, diversity, and leadership in mathematics education. He holds a PhD in curriculum and instruction from the University of Wisconsin–Madison and an M.A. in mathematics from the University of Montana.

Sandra I Musanti

Sandra I. Musanti is a visiting professor at the Center for Interdisciplinary Studies in Education, Culture and Society, School of Humanities, Universidad Nacional de San Martín, Buenos Aires, Argentina. She also serves as consultant for the Ministry of Education of Argentina. Her research interests include teacher education, teacher development, teacher collaboration, and bilingual education. Recently, she has published several papers on teacher professional development and collaboration situated in contexts of linguistic and cultural diversity. She obtained her PhD in Education at the University of New Mexico. She is a former Fulbright Scholar, and completed a postdoctorate fellowship at the Center for Mathematics Education of Latinos/as (CEMELA) sponsored by the National Science Foundation.

Sylvia Celedon-Pattichis

Sylvia Celedón-Pattichis is an Associate Professor in the Department of Language, Literacy, and Sociocultural Studies at the University of New Mexico and is a Co-PI of the Center for the Mathematics Education of Latinas/os (CEMELA). Her research interests center on the linguistic and cultural influences on the teaching and learning of mathematics, especially with

Latina/o student populations. She obtained her PhD in Curriculum and Instruction with areas of specialization in bilingual and mathematics education from the University of Texas at Austin. Prior to her university work, she taught high school mathematics in Rio Grande City, Texas. Her research has been published in the *Bilingual Research Journal*, *Journal of Latinos and Education*, and *Middle Grades Research Journal*.

William Zahner

William Zahner is a doctoral candidate in the education department at the University of California at Santa Cruz. His research interests include mathematics learning in small group discussions, assessment, and examining the mediation of language in mathematical reasoning. His work has appeared in *Mind Culture and Activity* and will appear in *Mathematical Thinking and Learning*.